LIGHT, FREEDOM AND SONG

LIGHT, FREEDOM AND SONG

A Cultural History of Modern Irish Writing

DAVID PIERCE

YALE UNIVERSITY PRESS
NEW HAVEN AND LONDON

For information about this and other Yale University Press publications, please contact:
    U.S. Office: sales.press@yale.edu   yalebooks.com
    Europe Office: sales@yaleup.co.uk   www.yalebooks.co.uk

Designed by Ruth Applin
Set in Minion by J&L Composition, Filey, North Yorkshire
Printed in China through Worldprint

ISBN 0-300-10994-6

Library of Congress Control Number 2005932337

A catalogue record for this book is available from the British Library.

Endpapers: Boazio's Map of Ireland 1599. Courtesy of the British Library.
Frontispiece: Detail of Dancing on the pier, Clogher Head, County Louth, 1935.
p.vi: Detail of Gravediggers, Glasnevin, by Evelyn Hofer.

10 9 8 7 6 5 4 3 2 1

For my elder brother John,
my neurosurgeon Gerry O'Reilly,
and in memory of Rosaleen Eagleton (1913–2002)

Contents

Acknowledgements

The extract from an unpublished letter by Fred Ryan in Chapter 2 is the property of the National Library of Ireland and has been reproduced with the permission of the Council of Trustees of the National Library of Ireland. Extracts of unpublished prose by W. B. Yeats in Chapter 5 appear by permission of Professor R. F. Foster, authorised biographer, A. P. Watt Ltd on behalf of Michael B. Yeats, and Colby College Special Collections, Waterville, Maine.

It's a pleasure to record a debt of thanks to the following individuals who have helped me track down information or clarify various lines of argument: Margot Banks, Terence Brown, Eamonn Cantwell, Vincent Cheng, Corinna Cunningham, Margaret Davis, Terry Dolan, Donal Foley, Rosa González, Mary Haugh, Jacqueline Hurtley, Ellen Carol Jones, Harry Marten, Jim McCord, Bill McCormack, Tina Moran, Johanne Mullan, Fergus O'Donoghue, S. J. Fintan O'Toole, Richard Pearce, David Powell, Una Quinn, Jörg Rademacher, Chris Ridgway, John Smurthwaite, Alistair Stead, George Watson, and Ian Kennedy White. This book would not exist in the shape it does but for the advice of several anonymous readers, and I thank them all. A special word of thanks to Brendan Kennelly.

I would also like to thank those individuals and organisations who have allowed me to use their work as illustrations. In particular, Robert Ballagh, Margaret Early, Peter Fallon, Margo Harkin, Dan Harper, Evelyn Hofer, Neil Jordan, John Minihan, Derek Speirs, John Stafford-Langan, Martyn Turner and Sean Walshe deserve special mention. Every effort has been made to ascertain and acknowledge ownership of illustrated material; any errors or oversights will be rectified at the earliest opportunity.

I have also benefited from the opportunity to present various sections of the book at James Joyce symposia and at Irish conferences in London, Aberdeen, Trieste, São Paulo and Almería.

Finally a word of thanks to Robert Baldock and his team at Yale University Press in London. My third book with Yale has given me the same joy as the previous two. As ever, my chief debt is to my immediate family, to Mary, my constant companion and editor, and to my son Matt, who's never far from my thoughts.

Abbreviations

FW   James Joyce, *Finnegans Wake* (1939; London: Faber and Faber, 1964). The page number is given first, followed by line number.

U   James Joyce, *Ulysses: The Corrected Text* (ed. Hans Walter Gabler with Wolfhard Steppe and Claus Melchior) (London: The Bodley Head, 1986). The chapter number is followed by line number.

VP   *The Variorum Edition of the Poems of W. B. Yeats* (ed. Peter Galt and Russell K. Alspach) (1957; New York: Macmillan, 1971).

Chapter 1

The Harp Without the Crown

She was going out from us, becoming strange, becoming possessed.
– Seamus Deane, *Reading in the Dark* (1996)

In this re-reading of modern Irish writing I am intrigued by what I perceive as a cognate set of pairings: loss and struggle on the one hand, and the harp and the crown on the other. Speaking broadly, texts such as James Joyce's *Dubliners* (1914), Elizabeth Bowen's *The Last September* (1929), Brian Friel's *Translations* (1981), Frank McGuinness's *Observe the Sons of Ulster Marching Towards the Somme* (1985), Sebastian Barry's *The Steward of Christendom* (1995), or Glenn Patterson's *That Which Was* (2004), are concerned with loss or its consequences. Texts such as Joyce's *A Portrait of the Artist as a Young Man* (1916) or *Ulysses* (1922), Samuel Beckett's *Krapp's Last Tape* (1958), Christy Brown's *Down All The Days* (1970), Jamie O'Neill's *At Swim, Two Boys* (2001), or John McGahern's *That They May Face the Rising Sun* (2002), are about struggle of one kind or another. Some texts, such as Anne Devlin's *After Easter* (1994), show how struggle stems from a sense of loss; some, such as W. B. Yeats's *Cathleen ni Houlihan* (1902), transform loss into struggle; some, such as Conor McPherson's *Shining City* (2004), counter loss with endurance; and some, such as Seamus Heaney's *North* (1975), are nicely poised between loss and struggle, between history and hope.

The other pairing, the harp and the crown, prompts a different train of thoughts. The harp by itself is the traditional symbol of Ireland, much older than the fifteenth-century harp on display in the Library of Trinity College Dublin. As a musical instrument it is nearer to culture and the arts of peace than the imperialism and militarism emblazoned in the crown. In Tom Moore's *Irish Melodies* (1807–34), the harp acquired a particular inflection by its twin association with the source of Romantic inspiration and the politics of Irish freedom. In one of his disarming songs, 'Dear Harp of My Country!', which gave me the title of my book, Moore lovingly addresses the harp as if it were a person trapped in prison: 'In darkness, I found thee,/The cold chain of silence had hung o'er thee long.'[1] In his

Opposite page
Detail of an Edwardian postcard, all the emblems in place.

autobiography, *Harp* (1989), John Gregory Dunne reveals that for Irish-Americans the harp could be less romantically conceived, for it has been not only a badge of group identity but is also close to a disparaging stereotype: 'I am a harp, that is my history, Irish and Catholic, from steerage to suburbia in three generations.'[2]

The crown is the traditional symbol of England and primarily connected with kingship and the exercise of power. The crown is worn, not played; it is positioned on the head of the body, and plots a never-ending circle. Embodied in its iconography is the triumph of wealth and legitimacy, the close identity between monarch and people, and an image of politics that fuses the hereditary principle, continuity and display. Unlike the harp, the crown is both symbolic and singular: there is only one crown and one individual fit or otherwise to wear it. Inscribed in the crown is both the achievement of history and the uncertainty of the future, a tension more in evidence in centuries past than in the present. Thus, at the end of the Tudor dynasty, the issue of succession created a crisis that was resolved only by importing a king from Scotland (who believed in the Divine Right of Kings). Not for nothing is a large part of the theme of kingship in Shakespeare concerned with usurpers, with the hollow crown, with clothes that don't fit, and with the distinction between office, role and person.

Shakespeare has a Scottish play, *Macbeth*, but no Irish play. At the time he was writing, as Baptista Boazio's detailed map of *Irelande* (1599) serves to illustrate, Ireland belonged to various chieftains and overlords, but their land was being systematically confiscated by Queen Elizabeth and given to her friends, courtiers and adventurers such as Walter Raleigh and Edmund Spenser. The dispersed centres of power in Ireland were no match for a united kingdom. From the coloniser's perspective, the colonial encounter, the meeting between the female harp and the male crown, commences offstage, with the brutal expression of power, with the entry of the Protestant stranger into Catholic and Anglo-Norman Ireland, and with dispossession. In Ireland it was centre stage, for the Elizabethan Plantation of Munster resulted in what the Gaelic writers at the time came to call the *longbhriseadh* or shipwreck of the Irish nation, and it was followed in the second half of the seventeenth century by the Ulster Plantation and the introduction of a distinctive drumbeat, which can still be heard to this day. In the eighteenth century, the descendants of the English and Scottish settlers learnt to call Ireland their nation and went on to establish their own parliament in Dublin, which ran from 1782 until it was abolished, in the aftermath of the French Revolution, by the Act of Union in 1801. Thereafter, the national ideal passed increasingly into Catholic hands, but not before the leader of the Irish Parliamentary Party in the 1880s – a Protestant landlord, Charles Stewart Parnell, the 'uncrowned king of Ireland' – almost succeeded in winning Home Rule from the crown. Independence followed in the next generation but unity did not, for partition divided Ireland into twenty-six counties, which formed the new State, and six counties of Ulster's nine, which refused to surrender their union with the United Kingdom.

Power and possession, assimilation and resistance, has characterised the colonial encounter since its inception. As Speaker in the newly convened Irish House of Commons in October 1614, Sir John Davies deployed a vocabulary and imagery designed to pacify his opponents among the recently dispossessed Irish, but in the richness of his language he merely called attention to the force of history and to the problems of ever ruling Ireland through consent:

> And this excellent cure [joining together the 'limbs' of Britain and Ireland] hath been performed by the wisdom and goodness of His Majesty, who in all his actions doth make good that word of his 'Beati pacifici' [Blessed are the peacemakers], and who, finding the strings of his harp of Ireland in discord and out of tune, hath not by hard wresting broken them, but by gentle and easy winding brought them to a concord; and though in the tuning of this instrument there hath been a little jarring and harshness at the first, yet now the strings are set right by so happy and skilful a hand, we hope that the music that shall follow shall be the sweeter.[3]

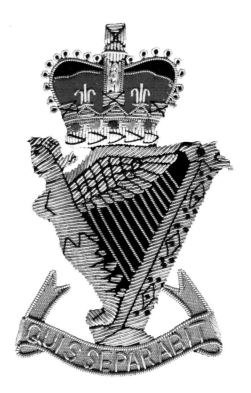

For many centuries, from its introduction in 1534 in the reign of Henry VIII, the harp and the crown – or rather the uneasy alliance between the two – graced British coins, was the emblem of choice adopted by various regiments of the British Army, and was worn with pride as a cap badge by the Royal Irish Constabulary until Irish Independence in 1922 and by the Royal Ulster Constabulary in Northern Ireland until its abandonment in 2002, in the aftermath of the Belfast Agreeement. For loyalists and unionists, the union between the harp and the crown inspired or inspires allegiance; for republicans and some nationalists, disaffection. But the harp never surrendered its ambition (and neither did the crown). Wherever the Irish fought, served, or pitched tent – and the Irish, we need little reminding, 'knocked at every nation's door'[4] – the harp

A striking badge with the motto prominently displayed. 'Quis separabit' (Who shall separate [Great Britain and Ireland]) was a favourite motto of British regiments with an Irish connection. As the argument of my book suggests, one answer is 'modern Irish writing'.

was their musical accompaniment, and it signalled not the separation but the many-layered interpenetration of culture and politics from pride to resistance, from chains to freedom, from assigned to individual identity and back again, from Tammany Hall to the White House. In 'Down Erin's Lovely Lee', a Fenian song dating from the 1860s, the hope expressed by the rebels driven out of Ireland as they sailed down the River Lee in Cork on their way to America is that one day their country might see the harp without the crown; an Ireland free, that is, from British rule.[5] The title to this introductory chapter is taken from this little-known song, but it shouldn't be thought that my book offers an unreconstructed Fenian view of modern Irish writing, for there is a counter-current also at work: Ireland may be a separatist issue but it is almost impossible to handle in a separatist way.

In the colonial context the border area between politics and culture is constantly criss-crossed, so that loss and struggle belong to politics as much as to culture. In some texts, the interpenetration is so strong that it has a tangible quality. There is a highly-charged scene in Seamus Deane's novel *Reading in the Dark* (1996), for instance, when the narrator's mother stands on the stairs looking out of the lobby window, whispering to herself, her mind fixated on burning. It is a moment of intense loss, especially for the narrator's Derry Catholic family, and is beautifully rendered by Deane in the haunting sentence: 'She was going out from us, becoming strange, becoming possessed.'[6] The loss of a mother for a boy, the loss of a wife for a husband, the loss of a past free from guilt – loss builds as the significance of a family secret concerning an act of betrayal during the Troubles in the 1920s leads to tragic consequences. As he attempts to make sense of a sectarian world consuming everything it touches, the boy is left reading in the dark. But Deane's remark has a wider resonance, for behind the boy's plight can be heard the sounds of what happened to Ireland as a whole under the colonial encounter: 'She was going out from us, becoming strange, becoming possessed.' As the land is confiscated, the familiar is defamiliarised, with the colonial subject becoming strange even to himself as the stranger enters the land. The boy's mother is possessed by ghosts, but now 'possession' accrues other meanings, not only the more straightforward one of ownership but also the one allied to Yeats's *Cathleen ni Houlihan* (1902), the dream of the colonised for liberation, for a return of what was lost, for the transformation of Ireland, the Poor Old Woman, into a beautiful queen. What Deane's novel insists on is something less utopian, namely the anguish, the loss of a familiar/family world, the emptying of a future of dreams, and the bitter residue, the story of how the mother will never return to herself.

'Always historicise!' is Fredric Jameson's celebrated call to arms.[7] In the Irish context, as *Reading in the Dark* indicates, the comment is somewhat redundant, for it is almost impossible not to feel the force of history everywhere in the culture. So pervasive is its presence that it produces striking, and even what might be considered extreme, responses, as with James Joyce's Stephen Dedalus, for whom history represented not the wisdom of the ancient world but a nightmare from which he was trying to awake (*U* 2:377). Or we could consider Eavan Boland's memorable phrase, 'outside history', and her complaint against the exclusion of women and the whole area of domesticity from the boys' own story of Irish history.[8] Drawing a line under history or escaping into the eternal present of landscape or nature has rarely, if ever, been possible, so to insist on historicising is less radical than it sounds. The real issue is not Jameson's injunction to historicise but the need to devise a sensitive framework that is not overwhelmed by history and which doesn't assume that the task is finished when all the marginal groups are recuperated from history; a framework, in other words, which makes sense of both legacy and reciprocity in the colonial relationship and which does justice to the system of injustice as a whole.

The colonial relationship between Britain and Ireland can be understood in a number of different ways, of which clash is the most obvious. A hundred years ago, the Irish nationalist ideologue D. P. Moran believed in the clash of civilisations between the Saxon and the Celt, but my own study is better served by the word 'encounter' and an attention to culture, not civilisation.[9] What clash doesn't allow for is common ground, markings other than black and white, and the intervention of politics. In every encounter something happens, or something else happens. Hovering over any attempt at ethnic cleansing in the North in the last thirty years is the irony that two of the opposing protagonists, Martin McGuinness and Ken Maginnis, shared almost the identical surname. A more sophisticated way is unwinding. The visionary Yeats, spanning two states and two literary generations, imagined that, 'Each age unwinds the thread another age had wound . . . all things dying each other's life, living each other's death'.[10] This has the merit of neatness and suggestiveness but it does not really square with what happened in modern Irish history, whether at the time or subsequently. In the 1920s, modern Ireland inherited a house the Irish formerly owned, but in reclaiming that house a dispute arose among the warring brothers about ownership, rendering any clean break with the past (or image of a spool) impossible. The legacy of colonialism lingered long after 1922, as did memories of colonialism, and when the Troubles in the North erupted in 1968, the spectre of British imperialism again threatened the stability of the whole island. So unwinding is not really an appropriate metaphor.

A third way is interconnectedness. In a poem entitled 'According to Pythagoras', Michael Longley refers to the 'fundamental interconnectedness of all things'.[11] The phrase is deliberately stiff, being an attempt to capture the bluntness of Pythagoras, but there is nothing leaden about the idea. My own sense of interconnectedness when thinking about colonialism tends to focus on a dialectical relationship rather than on cosmology or an essentially personal view of the universe. Interconnectedness is allied with my argument, but it needs to be supplemented by something less diffuse. In the colonial context at some stage the coloniser and the

The Crown Without the Harp. A fading mural in Belfast dating from the 1940s, with the kerbstone suitably adorned to match in red, white and blue. Photographer: Geoff Howard. Courtesy: Camera Press, London.

Left: Henry VIII harp groat, 1534–5. This was the first coin to carry the harp and the crown. It also carried the initials H and A for Henry and Ann Boleyn.

Middle: Copper coin from the reign of Queen Elizabeth I [Seaby 6510]. On one side of the coin E and R can be deciphered, on the obverse the harp and crown and the date 1601, the year which witnessed the defeat of the Irish earls Hugh O'Neill and Hugh O'Donnell at the Battle of Kinsale. With the accession of James I in 1603, the harp was included on the royal coat-of-arms as a sign of the crown's consolidation over Ireland. In the seventeenth century, the harp with a winged female figure, surmounted by an English crown, acquired emblematic status.

Right: Struck later than its date suggests, this token displays on one side the harp and crown, newly joined under the Act of Union, and on the other side Britannia holding an olive branch and trident, a union shield at her side, a ship on the seas in the distance. Courtesy to John Stafford-Langan for all these coins.

colonised rise and converge, as Flannery O'Connor puts it in her Southern short story about race and the eventual confrontation between white racist attitudes and the black individual, how 'everything that rises must converge'.[12] This is what happened when Gerry Adams, the Sinn Féin leader who famously had been denied the oxygen of publicity by Margaret Thatcher, was invited to Downing Street to shake hands with her successor. One drawback with this kind of interconnectedness is that it is driven by the consciousness of harmony and resolution, a consciousness which can give the appearance of being either too remote from actual conflict and injustice or too future-directed. The past and present are simply on the way to the future, and loss and struggle are there to be overcome, not to be valued or cherished in themselves.

The emphasis in this book is on an encounter, on the mobile and affecting image of the harp and the crown, and on the dynamic concept of a changing relationship, at the heart of which is loss and struggle. How the colonial encounter between Britain and Ireland is reflected in modern Irish writing in English is the question I set myself at the outset of this study. My aim has been to trace and delineate, to draw out and underline, to complicate and make sense of the legacy that encounter has bequeathed us. How did Irish writers cope with the Great

City Arms, Dublin.

This postcard of Dublin around 1900, on the eve of the new tramway system, provides a graphic view of the colonial encounter. Behind the imposing statue of the nationalist hero Daniel O'Connell stands the English hero Lord Nelson on his pillar, which in the 1880s was the fourth highest obelisk in the world. In the 1900s Sackville Street was in the process of being changed to O'Connell Street. In the 1960s Nelson was blown up by republicans; today the spot he once occupied boasts a spire, designed by an English architect, pushing 400 metres into the postcolonial air.

Famine, with the struggle for independence, with the violence of the Troubles, and with a history that did not live up to expectations? A stress on the colonial encounter not only allows scope to shed light on the hyphen which divides and joins Anglo-Irish literature but also acts as a pointer to the way modern Irish writing learnt how to become in part independent and to develop its own system of exchange.

As indicated above, the title of my book 'Light, Freedom and Song' comes from Moore's melody 'Dear Harp of My Country' (1815), composed during an earlier period in that encounter:

> Dear Harp of my Country! in darkness I found thee,
> The cold chain of silence had hung o'er thee long;
> When proudly, my own Island Harp! I unbound thee,
> And gave all thy chords to light, freedom and song!

'Light, Freedom and Song.' Edwardian postcard which included the lines from Tom Moore's song 'Dear Harp of My Country'.

Dear Harp of my country, in darkness I found thee,
  The cold chain of silence had hung o'er thee long,
When proudly, my own Island Harp! I unbound thee,
  And gave all thy chords to light, freedom and song.

The lines, the words with music, have rightly moved generations, for Moore understood the power of emotions and how these are wrapped in the simplest of phrases which are then unwrapped to reveal as here 'light, freedom and song'. The intensity, as indeed the nostalgia and the pleasure, belongs in a sense to the future, for Moore's work enters the culture as a utopian gesture, as hope deferred. Modern Irish writing is heir to this particular Romantic tradition, and even in its darkest moments it retains a struggle for articulation, an awareness of itself as different, and a commitment to a world free of the colonial encounter. If much of the story I have to tell is about the dark and the cold chain of silence, Moore reminds us of an accompanying chord that Irish writers have continued to strike in the cause of culture and humanity.

Outline

This book is divided into three sections with companion chapters in each section. The first section, 'Defining Contexts', which has three chapters, is devoted to providing key frames or reference points. In an introductory chapter on the hybrid character of modern Irish writing, I draw attention to some of the ways language, culture and history have been affected by the colonial encounter. In Chapter 3, in keeping with my concern for loss, I reflect on the greatest manifestation of loss in modern Irish culture, namely the Great Famine of the 1840s. This chapter surveys the nightmare view of Irish history, exploring how Irish writers and others have coped with a sense of loss in the culture. Anyone walking the hills of Ireland or boating down its inland waterways cannot but be struck by the absence of people and by the irony that part of the pleasure derives from a landscape empty or – more worryingly – emptied of people. The irony is well-captured by Boland in 'That the Science of Cartography is Limited', a poem that focuses on a road built by Famine victims which is now covered by a wood, a road that in fact ended when the victims died. Boland imagines their world without a horizon, noticing how maps of Ireland are in this respect indeed 'limited'.[13]

In 1841, in the census before the Great Famine of 1845 to 1852, the population of Ireland was over eight million, but by 1851 that figure had

6,548,000
1840

2,953,451
1946

2040
????

This sketch is taken from John O'Brien's study *The Vanishing Irish* (1954). Fortunately, as 2040 comes into view, such fears of the vanishing Irish have receded.

been reduced to six and a half million. According to the 2001 census, the population of Ireland, north and south of the border, is now more than five and a half million, with over 3,839,000 in the Republic and 1,685,000 in the North. Ireland is unique among the countries of Europe in possessing today a population lower than it had in 1841, and only since the 1960s has there been any sign of increase. By contrast, in 1841 Britain's population was eighteen and a half million; today it is nearly sixty million. If Ireland had grown at such a rate, its population would now be over twenty-five million. In 1954 a book appeared with the title *The Vanishing Irish*, in which the fear was expressed that if the decline continued, 'the Irish will virtually disappear as a nation and will be found only as an enervated remnant in a land occupied by foreigners'.[14] Half a century later that gloomy prognosis has proved false, but the image of the Irish who vanished still haunts the imagination.

Christine Kinealy argues that Ireland never recovered demographically from the Famine and that psychologically 'it is only beginning to be recognised that the scars left by this tragedy have been deep'.[15] Identifying the scars is no easy task, partly because in one sense they are invisible: starvation no longer stalks the Irish countryside; the fields are well-stocked; abandoned houses, when not replaced by those seeking second or retirement homes, add character as ruins; and emigrants take their story with them. Only the fragile status of the language the people spoke for two millennia remains to taunt us. Kinealy's interest in psychology is a reminder that effects can be felt even when a history cannot be traced. The Famine is part of the colonial encounter but it also belongs to something less amenable to classification, namely the difficulty of establishing an adequate discourse for an event that threatened to destroy not just a people but the pysche of a people (which can then be seen as belonging to that encounter).

Beginning this account with the Famine is a way of signalling a concern with loss and with what got lost in the culture. In 1990, a tourism consultancy study proposed five large headings or themes under which to group Irish heritage attractions – live landscapes; making a living; saints and religion; building a nation; and the spirit of Ireland.[16] This is too upbeat by far to cope with the Famine and serves to remind us both of the limits of cultural tourism and of the importance of certain 'themes', remaining outside the culture even as we seek to include them. In one of his poems, Thomas Kinsella speaks of the Famine as being 'unsimplifiable'.[17] The facts are simple – so many died, so many emigrated – but the event resists assimilation, and, even as the story is retold, the tragedy lacks a final act of retribution or reconciliation or the kind of satire on display in Jonathan Swift's *A Modest Proposal* (1729). Perspective is what the historian seeks but there is something unyielding about the Famine. The Great War in the United Kingdom and elsewhere in Europe has been partly absorbed by annual commemorations and monuments to the dead, but the victims of the Famine are only fitfully recalled in Ireland and their identity remains for the most part unknown.

The Famine serves as a reminder that tradition, as understood in a literary sense, is not always appropriate when embarking on a critical investigation into modern Irish writing in English. In structuring the book the way I have, with Chapter 3 focusing on deprivation and Chapter 4 on the march of a nation, my intention is to present an account that is twin-tracked, in which one section is geared to tracing cultural responses to material circumstances, while the other focuses on scrutinising the ideological formation and trajectory of nationalist ideas. The relationship between material circumstances and nationalist ideas, or between base and superstructure, to invoke Marx, between James Connolly and Patrick Pearse, seems to me the underlying and continuing issue in modern Irish culture, and, because it is enduring, it is as radical in its own way as what can then be seen as the temporary conflict between the harp and the crown. The colonial encounter deceived the colonised into thinking that loss could be overcome with independence. Only occasionally were other voices to be heard, as when the first Editorial in *The Irish Commonwealth* (1919) – significantly entitled 'Ourselves', a rejoinder, that is, to Sinn Féin and its exclusive emphasis on nationalism – proclaimed, a little forlornly but still with a residue of truth: 'For Ireland, as for the rest of Europe, social issues will soon dominate the situation.'[18] In advancing the claims of nationality, both the generation which created the Revival and the generation which inherited it tended to ignore the issue of material circumstances. Images of labour in modern Irish culture are few and far between, an absence which has had real political effects.[19] James Connolly worked tirelessly to promote the link between the two but after his execution in the aftermath of the Easter Rising, such a link was placed on indefinite hold and his agenda was largely sidelined. North and south of the border, 'Labour must wait' – de Valera's effective rebuke – has been a cry of contention ever since.

Chapter 4 is devoted to cultural nationalism in the period from the 1890s to the 1920s. With four Nobel Prize-winners for Literature – Yeats, Shaw, Beckett, Heaney – and five if the Irish-American dramatist Eugene O'Neill is included, and a fair sprinkling of Booker Prize-winning novelists and runners-up, Irish writing is now at the forefront of world literature. Ireland in 1890 gave little sign of the great period to come. The significant names in nineteenth-century Irish verse were represented by Thomas Moore, Samuel Ferguson and James Clarence Mangan. The novel could boast Maria Edgeworth, the pre- and post-Famine novelist William Carleton, as well as the tradition of the Irish Gothic novel from Charles Maturin, author of *Melmoth the Wanderer* (1820) to Sheridan Le Fanu, author of *The House by the Churchyard* (1863), and on to the reclaimed Irish writer Bram Stoker, author of *Dracula* (1897). The leading figure in drama was Dion Boucicault, author of *The Colleen Bawn* (1860), *Arrah-na-Pogue* (1865), and *The Shaughran* (1875). With one or two exceptions, this is not a list of names to command the world's attention for long, and we might well concur with George Moore's observation on

the eve of his return to Dublin in 1901: 'Strange that Ireland should have produced
so little literature, for there is a pathos in Ireland, in its people, in its landscapes,
and in its ruins.'[20] Such a rise to prominence of modern Irish writing in the twentieth century calls for explanation, and the view advanced here is that it stems from
an intensification at both the political and cultural levels in the colonial encounter
between Britain and Ireland.

In Tom Stoppard's play *Shipwreck* (2002), the literary critic Vissarion Belinsky is
animated by the thought that, 'People are going to be amazed by Russian writers.
In literature we're a great nation before we're ready.'[21] The first sentence could also
apply to Irish writers, but the second sentence – Belinsky is thinking of Gogol,
Pushkin, Dostoyevsky – is one to ponder in the Irish context. Russia was already a
nation-state, if not a 'great nation', when its major writers came on the scene, but
modern Ireland did not become a nation-state until 1922. The issue of readiness is
rarely asked in the context of culture – though it has been in historical accounts of
the transition with the outgoing British administration – and it would be difficult
to supply an answer, given that the achievement of the Revival was followed so
rapidly by the Irish Civil War. Part of the problem with the comparison lies in this:
modern Ireland has produced great writers but these writers do not or did not in
themselves produce either a nation or a great nation. Twentieth-century Irish writers were at the forefront of modern literature, but, except for someone like Yeats,
'great nation' status rarely featured as a political ambition. The battle-cry of the
republic-in-waiting was 'A Nation Once Again' or 'the harp without the crown',
independence or autonomy rather than greatness. So the relationship between literature and nationalism in Ireland is different or more complex, where time-
frames both overlap and co-exist, where the word 'accompanying' is as much in
evidence as 'foreshadowing', and where the phrase 'great nation' seems strangely
out of place.

Cultural nationalism as a concept is also explored in the context of recent
debates over nations and nationalism. Political nationalism – as with Parnell and
his Irish Parliamentary Party in the 1880s – is concerned directly with the achievement of political independence; cultural nationalism – as with Douglas Hyde's
Gaelic League – is concerned with the achievement of cultural independence.
These distinctions are not water-tight, and, equally, the relationship between the
two, when it exists, merits investigation. Yeats's late question, 'Did that play of
mine send out/Certain men the English shot?' (*VP* 632), which he asked in 1938
about *Cathleen ni Houlihan* (1902) and that play's effect on those who fought in
the 1916 Rising, constitutes a reminder of their proximity both in historical and in
conceptual terms. It was Maud Gonne's belief that without Yeats, without the
Revival he helped bring about, there would have been no Rising.[22] I don't pursue
that line here, for I have two other objects in mind: one is the uniqueness of
Ireland to the debate about nationalism, the other the common ground Ireland

shares with other modern nations. Ireland's uniqueness means that generalisations about the development of modern nationalism need to take account of discontinuities and exceptions to the rule – the specific history that Ireland has enjoyed – while its commonality means that the 'naturalness' of nationalism needs to be at once understood, valued, and overcome. With this in mind, I have therefore deployed not only Irish figures but also modern European thinkers, from Ernest Renan to Ernest Gellner.

The middle section of the book, 'Fields of Play', addresses the colonial encounter from the perspective of the two Irish writers who define the age: Yeats and Joyce. In the subversive 'Lessons' chapter of *Finnegans Wake*, where Joyce 'answers' Yeats's gyres with a sketch of two overlapping circles, intended to represent the female genitalia, the two are yoked together as a couple: 'a daintical pair of accomplasses! You, allus for the kunst and me for omething with a handel to it' (*FW* 295:27–8). The portmanteau words betray a child-like playing with words and cross-gendering: 'daintical' carries both 'dainty' and 'identical' and 'accomplasses' simultaneously suggests the words 'accomplice', 'compass', and 'lasses'. The stress on identity, gender and transgression is continued in Joyce's schoolboy playing on the German word *kunsthandel* or 'art dealer'. Yeats was always for the *kunst* (for Art, for women), while Joyce is for music, but, being more down-to-earth, Joyce is also for anything with a handle to it (commerce, the male body or friendship, 'omething'). Chapters 5 and 6 are also to do with unpacking but they afford a more straightforward enquiry, one that is specific and New Historicist in direction. In one chapter I concentrate on 'Easter 1916', a familiar poem that has received a considerable amount of critical attention, and in the other on a lighter topic, 'Joyce and cricket', that has received almost none. It is clear from reading these chapters that as an interpretative framework the colonial encounter, if properly handled, is more subtle than might be at first thought and has the capacity to shed light on both the familiar and the unfamiliar.

In any debate about cultural nationalism in Ireland, the figure of Yeats, the subject of Chapter 5, looms large. This is especially true of his views on the origins of the Revival. The classic contextual interpretation regarding the Revival, and one that still informs much thinking in this area, is Yeats's, that with the fall of Parnell in 1890 a space opened for the rise of literature.[23] In a moment of what he imagined was 'supernatural insight', it came to Yeats in the early 1890s that Ireland would be 'soft wax for years to come'.[24] What he meant by this was that literature could now distinguish itself from propaganda verse and political rhetoric and would therefore be free to develop along its own lines, allowing her writers to 'think of Ireland herself'.[25] In seeking to drive a wedge between literature and politics, Yeats ensured that the terms of the debate were largely his, but he also stimulated an antithetical movement, namely the return of literature to a political setting. Thinking of Ireland was at this time essentially prescriptive and therefore of necessity political. Thus the plays Yeats sought for his new theatre in Dublin addressed Sligo rather than London, the ennobling past rather than the jaded present, and Art rather than the box office. The result was less than inspiring. According to one commentator, the phrase that best summarises the Abbey Theatre's plays in its early years is 'rural backwardness and national introspection'.[26] While not entirely accurate, such an observation contains some truth, for this was the period when *John Bull's 'Other Island'* (1904), Shaw's incisive satire on the colonial encounter between Britain and Ireland, was commissioned and then rejected by Yeats, in part because it did not conform to Lady Gregory's desire for plays with 'an apex of beauty and a base of realism'.[27]

Yeats himself was given to extremes, which inevitably pitched him into politics. In his Dedication to George Russell at the beginning of *The Secret Rose* (1897), a collection of stories about Red Hanrahan, Irish folklore and the occult, Yeats suggests that his overriding subject is 'the war of spiritual with natural order'.[28] Such an inflammatory remark was given a keener historical edge in *Cathleen ni Houlihan* (1902), a play which Stephen Gwynn thought at the time shouldn't be performed 'unless one was prepared for people to go out to shoot or be shot', an issue which, as we have seen, concerned Yeats in later life.[29] As Raymond Williams once observed about George Orwell, it is not so much what Orwell wrote as what wrote Orwell that needs investigating. The remark is not an exact fit for Yeats but it can be adapted. The continuing task facing the critic of Yeats is not just to understand but also to see through the terms of his argument. If the Revival is a product of cultural nationalism, at the heart of cultural nationalism is Yeats. To attend to Yeats is to be involved in unravelling, so that the construction of Yeats is inevitably also a form of deconstruction. The same is true of cultural nationalism, which in Ireland has until the 1920s the look of the future about it but which thereafter never quite shakes off the sense of it all being over.

'Easter 1916', the main focus of Chapter 5, is a richly emblematic 'green' poem. Hidden and on display are Yeats's competing loyalties. On the one hand there is his provincial Protestant Sligo background, a background where of an evening, as he tells us in *Reveries Over Childhood and Youth* (1916), he would proudly run up the Union Jack in his garden; on the other hand there is his attraction in middle age to the rebels' sacrifice and to their motivation and cause. On the one hand, there is conversation at his various clubs in Dublin and London; on the other hand, there is dramatic action outside, on the streets. On the one hand, he imagines Ireland as motley, the colour worn by clowns, under a colonial cloud; on the other hand, the Easter Rising dramatically unfurls again the green flag of nationalist Ireland. In 'September 1913' he considered heroic Ireland 'dead and gone' but now discovers he was wrong, so wrong that he declares quite categorically that not only 'now' but also 'in time to be' Ireland had been 'changed/Changed utterly', where the unstressed final syllable of 'utterly' is made to rhyme with 'be' and so given an extra insistence, as if to dispel doubt. It's a poem about gestures and about change, change from one state to another – in personal attitudes, the natural world, Irish history, and Anglo-Irish relations – and it is as if the whole historic burden of the colonial encounter is being weighed again in his mind. In focusing on the fifty-one-year-old poet's response to Year One in modern Irish history, my intention is to draw out something of the complexity not only in the man but also in the hybrid culture that produced him. The poem also gives voice to tensions, especially in the area of gender and nationalism, and I return to these again in my chapter on the 1980s, for, as Boland's concept of 'outside history' indicates, the categories of the harp and the crown stand in need of extension and qualification.

Chapter 6 is devoted to Joyce and cricket in the light of the colonial encounter. Cricket is a game that once belonged exclusively to English gentlemen. In the Victorian period it became associated with the spread of Empire and tends therefore to be played only in countries of the former British Empire. Beyond small pockets, such as Philadelphia in the period between the 1840s and the Great War, interest in the game in the United States never took off.[30] In Ireland it did, but geographical proximity and the colonial encounter ensured it never became a national game. In the *Freeman's Journal* – a Dublin newspaper consulted by Joyce when writing *Ulysses* – the scorecards for some three cricket games played in Ireland (along with eight English county matches) are recorded on 16 June 1904, testimony to considerable interest at the time: this was indeed the golden age of cricket in Ireland.[31] For countries which play the game today, cricket has largely shrugged off its colonial image; indeed, its centre has shifted in part to the Indian sub-continent (where it unites countries that have nuclear weapons trained on each other). As for those labouring under the illusion that cricket is a minority sport, it is worth citing a remark made by Ramachandra Guha about test-match encounters between India and Pakistan: 'When [Sachin] Tendulkar is batting against the Pakistani swing-bowler Wasim Akram, the television audience exceeds the entire population of Europe.'[32]

Wherever the game was played, over time it produced different responses. The phrase Guha uses to describe the status of cricket in the changeover from colonialism to independence in India is '[t]horoughly domesticated' (p.xiii), so domesticated that a recent US Ambassador to India, lamenting the fate of baseball in the sub-continent, noticed how India seems 'impervious to American influence' (p.438). In the West Indies, cricket wasn't just domesticated; it was part of a long-term anti-colonial and nation-building enterprise, which culminated for some in the ambition to score a century at Lords. *Beyond a Boundary* is the title of C. L. R. James' book on cricket in the Caribbean, and when juxtaposed with what happened to the game in Ireland the phrase is especially suggestive, as my discussion of the topic serves to illustrate. There was never any ambition on the part of the colonised subject in Ireland to hit a hundred runs in London, but there was an issue with boundaries and borders and with the kind of games – linguistic, real and symbolic – they were forced to play with the coloniser. In keeping with the movement outward, I begin Chapter 6 with the sounds of cricket on the school playing fields of Victorian Ireland in *A Portrait of the Artist as a Young Man* and end with *The Crying Game*, the Irish director Neil Jordan's film about postcolonial identity. This film, we might recall, keeps returning to the cricket jumper worn by Jody, the black British soldier from Antigua, a jumper that haunts Fergus at each stage in his relationship with Jody's partner, Dil. Like Joyce, Jordan, two genera- tions later, could discern something of the complexity at the heart of cricket as a metaphor for the colonial encounter beyond a boundary.

In Ireland, cricket has had a checkered history, especially in the transition from dependency to independence, but this was less marked at Joyce's old school, Clongowes Wood, where the game is still played today. Similarly, Joyce's one-time protégé, Samuel Beckett, played cricket for Trinity College Dublin in 1925–6 and one of his regrets about living in Paris was not seeing his favourite game more often. If Ireland had been allowed room to advance independently of Britain it might have developed a keen interest in the game for its own sake, just as in recent years it has done for rugby and English soccer. As it is, watching cricket being played at Trinity in the heart of Dublin today remains a slightly bizarre – that is, a quintessentially postcolonial – experience, not least because a university formerly noted for its Englishness is now given over to marketing things Irish (of which cricket isn't one). What intrigues me is how cricket features in Joyce's writings and how it is used in his depiction of the colonial encounter; how what appears an easy target for the colonised can become, in sensitive hands, an ally in a struggle for a much wider liberation. From the 'pick, pack, pock, puck' sequence of sounds in *A Portrait of the Artist as a Young Man*, published the same year Yeats composed 'Easter 1916', to a famous passage on cricket in *Finnegans Wake*, Joyce betrayed an affection for the game which straddled the colonial divide and which allowed him room, unlike the English house system of his Irish boarding-school, to wrest some form of ownership from the imperial sphere of influence.

Chapter 7, 'Ireland in the 1930s', and Chapter 8, 'Ireland in the '1980s', are com- panion chapters which take forward the historical argument of the book. The 1930s was the first full decade when the harp – in the Irish Free State that is – was heard independently of the crown. Fifty years later, the colonial encounter in the North returned with a vengeance, arresting the forward momentum of history and reawakening old patterns and responses. The contrast between the two decades is especially apparent if we recast time as space, the 1930s as the West, the 1980s as the North, and compare attitudes to the West with identity issues in the North. In a documentary film such as Robert Flaherty's *Man of Aran* (1934), the sleepy West received an ethnological makeover, with the Canadian outsider seeking to impose a vision on the people now seen as natives. By contrast, in the 1980s, the cock of the North never stopped crowing and threatened to wake up the whole island of Ireland. In the 1930s, the impact of censorship increased the sense of disenchantment; in the 1980s in the North it wasn't disenchantment but noisy despair which became the emotional accompaniment to political deadlock. Juxtaposing these two decades serves to highlight what Joyce referred to as the 'same renew' (*FW* 226:17) quality of modern Irish history, as well as the different ways in which writers and other artists faced the challenges of history.

For generations, fear of the 'word' and taboos associated with images of the body helped define Irish Catholic thinking, but in the 1930s such fear became enshrined in the new State. The implementation of censorship in the 1930s, together with the economic war fought with Britain over compensation claims for land annuities, are graphic reminders of a continuing colonial legacy, as if the harp sought to block the worldview of the coloniser. The idea of a border acquired a new meaning, no longer now simply associated with a political border between the Free State and the North but, more significantly, with the cultural border between Ireland and the outside world. The 1930s posed the awkward question: after Independence, what then? Censorship supplied one answer and, as I draw out in this chapter, it overshadows each of the four areas I discuss: the influence of de Valera, the image of the West of Ireland in film and literature, the issue of emigration, and the recuperation of the self. De Valera's small island view of Ireland needed protecting from the new world of the cinema and radio; the image of the West was contested as if it embodied an ideal of Irishness threatened by modernity, as if it were the displaced harp; people emigrated in the 1930s not just for work but also on account of censorship and claustrophobia in the culture; and censorship called forth its opposite, namely the recuperation of the self outside the Church's control. In considering the legacy and the limitations of de Valera's worldview, I also survey Irish writing during and after the Second World War, examining in particular the work of Elizabeth Bowen, Francis Stuart, and John Hewitt, transitional writers who expressed complicated allegiances, especially towards the harp and the crown.

Among the contradictory forces at play in the 1930s, some sought a return of Ireland to the past, while others broke new ground. In the cloud-filled canvases of Paul Henry, in the tawny-coloured reassuring postcards of Maurice Wilks, in the quiet autobiographical reflections in Mary Carbery's *The Farm By Lough Gur* (1937), and in the even quieter sketches of life in the Glens of Antrim in Hubert Quinn's *Dear Were The Days* (1934), what we witness is a deep resistance to, or a reluctance to engage with, the forces of history. But retreat wasn't the whole story, for the turn in the culture was not so much escapist as inward, and it was the journey inward which permitted writers the freedom to discover their own voices, away from centres of power. They also discovered that, in spite of Independence, history was subject matter they couldn't let go. On display throughout Chapter 7 is

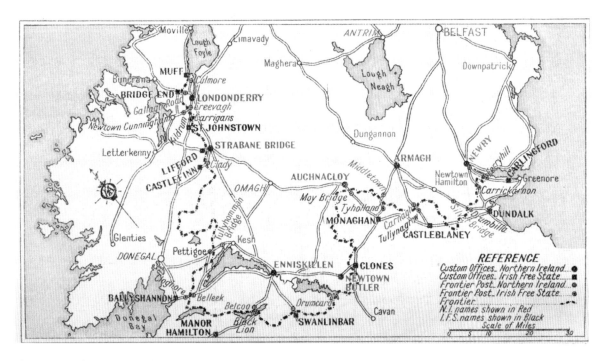

the tension between the hopes of a previous generation and the perceived failure of the present, between the reality of independence and a history of dependency, between images of Ireland generated from within the culture and powerful images now coming from abroad.

At the same time, it is evident that the 1930s was a decade when modern Irish culture began to change direction, reconfiguring again the relation between loss and struggle. The decade opens with Kathleen Coyle's psychological novel *A Flock of Birds* (1930) and closes with Sean O'Faoláin's 'Irish-American' novel *Come Back to Erin* (1940), which are both unduly neglected novels. In between came the outpouring of the last generation of Blasket Islanders, the launch of the Irish Folklore Commission, the rewriting of the West of Ireland in social or materialistic terms, a renewed interest in forms of social life outside of conventional politics, the reassessment of the relationships between the private and the public spheres and between the local, regional and national, the beginnings of an environmental conscience, as can be discerned in Monk Gibbon's *The Seals* (1935), the later, and arguably the most remarkable, poetry of Yeats, and two texts – Flann O'Brien's *At Swim-Two-Birds* (1939) and Joyce's *Finnegans Wake* (1939) – which ensured that the Irish contribution to postmodernism was in place forty years before that term was called on to define a style or period.

Because the title of the first chapter of this book is taken from a Fenian song, I am conscious that I might seem to be relegating the North to the narrow ground it

Red and Black. Ireland with and without the crown in the 1930s. The 1930 *AA Handbook to Ireland* referred not to the border but to the frontier between the Irish Free State and Northern Ireland. The absence of straight lines on the map belied such extreme language.

occupies. Chapter 8, 'Ireland in the 1980s', seeks to redress this, for its focus is the
North during the period of the hunger strikes, a bleak period in relations between
Britain and Ireland. In assessing how Northern writers, especially those from a
nationalist background, have responded to the Troubles, I concentrate on the
poetry of Heaney and Padraic Fiacc, Pat Murphy's film *Maeve* (1981), and a selection of Troubles fiction. The topics considered include random sectarian murder,
the 'neighbourly murder', the deadly proximity of intimacy and distance, and the
relationship between the novel and history, topics which suggest something of the
difficulty for such writers in establishing a space free from pain, politics, or loss.
Like the 1930s, the 1980s also witnesssed a period of adjustment, especially in
social and cultural terms. With the entry of new discourses such as feminism and
the European ideal, the turn was not now inward but outward, as people
attempted to connect with a world outside the harp and the crown. But adjustment did not dissolve loss, or the history of the Famine, or the colonial encounter.
When politicians and contemporary historians insist that the world moves on, the
world often decides otherwise, and nowhere was this more true than of the North
in the modern period.

Politically, the 1980s also threw into sharp relief relations between Dublin and
Belfast and increased the pressure for a reassessment of the historic colonial legacy.
The legitimacy of the two states (or 'statelet' as the North is sometimes called by its
detractors) has been subject to intense scrutiny. Whether or not nationalism in the
Republic has from its inception been complicit in imperialism is a question that
never quite goes away. Was the Easter Rising a putsch that advanced Catholic interests at the expense of either Home Rule within the United Kingdom or a united
Ireland? Has Northern republicanism anything in common with de Valera's 'four
glorious years' from 1917 to 1921, when Sinn Féin won a massive landslide victory
and popular support in Ireland? Was it inevitable that over three thousand people
had to die as part of the price for the collapse of the unionist system in the North?
Can the Good Friday Belfast Agreement of 1998 create the conditions in which the
double minority (of nationalists in the North, and of unionists in the context of
Ireland as a whole) might enjoy living together? Given the troubled history in relations between the harp and crown, such questions are pressing, and it has not
always been possible to discern the shared cultural terrain between Dublin and
Belfast, or indeed between Britain and Ireland, in the continuing fragmentation of
the United Kingdom.

Culturally, there has been a constant movement between the South and the
North, for, unlike border custom-posts, ideas cannot be neatly disposed of. One of
the characters in Coyle's *Youth in the Saddle* (1927), a novel that moves back and
forth between Derry and Dublin, pointedly remarks that 'Hedges couldn't alter the
air you breathed',[33] that there are more basic things in the world and in the culture
than political borders. With this in mind, in my chapter on the 1980s, I reflect on

the representation of the body and on the idea of bodily secrets at work in both parts of Ireland. At the outset, what intrigued me was this: while in the North the male body as victim was acquiring notice, in the South it was the female body as object on display. (*Maeve*, a film set in the North about feminism and republicanism, complicates, but doesn't destroy, this initial insight.) At the time of the hunger strikes and the dirty protest in the H-Blocks and in the women's prison in Armagh, the body, as a symbol of utter negation pleading before the bar of international opinion, suddenly hit the headlines. The IRA hunger strike by male prisoners – impossible not to connect with the Famine or indeed with censorship – was an action without words but it spoke a language understood by millions. In the same years in film, painting, and literature in the South, the body, especially the female body, was also receiving renewed attention, for instance in the fiction of Maeve Kelly, the poetry of Ethne Strong, and in the work of painters such as Micheal Farrell and Robert Ballagh, and the issue I seek to explore is the connection between the two – between politics and gender, domination and resistance, republicanism and feminism, repression and expression in the aftermath of censorship, and between secrecy and disclosure, loss and struggle, the North and the South.

How writers have responded to the postmodern condition and to a history largely circumscribed by the harp and the crown is at the centre of my concluding chapter. The burden is increased in Ireland, for anyone putting pen to paper after Yeats, Joyce, and Beckett is forced to think carefully about the word 'after'. With the image of endgame, the title of Beckett's 1958 play, still troubling the scene, contemporary writers continue to live under several shadows in a kind of afterlife, ever conscious of a great period in literature preceding them. However, unlike a previous generation, they seem less overawed by their predecessors and also less overawed than their predecessors. In his choice of *At Swim, Two Boys* (2001) for a title, Jamie O'Neill consciously parades his debt to O'Brien's *At Swim-Two-Birds* (1939), but in some respects the comparison ends there, and we sense that his title represents a way of freeing himself from debts to the past. As the protagonist in John Banville's novel *Eclipse* (2000) remarks, with the sigh of someone who has spent a lifetime playing parts in the theatre: 'Life, life is always a surprise. Just when you think you have got the hang of it, have learnt your part to perfection, someone in the cast will take it into their head to start improvising, and the whole damned production will be thrown into disorder.'[34] Even if it remains out of reach for his protagonists, Banville is preoccupied with the issue of personal authenticity and its related rhetorical procedure, 'improvising'. Other writers, such as Derek Mahon, see their task as taking the contemporary pulse, and address in a more direct fashion the afterlife of literature and the postmodern condition, now understood in terms largely other than national identity or, indeed, struggle and loss.

The process of repositioning literature is part of the responsibility of both writers and critics, and if there is still room for the new, then some of it will be located in a process of endless recycling and in the continuing undertow of the colonial encounter. I close my concluding chapter with a separate section devoted to the work of John McGahern, a writer who, in part because he has attended to loss and struggle, has revived in a special way the matter of Ireland. From his watery outlook beside a lake in the Irish Midlands, away from the centres of power in Dublin, the once-banned novelist has invested in a long-term critique of what constitutes reality in modern Ireland. Central to that critique is the tension between pattern and change, between the iterative present and the eruption of a revolutionary past, between the straitjacket of patriarchy and the possibility of desire. The uncomfortable question that Moran, the male protagonist in *Amongst Women* (1990), asks about the struggle for Irish independence in the 1920s in which he took part is: 'What was it all for? The whole thing was a cod.'[35] In refusing to look away, McGahern reminds us of the power of history as well as of the struggle or obligation to deconstruct its power, and he thereby gives another twist to Jameson's injunction by returning us to the present, our senses renewed, able again for a time to face the rising sun.

PART ONE

DEFINING CONTEXTS

Chapter 2

The Hybrid Character of Modern Irish Writing

> Dere's more to Oireland dan dis.
> – Alan Partridge

This chapter is concerned with the contexts that have shaped the hybrid character of modern Irish writing. I touch on four areas – history, language, representation, and culture – with different intentions in mind in each case. History features prominently in modern Irish writing as both context and subject, presenting its writers with a challenge and a theme. In this section on history, which is written for those less familiar with its contours, I provide a basic summary of the trajectory of modern Irish history since the fall of Parnell in 1890. This is a schematic and descriptive account, which highlights Irish history's dual or hybrid character as the harp moved from a colonial country to an independent State in the 1920s. The section on language is also descriptive but is more selective in its choice of examples. My concern is with the specific kinds of language found in modern Irish writing and with how they relate to hybridity and the colonial encounter. Representation, the focus of the third section, concentrates on stereotypes of Ireland and on how writers have responded to and worked the hybrid landscape. In a final section, with a view to clarifying the distinctiveness of my own book, particularly with regard to the idea of culture and the dark, I outline my differences with the ideas of F. S. L. Lyons as they are formulated in *Culture and Anarchy in Ireland 1890–1939* (1979). Together, the four sections of this chapter are designed to contextualise and lay the groundwork for the study which follows.

History

The emphasis in postcolonial theory on hybridity provides a useful way of thinking about relations between Britain and Ireland.[1] In the colonial context, as 'Easter 1916' reminds us, it is never easy to determine where history ends and literature begins, or indeed what constitutes the separate fields of the harp and crown.

Opposite page
Detail of Bing Crosby from an album cover of *When Irish Eyes are Smiling.*

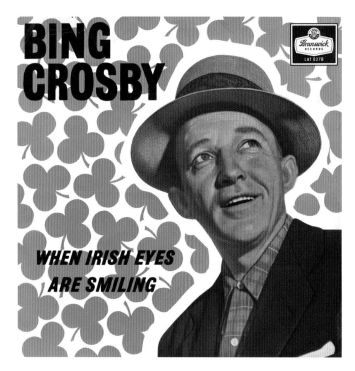

Images of hybridity focus the mind, but, as these two images suggest, hybridity is almost always a form of alterity, of elsewhere. Ever since Chancey Olcott's great hit of 1913, Irish eyes have been smiling on the world. No one in the twentieth century was better at rendering Irish sentimentality than the great American crooner. On this album, Bing goes in search of sunsets on Galway Bay, the philosophical conundrum posed by the impossibility of buying Killarney (an example of the American sublime?), and taking Kathleen home again to where her heart has ever been. Gay Byrne, meanwhile, for a generation dominated the Irish media with a weekly chat-show *The Late Late Show*. In a world of reciprocity and cross-cultural images, the Irish, with a history of colonial relations behind them, are as adept as anyone in defining others. They are also capable of relegating Joyce, Yeats, Wilde and Beckett to 'cultural Dubliners', a phrase that is closer to the tourist brochure than to the alterity of the dark. Courtesy of *RTE Guide*.

Indeed, history features so prominently as a topic or theme in modern Irish writing that its pervasiveness can be frustrating for those who come to literature to get away from history. As *Finnegans Wake* never stops insisting, 'waz iz' (*FW* 4:14), the past is present, the present is past, what was is. For the colonised, history is invariably foreground; for the coloniser, or those who inherit the colonial mantle, the perceived task is to relegate it to background, to draw a line under Irish history as British Prime Ministers before and after Harold Wilson sought to do. Such attitudes in their own way constitute a complex ideological response to the hybridity which has joined the limbs or fates of Britain and Ireland, for, whether one supports a unionist or a separatist agenda, it is difficult to visualise twentieth-century Irish history in isolation.

In considering the influence of the colonial encounter on the course of modern Irish history, four aspects can be noted. Firstly, Irish history is not quite in sync with European history. The two world wars dominate most histories of twentieth-century Europe, but this is not the case with the Republic of Ireland (which, prior to 1949, was called the Irish Free State). The Great War presented Irish nationalists with an opportunity, for England's difficulty was, according to the well-worn adage, Ireland's opportunity. During the Second World War, the Republic of Ireland remained neutral, refusing to side with the colonial power it had confronted in the War of Independence in 1919 to 1921. So, to a large extent, the Republic remained outside the formative experience that most Europeans lived through in the twentieth century. This is not the case with Northern Ireland. At the Battle of the Somme in July 1916, over five thousand Ulster Protestants lost their lives in the first two days alone, and in four nights in April to May 1941, nearly a thousand people were killed and over fifty thousand houses destroyed in raids on Belfast by the German Luftwaffe. Secondly, modern Irish history has been preoccupied with nationalism, an issue which, ironically, has been central to the twentieth century not so much in Europe, at least until the advent of Balkanisation, as in the wider world. So, while Ireland may have been out of sync with European history, its own history has chimed with what has occurred subsequently outside Europe, not least in countries that witnessed anti-colonial struggles. Thirdly, when, in recent decades, post- or late- became a preferred prefix in thinking about modern history – as in post-industrial, post-modern, late-modernity, and post-colonial – Ireland again bucked the trend and entered on a modernising project as if it was starting afresh the business of money-making and becoming a modern nation. Lateness as a historical concept has only rarely been troubling, though this is less true in the cultural domain (see my Conclusion). Indeed, in the 1990s, after decades of poor economic performance, the Celtic Tiger, as the remarkable growth of the Irish economy in the 1990s has been called, threatened to overturn history (and the talk of history) and in the process produce living standards higher (for some) than those enjoyed in the UK, the former colonial power. Fourthly, Ireland is now more in sync with Europe than its former colonial master is, and this has brought benefits. Were it not for its membership of the European Union, the ending of recent economic success in the wake of 9/11 and the subsequent global downturn could have made Ireland more exposed to external historical forces than it has been at any time since the Great Famine in the 1840s. Whether it retains its cherished independence in foreign affairs, only history can determine.

If we turn to the more specific details of dates and periods, we can begin with the fall of Parnell in 1890, an event which marked a decisive turn in modern Irish history. Constitutional nationalism was undermined and a clearing made for militant nationalism and the forceful break with Britain. As leader of the Irish Parliamentary Party at Westminster, Parnell played a skilful game with the two major British political parties, the Liberals and the Conservatives (as well as with the Unionists), and very nearly achieved Home Rule for Ireland. But when he was cited as a third party in a divorce case involving Kitty O'Shea, the wife of one of his MPs, Parnell was hounded from office. The Irish Parliamentary Party split over the issue, never recovering its earlier unity, and Home Rule was effectively shelved until 1912–13 when it was revived under the leadership of John Redmond. But the Party's own fortunes never revived. In its heyday under Parnell it had over eighty members, but in 1918 it secured only six seats in an election that witnessed a landslide victory for Sinn Féin, the party associated with the 1916 Easter Rising.

The Easter Rising, the event that changed the course of modern Irish history, had its origins in the perceived failure to win Home Rule by constitutional means. In January 1916, the Irish Volunteers, under the leadership of Patrick Pearse, and the Irish Citizen Army, led by the international socialist James Connolly, came together to plan for a military rising against the British. Part of the plan, which is discussed more fully in Chapter 5, seems to have been to hold certain key positions around Dublin for enough time either to allow Volunteers on the outskirts to entrap the British Army or, perhaps, to hold out long enough to call on the United

Robert Ballagh's striking design for Patrick Pearse's commemorative stamp. The Easter 1916 leader is here linked with the French Revolution and Delacroix's painting *Liberty Leading Her People*. Reproduced by kind permission of the artist.

Evelyn Hofer's 'Revolutionaries', as the caption reads in Victor Pritchett's *Dublin: A Portrait* (1967). Courtesy of the photographer.

States Government to pressurise the British Government into granting their demands. The Rising in April 1916 was quickly put down, and the leaders were arrested and, within a matter of weeks, executed. At the time, the Rising was deeply unpopular in Ireland, not least because of the thousands of Irish soldiers fighting in the trenches in France, but the summary executions changed the public mood

and the leaders were transformed into martyrs for an ancient cause. The Easter Rising became Year One in modern Irish history, and each subsequent generation has felt obliged to revisit the site of its origins. Until 1966, the fiftieth anniversary, the event was honoured without qualification, but since then opponents of this tradition, tired of old-style nationalist rhetoric, have become more vocal.

As soon as the Great War ended, another war began in Ireland, this time between the Irish Republican Army and the forces of the crown. These forces included the Black and Tans, who gained a fearful reputation for terrorising the Irish people. It was a guerrilla war, waged throughout the countryside with Michael Collins playing a key role as strategist. Known in Ireland as the War of Independence, it ended with the Treaty negotiations in London in December 1921, when twenty-six counties of Ireland became the jurisdiction of the Irish Free State. With the enactment of the Government of Ireland Act in 1920, control of the other six counties (two-thirds of the province of Ulster) had passed to a new (Unionist) government at Stormont. The War of Independence ended in partial independence, therefore, and created a split bet-ween those who accepted and those who rejected the Treaty, the Free Staters (under Arthur Griffith and Collins) and the Republicans (under de Valera). This led, in 1922–3, to the Irish Civil War, with former comrades-in-arms fighting each other and the new Government (Cumann na Gael, which later became Fine Gael) involved, like its predecessor, in executing leaders.

De Valera survived defeat, came in from the cold, and went on to take his Fianna Fáil party into government in 1932. Until his death in 1975, de Valera, as Taoiseach (or Prime Minister) and later as President (from 1959 to 1973), dominated Irish life

THE LISTENER, JULY 2, 1953. Vol. L. No. 1270.   PRICE THREEPENCE

The Listener

Published every Thursday by the British Broadcasting Corporation

J. Allan Cash

The Houses of Parliament, Stormont, where, during the State Visit to Northern Ireland of the Queen and the Duke of Edinburgh, Her Majesty will today receive and reply to addresses of loyalty

In this number:
The Bamboo Curtain (G. J. Yorke)
Can Weather Experts Help Our Crops? (Lionel P. Smith)
Science and Responsibility (John Perret)

'Her Majesty will today receive and reply to addresses of loyalty.' An extraordinary time-warped sentence from the front page of the BBC weekly *The Listener*, 2 July 1953. A reminder not so much of the Britishness of Northern Ireland as of an Empire overseas where professions of loyalty were often a sign of internal disorder.

From the White Cottage to the White House

THE CAPITOL, WASHINGTON

Céad Míle Fáilte a Seáin

BELFAST

GALWAY

DUBLIN

CORK

DUNGANSTOWN

THE KENNEDY HOMESTEAD
CO. WEXFORD

SEAN Ó SHEA.

Commemorative postcard of 'Sean's' visit to Ireland in 1963.

and made the Fianna Fáil party the natural party of government. Put simply, to understand de Valera is to understand much of modern Irish history. In the 1930s, he presided over an economic war with Britain, a new constitution in 1937 that privileged the Catholic Church, and a political turn inwards that continued until the 1960s. He resisted attempts by Churchill to make Irish ports available to allied shipping in the Battle of the Atlantic, and was steadfast in ensuring Irish neutrality during the Second World War. His 'comely maidens' speech in 1942, which I discuss in Chapter 7, provides a position statement about his view of Ireland, depicting the people in cosy homesteads, satisfied with frugal comfort and spiritual nourishment.

If Robert Lowell characterised 1950s America as the 'tranquilised' decade, then the only sound that could be heard in 1950s Ireland was either the echo of the future, an echo well-captured by Maeve Binchy in her nostalgic novel *Echoes* (1985), or, more faintly, the tramp of emigrants to the ports. Indeed, with fifty thousand people a year leaving, one commentator thought Ireland might in time vanish from the face of the earth. But this didn't happen. In 1955, Ireland became a member of the United Nations, in 1956 it confronted a reassuringly familiar balance of payments crisis, and in 1959 de Valera stepped down as Taoiseach. More ominously, in Northern Ireland, Ian Paisley founded the Free Presbyterian Church of Ulster, and in 1957 a new IRA border campaign began. The 1960s marked a more clearly defined (American-inflected) transition in modern Irish history, beginning with the election of John F. Kennedy to the White House and ending with civil rights marches in the North and the advent of the recent Troubles. This was a decade when Ireland applied unsuccessfully for membership of the European Economic Community, when RTÉ (Radio Telefís Éireann) was launched, and when economic reforms were accompanied by a rapprochement between Dublin and Stormont. It was also the decade when one of Dublin's most famous landmarks – Nelson's Pillar – was blown up by republicans.

The 1970s were dominated by the Troubles, the highlights of which included internment in 1971, Bloody Sunday, followed by Bloody Friday, in 1972, the Sunningdale Agreement in 1973, the Loyalist Workers' Strike in 1974, the assassination of the British Ambassador to Ireland in 1976, the murder of the Queen's cousin Lord Mountbatten in 1979, and then, in 1984, the attempt to assassinate Margaret Thatcher at the Conservative Party Conference in Brighton. As my chapter on the 1980s emphasises, the Troubles continued to dominate news coverage of Ireland throughout the rest of the century, but there was also other news, most notably the emergence of a feminist agenda in public discourse and the decline of the Church's power and influence, a decline that accelerated in the 1990s with revelations about paedophilia among the clergy. The 1990s also saw the unbelievable happen. In 1992, a Catholic bishop resigned after admitting to fathering a child, and in the same decade vocations to the priesthood almost completely dried up – and this in a country that supplied Britain and the rest of the world with clergy. We know we are in a different period of history when a contemporary playwright sees fit to describe a priest as 'a nice, uncomplicated man and celibacy causes him no problems'.[2] Also of note have been the various tribunals investigating corruption among politicians, the most senior figure to be arraigned being Charles Haughey, who served as Taoiseach for several terms from 1982 onwards. In the 1990s came the Celtic Tiger, making Ireland the third richest country in Europe by 2001. Arguably the most high-profile event in recent years, which has extended our understanding of 'event' as a moment bound in time, has been the 1998 Good Friday Agreement, which signalled not so much a point of closure on decades of violence as a late stage in a hopeful return to constitutional politics in Northern Ireland.

History in Ireland has run along two tracks, at times parallel, at times sectarian, one associated with the Republic or the South, the other with the North. Geography suggests that the island of Ireland should be one country, but history, or more properly the colonial encounter, has decided otherwise – at least for the time being. The past has produced a culture that is essentially hybrid but a politics which is often set on abolishing hybridity in the name of some undivided truth. As a result, it has been the historic role of writers in Ireland to occupy a space between culture and politics, to intervene, that is, and provide a counter to set against the driven quality that has characterised much of modern Irish history.

Language

One of the most revealing linguistic encounters between Britain and Ireland in modern Irish writing occurs in chapter 5 of Joyce's *A Portrait of the Artist as a Young Man*. The Dean of Studies at Belvedere College, an English Jesuit, is engaged in lighting a fire in his study, and confesses to one of his pupils, Stephen Dedalus, his ignorance of the word used in Ireland for 'funnel': 'Tundish! Well now, that is interesting!'[3] For the Dean, *tundish* is 'interesting', a word whose irony is underlined for us by the insertion of an exclamation mark, as if what he is hearing is a quaint dialect of the imperial language. The 'fire' scene recalls the Christmas Dinner argument over Parnell and the heat from the 'banked' fire. It, too, has been carefully prepared by the narrator, who informs the reader that the age of Tone and Parnell has receded, and that nationalist Ireland is now being educated by English Jesuits ignorant of Hiberno-English and the Dublin working-class suburb where, according to Stephen, perhaps with tongue-in-cheek, the best English is spoken. That a relatively obscure word – actually, a Middle English word meaning 'dish' – carries so much weight is a reminder less of two countries divided by a common language (which was Shaw's view of Britain and the United States) as of the stored resentment of the Irish for the English coloniser, a resentment that can be readily activated when called for.

Joyce forces the language issue on the reader, forces the reader, that is, to pay attention not just to individual words and punctuation marks but, more importantly, to the complex tension between language and power. On the one hand, the language Stephen speaks is 'an acquired speech' (p.189), and he notices how different words such as 'home, Christ, ale, master' sound on the Dean's lips. On the other hand, while 'home' might sound different in standard English and Hiberno-English and become a weapon for a young malcontent to use against his superior, it hardly constitutes a defining line between difference and separation or, indeed, a call to the barricades. Joyce is thoroughly apprised of the contradictions involved in extrication for the colonial subject. Elsewhere in the book Stephen declares that the best prose stylist in English is Cardinal Newman, the English convert who became the first Rector of Joyce's university; so imbued with English models is Stephen's consciousness at this stage that an Irish writer such as Wilde is not even considered as a possibility. This dilemma runs through the early part of the book which follows, for the colonial encounter ensured that the use of English in Ireland was at once a separatist issue but one that was also almost impossible to handle in a separatist way.[4]

Colonialism, then, created the hybrid conditions in which a Hiberno-English vocabulary could flourish separately from the crown, in two senses. *Tundish* is a reminder of contention across the divide; elsewhere, especially in today's postcolonial climate, writers operate under a single spotlight where they can deploy words with a different denotation to standard English, without having to gloss them. One example will serve for many. In 'Hermes', a recent elegy by Bernard O'Donoghue, a popular local figure, Denis O'Connor, is affectionately recalled and compared to Hermes 'bearing messages/from the past'.[5] Denis's various achievements are commented on, including his ability to sing and to play the mouth-organ, and his physical agility. Then in a final stanza, another kind of 'message' is inserted into the poem, full of a charge that will be missed by those unfamiliar with its (pervasive) use in Ireland. One December night, Denis was looking for a lift 'To help you get your messages up home', where 'messages' signifies 'groceries' or 'shopping'.[6] It's a tender moment, a dropping into an informal register before the final two lines, when we hear Denis mumbling, 'Christmas is the worst time of all/For the person living on their own.' 'Messages' also appears in Banville's novel *Mefisto* (1986), but with a difference, for here it is employed by the Mephistophelian Felix to denigrate Gabriel's backward schoolboy friend Clancy, now a delivery boy, who has brought some messages from the local shop. '– What is the fellow talking about? . . . . – The grocery messages, Clancy said. . . . – Oh, *groceries*, Felix said, with a little laugh.'[7] The cruelty continues when the illiterate Clancy is asked to read out the list of messages. 'Oh, go on then, he said to Clancy, take your stuff around to the back door.'

'Messages', a 'back door' word, acts as a solidarity marker but it also reminds us of the stratification of contemporary Irish society in terms both of social class and of the divide between an urban and a rural culture. With the removal of the crown from the Republic, certain attitudes lingered or intensified as if the Pale's legacy, the historical line that separated Dublin from the rest of the country, still continued. In a recent survey that focuses on the harp without the crown, the journalist John Waters stresses the confrontation between the Dublin 4 liberals or modernisers and the traditionalists or supporters of Rural Ireland, the one intent on putting a space between today's Ireland and the past, the other wedded to Ireland's uniqueness in the modern world.[8] Among the many terms of abuse in *Cell* (2000), Paula Meehan's play set in a women's prison in the Republic, is *culchie*, the word used by city-dwellers, especially Dubliners, when they want to denigrate someone from the country. In *A Dictionary of Hiberno-English* (1999), Terence Dolan outlines the (uncertain) origins of this particular word, a word that also has a generous number of synonyms, including: muckers, boggers, greenbacks, woollybacks, rednecks, wellywarriors, bogtrotters, mucksavages, feckin' counthry boyos and clodhoppers.[9] 'The culchies have everything,' complains the Northside Dubliner Jimmy Rabitte in Roddy Doyle's *The Commitments* (1988): 'An' Dubliners are the niggers of Ireland.'[10] 'Country people,' thinks Macca, the Dublin streetwise kid in Ursula Rani Sarma's play *Touched* (2002), 'they're all fucking twisted . . . touched and twisted.'[11] Such a richly discriminating vocabulary suggests we are close to an ideological trouble-spot in Irish culture, as if the rural and the urban, the displaced harp and the crown, are still in dispute over claims to the territory or image of Ireland.

In a recent humorous sequence with a suitably non-PC title, 'Cries of an Irish Caveman', (2001), Paul Durcan enters this debate in his own inimitable way. Focusing on the animal in the field and without the help of Hiberno-English, he deliberately reverses conventional subject–object relations by providing a rare excursion into 'bovinity' or the mind of the cow. In one poem the cow, after 'the umpteenth muckout', is taken by surprise, 'Not by bovinity/With which I am by millennia ossified/But by the colossal naïveté of my bovinity'.[12] This is an expert stroke – the juxtaposition of a sophisticated linguistic apparatus, including a French word with two accents, and the use of a half-rhyme that could become a full-rhyme, either making *bovinité* rhyme somewhat grandiosely with 'naïveté' or drawing into word association 'bovinity' and 'divinity'. Like the American poet Denise Levertov in her 'pig' poems, Durcan manages to dignify the animal that watches the world go by, whether ruminating in the fields on affection or 'modelling my live meat in the cattle mart', knowing that all that counts with the farmers is 'my dead meat' (p.145).

A word, phrase or syntactic structure can betray a whole attitude or indeed a whole culture, but articulation, as the Lancashire-Irish writer Bill Naughton constantly reminds us in his plays and autobiographies, is also a form of resistance.[13] It was only natural that one of the Prefaces to the prestigious ten-volume anthology *Irish Literature* (1904) – in its day the *Field Day Anthology* (1991; 2002) – should be J. F. Taylor's essay, 'The Irish School of Oratory'.[14] The importance of articulation and oratory in a colonial context cannot be overestimated, and perhaps it is for this

The importance of articulation. The sense of injustice is palpable in this photo by Derek Speirs of a dispute at University College Dublin in July 1985 involving cleaning staff and members of the Irish Transport and General Workers Union. Courtesy of the photographer.

reason that modern Irish writing is a literature of the spoken voice. When, in the 1920s, Joyce was asked to read something from *Ulysses* for a gramophone recording, interestingly he chose the Taylor speech from the newspaper episode. Almost every contemporary Irish poet, from Durcan to Longley, Boland to Heaney, has a distinctive delivery voice. Some poets, such as Rita Ann Higgins, are close to being performance poets; others, such as Michael Donaghy, who at venues would read his often dense verse without a script in front of him, are quite mesmerising and in the process return one to the page to reconnect the ear with the eye.

J. M. Synge understood this better than most. When Christy Mahon settles into life at the Flaherty shebeen in *The Playboy of the Western World*, he imagines it would be a fine place 'to be my whole life talking out with swearing Christians'.[15] 'Swearing Christians' is a taboo-busting phrase that must have delighted the Protestant-born unbeliever, for in their invocations and curses the country people did know how to swear, even if his Dublin audiences didn't want to recognise that fact. More recently, in Martin McDonagh's satirical play *The Lonesome West* (1997),

In this scene from the Hull Truck performance of Martin McDonagh's *The Lonesome West* in March 2005, directed by Gareth Tudor Price, Valene (Michael Glenn Murphy) taunts his brother Coleman (Ged McKenna) with a cheque on returning home after burying their father. Meanwhile, the priest (Vincent Patrick), behind him the gun and the crucifix and Valene's religious statues, fingers his glass of poteen for comfort. London-Irish McDonagh spent his summers in Ireland, where he learnt, like Synge before him, how English is spoken in Ireland and how to give voice to the theme of the exotic, the marginalised and the abandoned. He also developed a mind ferocious in pursuit of the ordinary. Photo by Adrian Gatlie.

when Girleen discovers Valene has short-changed her, she shows herself equal to the brothers in self-expression: 'You're the king of stink-scum fecking filth-bastards you, ya bitch-feck, Valene.'[16] Performance extends to the novel. At a get-together with neighbours in Christy Brown's novel of the Dublin slums, *Down All the Days* (1970), the newly widowed Red Magso, her eyes on the ceiling, a whiskey bottle in hand, invokes her dead husband with a mixture of fluency, irreverence and vulgarity: 'I hope you're with God in heaven tonight, but I know in my heart it's down in the quare place you are with a red-hot poker up your arse and you screaming for mercy and finding none!'[17] Patrick McCabe is a brilliant reader of his own work, as if the writing – as true of *The Butcher Boy* (1992) as of a short story such as 'The Turfman from Ardee' (2001) – had been intended from the outset for adaptation or performance.

The proximity of articulation, resistance and betrayal in the Irish context has ensured that no Irish writer could have coined the phrase 'the medium is the message', but the matter doesn't rest there. Irish writers have been fortunate in having another language to exploit. *Translations* (1981) is the name Brian Friel assigns to the relationship between languages, as a way of signalling that his play, which begins in a classroom with students learning a classical language, isn't so much an adaptation of an original script as a study in difference arising from the colonial encounter between Britain and Ireland. In the 1830s when the play is set – before, that is, the Great Famine – Ireland was bi-lingual, but thereafter Irish began its long decline until today, when it is spoken only in pockets of the countryside. But the ancient language of the harp, which received welcome State support with the establishment in 1996 of *TG4*, an Irish-language TV channel, remains an important resource for writers.[18] The success of James Stephens's *Reincarnations* (1918) – he deploys the suggestive 'reincarnation' rather than the stiff 'translation' – lies in part in his forceful rendering of poems by the seventeenth-century Gaelic poet Dáibhí Ó Bruadair.[19] Austin Clarke's skilful manipulation of assonance, internal rhyme and intricate vowelling patterns is perhaps the most striking example of a modern poet criss-crossing the two languages. Ciaran Carson, in his translation of *The Inferno of Dante Alighieri* (2002), makes telling use of Hiberno-English, including eighteenth-century Irish ballads in English. Elsewhere in his writing Carson raids Patrick Dinneen's great Irish-English Dictionary for linguistic connections, while Yorkshire-based poet Ian Duhig in 'From the Irish' has Dinneen in mind when he wittily plays on the idea of loose and literal translations.[20]

The situation is greatly enriched by the presence of some fine contemporary Irish-language poets, whose work has in turn been translated into English by leading poets such as Michael Hartnett, Paul Muldoon and Seamus Heaney. Nuala Ní Dhomnaill has inherited the aspiration and freedom of a tradition that is flexible and close to a popular imagination. As she writes in 'Ceist Na Teangan' (The Language Issue), she placed her hope in the little boat of the language and watched it float away, 'not knowing where it might end up;/in the lap, perhaps,/of some Pharaoh's daughter'.[21] Such freedom, I suggest in my Conclusion, is also apparent in the verse of Cathal Ó Searcaigh. Few modern poets have better captured the drifting London scene than Ó Searcaigh, whether Euston Station, gateway for Irish exiles, where he describes himself 'sitting uncomfortably/on my hold-all of dreams', or Covent Garden, where he watches the 'done-in tourist head for pubs'.[22] What unites these poets is a willingness to take risks and not be hidebound to traditions or to prejudices about what constitutes tradition.[23] Often in the translation our attention is drawn to older uses of a word or its etymology, to a world that predates the colonial encounter or the coming of a hybrid culture. Ó Searcaigh's 'An tAngelus' (The Angelus), for example, opens with an image of the sky as 'ór Mhuire' or 'marigold'.[24] In a poem about spring sowing and the chapel bell ringing out the Angelus across the fields, it is fitting that Mhuire or Mary, the subject of the Angelus – 'the Angel of the Lord declared unto Mary. . .' – is mentioned by name. When translated into English, more than poetry is lost, for the link between *mari* (Mary) and 'gold' becomes less explicit and hence the link between the natural and religious worlds is also weakened.

In contrast to what obtained during the period of the Revival, which is discussed in Chapter 4, the Irish language, far from simply being part of some separatist project, has in recent years been vital in filtering or softening the presence of the crown, not least in making Hiberno-English easy on the ear. In *Down All the Days* (1970), Red Magso employs the speech rhythms of Hiberno-English, the language of English as spoken in Ireland, and her tagged-on clause – 'and you screaming for mercy' – links her to the lyrical sing-song language of Synge's plays. Such language use – even in the confined environment among the Dublin poor – is a reminder that Irish syntax and Irish expressions inform Hiberno-English in a particularly fertile way. What we are listening to is a specific kind of English, at once highly articulate and rooted in two languages, capable of carrying, as Girleen demonstrates, a whole string of epithets and compound-words before the end of the sentence is reached and the onslaught fully expelled from the lungs. By way of a caution, in case we thought the language was quaint or quaint without reason, Carson in 'The Irish for No' alerts us to how Irish speakers frequently avoid using 'yes' or 'no', preferring instead expressions such as 'it is' or 'it isn't' in response to a question, for this is indeed how agreement or disagreement is voiced in Irish.[25] As for macaronic verse, a distinctive feature of hybridity in eighteenth-century verse and song, where lines of English and Irish are run together, this is now rare in a country that is no longer bi-lingual.[26]

Regional accents have also been affected by the colonial encounter and its aftermath. In Northern Ireland, there has been a strong commitment to an Ulster speech community, as demonstrated by the early dialect plays of St John Ervine such as *Mixed Marriage* (1911), Christina Reid's Protestant domestic working-class plays, or John Morrow's journalistic prose pieces in *Northern Myths* (1979). The energy of such writing springs from a confident sense of a regional identity, which is inseparable from how people speak.[27] As part of their colonial inheritance, Ulster writers also enjoy access to individual Scots-Irish or Ulster-Scots dialect words or phrases, access which can be used with particular effect. 'Hoke it out' says one of the characters in Stewart Parker's play *Pentecost* (1987) in reference to poking a fire, and we sense that such a pointedly home-spun phrase links with the play's wider theme of wresting meaning from the fire of history. Other words or phrases have a lighter but no less distinctive touch. In his poem 'The Factory', an affectionate tribute to fellow-poet Brendan Kennelly, Longley inserts *hurlygush* to describe the latter's voice, a Scots-Irish word, he explains in a note, meaning 'a noisy rush of water'.[28] When it comes to the invented as opposed to the inherited word, Muldoon's *quoof*, a word used in the Muldoon County Armagh family to refer to a hot-water bottle, is testimony to the difficulty of adding words to the language.[29] Elsewhere in Ireland, the Cork accent – or perhaps we should say, simply, Cork – came to prominence in the 1930s in the work of the Cork realists Joseph O'Connor and Sean O'Faolain, and, in recent years, with the pressure on to find new subject-matter, other accents have also come to the fore. Marina Carr, for example, has added the Midlands accent to the linguistic pot and reveals an Ireland less pleasant to the mind or ear, as when Dara in *On Raftery's Hill* (2000) tells Sorrel: 'Me father's wan sad picnic in the rain. He never speaks to me mother, just kind a grunts and pints and sits in the corner drinkin cans a condensed milk and sighin to heeself'.[30] This is a world where if 'ya like radin' you want 'buuks' and where the most savage remark sounds even more savage spoken thus: 'We're a band of gorillas swingin from the trees' (p.58).

The language of modern Irish literature, therefore, is bound up with the colonial encounter or its legacy, and it yields enormous riches for the cultural historian and attentive reader alike. From the spare, refreshing language of Beckett to the *hurlygush* of Kennelly, from the superbly polished language of Wilde to the language of discovery in the fiction of Kathleen Coyle, from the look of performance that characterises the language of Yeats's verse to the conscious relish for the written word in Banville's fiction, modern Irish writing has never lacked interest or variety, so that even a small word such as *tundish* or 'messages' can carry within its microcosm the whole hybrid world of the harp and the crown.

Representation

Stereotypes have played an active role in the colonial encounter between Britain and Ireland. Never far from a discussion of Ireland in English pubs is the issue of racial stereotypes. *Rotten: No Irish, No Blacks, No Dogs* (1993), the title of John Lydon's London-Irish autobiography, is a hard-hitting reminder of a once not uncommon notice, used to advertise rooms to let in the imperial capital. Irish jokes, or rather anti-Irish jokes, have enjoyed a long history. A 1980s cartoon post-card depicts a crude English comedian, on stage, about to crack an Irish joke that begins, 'There were these thick Paddies . . .'. In the background are the figures of Wilde, Yeats, Joyce and Brendan Behan. The point is well-made: stereotypes linger long beyond their sell-by date and behind the knowing humour lies an empire of ignorance. A recent Alan Partridge television sketch included a discussion with two Irish programme-makers from RTÉ in which the gaffe-prone Norwich radio presenter reveals a characteristic mixture of ignorance and more ignorance:

> Yeah. I think the Irish are going through a major image change. I mean, the old image of Leprechauns, shamrock, Guinness, horses running through council estates, toothless simpletons, people with eyebrows on their cheeks, badly tar-macced drives – in *this* country, men in platform shoes being arrested for bombings, lots of rocks, and Beamish. I think people are saying 'Yes, there's more to Ireland than this. Dere's more to Oireland dan dis.'[31]

TWO FORCES.

A century earlier, in the vicious cartoons of John Tenniel in *Punch*, the Irish were represented as 'white Negroes', with simian features, a protrud-ing jaw, a receding forehead and thick lips, who were short in the leg department, and closer to the ape than to the civilised world. It was a view confirmed by the measurements of phrenologists and physiognomists, one of whom even sug-gested that Irish eloquence resembled the bark-ing of dogs.[32] In Victorian fiction, the language the Irish spoke was peppered with 'begorrah', 'darlin', 'top-of-the-morning', and 'says I to meself', adding local colour to narratives from which they were largely excluded. Poor Paddy lived in squalor, kept pigs in the house, subdi-vided his land, lived off potatoes, went to Mass

John Tenniel's colourful view of the Irish as Anarchy, the Simian features complete with low forehead, protruding jaw and hostile posture. In contrast, Britannia stands morally upright, treading on the agrarian agitation of Michael Davitt's Land League, in one hand the sword of the law, on her arm a weeping Hibernia seeking protection from the brute. *Punch*, 29 October 1881.

on Sundays where he bowed his head to the priest, believed in fairies, drank to excess, was prone to raising his cudgels and being generally troublesome. He never rested until his Bridget had produced ten or more children for him. As if to confirm that one kind of resentment in the North is shared across the sectarian divide, it took a Belfast Protestant, Christina Reid, to write a play with the title *Did You Hear That One About the Irishman . . .?* (1985).[33] It's a view shared by Lorrie in David Park's recent novel *Swallowing the Sun* (2004). Asked why she has returned home to Belfast, she replies that she was 'tired of being a Paddy' in London, tired of her accent sounding strange on her ears.[34]

When investigating stereotypes in modern Irish literature, we soon uncover a picture more varied than might be imagined: negative stereotype, positive stereotype, recognisable type or situation, familiar situation, familiar elements, unfamiliar aspects, unmarked features, rounded individuals and the wholly unique. Irish writers rarely reproduce the known stereotype pure and simple but typically move back and forth across the spectrum. When Broadbent, a stereotype of the no-nonsense Englishman, declares admiringly to Nora, a stereotype of an Irish colleen, in *John Bull's Other Island* (1904) that 'all the harps of Ireland are in your voice', we know for certain that illusion will get the upper hand. And the very next moment he obliges: '(She laughs at him. He suddenly loses his head and seizes her arms, to her great indignation)'.[35] In a play such as *Juno and the Paycock* (1923), Sean O'Casey transforms the negative stereotype, such as the work-shy Dubliners Paycock and his buddy Joxer, into engaging participants in a larger tragic-comedy. 'I'm telling you . . . Joxer . . . th' whole worl's . . . in a terr . . . ible state o' . . . chassis!' is one of the least classy but most quoted lines from modern Irish literature – a stereotype of Dublin drunken ignorance posing as wisdom.[36] Mary is the positive stereotype, a single hard-working young Catholic woman who looks to education for escape, but whose career is damaged by an unwanted pregnancy. In *The Playboy of the Western World* (1907), Synge manages to hold together and to reverse negative and positive stereotypes, so that Christy, who begins as a wimp, ends as a hero, while his father, who begins as a cruel god, wakes from the dead and learns to love his rebellious son.

The priest in Martin McDonagh's *The Lonesome West* (1997) is a recognisable type, no longer the stereotype of the reassuring priest as portrayed by Spencer Tracy or Bing Crosby in Hollywood films of the 1940s, but more like the post-Vatican-II-Father-Ted type of priest, anxious to mix in with his parishioners but in the end defeated by their unresponsiveness and wicked talk and behaviour. The play also contains familiar elements for satire: the claustrophobia of rural Ireland, a pair of feuding brothers, ugly cottage interiors where nothing coheres, a lifestyle defenceless against television and the media, where more attention is paid to the brand of crisps bought from the local shop than to murder committed in the family. We could be forgiven for thinking there is nothing behind the emptiness and bickering except humour at the expense of others, but this is part of the play's attraction, not to give an inch to sentimentality or easy paraphrase. Mairead in *The Lieutenant of Inishmore* (2001), McDonagh's play about torture and the darker side of Northern Republicanism, is a recognisable type of Republican activist and close to a stereotype. With her close-cropped hair, white T-shirt, sunglasses, and a personality to match, humourless, battle-hardened, and in flight from her emotions, she is not unlike Jude, another stereotype, from Neil Jordan's *The Crying Game* (1992). Very few characters or situations in modern Irish literature lie outside the known or familiar. Even extremes are quickly identified and accommodated, as when the torturer Padraic tells his distended victim: 'If I hadn't been such a nice fella I would've taken one toenail off of separate feet, but I didn't, I took two toenails off the one foot, so that it's only the one foot you'll have to be limping on and not the two.'[37] It is a measure of McDonagh's understanding of stereotypes that the longer certain passages continue the funnier they sound, until in the end we are not sure what we are laughing at.

The best writers work the hybrid landscape, or, in Joyce's case, the imagined hybrid landscape. Leopold Bloom, the main protagonist in *Ulysses* (1922), is both Jewish and Irish. *Ulysses* is set in Dublin in 1904, at a time when Jews numbered no more than some 2,200, and yet 'allroundman' Bloom, the advertising agent whose family came from Hungary, performs the roles of Odysseus, Everyman, *l'homme moyen sensuel*, and the Irish Outsider. Identity is shown repeatedly by Joyce, often in a single move, as both constructed and deconstructed. As for Bloom's Irish Molly, she is quickly slotted into a certain type, whether as earth mother, sensuous female body, or Penelope, the patient wife of Odysseus. But her identity, while seemingly specific, is in fact slightly obscure, as if Joyce, by not telling us everything, wants to insist that a person's identity is often

9387   MY IRISH MOLLY O. 2.   ROTARY PHOTO, E.C.
Molly dear, and did you hear I furnished up a flat?
Three little cosy rooms, and bath, with "Welcome" on the mat
It's five pounds down, and two a week I'll soon be out of debt.
It's all complete except they haven't brought the cradle yet.
Molly, my Irish Molly, my sweet acushla dear!
I'm fairly off my trolley, my Irish Molly, when you are near.
Springtime, you know is ring time
Come, dear, don't be so slow!
Change your name, go on, be game,
Begorra! and I'll do the same,
My Irish Molly O.
WORDS BY PERMISSION OF MESSRS. FRANCIS DAY & HUNTER, W. JEROME, AND J. SCHWARTZ.

'I'm fairly off my trolley, my Irish Molly, when you are near.' While not exactly Molly and Bloom, the Edwardian song is a reminder that their idea of their relationship is informed by what they saw and heard in popular culture.

Left: The Royal Dublin Fusiliers, which was raised in 1661 to protect the East India Company in Madras, was stationed in Gibraltar from 1874 onwards. It was later disbanded in 1922, following the formation of the Irish Free State. In the 'Circe' episode of *Ulysses*, 'Major' Tweedy reappears in 'bearskin cap with hackleplume and accoutrements, with epaulettes, gilt chevrons and sabretaches, his breast bright with medals'. Joyce understood precisely the workings of colonialism when he has Molly in the 'Penelope' episode reflecting on her childhood and sexual awakening among the fiery boys in uniform.

Below: Angeline Ball as Molly in Sean Walshe's film *Bloom* (2003). In a departure from Joyce's novel *Ulysses*, the film begins with Molly, the woman who is both Calypso and Penelope, both temptress and long-suffering wife, a concert singer who also sings for her supper. Courtesy of Odyssey Pictures.

based on hearsay and rumour and not to be confused with official records in a Register Office. In the music episode 'Sirens', which takes place in the afternoon in the Ormond Hotel, her identity is discussed by Simon Dedalus and his drinking partners. 'Irish? I don't know, faith' (*U* 11:510). The issue is raised but then discounted, and Simon continues 'From the rock of Gibraltar. . .all the way.' With

Boylan on his way to see if Molly will go all the way, the insertion of the elliptical points is presumably intended as an innuendo – unlike the French translation which has *en ligne droite* (in a straight line) and no elliptical points.[38] And, as if to confirm that it is an innuendo, the same phrase appeared in Bloom's thoughts in the earlier breakfast episode, 'Calypso' to refer to the bed on which Molly is lying, how it came all the way from Gibraltar and how it 'jingled', a word associated throughout the novel with Boylan (*U* 4:59–60). Molly's father, who bought the bed in an auction while stationed in Gibraltar, possesses the suitably Penelopean name of Tweedy and is an officer in the Royal Dublin Fusiliers, perhaps a lowly sergeant-major and not the major which the phrase 'I rose from the ranks, sir, and I'm proud of it' (*U* 4:63–4) might lead us to believe. Her mother, who seems to have abandoned Molly as a child, is a Spaniard with the colourful, if implausible, name Lunita Laredo (the little moon of Laredo). In her entertaining monologue at the end of the novel, Molly, the colonial subject with the Spanish eyes, wanders in her mind back and forth between the English garrison of Gibraltar – where she was raised – and the colonial city of Dublin. So natural, so lacking in hybridity, does she appear that we assume all kinds of things, including a voice full of the broad vowels of the West of Ireland, where Joyce's partner, Nora Barnacle, on whom she is in part modelled, came from, but this is to forget that she is the product of Joyce's 'meandering male fist' (*FW* 123:10) and comes to life amid the shadows in the interplay between the spoken and the written and in a border region somewhere between cliché, word association, and stereotype.

As Paul Muldoon and the photographer Willie Doherty remind us, the Troubles need careful handling. 'Ireland', a five-line enigmatic poem by Muldoon, deliberately plays on the menace that is sometimes associated with today's image of the North. A car (a Volkswagen) is parked in a gap, ticking over, and you wonder if it's nothing more than lovers 'And not men hurrying back/Across two fields and a river.'[39] Why is the car a Volkswagen? Is the river a symbol, and if so, of what? Ditto for two fields, and why two? But, unlike Doherty, Muldoon is nothing if not indirect, and the question he poses turns out to resemble a piece of advice – don't jump to conclusions. Doherty, on the other hand, works deliberately with clichés, as in *Border Incident* (1994), a famous image of a burnt-out car on a country lane that is designed to elicit a targeted response.[40] In the still, held moment, Doherty invites the spectator to go through a set of responses as if representation itself was his theme, and perhaps what he asks us is to interrogate the stereotypes we have of the Troubles. Keep looking, he seems to say; this, in one sense, is all there is, so any interpretation must come from you. In supplementing the image, we (or is it 'I as spectator'?) find ourselves becoming slightly uneasy for, in the words of Doherty himself, 'the viewer is compelled to move beyond the immediate surface of the photograph and to examine the specific details of social and economic experience embedded within the image'.

Willie Doherty's *Border Incident* (1994). A country lane, a burnt-out car with peeling paint and no windows, surrounded by fields. By detaching the image from its context, Doherty manages to co-opt the viewer into a possible crime scene. Cibachrome on aluminium. Collection Irish Museum of Modern Art.

Stereotypes, as Michael Pickering has recently observed, need to be distinguished from categories.[41] Without categories, structured ways to observe the world, we would be lost. Stereotypes, on the other hand, need watching. The Other receives particular attention, but archetypes are left unscrutinised by Pickering, as is the relationship between stereotypes and archetypes. The association of the Other with a contemporary form of theorising the archetype is therefore missed, as is the classic assimilation of the fearful Other into reassuring stereotype. Stereotypes tend to operate in an ethical domain or discourse on power, archetypes in the world of myths and an informing imagination. But in the hybrid Irish context, the picture is complicated by the colonial encounter. Stereotypes represent the crown's view of the harp, while archetypes embody the harp's view of itself. Cathleen ni Houlihan is an archetype and her (sovereign) figure, with its association of the eighteenth-century *aisling* or visionary tradition, can be encountered everywhere in modern Irish literature. In Yeats's play of that name she is the revolutionary woman calling Ireland to arms against the crown. In Edna O'Brien's *The Country Girls* (1960), at the moment when Mr Gentleman whispers in Caithleen's ear 'Show me your body'– arguably the moment when the 1960s in Catholic Ireland begins – the figure assumes a real body and with it a betrayal and a fall to earth.[42]

Priests (or ministers) are at times closer to stereotypes, but the best novels, such as George Moore's *The Lake* (1905) or Gerald O'Donovan's *Father Ralph* (1913) or Francis Stuart's *Redemption* (1949) or Richard Power's *The Hungry Grass* (1969),

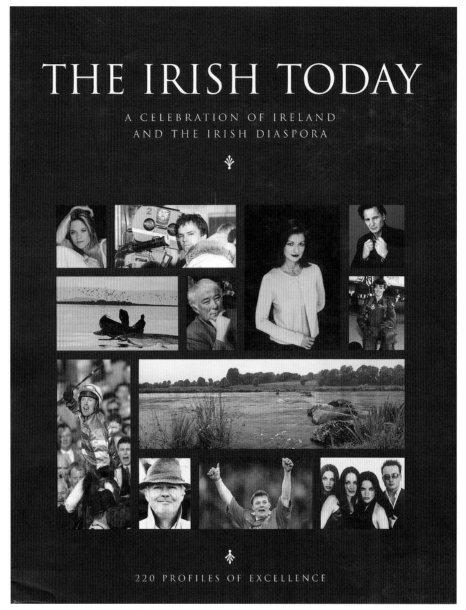

One version of the Irish today. Istrabaq and Charlie Swan at Cheltenham races 2000, Eileen Collins the first woman pilot on the space shuttle, Maureen Dowd a *New York Times* columnist, Neil Jordan the film-maker, the actor Liam Neeson, Daniel Patrick Moynihan ex-Senator and friend of the Kennedys, Brian O'Driscoll brilliant rugby union player, the Corrs, Seamus Heaney, the River Shannon at Castle Connell. There's nothing quite like the river of success to do away with the past. This handsome book, edited by Sonya Perkins, was published by Cadogan Publication in 2000.

or Glenn Patterson's *That Which Was* (2004), are more subtle in their representation. Some themes, such as land and inheritance, prominently displayed, for example, in Padraic Colum's play *The Land* (1905), John B. Keane's *The Field* (1965) or Tom Murphy's *The Wake* (1998), have threatened at various points to become archetypes, so close is land-hunger to Irish experience. The more conventional archetypal idea of the earth as sacred or as sacred mother can be observed in 'The Ploughing of Leaca-na-Naomh' (1916), a short story by Daniel Corkery about the evil that befell a family who ploughed a field belonging to the saints, or in the bog poems of Heaney, or in the religious verse of Joseph Campbell, but, given the religious nature of Irish life, such a theme is less prevalent than one might suppose.

The particular animus against stereotypes in Ireland, especially in the cultural domain, derives in part from a subject people – and in some respects this is also true of Northern Unionism – throwing off the yoke of the coloniser. Indeed, running through this book is a series of arguments or responses about how a culture-in-opposition learned to be itself, to live without the crown. As I explore in Chapter 4, on cultural nationalism, the issue involves in particular the wresting of eloquence away from barking dogs to Wilde's view that the Irish – and this includes the Northern Irish – are among the best talkers since the Greeks. One temptation today, stemming in part from the influence of the United States, is only to latch onto success stories, even when, as with Frank McCourt's memoirs, they are couched as sob stories. As the literature of the poor in fact suggests – the list would include Patrick MacGill's *Children of the Dead End* (1914), Timothy O'Grady's *If I Could Read the Sky* (1997), Paul Smith's neglected novel about slum life, *The Countrywoman* (1962), James Plunkett's lively reconstruction of the 1913 Dublin Lock-Out in *Strumpet City* (1969), Patrick Galvin's *Song for a Poor Boy* (1990), Dermot Bolger's affectionately drawn novel about travellers and traditional music, *Father's Music* (1997), and Jimmy Murphy's recent plays about navvies and publicans defeated by circumstance – not everyone could claim they had come through. And, as Brian Harvey's recent critique of contemporary Ireland for the Joseph Rowntree Charitable Trust and other studies remind us, Ireland isn't such a success story.[43] But the biggest temptation in the aftermath of the colonial encounter is to assume that the marketable commodity known as Irishness actually constitutes Irish reality.

Culture

Three meanings of the word 'culture' are highlighted by Raymond Williams in *Keywords* (1976): first, culture as 'a general process of intellectual, spiritual and aesthetic development'; secondly, culture as 'a particular way of life, whether of a people, a period or a group'; and thirdly, culture as 'the works and practices of intellectual and especially artistic activity'.[44] For F. S. L. Lyons, culture is essentially confined to the second meaning, which he believes is the one most relevant to the Irish context. According to Lyons, on the island of Ireland four cultures have been in conflict – 'clash' is a favourite word – for four centuries. These are: English culture, Anglo-Irish culture (embodied in Trinity College, the Dublin Horse Show, and the 'Horse-Protestants', as Brendan Behan memorably called them),[45] native Irish culture, and Presbyterian-dominated Ulster Protestantism. There is no doubt that this particular meaning of culture, which is close to ethos or atmosphere, can be very powerful. In Thomas Murphy's play *The Wake* (1998), for example, Finbar, we are told, is 'the product of a culture', that is, he has been put into care as youngster, brutalised there and abused by the Christian Brothers.[46] Murphy is also able to broaden his critique, as when he writes of Henry, the dropout lawyer, that '[t]he culture has defeated him' (p.22), meaning Irish society as a whole.

There are problems, then, with Lyons's starting-point. His view of culture lacks movement, and, unlike Murphy, he seems intent on submerging politics and power relations under the idea of culture as a counter between social groups or classes. No role is reserved for the idea of culture as a dynamic activity, whether that is understood in Arnoldian or Gramscian terms. Lyons's title, *Culture and Anarchy in Ireland*, which plays on Matthew Arnold's *Culture and Anarchy* (1869), is therefore at odds with his thesis, for Arnold well understood the ideological role for culture.[47] Put simply, according to Lyons, whatever Anglo-Irish people do or say represents their culture, so that even figures from the ruling class who were intent on distancing themselves from their social background, such as Lady Gregory or George Moore or, indeed, Yeats or Synge, are somehow destined to express nothing other than, or nothing more than, their origins. Equally, Lyons is either uninterested in, or unable to account for, the *intervention* of writers and artists in the culture. Against Daniel Corkery's insistence on only writing verse based on the old poetry, the Irish-language poet Seán Ó Ríordáin responded: 'But what can one do when things outside the tradition have gone into one – when the person is wider than the tradition?'[48] Arguably, the liveliest Irish writing in the twentieth century, from Kate O'Brien to Edna O'Brien – two very different novelists who, presumably, would be grouped by Lyons as 'the native Irish' – was concerned with transgression of one sort or another, with going beyond definitions, moral conventions, or gender stereotyping. The cultural historian or postcolonial critic needs to be alive to such moves, not least because all the writers worth reading have been making them.

Lyons's account is indebted to Yeats, the poet of disenchantment, rather than to the wild card that is Joyce. The young Joyce is banished early on from the scene: '[W]hile in an artistic sense he never really left his native city, his insight into the Irish paralysis, of which Dublin was the centre, denied him any hope of changing the fundamentals of the situation.' This clears the ground for Lyons to assert: 'Much of the cultural history of Ireland in the twentieth century was to be the his-

Elizabeth Bowen in front of Bowen's Court, the clouds billowing, the hay gathered into homely little cocks, and she striding out. No sign of the ruin to the house to come.

tory of their [the Anglo-Irish] disenchantment.'[49] With the exception of a great writer such as Elizabeth Bowen, whose novel *The Last September* (1929) effectively records the end of a social class in Ireland, there is little in the imaginative literature or the visual art of the period to support such a contention, or, if there is, it is that disenchantment was general all over Ireland. The tone running through Molly Keane's *Good Behaviour* (1981) is not disenchantment but good-humoured raillery that takes its cue from Maria Edgeworth's *Castle Rackrent* (1800).

The study which follows is largely concerned with Williams's third sense, with culture as artistic activity, and, where I do invoke the second sense as in my account of Yeats, it is to attend to the encounter, but not necessarily the clash, between different social groups or classes or national identities.

When the emphasis is on intervention and the colonial encounter, a different story emerges. Away from the gaze of the coloniser, Ireland discovered strangeness in art and the dark in literature. The strangeness is frequently of a piece, so that Sean Keating, Charles Lamb, Gerard Dillon, and the visionary landscapes of John Luke belong to a line that is recognisably Irish. However, the Irishness of a painter such as William Orpen presents difficulties for both the pro- and the anti-nationalist, for even when his subject matter is Synge-inspired his treatment can seem whimsical, off-key or decidedly irreverent, as in *An Aran Islander* (1912) or *The Holy Well* (1916). Determining the Irishness of the late paintings of Jack B. Yeats, or of the work of Modernists such as Mainie Jellet or Colin Middleton, or of the contemporary London-Irish painter Sean Scully, requires patience, but the strangest – and, on reflection, in some respects the most Irish – modern painter is Louis Le Brocquy, whose obsessive paintings of the heads of famous writers such as Yeats, Joyce, and Beckett play uneasily on the association of depth and death.

In contrast, modern Irish writing is not so much strange as familiar, but it is a familiarity based on the dark. In a period of reaction following the Act of Union in 1801, Tom Moore, as noted above, found the harp not only in chains but also in darkness. Róisín Dubh, Mangan's dark Rosaleen from the Hungry Forties, is a familiar image of Ireland, so familiar that we sometimes overlook its darkness. 'We begin in darkness,' the philosophical Kathleen Coyle declares in her childhood autobiography *The Magical Realm* (1942), 'a state that resembles blindness.'[50] Or as Stephen Dedalus, the Jesuit-educated artist contemplating writing the Irish epic, ruminates: 'Darkness is in our souls, do you not think?' (*U* 3:421). For, as Oscar Wilde suggested in 'The Portrait of Mr W. H.', the soul 'hides in the dark and broods, and consciousness cannot tell us of its workings'.[51] In national traditions of writing, themes have a habit not only of recurring but of reshaping our idea of tradition. The well-trodden path of modern Irish writers begins with the door into the dark, the title of Heaney's second volume of verse, and darkness is never far from the title page – for example, in O'Casey's *The Shadow of the Gunman* (1923), Liam O'Flaherty's dark, brooding novel *The Black Soul* (1924), F. R. Higgins's *The Dark Breed* (1927), Louis MacNeice's radio play *The Dark Tower* (1946), the Irish-American playwright Eugene O'Neill's darkest and most Irish play, *Long Day's Journey into Night* (1956), Thomas Murphy's *A Whistle in the Dark* (1961), McGahern's *The Dark* (1965), Jennifer Johnston's Troubles novel, *Shadows on Our Skin* (1977), Dorothy Nelson's novel about child abuse, *In Night's City* (1983), Deirdre Madden's *One by One in the Darkness* (1996), Seamus Deane's *Reading in the Dark* (1996), or Conor McPherson's ironically entitled dark play, *Shining City* (2004).

Darkness is there as a given or there to be explored, as in Seán Ó Ríordáin's 'Claustrophobia', a poem that struggles towards the completed self against the night that is forming from him. In Beckett's *Krapp's Last Tape* (1958), at precisely the moment when Krapp, a pool of light above his head, is about to reveal 'the

From the door into the dark to seeing things. Playful Heaney poster that appeared in the *Frankfurter Rundschau* for the Frankfurt Book Fair, October 1996.

belief I had been going on all my life', he curses and winds the tape forward: 'clear to me at last that the dark I have always struggled to keep under is in reality my most–'.[52] Blind, with a bloody bandage over his eyes, Hamm in *Endgame* (1958) sits in the theatre like some figure from a forgotten outpost of an abandoned empire, an image of the darkness now gathering to witness the 'endgame' for the West. Darkness as a cloak, whether defined in moral or epistemological terms, is the subject of Banville's *Shroud* (2002). Set in Turin, the city where the Holy Shroud is periodically exposed and its authenticity challenged, Banville's novel takes for its subject the 'shady, not to say shrouded, past' that Axel Vander, the Paul de Man figure, concealed from the world about his pro-Nazi writings during the Second World War.[53] In *On Raftery's Hill* (2000), Marina Carr's topical play on the contemporary theme of incest, darkness provides for one sister a cloak for her father's abuse and for the other sister a retreat. Dinah is happy to go along with her father's approaches: 'So we do ud from time to time, allas in the pitch dark, never a word, ud's nowan's bleddy business. Who's ud hurtin?'[54] The sensitive Sorrell is more reflective and turns to the dark for articulation: 'The world's gone ouh like a ligh and I can't see righ abouh anything any more'(p.54).

When Henry James travels from Dublin Castle to the Royal Hospital at Kilmainham in Colm Tóibín's quietly evocative historical novel *The Master* (2004), he feels not unlike his English hosts, surrounded by the 'hostile stares and dark accusing eyes' of the native Irish.[55] Appropriately, the final word (as a stage direction) in Frank McGuinness's *Observe the Sons of Ulster Marching Towards the Somme* (1985) is '*Darkness*', the fate that befell the 'dying breed' who fought for the 'Protestant gods' of Ulster in the Great War.[56] In a recent interview Michael Longley reveals a hope that his Mayo poems may 'irradiate the northern darkness'; a decade previously in the title poem, 'The Ghost Orchid' (1995), he shows darkness accruing a positive value: 'Just touching the petals bruises them into darkness.'[57] In Medbh McGuckian's 'She is in the Past, She has this Grace', a daughter, looking at her mother in old age, wonders what she is thinking: 'She is in dark light, or an openness/That leads to a darkness.'[58] McGuckian's pursuit of images takes her across the pauses of darkness between lines, and the reader pauses in the dark with her.

When the lights are extinguished in the work of the English novelist D. H. Lawrence, touch becomes the vital sense. For post-Romantic or post-Independence Irish writers, blindness or the dark leads, at times unannounced, to an empty stage and the piercing rage of a Lucky against meaninglessness or madness in Beckett's *Waiting for Godot* (1954), the inconsolable lament of Francis Hardy against chance or circumstance in Brian Friel's *Faith Healer* (1980), or the believer's despair before the onset of unbelief as when, the Troubles all around her, Marian in Stewart

Gravediggers, Glasnevin, the setting for Joyce's 'Hades'. Evelyn Hofer's photograph provides a nice take on those responsible for the long-term preservation of the dark.

Parker's *Pentecost* (1987) concludes that God's eyes have been put out: 'He only exists in the dark now.'[59] Elsewhere, in *The Mai* (1995), Marina Carr writes of 'the dark, formless, strangely inviting . . . house you build when you've nowhere left to go',[60] while in Sebastian Barry's *Our Lady of Sligo* (1998) the dark assumes an identity with the ruins of Mai's memories and looks. Away from the stage, as Paula Meehan has rightly noticed in her poem with the suitably intimate title 'Pillow Talk', 'the dark has no end to it'.[61] Or as one of the characters in Kathleen Coyle's novel *There Is a Door* (1931) declares: 'I believe in the dark, young man. Night is a necessity. It contains all origins under its cover. God went wrong when he broke off half his Kingdom and called it Day.'[62]

The dark as a motif reminds us that culture cuts across or undermines neat blocks or categories. Identifying its location is no easy task, for the dark is neither anarchy nor opposed to culture – though it might become either or both. How the dark belongs to hybridity or to the colonial encounter, or whether indeed it is another word for that encounter, or why Irish writers from different backgrounds are attracted to the dark are also questions that are difficult to resolve. I raise the issue here to suggest how an enquiry into the colonial encounter in modern Irish writing requires a more dynamic theory of culture than the view advanced by Lyons. Although I do not address the question in such a direct way again, the dark casts its shadow throughout the chapters which follow.

Chapter 3

THE GREAT FAMINE AND MODERN IRISH CULTURE

So it was a terrible calamity.
And the result of it is to be felt to this day.
Emigration: any of them that was able to leave the country,
they went out of it.
– Hugh Nolan, cited in Henry Glassie, *Passing the Time in
Ballymenone* (1982)

We are the Silent People.
How long must we be still,
To nurse in secret at our breast
An ancient culture?
– Walter Macken, *The Silent People* (1962)

Do our numbers multiply
But to perish and to die?
Is this all our destiny below,
That our bodies, as they rot,
May fertilise the spot
Where the harvests of the stranger grow?
– Denis Florence MacCarthy, 'A Mystery' (1847)

Opposite page
An abandoned stone
cottage surrounded
by a patch of grass
constitutes the Famine
Memorial, Battery
Park City, New York,
which opened in 2002.
Designed by Brian
Tolle, the Memorial
looks in one direction
across to Ellis Island
where Irish emigrants
after 1892 were
processed; in the other
direction, it looks up
Vesey Street to the site
where the World Trade
Center formerly stood.
Photo by the author.

If the trajectory of cultural nationalism is forward, then discourse on the Great Famine moves in the opposite direction, and it is partly for this reason easier to track the momentum of cultural nationalism than it is to chart the legacy of the Famine. Nationalists have had difficulty broaching the topic, not least because talk of building a nation on the back of such a cataclysm seems singularly inappropriate. Among the debates listed by the Jesuits in *A Page of Irish History: Story of University College Dublin 1883–1909* (1930), I have been unable to locate a single specific reference to the Famine.[1] The Christian Brothers' school textbook *Irish*

The New Revised History of Ireland

In 1847, two peasants debate the benefits of a low starch diet.

'Pages from History', a sketch by Robert Ballagh. Courtesy of the artist.

History Reader, published in the same year as the 1916 Rising, plays down the tragedy, simply stating that 'the details of this dreadful famine need not be dwelt upon'.[2] The Famine is a 'dangerous history',[3] as Kinealy has recently pointed out, which is a useful way of thinking about the theme of loss, and hovering over this chapter is another dangerous history taken from the twentieth century, namely the Nazi concentration camps and the issue raised by Theodor Adorno of putting pen to paper after such horrors in Europe. The historian Cormac Ó Gráda believes the Famine is central 'not only to Ireland's history, but to British political and European demographic history, and to the world history of famines'.[4] This, too, is right, for although often neglected as a topic in Britain, the Famine is part of British history – there is no more telling proof of this than a modern British Prime Minister apologising for what happened – part of the Hungry Forties, part of the colonial encounter, part of the continuing 'news from Ireland',[5] and, if Britain was not entirely to blame, the Famine nevertheless advanced the day when the UK would no longer rule Ireland.

Until the advent of revisionist historians, a simmering resentment against the British Government and its failure to act underlay most Irish accounts of the Famine. 'Murdered by order of Lord John Russell' (the British Prime Minister at the time) is how Catherine Loftus, an Irish-American orphaned survivor of the Famine, recalled the fate of the victims.[6] In spite of its title, there is therefore no mystery about Denis Florence MacCarthy's poem 'A Mystery', lines which form one of the epigraphs at the start of this chapter. Every ship exporting food from Ireland was perceived as committing an act of betrayal against the people of Ireland. The question of whether there has been any consistent development or progress through time in literary and cultural responses to the Famine is harder to determine. Motifs recur, and I return to these in my concluding remarks, but each period has tended to see the Famine in slightly different ways. According to Christopher Morash, 'Every Famine text partakes of other discourses, whether militant nationalism (Mitchel and Walsh), Catholic social policy (Conyngham and Guinan) or simply commercial horror fiction in the case of Alan Ryan's *Cast A Cold Eye*.'[7] As recent novels such as Brendan Graham's *The Whitest Flower* (1998) or Joseph O'Connor's *Star of the Sea* (2003) indicate – and this is also in evidence in Máighréad Medbh's long verse sequence *Tenant* (1999) – the effort at reconstructing the Famine, where the stress is placed on loss rather than on struggle, still attracts imaginative writers. This has been a dominant mode, but there have also been attempts to reflect on the presence of the Famine in modern Irish culture. I begin at the head of the procession with the agenda-setting Edmund Spenser, for he did more than any later historian to link Irish Famines with the colonial encounter between Britain and Ireland.[8]

Spenser's Elizabethan View

In 'A Brief Note of Ireland' (1598), Spenser observed: 'Great force must be the instrument but famine must be the meane for till Ireland be famished it can not be subdued.'[9] Spenser's extraordinary remark flags up an important truth: writing about the Famine requires something other than the usual kind of historiography. Adorno believed that 'To write poetry after Auschwitz is barbaric'.[10] Can something similar be said about the Famine? In one respect, the answer should be yes. It *should* be the case, to take the least extreme view, that Irish literature was permanently altered by the Famine. Thomas Kinsella, one of the chief advocates of such a view, came to the conclusion that '[S]ilence, on the whole, is the real condition of Irish literature in the nineteenth century'.[11] He is thinking in particular of the loss of Gaelic, but Kinsella, as I explore below, is one of the few writers to register the seismic effect of the Famine on the culture. Part of my argument in this chapter is that we should not ignore the ethical dimension the Famine has bequeathed to us. For all of the seventy million people who claim Irish descent are survivors of the Famine, and although it is now too late to do more than trace a family line it is still not too late, in the words of George Steiner, who had a different tragedy in mind, 'to imagine backward, to enter hell by act of imaginative talent'.[12]

Arguably the most visually arresting description of hunger in the whole of Irish writing can be found in Spenser's *A View of the Present State of Ireland* (1596), first published in 1633.[13] This is Irenius (man of Ireland, 'Ireland man', or possibly peace) describing to Eudoxus (man of good judgment or repute) the 'late wars' in Munster in the confident prose of an Elizabethan courtier:

> [N]otwithstandinge that the same was a moste ritche and plentifull Countrye full of Corne and Cattell that ye woulde haue thoughte they Coulde haue bene able to stande longe yeat ere one yeare and a haulfe they weare broughte to soe wonderfull wretchednes as that anie stonie harte would haue rewed the same. Out of euerie Corner of the woods and glinnes they Came Crepinge forthe vppon their handes for their Leggs Coulde not beare them, they loked like

The remains of Spenser's Castle at Kilcolman, County Cork. A graphic reminder of history returning to nature. Photo by Dan Harper.

Anotomies of deathe, they spake like ghostes Cryinge out of theire graues, they did eate the dead Carrions, happie wheare they Coulde finde them, Yea and one another sone after, in so muche as the verye carkasses they spared not to scrape out of theire graves. And if they founde a plotte of water Cresses or Shamarocks theare they flocked as to a feaste for the time, yeat not able longe to Continve thearewithall, that in shorte space theare weare non allmoste lefte and a moste populous and plentifull Countrye sodenlye lefte voice of man or beaste, yeat sure in all that warr theare perished not manie by the sworde but all by the extreamitye of famine which they themselves had wroughte.[14]

Spenser spent eighteen years in Ireland in various State employments, beginning in 1580 as Secretary to Lord Grey, the Lord-Deputy of Ireland. In 1589 he was rewarded with a three thousand acre estate at Kilcolman in County Cork. Here he is describing the war of resistance by the native Irish against the confiscation of the Desmond lands in Munster from 1579–83. The colonisers, the 'New English', resorted to a scorched earth policy and starved the Irish into submission – hence famine is a better word in this context than hunger. But the responsibility for this is laid at the door not of the ruthless Lord Grey but of the native Irish, who are thus the cause of their own misfortune.

The passage is frequently cited by commentators and is included by Yeats in his Introduction to *Poems of Spenser* (1906). 'His genius was pictorial,' writes Yeats, his prose 'powerful and subtle . . . full of youthful energy.'[15] The burden of Spenser's remarks on Ireland is more problematic, and Yeats, who was not given to voicing humanitarian views, does his best to muster a defence: 'When Spenser wrote of Ireland he wrote as an official, and out of thoughts and emotions that had been organised by the State' (p.xxxii). But Yeats, who in 'Easter 1916' deployed a similar image of transformation, is forced to concede that there are moments when 'one can read neither Milton nor Spenser, moments when one recollects nothing but that their flesh had partly been changed to stone' (p.xxxviii). Constantia Maxwell in *The Stranger in Ireland* (1954) is more generous: 'Spenser's *View* has been described as intolerant and high-handed, but he had more humanity and more sympathy with the Irish than he has been credited with by Irish writers.'[16] More recently, the Irish historian Nicholas Canny, who is more radical than Yeats in that he sees *A View* not as separate from but as 'a logical sequel' to *The Faerie Queene* (1590–6), has staged a more subtle defence of Spenser.[17] According to Canny, Irenius is deliberately provocative in order to persuade court officials that 'there was no point in the crown undertaking any further military action in Ireland unless there was a firm determination to proceed with it' (p.51).

Canny goes further than most commentators and argues that Irenius and his creator Spenser were 'moved to pity by the terrible scenes of starvation'. What seems clear is that for 'Spenser and Ireland' we should read 'Spenser and Contradiction'. Spenser is an adept at observing the 'wilde Irishe', even choosing to insert the adjective 'wonderfull' before 'wretchednes'. This is 'culture' looking at 'nature', or rather, from today's postcolonial perspective, cruel Prospero being exposed for what he is by a wretched Caliban. But, as the editors in a recent edition of *A View* suggest, particularly in reference to the status of bards in Gaelic society and to Irenius's criticism of the Crown, Spenser complicates the simple opposition between the civilised English and the barbarous Irish.[18] In the Dedicatory Epistle to *The Shepheards Calender* (1579), Spenser (or his unknown representative, EK) makes a strong plea for not being ashamed of one's mother tongue and for not assuming that people speak gibberish when it is not immediately understood:

'Much like to the Mole in Æsopes fable, that being blynd her selfe, would in no wise be perswaded, that any beast could see.' Language for Spenser is something that is imbibed with 'Nources milk', linked with the country of one's birth, to be honoured and valued and beautified. In *A View* he attacks the Anglo-Normans (the Old English who had settled in Ireland in previous centuries) for allowing their children to learn Irish from their nurses (p.119). No mingling, no half-measures, but the overthrow of Gaelic customs and language is the social engineering Irenius proposes. For Spenser not to see the contradictions in such a policy presents a problem for the modern reader, especially given that he writes with such power and sensitivity about language and identity.

The passage above stands as a crux in our understanding of early colonial attitudes towards Ireland. On the one hand, it is tempting to conclude that the passage lends itself to the more straightforward view across time, one which doesn't have recourse to the lack of squeamishness among the Elizabethans or to the limits of their humanism. On the other hand, the lingering fascination with corpses, dying bodies, and images of transformation carries an Elizabethan signature, itself indebted to Ovid and Machiavelli. Spenser can, however, expose the wooliness in our thinking about famine, especially if we thought famine was only or primarily to do with geography or civil war. For if the forces that produce modern famines are the result of trading inequities or the manipulation of commodity prices or global warming, and we stand idly by, then it would be hypocritical to condemn Tudor ideologues, who could cope with extreme situations by denying a common humanity or by appealing to a higher good. Extremes meet, especially in Ireland. Centuries before the Great Famine – or indeed the Jewish Holocaust – literature had in its possession an *awful* language to describe widescale horror, a language that was never in fact bettered when a far worse catastrophe visited Ireland in the 1840s.[19] The extent to which the civilised Spenser believed in barbarian ideas remains open to interpretation, but once uttered, certain things cannot be unsaid, just as, once a people have been starved, they develop somewhere a habit of not forgetting. Spenser injected into all subsequent discourse on famine in Ireland a sinister note, albeit perhaps an honest one, and, when famine returned with a vengeance in the nineteenth century, nationalists needed little persuading to seek out a hand that lay behind it. As for Spenser, revenge came more swiftly, for in 1598 he and his family were burnt out of his castle. A year after returning to London, he died in penury.

Nineteenth-Century Observers

Two-hundred-and-fifty years later, at the time of the Great Famine, the picture of hell was repeated, but now writers, although fascinated by the half-state between life and death, were motivated more by Victorian pity than Elizabethan power play:

'One beholds only shrunken frames scarcely covered with flesh – crawling skeletons, who appear to have risen from their graves, and are ready to return frightened to that abode.'[20] So writes a correspondent in the *Illustrated London News* in 1849. Another witness also tries to distinguish forms of living death: 'not yet dead, but more terrible to look upon than if they were dead'.[21] Cecil Woodham-Smith, the great historian of the Famine, tells us that by April 1847 'children were looking like little old men'.[22] In his historical novel *Glenanaar* (1902), Canon Sheehan includes a description of the Famine which in its conventional language reminds us both of the workings of folk memory and also of how easy it was to slip into a familiar way of writing: 'Gaunt spectres move here and there, looking at one another out of hollow eyes of despair and gloom. Ghosts walk the land.'[23] When Herbert Fitzgerald enters a peasant's cabin seeking shelter from the rain in Trollope's *Castle Richmond* (1860), he discovers a woman squatting on the earthen floor with a child. He does not realise at first how close she is to death, but if he had had more experience of famine conditions, the narrator informs us, he would have realised that the fallen skin on her cheek and her dragged mouth indicated that 'the mark of death was upon her'.[24] This is a literature of the last hour, a witness to the trauma of history, a witness to a history that was taking place for many victims with no witness.

In his description of the interior cabin scene in *Castle Richmond*, Trollope, his nerves settled by belief in Providence, does not flinch from the task, but in his case the tone is reverential, not cruel or anxious, as Margaret Kelleher has recently implied.[25] Of all the passages written about the Great Famine this is arguably among the most moving, a reminder that the colonial encounter doesn't always

The Famine left some villages not so much deserted as destroyed. *Illustrated London News*, 15 December 1849.

stack up as it should. Suddenly the narrative falls away and onto the stage there appears Lear's 'unaccommodated man', or in this case woman, no more than this, 'jist as yer honour sees it' (p.359). A cold, dark cabin, a woman in rags, eyes 'with a dull, unwholesome brightness', 'hardly capable of suffering', a child in arms, cold. Herbert, moved to administer to her immediate wants, sees something in the corner of the room:

> Seeing this he left the bridle of his horse, and stepping across the cabin moved the straw with the handle of his whip. As he did so he turned his back from the wall in which the small window-hole had been pierced, so that a gleam of light fell upon the bundle at his feet, and he could see that the body of a child was lying there, stripped of every vestige of clothing.
>
> For a minute or two he said nothing – hardly, indeed, knowing how to speak, and looking from the corpse-like woman back to the life-like corpse, and then from the corpse back to the woman, as though he expected she would say something unasked. But she did not say a word, though she so turned her head that her eyes rested on him. (pp.359–60)

It is a chilling moment, with the reader seeing everything through Herbert's eyes. The scene possesses a cinematic but not a voyeuristic quality as the camera pans round the room. The tension builds, and we are drawn into this chance encounter between Herbert and the woman. The passage exhibits nothing of Spenser's 'wonderfull wretchednes', the object here denying the subject safety in language. The woman remains silent, but 'so turned her head that her eyes rested on him'. The position of 'so' captures precisely the moment as the spotlight shifts from Herbert to the woman and from the woman back to Herbert. The scene permits no fall-back position, no room for any reassuring phrase such as 'historical background' or 'setting', and little attempt is made by the author of *Castle Richmond* to integrate such a scene into the wider narrative. Indeed, even if he had adopted 'A Tale of the Famine Year in Ireland' for his title (which he had in mind), the tragedy of the Famine would have remained unintegrated.

William Carleton's *The Black Prophet* (1847), set in 1817 at a time of an earlier famine, struggles magnificently to do justice to the Famine then unfolding. Its best scenes are vignettes of the *gombeen* man (Irish for 'usurer') Darby Skinadre, as well as tender moments when we catch a glimpse of hunger victims such as Margaret Murtagh and her baby born out of wedlock dying amid destitution and destitute neighbours. 'They had placed it by her side, but within her arm, so that by this touching arrangement all the brooding tenderness of the mother's love seemed to survive and overcome the power of death itself.'[26] Later in the novel there is another poignant mother-and-child scene which slices through the narrative as if the pressure is too much for recasting the material in imaginative terms:

Stretched out in this wretched and abandoned hut, lay before the good priest and his companion, a group of misery, consisting of both the dying and the dead, to wit, a mother and her three children. Over in the corner, on the right hand side of the fireplace, the unhappy and perishing creature lay, divided or rather torn asunder, as it were, by the rival claims of affection. Lying close to her cold and shivering breast was an infant of about six months old, striving feebly, from time to time, to draw from that natural source of affection the sustenance which had been dried up by chilling misery and want. Beside her, on the left, lay a boy – a pale, emaciated boy – about eight years old, silent and motionless, with the exception that, ever and anon, he turned round his heavy blue eyes, as if to ask some comfort or aid, or even some notice from his unfortunate mother, who, as if conscious of these affectionate supplications, pressed his wan cheek tenderly with her fingers, to intimate to him that, as far as she *could*, she responded to, and acknowledged these last entreaties of the heart; whilst, again, she felt her affections called upon by the apparently dying struggles of the infant that was, in reality, fast perishing at the now exhausted fountain of its life. (p.272)

Carleton's plot-filled narrative gets in the way of such moments. The famous paragraph in Charlotte Brontë's *Shirley* (1849) told from Caroline Helstone's point of view – beginning 'A lover masculine' and including 'You expected bread, and you have got a stone' – pierces the text as if the author's own predicament as a woman was on display.[27] In *The Black Prophet* we sense not so much an eruption as contact with material which informed the novel from the start but which was overlaid with intrigue and the demands of a reading public for a strong story-line.[28] Part of the problem for native Irish novelists such as Carleton in the nineteenth century was the unequal relationship between author, subject matter, and audience, an imbalance which largely resulted from the colonial encounter. Too often, the author's stance was: 'Here is an awful picture of the rural poor in Ireland. You in Britain and elsewhere should know about it, but I am going to dress it up in a story with a love intrigue for easier consumption.' Such a stance meant that the narrative was frequently at odds with its background, which was also, effectively, its displaced foreground. Among Irish Famine novels there is nothing as fully achieved as Knut Hamsun's compelling first-person novel *Hunger* (1890). On the other hand, for the critic, the uneven texture of nineteenth-century Irish fiction has meant that the link between ideology and literary form can be more forcefully exposed.[29]

James Clarence Mangan (1803–49), who was for Joyce 'a romantic, a herald manqué, the prototype of a nation manqué',[30] has long been associated with the Famine. In the 1930s the association was underlined by Louis D'Alton in *The Man in the Cloak* (1937), a moving play about the poet set against famine stalking the countryside and cholera threatening his home life in Bride Street, Dublin. D'Alton brings out how Mangan, who enjoyed 'moments of genius in years of mediocrity', becomes a riddle even to himself, and how, in embracing death, his hope is that one of his songs 'may shake down an empire'.[31] The association is so pervasive that Mangan's modern biographer has felt obliged to distance him from the Famine, arguing that a poem such as 'The Funerals', although prompted by the contemporary reality in March 1849 when it appeared, was in fact about the poet's state of mind in 1839.[32] There is merit in drawing such a distinction but Mangan himself was largely responsible for enforcing the link between the personal and the public:

> Swiftly – not as with march that marks
>   The earthly hearse,
> Each FUNERAL swept onward to its goal –
>   But, oh! no horror overdarks
> The stanzas of my gloomsome verse,
>   Like that which then weighed down my soul!
>
> It was as though my life were gone
>   With what I saw!
> Here were the FUNERALS of my thoughts as well!
>   The dead and I at last were one!
> An ecstasy of chilling awe
>   Mastered my spirit as a spell![33]

Mangan couldn't resist intensifying words such as 'overdarks' or artificially yoking together emotional opposites such as 'chilling' and 'awe', as if the reality of loss was too much for ordinary language to cope with. The author of another poem on abjection with the title 'The Nameless One', he was also given to fusing or collapsing identities, never more so than in his most famous poem 'Dark Rosaleen'. In the *Dublin University Magazine* in 1834, Sir Samuel Ferguson, in his review of James Hardiman's *Irish Minstresly* (1831), argued against an allegorical political reading of the Elizabethan Gaelic poem 'Róisín Dubh', the source for Mangan's poem.[34] But 'Dark Rosaleen', especially in its allusive symbolism, not only insisted on such a reading but also spoke directly to those enduring an extreme plight:

> The judgment hour must be nigh
> Ere you can fade, ere you can die,
>   My Dark Rosaleen.

Twenty years after the Famine, when Canon John O'Rourke visited Skibbereen, he discovered in the suburb of Bridgetown no longer a long row of houses but only 'detached blocks of three or four or half-a-dozen cabins here and there'.[35] One legacy of the Famine was not the deserted but, as a contemporary report in the *Illustrated London News* reveals, the 'destroyed' village, not the picturesque Goldsmith therefore, but something closer to the abjection of the harp and to the role of the crown in the disaster.[36] O'Rourke's account also includes an encounter with an old man who had lived through the Famine and its aftermath. In his unsentimental, down-to-earth series of responses, the old man offers a clue as to how the Famine was 'overcome':

> I accosted a man who was standing at the door of his humble dwelling: 'I suppose you are old enough,' I said to him, 'to remember the great Famine?' 'Oh! indeed I am, sir,' he replied, with an expressive shake of his head. 'Were there more people in Bridgetown and Skibbereen at that time than now?' 'Ay, indeed,' he replied, 'I suppose more than twice as many.' 'And where did they all live – I see no houses where they could have lived?' 'God bless you, sure Bridgetown was twice as big that time as it is now; the half of it was knocked or fell down, when there were no people to live in the houses. Besides, great numbers lived out in the country, all round about here.' 'Come here,' he said, earnestly, and we ascended the road a little space. 'Do you see all that country, sir?' and he pointed towards the north and west of the town. 'I do.' 'Well, it was all belonging to farmers, and it was full of farmers' houses before the famine; now you see there are only a couple of gentlemen's places on the whole of it. The poor all died, and of course their houses were thrown down.' 'And where were they all buried,' I enquired. 'Well, sir,' he replied, 'some of them were buried in the old chapel yard, near the windmill; a power of them were buried in Abbeystrowry, just out there a bit, where you are going to but –' he suddenly added, as if correcting himself, 'sure they were buried everywhere . . .'[37]

The 'expressive shake of his head', which O'Rourke takes care to include but not to gloss, is the old man's way of saying: 'Yes, I saw it all and here am I, a survivor of those dreadful times. I've lived to tell it all.' By not saying it, by not telling it, that is, the tragedy of the Famine is allowed a dignified space outside language. This is not the gesture of someone suffering Post-Traumatic Stress Disorder – though it could be an example of survivor guilt. The poor died, the houses were knocked or fell down. O'Rourke doesn't pursue the matter.

The old man's response is tied to the land and issues of ownership and he assumes this is what the outsider wants to hear. But such a response also conceals material and attitudes that could only be spoken about or fully understood within the parish or family. Thus the gesture screens as much as it reveals. 'I won't tell you more about those days,' says Sissy O'Brien's mother in Mary Carbery's *The Farm by Lough Gurr* (1937). 'The past is past, and the present is happy, thank God.'[38] Rural Ireland, the harp, did recover, its gestures and use of language – at least in one respect – intact. According to Emily Lawless, writing at another transitional moment in 1898, to hear the phrase 'Famine road' 'casually uttered is to be penetrated by a sense of something at once familiar and terrible'.[39] Within a short space again, the Famine became part of the Irish lexicon, as when Corney's father in Sean O'Faolain's novel *Bird Alone* (1936) is described as having 'the sharp look of the Famine'.[40] But the freedom inherent in such imagery was bought at a price, for, as the Irish-Australian historian and novelist Thomas Keneally has observed, after the Famine Ireland became 'a land of the solitary and the aged, pared to the limit'.[41]

As a footnote, not every allusion to famine by later Irish writers belongs to the Famine. In Kathleen Coyle's 'London' novel *Piccadilly* (1923) there is a reference to 'famine bread'; the heroine, in search of employment as a short-hand typist, fears she will be offered domestic work at the Labour Exchange, 'the famine bread of the professionally stricken'.[42] The phrase seems to have an Irish ring to it but in fact it is associated with the bread made from the bark of trees during famines in northern Europe, especially Scandinavia. However, it would be interesting to know if Coyle is drawing on a phrase heard in childhood in Derry in the late nineteenth century; its use and its associations certainly raise issues about the lack of resourcefulness shown by the Irish during the Famine.

Gerald Keegan's Famine Diary has been the subject of much interest, mostly negative. When published in 1992 it was thought that this was a true account from the period, but subsequently it was shown to be based on 'The Summer of Sorrow' (1895), Robert Sellar's story, which itself was based on accounts from the Famine years. In its defence, Christine Kinealy has recently argued that the Diary 'clearly filled a void, whilst demonstrating that the revisionist interpretation had failed to displace. . .the traditional nationalist interpretation of the Famine'.[43] At the very end of his Diary, his hand shaking from the fever that eventually kills him, Gerald Keegan bids a formal farewell: 'In reverent memory of all those who have perished in this holocaust.'[44] The use of the word 'holocaust' is proof enough that the Diary is a fake, and yet in its imaginative recreation of the Famine years James J. Mangan's text has much to recommend it. References to the effects of the Famine in Dublin, the use of Mangan the poet and the scenes on board the Famine ship all have a contemporary feel. When the Famine begins to take hold, Keegan, a village school teacher who struggles throughout the period of his Diary against the overwhelming force of his emotions and letting himself go, finds himself regretting 'the increasing indifference' he feels on witnessing yet another eviction (p.48).

The Diary would have been more effective if it had been allowed to stand as fiction rather than documentary and had been published alongside 'The Summer of Sorrow'. Robert Sellar's story, from a collection designed to 'convey in a readable form an idea of an era in the life of Canada which has passed – that of its first settlement by emigrants from the British Isles, based on real incidents in their humble lives', has been unduly neglected in the recent controversy.[45] Sellar's story is itself situated within a story about the author/narrator's encounter with an Irishman who has a copy of his 'poor nevy's book' but who seems more interested in another story about his early days of settlement in Canada, concerning how an old woman and a cow went missing. When the author/narrator begins copying the Diary, he learns more from the uncle about how it entered his possession. In the context of the colonial encounter there is something else worth noting. Surprisingly, given the pro-Irish sentiments of *Gerald Keegan's Famine Diary*, the discourse of 'The Summer of Sorrow' is a concerted attack, not on Britain but on the Canadian authorities, for mismanaging the crisis at the embarkation point at Grosse Isle, when Irish emigrants on board fever ships were refused permission to land and when thousands died 'for a lack of crust on Canada's shore' (p.457).

The Famine and the Revival

The Famine has cast a long, if at times unnoticed, shadow over modern Irish culture. On the face of it, Terry Eagleton asks a perfectly reasonable question: 'Where is the Famine in the literature of the Revival? Where is it in Joyce?'[46] Part of the answer is supplied by Margaret Kelleher, who cites Maud Gonne, Rosa Mulholland, Edith Somerville and Martin Ross and Emily Lawless.[47] But when Kelleher concurs that the Famine is absent in Joyce and Yeats, she risks overstating the case. Yeats's moody play *The Countess Cathleen* (1892) is set during a famine, while in *The King's Threshold* (1904) he tackled the story of the legendary poet Seanchan who, to restore his right to sit at the King's table, resorts to fasting. As an Irish anthologist, in *Representative Irish Tales* (1891) Yeats included Rosa Mulholland's intense, realistic, famine story, 'The Hungry Death'. As an editor and reader of William Carleton, the early Yeats repeatedly tapped into the Famine and pre-Famine Ireland and also into history-from-below:

> The history of a nation is not in parliaments and battle-fields, but in what the people say to each other on fair-days and high days, and in how they farm, and quarrel, and go on pilgrimage. These things has Carleton recorded.[48]

It was an important insight. Carleton's *Traits and Stories of the Irish Peasantry* (1830; 1833) provided Yeats with a 'recorded' image of pre-Famine Ireland which the Famine had in part destroyed. In his search for continuities between self and community, past and present, the people and the Court, Yeats discovered in Carleton not only 'the most Celtic eyes that ever gazed from under the brows of story-teller' but also a way of thinking about history that commanded – and still commands – attention.

When we turn to the imagery of Yeats's writing, there is frequently a scattered energy at work, as if some prior dispersal or emptying has occurred. His anti-bourgeois sentiments, too, stem not only from his father's influence, his Romantic heritage and Nietzschean pre-disposition, but also from the Famine. 'I want to be a vagabond, a wanderer' declares the main protagonist, Paul Ruttledge, in *Where There Is Nothing* (1902), and the imagery fills up with the roads that the Famine victims also took, Ruttledge's irresponsibility a counter to the settled life of Victorian drawing-rooms: 'They never meet one another. The roads are the only things that are infinite. They are endless.'[49] And it's natural for the audience to recall a Famine tableau when Ruttledge later vows: 'I pulled down my own house, now I go out to pull down the world' (p.1142). With the catastrophe of the Famine behind him, Yeats found little to delay him in the temperate zone. It is true that at one stage he would have liked to have composed something for an imagined fisherman, but this resembles an empty gesture rather than a genuine commitment. There is no 'Michael' in him and little recollection in tranquillity. He made his reputation as the dreamy author of 'The Lake Isle of Innisfree', but, constitutionally, Yeats is a poet energised by extremes rather than by margins, for whom any reverie or reassurance comes at a price. During the Irish Civil War, with the warring participants and danger all around him, he invites the honey-bees to 'build in the empty house of the stare' (*VP* 424). The gesture is consciously at odds with the situation. While he doesn't have the sharp look of the Famine, he does seem driven by Freud's repetition-compulsion to scenes of loss and deprivation, which then become the ground for some of his best lines. In *The King of the Great Clock Tower* (1935), immediately after speaking the lines of the Stroller's severed head, the First Attendant declares: 'O, what is life but a mouthful of air' (p.1004). The analogy belongs not only to the *sprezzatura* of the Renaissance courtier but also to a culture which had enjoyed a sustained intercourse with death and in this particular case to an observation he made as a young man in a review of Lady Wilde's *Ancient Cures, Charms, and Usages of Ireland* (1890), how the *sidhe* (the host of fairies) were at twilight, 'Nations of gay creatures, having no souls; nothing in their bright bodies but a mouthful of sweet air'.[50]

The presence of the Famine in Joyce's work is in many respects stronger. The first reference to the Great Famine in *Ulysses* occurs in the 'Nestor' episode when the Orangeman, Mr Deasy, attempts to gain credibility with the Catholic-educated Stephen: 'I saw three generations since O'Connell's time. I remember the famine in '46. Do you know the orange lodges agitated for repeal of the union twenty years before O'Connell did or before the prelates of your communion denounced him as a demagogue. You fenians forget some things' (*U* 2:268–72). Joyce filters this first reference to the Famine through a strained encounter between the smug owner of a school, a modern Nestor emptily parading the wisdom of the ancient world, and a penniless young teacher who needs an advance to see him through the day. What the remark affirms is not only the proximity of the Famine to 1904 but also how the Famine was not a discrete historical event but was associated with the

O'Connell period and the issue of Repeal of the Union. Deasy is on the defensive and Stephen, for all his feelings of dispossession, and though he has in the Famine a weapon of some power, characteristically declines to respond.

In the following episode, 'Proteus', perhaps with this conversation still reverberating, Stephen recalls the famine in Dublin in 1331: 'Then from the starving cagework city a horde of jerkined dwarfs, my people, with flayers' knives, running, scaling, hacking in green blubbery whalemeat. Famine, plague, and slaughters. Their blood is in me, their lusts my waves' (*U* 3:304–7). This striking passage is described by Kelleher as 'carefully distanced into medieval times',[51] a conclusion that is both right and wrong, for this is history being quickened from within, enacted before our eyes, being both the memory and the event. Deasy claims a link with the Famine years but Stephen has a quicker sense of history, one that reaches back to famines in the very distant past, famines which through the engagement of the imagination and a line running through his Irish genes also register with him as if they were still contemporary. What is missing from Joyce is a similar evocation of the Famine itself, for then the phrase carefully distanced into the Famine time would indeed be inappropriate.

Of course, not every reference to food evokes the Famine or evokes it in a direct or obvious way. In *Ulysses*, the Famine leaves its displaced mark in the talisman of the potato that Bloom carries in his pocket throughout the day. The potato links the fortunes of two races, the Irish and the Jews, the potato being for Jews a central dish in the ritual meal after a funeral, a relic, as we later learn, of Bloom's poor mamma (*U* 15:3513). It is also part of an Irish stereotype – every Murphy is a spud – so the displaced mark is also Joyce playing with a stereotype of the harp. In 'Calypso', Bloom, on leaving the house, is reassured by the presence of the potato, this time positioned first in the sentence both for emphasis and humour: 'Potato I have' (*U* 4:73). In 'Lestrygonians', the episode designed to induce a reaction against eating, Bloom links the police informer Corny Kelleher with an idiomatic expression: 'Drop him like a hot potato' (*U* 8:444–5). The same episode also contains a direct reference to the Famine entering Bloom's consciousness: 'They say they used to give pauper children soup to change to protestants in the time of the potato blight' (*U* 8:1071–3). 'Lestrygonians' also reminds us throughout of the link between food and sex. A paragraph beginning with wine leads naturally from grapes in Burgundy to Bloom's memory of Molly on Howth Head giving him seedcake into his mouth while kissing: 'Yum' (*U* 8:906). Less seriously, in the 'Circe' episode, the potato takes another bow, this time as part of Bloom's response to the Catholic litany, where the invocation begins with a kidney and ends with a potato: 'Kidney of Bloom, pray for us. . . . Potato Preservative against Plague and Pestilence, pray for us' (*U* 15:1941–1952).

Periodically, then, throughout *Ulysses*, a novel of struggle rather than loss, the Famine chord is struck. The Famine is part of the culture, Joyce seems to be saying, not to be regarded in terms of Thomas Kinsella's seismic gap or as an example of Freud's concept of latency – the time, that is, between the accident and the first appearance of symptoms – but rather to be accepted as a given. It transpires that the song Simon Dedalus sings at the beginning of *A Portrait of the Artist as a Young Man* – 'O, the wild rose blossoms/On the little green place' – is a Famine song entitled 'Lilly Dale'. It was presumably a favourite of John Joyce, who sweetened the words for his baby Jim by exchanging 'place' for 'grave'.[52] If Joyce wanted to wrap his novel in the clothes of the Famine, this would have made an excellent start, but he doesn't, preferring instead to reverse the significance of a private memory and a public event. As for the image of the old sow eating her farrow, again the association is not with the Famine, though it could have been turned by Joyce in that direction.

As his first stay in Paris bears out, suffering and pain were felt by Joyce initially in personal rather than cultural terms, but it is fitting that he made his fictional debut with a story containing 'stirabout', the porridge once associated with the Famine.[53] In 'The Sisters', the boy in the story crammed his mouth with stirabout to suppress his anger on hearing Old Cotter berating his friendship with the priest. Significantly, in *Lights and Shades of Ireland* (1850), the contemporary American commentator Asenath Nicholson uses inverted commas round the word now being newly annexed to the Famine: 'It is well known that among the many devices for the cure of Ireland's famine, the soup-shops and "stirabout" establishments, ranked among the foremost, and the most effectual for some time.'[54] In 'The Sisters', food and drink, as references to cream crackers, beef-tea, and a glass of sherry indicate, contribute to the portrait of pinched circumstance. Even the Eucharist is associated with duty rather than with celebration, and the priest also fails here. By contrast, 'The Dead' contains a celebrated paragraph on food beginning 'a fat brown goose lay at one end of the table', a paragraph that could only have been written by someone familiar with starvation.[55]

Dubliners, then, is framed by two stories in which food plays a conspicuous part, a reminder that its author came to consciousness in a country where deprivation and scarcity was a constant theme. Joyce is enough of a realist to concur with Bloom that 'Hungry man is an angry man' (*U* 8:662–3). He also knows that pinched circumstances, surrounded by stirabout and snuff, produce pinched mentalities and malapropisms, and that rich circumstances, surrounded by geese and Smyrna figs, produce expansive minds and high-flown rhetoric. But there he stops. For Joyce is only occasionally a systematic thinker or a political animal. Stephen's nightmare view of Irish history is deflected by the recourse of an exile: 'We can't change the country. Let us change the subject' (*U* 16:1171). For Joyce, culture exists as active response to circumstances, central to which are alternative and comparative viewpoints. Such an outlook carries him beyond nineteenth-century forms of reductionism or determinism and beyond the Marxist idea of economic base and ideological superstructure. As for the pattern of his own behaviour, this betrays its own form of determinism, for Joyce couldn't resist indulging himself. The potato that Bloom carries with him throughout the day is discovered in the 'Nighttown' episode at the top of the prostitute Zoe's stocking: 'Those that hide knows where to find' (*U* 15:5–6). In the context of the present discussion, it is a slightly blasphemous moment, for from an association with filial duty – and by extension the Famine – the potato has been dematerialised by Joyce into an object of sexual desire, a peepshow.[56]

O'Flaherty's *Famine* (1937)

For different reasons, Famine novelists in the nineteenth century tended to underplay the brute show of force, preferring, as with William Carleton, who emphasises the evils of the usurer and the uncaring attitudes of land agents, to attend to the wider social and historical picture. Liam O'Flaherty, who gathered material for *Famine* from the Rev. John O'Rourke's account, adopts a stronger line and records how a whole community effectively died under the onslaught of the Famine. The agent is killed, the doctor dies of plague; with no customers the shopkeeper Hynes retreats to the local town to face an uncertain future. Gleason the weaver loses his mind, Michael dies after a long illness, Thomsy is eaten by dogs, Sally kills her three children to prevent further suffering, Ellie, the agent's housekeeper, is forced to emigrate after news that Chadwick has been abusing her, and the final scene shows the patriarchal figure of Brian Kilmartin digging a grave for his wife and collapsing on his spade. Only Mary and Martin, a stone from the family hearth in their pockets, escape from the deluge by emigrating. To deepen the sense of tragedy, O'Flaherty repeatedly stresses the ironies. After eating some bread distributed by the Quakers, Patsy O'Hanlon's stomach swells up and his eyes become like the eyes of a corpse; he goes out to relieve himself in a ravine used by the family as a privy, accidentally tumbles down and dies. He is discovered by his children 'doing "little pigs" up on the mountain at the back of the house'.[57]

As with Spenser, O'Flaherty's discourse mixes description, context, cause, and responsibility. But in his descriptions of the drunken lawlessness and lasciviousness of Chadwick the agent (a familiar figure in O'Flaherty's fiction), O'Flaherty, as if he was in search of an ideological formation more universal than the colonial encounter, betrays the undue influence of nineteenth-century primitivism and naturalism. When the doctor, for example, arrives to attend to Mary's brother-in-law, he can't take his eyes off her. Nothing develops between the two and it obstructs the ongoing narrative, simply revealing a subtext of sexual desire in the novel that is not directly expressed. Mary's sister, Ellie, finds herself sexually compromised by Chadwick the agent, denounced from the altar, and forced to flee the district. Such hints at an interior life are pointers to another novel inside its covers, but here the main story is threatened by the influence of Zola. However, because most accounts of the people who died tended to emphasise their status as victims, the attempt to provide a human dimension to the Famine – human, that is, in terms of sexual drives – is a welcome shift of emphasis on O'Flaherty's part away from loss to struggle. Not for nothing did Sean O'Faolain remark on its publication that *Famine* was 'the best Irish historical novel to date', a puff that still to some extent holds true.[58]

It would be wrong to see, therefore, only loss or defeat. Sporadic rebelliousness punctuates famine novels from Carleton to O'Flaherty. *Famine* reconstructs several high-energy scenes of resistance by the people – against Chadwick, the agent, against John Hynes, the home-grown gombeenman, against the Repealer, Father Roche and against the charity of the Protestant parson, Mr Coburn. In this sense, *Famine* is closer to the resistance that is well described by Ciaran Ó Murchadha in a recent study of Ennis, County Clare during these years.[59] Having been brought up on the Aran Islands, where his father, during the Land War in 1880, had once driven his landlord's cattle over the cliff into the sea, O'Flaherty had a special personal insight.[60] Where Carleton addresses his novel to the British Prime Minister in the hope of winning his support, in post-Independence Ireland O'Flaherty makes no such appeal. If anything, his aim is more home-grown: it is to expose the various weak character traits such as cowardice, as typified by Hynes the doctor; the failures of upwardly mobile social classes as they departed from their roots in the people; the false move, as presented by O'Connell's Repeal movement, and the collusion of the Catholic Church in fostering quietism and not rebellion. The contrast with Louis J. Walsh's Famine novel *The Next Time* (1919), which carries for its subtitle *A Story of 'Forty-Eight*, is most apparent at this point, for nothing stills the ongoing momentum of Walsh's backward-looking novel, which begins with Catholic Emancipation in 1829 and ends with the protagonist's death and his looking to the future: 'We won't fail the next time, Jim – sure we won't?'[61]

Death and defeat stared the Famine generation in the face. 'There's another name for the stranger,' says Sean the Fool in Gerard Healy's doom-laden play *The Black Stranger* (1945). 'They're calling him the reaper now.'[62] 'The poor!' declares a bewildered Sally O'Hanlon towards the end of O'Flaherty's novel, 'Why did God ever pester the world with them?' (p.340). Eviction, the workhouse, emigration – these were the options facing the rural poor. In *The Black Prophet* Carleton stresses another trefoil – famine, disease and death. Whatever the series, in the 'valley of dry and rotting bones', as 'Andrew Merry' memorably puts it in her novel *The Hunger* (1910),[63] death beckoned for over a million; death by typhus or dysentery, death in a cold cabin, death by the roadside, death at the ports, and death on board the coffin ships to North America. In a Famine narrative, by the time we reach the sentence 'The great hunger has come', it is already too late.[64]

The Famine and the Poets

Patrick Kavanagh and Thomas Kinsella offer contrasting views of the effects of the Famine on modern Irish culture. Twenty years after Independence, with the publication in 1942 of *The Great Hunger*, the screams of the Famine can be heard again, only this time it is the scream of the small farmer, 'an impotent worm on his thigh', crying out for sexual contact.[65] The association with the Famine in the title is particularly striking. When the poem was first published in *Horizon* it carried a backward-looking title, 'The Old Peasant'. In altering it to *The Great Hunger*, Kavanagh at once widened the scope and interpretation, for a metaphorical reading of the poem could now accompany the story of Maguire stuck in the clay of provincial Ireland where 'The hungry fiend/Screams the apocalypse of clay/In every corner of this land'. But, as if to stress that his complaint was a modern one, Kavanagh takes care to avoid detailed references to the Famine, and this in spite of the eviction of his own family from their cottage in County Monaghan at the time of the Famine. Indeed, according to his brother Peter, 'No element of politics or of sociology entered consciously into the writing of these poems.'[66]

Shifting the focus in this way was not so much a betrayal of the record as a way of gaining attention. For Kavanagh, twentieth-century Ireland is confronting as powerful a famine as it faced in the nineteenth century, only now it is to do with bodily desire or the search for 'flesh', which he describes at one point in the poem as a 'thought more spiritual than music/Among the stars'. The poet sets the scene as he means to go on: 'Clay is the word and clay is the flesh'. This gives us the whole poem, for, like his predecessor, the author of St John's Gospel, but with a difference, Kavanagh is set on exploring the meaning of the Word made flesh. There is a rooted quality to Kavanagh's language and imagery, but his parish is the world. The scream is heard not in the sentimental and clichéd 'four provinces of Ireland' but in the deliberately toned-down 'every corner of this land'. This is the harp post-Independence, where critical headlines which startle are beginning to find expression in the culture: 'No hope. No lust.' This is not the *culchie* country as imagined by the city but more like the revenge of the country on the whole country. How different is this structure of feeling from the pre-Famine world of Brian Merriman, whose bawdy long poem on love and celibacy, 'Cúirt an Mheán-Oíche' (*The Midnight Court*), which was composed about 1780 and newly translated by Frank O'Connor in 1945, contained lines such as 'Let lovers in every lane extended/Follow their whim as God intended'.[67] Too late for that kind of pastoralism. Don't blame anyone else, Kavanagh seems to say. When introducing a reading of the poem on BBC radio in May 1960, Kavanagh characteristically took care to distance himself from it by claiming the poem was 'stuck in the ground', 'not completely born', with 'no laughter in it'.[68] Tragedy, he argued, was underdeveloped comedy, but he concluded on a potentially tragic note by observing that while changes in farming practices had

Patrick Kavanagh harvesting in the early 1930s, a scythe tucked under his arm, his shirt collarless but top-buttoned, his hair slightly dishevelled and already beginning to recede, and two young animated women binding up stooks of corn. Kavanagh looks directly into the camera, slightly quizzical but without anger, as if he already knew he would one day write that here in the fields 'is the source from which all cultures rise'. Photo (slightly overexposed) taken from Patrick Kavanagh, *November Haggard* (1971).

occurred, with the horse being replaced by the tractor and the cart by the trailer, 'the life as lived there remains practically the same – sad, grey, twisted, blind, just awful'.

For Kinsella, the Famine is part of a larger argument associated with silence, the loss of Irish, and the colonial encounter:

[S]ilence, on the whole, is the real condition of Irish literature in the nineteenth century – certainly of poetry. ... If I look deeper still, further back, in the need to identify myself, what I meet beyond the nineteenth century is a great cultural blur. I must exchange one language for another, my native English for eighteenth century Irish. After the dullness of the nineteenth century, eighteenth century Irish poetry seems to me suddenly full of life: expertise in the service of real feeling – hatred for the foreign land-owner; fantasies and longings rising from the loss of an Irish civilisation (the poets putting their trust in the Stuarts or the Spanish fleet or even the Pope of Rome); satires, love-songs, lamentations: outcries of religious fervour or repentance. . . . Here, in all this, I recognise simultaneously a great inheritance and a great loss. The inheritance is mine, but only at two enormous removes – across a century's silence, and through an exchange of worlds. The greatness of the loss is measured not only by the substance of Irish literature itself, but also by the intensity with which we know it was shared; it has an air of continuity and shared history which is precisely what is missing from Irish literature, in English or Irish, in the nineteenth century and today.[69]

Kinsella is a more systematic thinker than Kavanagh, arguing that modern Irish culture is the product of the 'gapped tradition' and that its great modern poet, Yeats, is 'isolated in the tradition', isolated from a people who speak another language and 'whose lives, therefore, he cannot touch'. Kinsella invariably situates his predicament in historical or cultural terms and these remarks are no exception. In 'Nightwalker' he writes:

> A dying language echoes
> Across a century's silence.
>   It is time,
> Lost soul, I turned for home.
>   Sad music steals
> Over the scene.
>   Hesitant, cogitating, exit.[70]

'Nightwalker' – the title links with my discussion of the dark in the Introduction – is a characteristic Kinsella journey through Irish history. The poem opens with a reference to the Joyce Tower at Sandymount, an appropriate setting for a sequence of ironic and ambivalent reflections on the theme of dispossession. In the second section, Kinsella recalls a school lesson where he was taught by the Christian Brothers that 'Her Majesty' Queen Victoria:

> Gave us the famine – the starvation, as Bernard Shaw,
> A godless writer, called it more accurately.
>
>   A hand is laid on my brow.

A voice breathes: You will ask are we struck dumb
By the unsimplifiable. Take these . . .
Bread of certainty; scalding soup of memories,
From my drowsy famine – martyrs in a dish
Of scalding tears: food of dragon men
And my own dragon half.[71]

'The traumatised,' writes Cathy Carruth in *Trauma* (1995), an enquiry centred on Holocaust victims, 'carry an impossible history within them.'[72] 'Nightwalker' is not itself a traumatised poem, but Kinsella does raise the issue of the Famine as trauma in Irish culture. In the face of such enormity the poet feels the hand of the past on him, and he formulates the response not as emotion but as question. His response in turn is equal to the task. Take these (and eat of it, all of you). It is an act of homage, which consists of 'bread of certainty', an awkward collocation but one that is arguably of equal interest if applied to the Eucharist or the Famine. Like the Eucharist, the Famine is unsimplifiable but nevertheless certain for the poet (or school-teacher). The next phrase 'scalding soup of memories' conjures up the image of 'soupers' trying to convert the poor victims to Protestantism, behaviour which would have been roundly condemned by the Christian Brothers. The memories scald the mind and the protagonist is at one with the victims. The phrase 'my drowsy famine', which Kinsella cut from his *Collected Poems* (1996), presumably refers to the classroom scene, implying that in its retelling the history of the Famine has lost its power to disturb. But then there is a jolt and the voice pronounces the victims martyrs. 'Martyrs' is a strange word to apply to the victims, and yet, on reflection, it is not inappropriate. The victims were martyrs, witnesses to horror or to the future. Kinsella, the poet of loss and the awkward silence, is not always successful with what he tries, but he challenges the reader to make sense of his verse as both argument and experience, and his questioning, self-critical approach is particularly suited to a belief in the gapped tradition that he sees as constituting the legacy of the Famine.

There is another way for the modern poet of addressing the Famine as unsimplifiable. When the contemporary poet Brendan Kennelly imagines words emigrating through Judas's mouth in a poem entitled 'Lips', his thoughts turn to silence and hunger as if some primordial Irish reality is crying out for expression:

The words escape into the darkness
Like hunger-strikers finding the gates open
Or cries of children swallowing hunger
On a mountain of excrement and death.[73]

Only an Irish poet could produce such a sequence of images. Words, darkness, hunger-strikers, children, hunger, excrement, death, and all in four lines. Only in an Irish context, with a history of famine and hunger, could all these images – including the dark – cohere and not sound invented or strained. In a collection of poems about Judas, the most cast-out of any outcast in Western culture, the poet in prison identifies his words firstly with hunger-strikers and then with children crying not in the wilderness but on the mountains, where they swallow not air but hunger. The ground of both images is hunger, and, appropriately, Kennelly in these lines deliberately chooses to stress the physical reality rather than the symbolic meaning.

In the work of the American poet Susan Howe, the spectre of the Famine comes face to face with contemporary postmodernism. The oddness of the juxtaposition is handled with considerable skill by Howe, so that the marginal becomes central, the familiar is defamiliarised, and loss turns into struggle. As a child in her great-aunt's garden beside Killiney Bay near Dublin, Howe first heard James Mangan's poem 'Roisin Dubh' ('Dark Rosaleen'). For Howe, Mangan in his self-conscious modern manner is an exemplary figure, and she exploits Herman Melville's 'marginal' comments on Mangan to write about Mangan himself. In 'Melville's Marginalia' (1993), she provides not only a chronology of his life under the heading 'Parenthesis', a word with considerable status, but also a separate entry on the Famine. For Howe, Mangan is 'Marginal. Belonging to the brink or margent'. That is, he is both on the edge of something, on the brink, peering over the abyss, but also close to the edge of writing, the margins of writing, close, that is, to the notes the postmodernist poet herself is investigating and reconstructing. She pictures Mangan as a librarian:

A spectral creature on a ladder
All his soul was in the book
In his arms
Roisin Dubh means Ireland
On earth I guess
I am bound by a definition
Of criticism[74]

Mangan has been frequently depicted as a spectral figure – indeed, 'spectral-looking' is how he is described in the passage Howe quotes from a nineteenth-century editor of Mangan.[75] Howe refers to Mangan's 'corpse-like features', and, later, immediately following lines on his quiet death in Meath Hospital and his paltry funeral in Glasnevin, a series of words appears, as if to capture something of Mangan and the fate of the Irish: 'Drudge dole pauper famine'. Howe works all this historical association into a poem with a decidedly postmodern agenda, free in its own way from the colonial encounter, but not free from a sense of loss. A creature raised above the earth, Mangan is not so much self-possessed as someone in possession of his soul, which is linked here to books, books in his arms, that is, to libraries, and to the following line of verse; to poetry. According to John Mitchel, Mangan 'lived solely in his poetry – all the rest was but a ghastly death-in-life'.[76] The conventional reading is that 'Dark Rosaleen', the little black rose, is an image of Ireland. Howe, who is intent on widening and undermining conventional readings, also does more with this idea and we infer that the line 'Roisin Dubh means Ireland' must signify something else or more than this. Mangan, the creature on a ladder, is a visionary poet, and perhaps the dark Rosaleen figure is not bound by 'Ireland'; on earth perhaps she is, but Mangan is on a ladder. The spectral figure then comes to take up in his arms his book learning and his craft as a poet. Not death, therefore, but an image of literature wrested from the earth, an answer, among other answers, to the lines in MacCarthy's 'A Mystery':

> Is this all our destiny below.
> That our bodies, as they rot,
> May fertilise the spot
>   Where the harvests of the stranger grow?[77]

Staging the Famine

Tom Murphy's historical reconstruction of the Famine is concerned more with the response of the harp than with the crown's role in the disaster. *Famine* (1968) begins in language which is deliberately heightened, poetic, and ritualistic: 'Cold and silent is now her bed. . . .Damp is the blessed dew of night.'[78] In this first scene, with a field of potatoes for background and the death of a young girl in the Connor family for frame, Murphy offers a survey of attitudes. John Connor wonders what it matters in the scale of values if the potatoes are blighted when his daughter is dead. Fr. Horan, who resorts to testing one of his parishioners through an exercise from the catechism, expresses the bland optimism of churchly wisdom: 'Trust in God' (p.9). Others search for meaning and deliverance through the great liberator Daniel O'Connell – but later in the play someone notes that his achievement in winning Catholic Emancipation in 1829 failed to prevent the Famine. Memories of previous famines help the villagers in their attempts to get a measure of the Great Famine, but such memories actually prevent them from realising the enormity of the new situation. The villagers search for answers and for causes, considering how it might have been helpful for them to eat the seed potatoes rather than plant them, and how they should have sowed them deeper.

For Murphy, it is the tragic strain, especially evident in his attention to details, rather than the colonial encounter, which dominates. It's as if the latter had been confined to history, but Murphy still has an argument with his own people. He repeatedly highlights the link between irony and tragedy, showing how burials

prompted generosity of spirit that couldn't in fact be afforded. When Mark keeps
repeating the word 'speckeleens' in his description of the potato flowers as if
unaware of the implications, the audience finds this disturbing not, as he thinks,
reassuring. Mickeleen, full of revenge against the system of landlordism in Ireland,
is the realist: 'Ye don't want to see, but in a day or three, the smell will blind ye into
seeing!' (p.13). But when he is accused of being a 'Jumper', that is, of converting to
Protestantism, his testimony becomes slightly suspect to the villagers. John and his
wife accept their fate, summed up in the phrase 'Welcome be the holy of God'. But
even in this first scene we infer that John, the natural leader of the village, will alter
his position as the famine takes hold. The scene closes with John's wife keening; it
is a return to the opening, and the sense of loss is poignant: 'She is gone forever. . . .
Cold and silent is her repose' (p.19).

Seamus Deane argues that the Famine 'resituated the relationships between
land, language, and national character'.[79] He might have had in mind *Translations*
(1981), a play pre-eminently concerned with pre- and post-Famine Ireland. While
set in the 1830s, it's a play about a watershed in Irish society, about the 'dreadful
gulf' that Asenath Nicholson anticipated in 1850.[80] Throughout the play Brian
Friel repeatedly hits the note associated with the title, drawing us into a deeper

Field Day Theatre Company (Left to Right):
Back Row: Ray McAnally, Stephen Rea, Magdalena Rubalcava, Liam Neeson, Bo Barton, Jonathan Tait, Shaun Scott.
Middle Row: Brian Friel, Mary Friel, Ann Hasson, Roy Hanlon, Margo Harkin, Finola O'Doherty, Brenda Scallon.
Front Row: Art O Briain, Mick Lally, Nuala Hayes, Paddy Woodworth, David Heap.

The original
programme for
Translations in 1980
carried a photograph
of Field Day, with
youthful-looking
Stephen Rea and Liam
Neeson. Photo by
Larry Doherty.

The opening night of *Translations* in Derry. Report by Paul Wilkins in *Hibernia*, 25 September 1980.

Field Day For Friel

On Tuesday night Brian Friel came home, when the Field Day Theatre Company, which he formed recently with Stephen Rea, presented in Derry Guild Hall the world premiere of *Translations*, which will prove to be one of Friel's finest and most characteristic plays. I was uneasy that, with the premiere in Derry, this might be an occasion of empathy, local piety, with general civic celebration sliding into self-congratulation. From the start of *Translations*, however, it was evident that what dictated this venue was not sentiment but theme. A play dealing with disparate cultures could perhaps find no surer test of its impact than with a Derry audience.

The play is set in a hedge-school in Ballybeg, in 1833, when local place names were anglicised by the military during the first Ordnance Survey of Ireland. Hence "Translations"—but the title resounds beyond this primary application to include the entire shift from an indigenous, Irish-speaking culture to the imposition of an English speaking one, translations embodied in two of the characters: Owen, the local boy who left for Dublin and has now returned as the Royal Engineers' interpreter, and Yolland, the young English officer who, having fallen in love with both Donegal and a native girl, strives to learn Irish.

A quotation from Heidegger prefaces the programme: "Man behaves as if he were the master of language, whereas in fact it is language which remains his mistress. When this relationship of dominance is inverted, man has recourse to strange contrivances". The play is about such an inversion and its victims. We are made aware repeatedly of questions of language and identity, not in an abstract manner, but as inherent in an historical situation and in individual lives: the mute Sarah being coaxed by her teacher, Manus, to speak her name for the first time; the bedraggled Jimmy Jack, "a 70-year-old infant prodigy", reciting from Homer and dreaming of goddesses; Hugh, master of the hedge-school; Tittler an entymologist, composing Latin verses and seeking appointment as headmaster of the new national school.

Friel uses a device which constantly reminds us of the gulf between peasantry and soldiers: when the local characters speak to each other in Irish, what the audience hears is (of course) both sides using English. Thus the division between them is all the more poignant and frustrating. This also makes some sections of dialogue very funny, though at times things came close to comedians patter, and one or two jokes about place-names were too obviously tailored for the Derry audience. But generally this device (unlike that of the narrator in *Living Quarters*) was pertinent and effective, stunningly so in a scene involving Yolland and Maire, where the place-names which compose his entire Irish vocabulary are used to woo her. This was the high point of the play, movingly portraying the situation's complexity—his only means of verbal communication with the girl is precisely what he has come to destroy.

Particularly notable performances came from Stephen Rea, showing great range as Owen; Ray McAnnally, authoritative and amusing as Hugh (a part which a lesser talent might have overplayed), and Mick Lally as Manus.

I am not completely certain of the validity of the ending, powerful though it is. But this is a play of great richness—richness of intellect, and of lyricism. Its strength is that it combines a penetrating view of Irish history with a truly universal subject: how words can "interpret between privacies". The distinguished first-night audience included Cyril Cusack, Seamus Heaney, Julie Covington and several national theatre critics, one of whom, James Fenton, remarked on the audience's enthusiasm, so rare in London. There was, however, nothing false about the final ovation. *Translations* is the most powerful of Brian Friel's recent plays.

Paul Wilkins

awareness of his theme, which, as ever, is articulated in essentially conceptual terms. This is shown in the classroom scene where the dead language of the classics is being translated into English (though we have to remember that Irish is the language of the play); in the fact that Máire is learning English so as to emigrate to America; or that Sarah is still learning how to speak; and that the drunken schoolmaster, Hugh, is lamenting the loss of Gaelic civilisation. It is also apparent when much is made of the mis-translation of local place-names for an Ordnance Survey; or when Hugh's son Owen returns to the parish as an Irish intermediary for English sappers, and so on. The shadow overhanging the whole play is the Famine, but this is only given specific form late in the play when Bridget detects the 'sweet smell' of the blight. 'Smell it!' she says, not realising it's the tents of the soldiers burning. And then adds, 'God, I thought we were destroyed altogether.'[81]

As it transpired, it was not soldiers but famine that destroyed that generation – though Friel raises a doubt or an issue in our minds as to the connection between the two forces. As is apparent in his other plays, such as *Dancing at Lughnasa* (1990), Friel is especially attracted to time-frames. The pathos in *Translations* stems from the audience knowing and his characters not knowing the next chapter in Irish history. In a play largely devoted to historical reconstruction, he captures a moment of people anticipating their fate, for this was the generation that came to be known to history as the pre-Famine generation. But there is something that can't penetrate the time-frame, the translation, and this seems to be Friel's point. His interest is not primarily in historical reconstruction, or in the more philosophical post-structuralist concept of *différance*, but in an essentially political (or is it apolitical in his case?) idea concerning our inability or failure to negotiate the terrain between past and present, one language and another, culture and politics, language and identity, or the harp and the crown.

Concluding Remarks

What made the Great Famine worse as a catastrophe was a hybrid culture which somehow got imprisoned, as Hugh remarks in *Translations*, in 'a linguistic contour which no longer matches the landscape of . . . fact': 'Yes, it is a rich language, Lieutenant, full of the mythologies of fantasy and hope and self-deception – a syntax opulent with tomorrows. It is our response to mud cabins and a diet of potatoes; our only method of replying to. . .inevitabilities' (pp.42–3). On the eve of the calamitous event that was to reduce Ireland's population from just over eight million to six and a half million, people were still playing host to the prophecies of Pastorini and St Columcille. Belief in Providence also disabled people from tackling their fate head-on. 'We must be content with what the Almighty puts upon us' was the phrase that impressed Asenath Nicholson.[82] In Peadar O'Donnell's *Adrigoole* (1929), a realistic novel set in the 1920s, which begins with a hiring fair in Strabane and ends in a famine death, a young girl in search of food dies after eating hemlock. Thereafter, the neighbours redoubled their prayer against the fever, action which 'was no doubt rooted', according to O'Donnell, 'in the '47 famine horrors'.[83] So strong was religious belief that some, such as John Hynes, find only guilt across the class divide. Haunted since childhood by a suspicion that God disapproved of him as a usurer, Hynes carries with him 'the peasant's conception of God, as the defender of the poor and the down-trodden'.[84] The Famine, as O'Flaherty's novel indicates, sorely tested the view that God was on the side of the poor, but there were enough revolutionary curates such as Fr. Geelan around to suggest that the disillusioning process would not be the legacy of the Famine years. As the deeply confused Hugh remarks at the end of *Translations*, 'My friend, confusion is not an ignoble condition' (p.67).

In Ireland, west of a line from Wexford to Sligo, and particularly in the south-west counties of Cork and Kerry, few saw very far into the future. The phrase used by an old man from County Kerry in his submission to the Irish Folklore Commission in the 1930s evokes something of the dreadful fatalism that wiped out a whole generation: 'People were fading like frost after frosty weather.'[85] More recently, in a section devoted to contemporary songs of the Famine, Cormac Ó Gráda notices how 'as the crisis deepened' so did the understandable 'communal fatalism'.[86] Few at the time were able to get a measure of things. Few were as percipient as Anna in Alexander Irvine's novel *My Lady of the Chimney-Corner* (1913), who has the Protestant Northerner's realism to discern that 'every hope has a headstone – a headstone that only waits for the name.'[87] Anna, who betrays not so much defeatism as the practical intellect ready to seize an opportunity, is an exception, and she has recourse to a proverb, the practical wisdom of the people: 'We don't cross a stile till we come to it, do we?' (p.27). In very few of the accounts, whether imaginative or documentary, is there to be found a phrase such as 'the right to live' or 'Ireland for the Irish'. The banner the people march under in Andrew Merry's *The Hunger* (1910) is 'WE ARE STARVING'.[88]

Part of the harp's imprisonment has its origins in the best aspects of Irish life, its sense of community and its generosity of spirit. A well-seasoned observer of the Irish poor on the eve of the Famine had this to say: 'No such phenomenon exists in Ireland as a people utterly regardless of the wants of their neighbours. The hearts of the poor Irish are glowing with kindness to one another, prompt and liberal, according to their means, in relieving one another in distress.'[89] In the eyes of a contemporary witness, the main effect of the Famine was not to create poverty, but to make the people 'so sad in themselves . . . and that it made many a one hard too.'[90] According to Patrick S. Dinneen, *gorta*, the Irish word for hunger, carries a series of other meanings including 'scarcity', 'famine', 'destitution', and 'stinginess'.[91] Stinginess is the odd one out and highlights an important cultural marker. It was impossible for famine to arrive without a loss of self-esteem, and not just the esteem that Spenser notices. As Peter McCarthy observes in Gerard Healy's *The Black Stranger* (1945): 'You see, no matter what they took from us before, they left us a bit of pride, a bit of dignity that we thought was secret inside ourselves an' couldn't be touched, in spite of all the laws and all the dispossession.'[92] William Carleton understood what was at stake here: 'There is scarcely anything so painful to hearts naturally generous. . .as the contest between the shame and exposure of conscious poverty on the one hand, and the anxiety to indulge in a hospitable spirit on the other.'[93]

Linked with *gorta* is the phrase *féar gorta*, the 'quaking grass' or 'starvation grass'. In Irish, famine had a folkloric dimension as well as a moral one. Quaking grass grew on soil where a famine victim was buried. Should an unwary traveller walk over the spot, death or hunger might be the result. 'Watch out for the *féar gorta* up in those hills' was advice heard in County Kerry.[94] Food had to be provided, as it were, for the victims of famine to eat. No one was ever quite lost to history. In *The Black Prophet*, Carleton makes much of the Grey Stone at the cross-roads of Mallybenagh, site of an unsolved murder some twenty-two years before the narrative proper begins. Here, the Gothic conventions of fiction and Irish folklore meet in a powerful embrace. Like quaking grass, the grey stone is a site of unresolved suffering, acquiring particular intensity because it plays on a popular imagination steeped in superstition. Ironically, a decade later, Carleton's post-Famine story 'Fair Gurtha; Or the Hungry Grass: The Legend of the Dumb Grass' (1856) is designed in part to remind readers of the superstitions of the past, which are now all but vanished.[95]

Why did the people not rise up against the crown? In one respect they did, only it took until the Fenian Rising of 1867, the Land War of 1879–82 and the Easter Rising of 1916 for the children to wreak their revenge for the terrible things that happened to their parents. Trollope's suggestion that it was a form of apathy is partly right but is too close to his own ideological, compromised position to accept as it stands. The Irish were fatally unprepared for *An gorta mór*, 'the great hunger'.[96] The type of agriculture, the system of land ownership, the subdivision of the land, the cultivation of the one root crop, the *laissez-faire* ideology dominating British Government thinking and policy, and changes in the Poor Law all conspired to make the Great Famine the single worst tragedy in nineteenth-century Europe. Equally, ranged against the poor were the forces of the state.[97] When Alexander Somerville, the author of *The Autobiography of a Working Man* (1848), arrived in Ireland in 1847 to survey conditions, the first thing he noticed was the armed police:

> One of the first things which attracts the eye of a stranger in Ireland, at least such a stranger as I am, and makes him halt in his steps and turn round and look, is the police whom he meets in every part of the island, on every road, in every village, even on the farm land, and on the seashore, and on the little islands which lie out in the sea. These policemen wear a dark green uniform and are armed, this is what makes them remarkable, armed from the heel to the head. . . . The only difference between them and the regular military is, that the military do not always carry guns and pistols primed and loaded, not always bayonets in their belts, not always swords sharpened. The Irish police never go on duty without some of these.[98]

Only a co-ordinated guerrilla army could have taken on the crown at this time and such a force didn't appear in Ireland until the War of Independence in 1919. The Young Ireland rebellion of 1848, led by John Mitchel, ended ignominiously in Widow McCormack's cabbage patch in County Tipperary.

The mother-and-child scene is a familiar motif in the oral tradition,[99] and it is appropriate that one of John Behan's Famine sculptures is entitled *Famine, Mother and Children*. Nothing could be more poignant than the child trying to suck from its dead mother. This is an image of Mother Ireland unable to feed her children, her griefs comparable to the real mother in George Cooper's contemporary poem 'The Irish Mother's Lament Over Her Child':

> The frost nips the bosom that fain would thee nourish,
> My thin blood is frozen, and closed every pore
> That Nature has framed my poor baby to cherish;
> Oh Erin! Oh Erin! *thy* griefs are as sore.[100]

The historical icon that best captures the Famine years is also that of a woman (Bridget O'Donnell) and her two children; it appeared in the *Illustrated London News* on 22 December 1849.[101] She stands shoeless in rags, her arms draped over her two children, looking out at the world almost expressionless. And she has a story to tell, though this is rarely noticed. The German artist Käthe Kollwitz, three-quarters of a century later, would have portrayed her more dramatically, perhaps with the mother shielding her children from the forces of history, but there is no attempt at this here. This is abjection, the end, the extinguishing of hope, no reservoirs of emotion to call on to fight through to the next stage, not even enough to plead for pity from the sketch-artist.

Similarly striking are the scenes of dogs digging up scattered bones buried insufficiently deep in the earth. Father Peter O'Leary records an incident from his childhood when Tadhg, the eldest son of Black Michael and Cathleen Purcell, killed a neighbour's cow for food to feed his desperate parents. After eating a meal Tadhg then removed the corpse of his dead brother from the corner of the cabin and buried him. Arrested by the authorities, he was transported, and his parents took to the roads. The sequel is no less harrowing:

> Some days after they had gone away, a neighbour was going past the cabin. He saw a hound, with something in his mouth, in the garden; the hound threw down the thing he had in his mouth and ran away. The neighbour came over and he nearly fell with the shock and the horror when he saw that it was a person's hand that the dog had in his mouth! Tadhg hadn't made the hole deep enough before he had put the body down into it.[102]

Carruth comments on 'the *literality* and nonsymbolic nature of traumatic dreams and flashbacks, which resist cure to the extent that they remain, precisely, literal'.[103] The recurrence of such images of dogs eating humans has something of this quality within the memory of the culture as a whole. It must have been a common sight, but the image was so disturbing that it is as if later generations felt traumatised themselves, 'the symptom of a history they cannot entirely possess'.

According to a recent historian, Mike Cronin, 'Each and every one of those individuals who died or left Ireland had a story to tell. . . . Many of the individual stories were left behind in the form of letters and diaries. . . . From such harrowing personal narratives and official observation, the lived experiences of the famine can be, at least in part, uncovered.'[104] But this doesn't square with his observation that 'roughly a million' died from starvation and a further million emigrated. (In fact, starvation was not the primary cause of death: dysentery, diarrhoea, dropsy, fever and other factors were.[105]) It would be more accurate to say that many of the Famine victims died without any witness and, worse, that many died without any record of their having lived. In a recent poem entitled 'that bread should be', the contemporary Yorkshire-based poet Maggie O'Sullivan, some of whose family are buried in the massive Famine pit in the Abbey Cemetery in Skibbereen, writes about this loss with a faltering catch in the voice, the single long dash allowed to speak across a century's 'hard plain howl':[106]

whole families without a trace my ———

James Mahony's sketch of Bridget O'Donnell and her two children. How she arrived at this state is a reminder that the Famine undermined the whole fabric of rural society. Behind with the rent, Bridget was evicted and dispossessed of thirty stone of oats. She then fell ill with fever and her house 'tumbled'. Given the last rites, she recovered and gave birth to a still-born child. Further misfortune followed when her thirteen-year-old boy died from hunger. Meanwhile, the corn she once owned was taken into Kilrush and sold. We don't learn what happened to her husband, nor indeed if she survived the Famine. See *Illustrated London News*, 22 December 1849. In Adrian Noble's London production of Brian Friel's *The Home Place* (2005), a play set on the eve of the Land War in 1878, this sketch of Bridget O'Donnell is recalled when the impoverished Mary Sweeney with two children enters the Big House and pleads for assistance.

Published by the Workers' Music Association in 1955, Galvin's anthology is a reminder of the great tradition that once encouraged thousands to support the cause of Irish nationalism.

We will never know the actual numbers who died. Was it a million or a million and a half? So the recorded moments, whether in literature or in other forms of writing, are the exception. As O'Sullivan rightly suggests, the story for most is an 'unstory', best represented also by a black line across a white page, where letters of a language should be. We are much closer, therefore, to Adorno's characterisation of those who died in the concentration camps, how 'it was no longer an individual who died, but a specimen'.[107] If the authors of *Lost Lives* (1999), the 1,600-page reference book containing the stories of the 3,636 people who were killed in the Northern Irish Troubles between 1966 and 1999, were to compile a similar record of all those who died in the Famine – that is, assuming the information were available – it would fill a small library.

Even if we knew the names of all the victims and all their stories, all the causes, all the names of those to blame, the Famine would still remain not so much unanalysable as outside our comprehension. The first time to my knowledge the word 'holocaust' is linked with the Famine occurs in *The Fall of Feudalism in Ireland* (1904), when Michael Davitt, the leader of the Land League during the Land War from 1879–1882, refers to 'the holocaust of humanity which land-lordism and English rule exacted from Ireland in a pagan homage to an inhuman system'.[108] This makes the Famine perhaps too comprehensible, part of a historical

A detail from Rowan Gillespie's *Famine*, a group of statues of six individuals clutching all their worldly goods, a dog at their heels, which was erected near the Custom House in Dublin to commemorate the flow of people out of Ireland a hundred and fifty years ago. Photo by Matt Eagleton-Pierce.

argument which is both too specific and too general. On the other hand, the use of the word 'holocaust' in *Gerald Keegan's Famine Diary* is in one respect, as we have seen, an act of betrayal but in another highly suggestive, for the Famine does invite comparison with the twentieth-century Holocaust. The Famine shares with the Holocaust huge numbers of victims, scenes of utter desolation, spectral images, and a long history of religious persecution. Moreover, just as the Holocaust is detached from its original meaning of sacrifice, the Famine, too, is rarely seen in terms of sacrifice. Differences also need to be noted. Unlike the Jews, the Irish have only intermittently held the position of the Other in western culture. As Zygmunt Bauman has rightly underlined, we are *possessed* by the memory of the gas chambers – which is not something that can be said about the Famine.[109] The literature of the Holocaust survivors, especially the second generation survivors, keeps expanding, but, as my reading here suggests, we miss first-hand accounts of the Famine. Much of famine literature is second-hand reconstruction, often without personal involvement – hence the misplaced excitement that greeted the publication of what was thought to be a lost diary from the period. Equally, the catastrophe of the Famine was not wholly man-made, and no one today could argue that the potato blight was sent to Ireland to destroy a quarter of the population. Many people, most notably Quakers, helped to reduce suffering. The workhouses were much despised but they were not concentration camps.

It's also unclear how *much* trauma Ireland suffered as a result of the Famine. Trauma victims from the camps are still with us and when they speak, they do so with authority. This is not the case in Ireland, where even records of the first-hand witness are rare and where contact with the primary experience can be achieved only through reconstruction. In contrast to the Famine, The Night of the Big Wind in 1839 was often recalled in oral folklore because it was safe. As Ciarán Ó Murchadha has noted, many of the respondents in the recordings undertaken by the Irish Folklore Commission between 1938 and 1945 'showed a marked reluctance to share what they knew. . . . But . . . nearly a century after the Great Famine, the children and grand-children of those who endured it and survived were still in possession of a coherent inherited memory of its horrors.'[110] A century and a half on, there has been a concerted effort to rediscover the Famine after years of neglect, which stems, in part, from the inherited burden of shame.

Persistence has an important part to play, for what we are dealing with here is a complex set of responses that need sifting. A recent historian has suggested that the use of the analogy between the Famine and the Holocaust 'emphasises the depth of feeling involved, and the extent to which historians are forced to bend the knee to the emotive issue'.[111] This is not quite right, and the image of bending the knee, which actually betrays an anxiety in the face of the enormity of the event, is revealing. As for the issue of emotions, when Richard Dimbleby, the first reporter into Belsen, began his broadcast, he broke down, and the BBC needed verification before they went ahead with his report.[112] At stake is not depth of feeling, for, clearly, witnesses to the Famine and the Holocaust were *overcome* by feeling, or, in Victor Pritchett's case, on seeing the bombed-out German cities in April 1945, 'stripped of every feeling'.[113] Later commentators and historians have a different responsibility, at the heart of which is also a need to respond, but to respond in a way which turns not only on what happened then but also on deciding what constitutes an adequate response now.

Feeling a sense of loss and recovering a sense of loss are not the same thing; one is an emotional, the other a rational response (which might lead to an emotional response). Equally, feeling, wanting to feel, being obliged to feel, or ascertaining what one ought to feel are all different, as is bad faith. As Eva Hoffman has recently reminded us in *After Such Knowledge* (2004), the path of a trauma in a person, in a culture, or in history, requires careful handling. '[T]his is exactly the crux of the second generation's difficulty: that it has inherited not experience, but its shadows.'[114] Some of these distinctions are also explored with considerable skill and honesty by Adrienne Rich about her Jewish-American background, a continent and a generation away from the Holocaust, but, with the exception of someone like Eavan Boland, it is rare to find anything equivalent in modern Irish writing.[115] However, in spite of all these qualifications, the importance of the comparison between the Famine and the Holocaust should not be downplayed. Indeed, just raising the issue tends to enforce the links. Let me end on this note. Just as the therapist listening to descriptions by an Auschwitz survivor is involved in what Carruth describes as 'a double survivor situation', meaning the person who survived and the one who is a proxy survivor, so, too, in reading accounts about the Famine we also are 'survivors' and we, too, if we have eyes to see, undergo something of the original trauma suffered by the victims.[116]

HOME RULE

Chapter 4

The Impact of Cultural Nationalism

When boyhood's fire was in my blood,
I read of ancient freemen,
For Greece and Rome who bravely stood,
Three hundred men and three men.
And then I prayed I yet might see
Our fetters rent in twain,
And Ireland, long a province, be
A NATION ONCE AGAIN.
– Thomas Davis, 'A Nation Once Again' (1845)

What ish My Nation?

In Shakespeare's *Henry V*, Captain Macmorris asks a question that has continued to reverberate in Ireland, especially in the period after the 1880s: 'What ish my nation?' Godwin Smith, writing in the *Contemporary Review* in 1885, refused to countenance the possibility that people of English extraction could press for Home Rule: 'What can be more ridiculous than to hear a man bearing the name of Parnell, Biggar, or Sexton, talk of driving the British out of Ireland?'[1] A generation later, in Shaw's anti-war play *O'Flaherty V. C.* (1915), with its ironic sub-title, 'Recruiting Pamphlet', Private O'Flaherty, home on leave after being awarded the Victoria Cross, voices his doubts about patriotism at General Sir Pearce Madigan's country estate in Ireland: 'It means different to me than what it would to you, sir. It means England and England's King to you. To me and the like of me, it means talking about the English just the way the English papers talk about the Boshes. And what good has it ever done here in Ireland?'[2] In the trenches during the Great War, the Irish soldier-poet Francis Ledwidge, lamenting the execution of Thomas MacDonagh after the 1916 Rising, must also have pondered his position.[3] More recently, in *A Star Called Henry* (1999), Roddy Doyle's historical novel about the period, the five-year-old destitute slum-dweller Henry Smart, who later fought in

Opposite page
Detail of Tom Merry's cartoon in *St Stephen's Review*, 10 January 1891.

Modern Irish writing begins with a bump. A month after the Fall of Parnell in Committee Room 15 at the House of Commons, Tom Merry performs one final, cruel twist of the knife on Gladstone and his association with the Irish Parliamentary Party. *St Stephen's Review*, 10 January 1891.

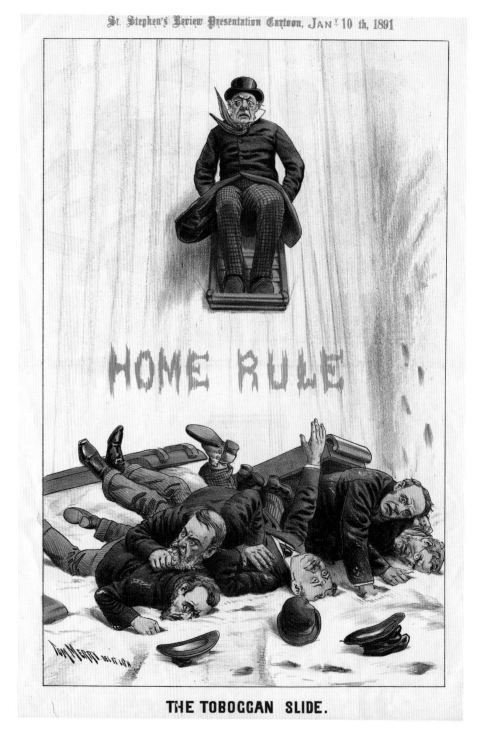

St. Stephen's Review Presentation Cartoon, Jan.ᵧ 10 th, 1891

THE TOBOGGAN SLIDE.

H. Capivez   IT'S A LONG, LONG WAY TO TIPPERARY   No. 5

The song, which was composed in 1912 by an American who had never visited Ireland, became a favourite with those on the home front as well as with those fighting in the trenches. The card was posted in October 1914.

the Easter Rising and then became one of Michael Collins's anointed, didn't even know he was Irish as he watched King Edward VII processing through the streets of Dublin in 1907.[4] All these 'curious sympathies',[5] shifting responses and allegiances, which were brought to a head at moments of crisis, were essentially the product of the colonial encounter between the harp and the crown, an encounter the historical accents of which can still be heard today, especially among Northern nationalists and Republicans. According to Bobby Sands, the song which lifted the spirits of Republican prisoners in the H-Blocks in the early 1980s was 'A Nation Once Again', the unofficial anthem of nationalist Ireland in the nineteenth century.[6]

Unlike Spenser, Shakespeare has little to say about the Irish, but in his play celebrating the triumph of the English over the French, he makes much of the sh-sound, the intruding Hiberno-English speech-marker often used – as here – in a patronising fashion: not what is but what *ish* my nation. Elizabethan Shakespeare also serves to remind us that Ireland as a nation predated the Elizabethan period. Free for the most part, unlike its neighbour, from occupation by the Romans, Ireland has its origins in antiquity, in the rivers and wells of mythology, in the survival of its ancient language, in its place-names, in its myths and sagas and in its sense of difference and resistance. Moreover, its bardic poetry and 'personality' was already in place before Shakespeare was born:

> 'I am of Ireland,
> And the Holy Land of Ireland,
> And time runs on,' cried she.
> 'Come out of charity,
> Come dance with me in Ireland.' (*VP* 526)

This is Yeats in his mid-sixties, renewing his commitment to *Tír na nÓg*, the mythical Land of Youth, in a poem developed from a fourteenth-century Irish-language dance song, 'Icham of Irlande'. Couched as an invitation by a woman who identifies herself with a spiritual Ireland of the saints but who also recognises the demands of the body and the pressure of time, this female *carpe diem* is a fine example not only of the 'perennialist perspective' on nationhood that Anthony D. Smith discusses in *The Nation in History* (2000) but also of how pre-modern Ireland could be evoked simply by the act of translation and made modern and enticing in the process.[7]

In spite of its antiquity – or, equally, because of it – defining the harp's distinctiveness has never been easy. Beguiled by difference, Yeats typically tends to assume or assert, rather than spend time proving his case. Throughout his career, he believed the Irish were a 'chosen race',[8] 'nearer than the English to the Mythic Age'.[9] As a boy, his mother taught him to feel disgust at the English lack of reserve, pointing out to him how they kiss at railway stations.[10] Bishop Berkeley's response to English empirical philosophy, cited by Yeats in the Irish Senate in the 1920s, was 'We Irish do not hold with this', and it summed up much of Yeats's defiant attitude to the world, a defiance that makes it impossible to believe that Yeats didn't have an English audience uppermost in his mind.[11] But, as is apparent in *On the Boiler* (1938), his last extraordinary prose rant against the modern world and the crown, we also need to bear in mind that such defiance could spill over into a form of barely disguised racism: 'The Irish mind has still in country rapscallion or in Bernard Shaw an ancient, cold, explosive, detonating impartiality. The English mind, excited by its newspaper proprietors and its schoolmasters, has turned into a hot-bed harlot.'[12]

In truth, as *John Bull's Other Island* (1904) repeatedly demonstrates, Shaw himself was better than Yeats at distinguishing English from Irish, not least, as Declan

HISTORY AND GEOGRAPHY.

MR. TATE.

1. Give with date a very short account of any land or sea battle where British arms were engaged (from, but exclusive of, the Conquest down to and including those of the present war) which you would consider of decisive influence on the history of the world, stating your reasons for holding that opinion.

2. State shortly for what the following personages were remarkable, approximately how long ago each of them lived, which of them, if any, were contemporary with each other, and which of them, if any, could be remembered by persons now alive :—Strongbow, Caxton, Milton, Marlborough, Edmund Burke, Goldsmith, Lord John Russell, Bismarck.

3. Give a short account, with principal dates, of the American War of Independence.

4. Starting from Dublin, and going south, enumerate in order all the Irish counties which touch the sea.

5. Illustrate by a rough map the position of the French and British lines on the Western front, showing the chief places near which they pass.

6. Mention the principal passenger steam-boat routes between Ireland and England, with the names of the chief towns through which one would pass between the English port of arrival and London.

7. Mention any four great rivers of Africa, indicating shortly their course, and into what seas or oceans they flow.

Mr Tate's entrance exam for Trinity College Dublin, January 1918. It took Trinity another half-century to shake off its Anglo image. From *The Dublin University Calendar for the Year 1918–1919.*

Kiberd has persuasively argued, in showing how the terms were subject to comic reversal.[13] Broadbent, the English entrepreneur, is more sentimental than the Irish, and, on his first encounter with the country, falls in love with an Irish colleen beside the romantic Round Tower in Rosscullen. Doyle, his Irish colleague long domiciled in London, exhibits the hard-headedness associated with the English, and feels compelled to expose illusions in Anglo-Irish relations wherever they appear. When Broadbent refers to 'the melancholy of the Keltic race' (a way of thinking advanced by the nineteenth-century French and English Celticists Ernest Renan and Matthew Arnold), Doyle, his Irishness touched, comes close to exploding: 'Good God!!! . . .. When people talk about the Celtic race, I feel as if I could burn down London.'[14]

At one level, Yeats's idealism and Shaw's realism shape up as opposites, but from another perspective the fairy king and the man given to sporting fashionable Jaeger suits belong together. There is an extreme quality about both their attitudes, as if the world could be put to rights by climbing on a soapbox (or a disused boiler on Sligo quays in Yeats's case). Unlike Yeats, however, Shaw knew his limitations, and to counter the 'efficient' intellect, his own included, he takes care to foreground the critique of the defrocked priest, Father Keegan, in *John Bull's Other Island*. An early commentator failed to see anything other than comedy in Shaw's portrayal of Keegan: 'a man of God who passes for a lunatic, a mystic who talks to grasshoppers, calls the ass and the pig his brothers, believes like a Buddhist in metamorphosis, and asserts that Hell is on earth!'[15] But from today's perspective, with his advocacy of green politics and with his attack on 'four wicked centuries' of capitalism and 'this foolish dream of efficiency',[16] Keegan sounds like an authentic – and still relevant – Shavian mouthpiece, outflanking both the harp and the crown.

If Ireland was the subject, London was frequently the viewpoint, so, from Shakespeare to Yeats and Shaw, attempts to distinguish the Irish from the English were inevitably shot through with misconceptions. Boazio's map of Ireland (1599) speaks louder than words. As with other maps of Ireland in the sixteenth century, the perspective is from London, with the South of Ireland to the left of the canvas and the West at the top. More than his predecessors, Boazio attends to the Irish dimension, providing a glossary for place-names in Irish, 'for the better understanding of the reader' as he innocently puts it, but, with its decorative and reassuring depiction of landscape, the map resembles a London estate agent's brochure, complete with symbols of the crown and quiet backwaters for the prospective planter to hunt and shoot and fish.[17] The task, therefore bequeathed to subsequent generations in Ireland was to right the map, as it were, reclaiming the plantations, and re-establishing a way of seeing adjacent, but not necessarily hierarchical, relationships between Britain and Ireland.

In tracking the development of cultural nationalism we need to bear in mind that from the outset the knife cuts both ways, that passionate realism frequently accompanied passionate idealism, and that Irishness, as Joyce, too, understood, was at once a natural feeling and a contestable concept. Whatever 'Judge Eglinton' claims in 'Scylla and Charybdis', the 'balancing' episode in *Ulysses*, the truth in this matter was almost certainly not 'midway' (*U* 9:1018). Joyce approached the question from the safety of exile but he understood the unnaturalness of his position, being, as he describes Shem in *Finnegans Wake*, 'An Irish emigrant the wrong way out' (*FW* 190:36). In the well-known scene in Barney Kiernan's pub in the 'Cyclops' episode of *Ulysses*, a scene which recalls the discussion in 'Sirens' about Molly's identity, Bloom is forced to defend himself against the charge that he is not really a harp: 'What is your nation if I may ask?' And the answer the modern-day Macmorris gives to the 'Citizen' is the deflating, moving, utopian end-stop which draws attention to the etymological roots of the word 'nation' in *natio* or birth: 'Ireland, says Bloom. I was born here.' This is Joyce providing another perspective on the harp and in particular on the meaning of 'attachment', a word that in one respect is simply functional (attach this to . . .) but which from another angle does service for some of our strongest 'attachments', not all of which are emotional.

To insist on the point – and insistence is largely the point – Joyce at this juncture in 'Cyclops' produces one of the many Rabelaisian satirical lists that thread their way though this episode as the Citizen and his associates berate Bloom for his non-Irishness:

> The muchtreasured and intricately embroidered ancient Irish facecloth . . . was then carefully produced and called forth prolonged admiration. . . . The scenes depicted on the emunctory field, showing our ancient duns and raths and cromlechs and grianauns and seats of learning and maledictive stones are as wonderfully beautiful and the pigments as delicate as when the Sligo illuminators gave free rein to their artistic fantasy long long ago in the time of the Barmecides. Glendalough, the lovely lakes of Killarney, the ruins of Clonmacnois, Cong Abbey, Glen Inagh and the Twelve Pins, Ireland's Eye, the Green Hills of Tallaght, Croagh Patrick, the brewery of Messrs Arthur Guinness, Son and Company (Limited), Lough Neagh's banks, the vale of Ovoca, Isolde's tower, the Mapas obelisk, Sir Patrick Dun's hospital, Cape Clear, the glen of Aherlow, Lynch's castle, the Scotch house, Rathdown Union Workhouse at Loughlinstown, Tullamore jail, Castleconnel rapids Kilballymacshonakill, the cross at Monasterboice, Jury's Hotel, S. Patrick's Purgatory, the Salmon Leap, Maynooth college refectory, Curley's hole, the three birthplaces of the first duke of Wellington, the rock of Cashel, the bog of Allen, the Henry Street Warehouse, Fingal's Cave – all these moving scenes are still there for us today rendered more beautiful still by the waters of sorrow which have passed over them and by the rich incrustations of time. (*U* 12:1438–1464)

Against such a list, the claims of Bloom to being a harp seem, at least at one level, fairly weak. But even if the reader has never visited it, s/he knows that the Maynooth college refectory can hardly compare with the monastic ruins of Clonmacnois, that the mention of Guinness's brewery must mean that other watering-holes are also listed (the Scotch house and Jury's Hotel), that Curley's hole must be vulgar (it is in fact the name of a bathing-place at Dollymount north of Dublin), that the three birthplaces of Wellington must include the stable that forms part of his reputed answer to the question about his Irish origins: 'If a gentleman happens to be born in a stable, it does not follow that he should be called a horse'. Joyce's intention is calculated to amuse by playing with (but not destroying) the idea of nationalism and identity. Nothing, we surmise – not Ireland's natural beauty nor her distinctiveness, nor indeed Bloom's otherness – merits so much adulation or attention, unless the aim is to expose the Citizen's soiled handkerchief bearing 'the rich incrustations of time'.

At one level, Bloom's response expresses Joyce's retort to one-eyed nationalism (and to the burgeoning mass tourist trade); at another level it shows Joyce, the one writer at this period who relished the hybrid character of Irish culture, ruthlessly mocking the pretensions of the Revivalists. But his critique goes further, in part because we cannot ever forget the natural feeling Joyce has for his native country, about which he never stopped writing. Even as he comes to the rescue of Bloom, he betrays the connection between the sentimentality of the citizen in search of home and the passion of the 'Citizen' in defence of homeland. It is true that, in an era of continuing ethnic nationalism, Joyce the civic nationalist is an appealing figure. After all, nationalism, as the civic nationalist understands better than the ethnic nationalist, needs to address matters which are at once less exciting and more problematic than establishing a seat of government, such as the prosaic, unheroic nature of everyday life, the relationships between father and son, or between the body and the mind, the increasing opposition in bourgeois society between the citizen and the artist, and the issues of marital infidelity and sexual desire. Such issues, Joyce seems to imply, cannot be enlisted into a party political programme or, indeed, made much sense of in the context of the harp and the crown – though they can be understood more easily in terms of loss and struggle. And the point is made without any passionate pleading on Bloom's part: the Odyssean hero is unceremoniously ejected from the cave by the Cyclops, but he has a home to go to and he cannot be driven out of the 'nation' to which he has laid claim.

In a recent poem entitled 'Testing the Green', Siobhán Campbell satirises a common topic in late-night conversations in a hotel, the porter still flowing, of 'who is more Irish than whom' (the test comes down to serving mass, milking by hand, saving hay into the night, seeing the '54 final and singing 'The Croppy Boy').[18] That the issue of chauvinism in Irish life rumbles on is also evident from Hugo Hamilton's recent memoir, *The Speckled People* (2003). The author, who is German-Irish by birth, recalls how at school in Dublin in the 1950s he was frequently called a Nazi and how his father changed the family name to Ó hUrmoltaigh: 'Our name is proof of who we are and how Irish we are.'[19] The father's assertion deserves noticing; he stresses not just who we are but how Irish we are. It is also worth contrasting with a similar question in, say, Britain, where arguably only the right-wing British National Party would be interested in how English a person was. Hamilton ends his memoir reflecting on his Bloom-like state but he arrives at a different conclusion from Joyce's hero, for he is no longer afraid of being German or Irish 'or anywhere in between. Maybe your country is only a place you make up in your mind' (p.295).

But this is to concede too much ground and to lose something of the natural feeling of the ethnic nationalist. The knife, we remember, cuts both ways. From his youth, Joyce as a writer was fiercely committed to transcribing the world he saw and heard, believing that if he could get to the heart of Dublin he would get to the heart of the world. Therefore his country was never simply a place he made up in his mind. In the opening line of his first published story in the *Irish Homestead* (1904), he includes a reference to 'Great Britain-street', where the down-at-heel sisters live.[20] For the experienced reader of Joyce the street-name is impossible to read without irony, without conjuring up an empire in decline. As both the ethnic and the civic nationalist might agree, virtually no area of Joyce's city is free from the scars of the colonial encounter. The sharpness of observation in Joyce's writing, and the intelligence informing it, cuts across, therefore, any neat division between ethnic and civic nationalism. As for Macmorris's famous question, Joyce deliberately turns the patronising *ish* back into standard English, signalling that here, in the claustrophobia of the Cyclops's cave, is an excellent place to begin what is in fact a joint critique of nationalism and imperialism in Ireland.

What is a Nation?

According to Virginia Woolf, the ground literature occupies 'is not cut up into nations; there are no wars there'.[21] What she doesn't say is that culture doesn't just occupy but actually constitutes a site of struggle. However, it remains a telling observation, and its relevance can be felt today much as it was in 1940, when such an essentially pacifist sentiment belonged to a wider strategy of resistance. But if Britain had been overrun by Nazi Germany, then her image of the common ground would have been effectively destroyed, and the call to trespass would have become part of a more militant form of resistance. Yeats stands on the opposite hill. 'There is no great literature without nationality, no great nationality without literature.'[22] Born into a country that was perceived by many of its people to be occupied by a foreign power, and convinced that art was not 'tribeless, nationless, a blossom gathered in No Man's Land',[23] Yeats spent a lifetime determined to reclaim independence and to 'nationalise' writing in Ireland. The point is worth underlining: without the colonial encounter Yeats would have lacked not just an important theme as a poet but also a significant part of his make-up as a person.

In 'What Is A Nation?', a famous lecture delivered at the Sorbonne in Paris in 1882, the nineteenth-century Breton Celticist Ernest Renan produced a succinct definition of a key term when thinking about cultural nationalism:

> A nation is a living soul, a spiritual principle. Two things, which in truth are but one, constitute this soul, this spiritual principle. One is the past, the other is the present. One is the common possession of a rich heritage of memories; the other is the actual consent, the desire to live together, the will to preserve worthily the undivided inheritance which has been handed down. Man does not improvise. The nation, like the individual, is the outcome of a long past of efforts, and sacrifices, and devotion.[24]

In many respects, the best adjective to encapsulate Yeats's attitude to Ireland is not so much 'loyalty' as 'devotion': he was devoted to its cause as if to a person or a church. Almost as if he knew his remarks would be applied to Ireland, Renan inserts between 'effort' and 'devotion' the word that has haunted modern Irish nationalism, namely 'sacrifice'. Renan's emphasis on a living soul and the desire to live together shifts the debate about nationalism away from the externalities of territories, nation-states and maps, and redirects it decisively towards cultural expression and subjective commitment, towards what Fichte in his *Addresses to the German People* in 1807–8 called 'spiritual dignity'.[25] As a Frenchman, Renan has in mind the disputed territory of Alsace-Lorraine, but his remarks have a wider application, and, while the terms are not Yeats's, the sentiments are.

With its ancient idealism, Ireland was a spiritual entity for Yeats, its history a 'living stream', as he calls it in 'Easter 1916'. Behind its history, dating back to the Druids and beyond, was 'a great tapestry',[26] which even Christianity could not obliterate. Its oral tradition contained a folk imagination and a store-house of memories unique in modern Europe. Needless to say, if that tradition had been as prominent in Victorian Britain as it was in Ireland, the adrenalin running though Yeats's blood would have been weaker. Renan's notion of an undivided inheritance was also important for Yeats and it belongs with his championing of the imagination of the poor and with his search for 'Unity of Culture'. The past was critical for cultural nationalists, who, under the twin emotionally charged principles of preservation and possession, transformed the enthusiasm of the antiquarian and academic interest into a more active engagement with the present. For Renan, a nation is like an individual; for Yeats, a nation is a family, complete with children whose limbs have the capacity, as during the Easter Rising, to 'run wild'.

When Yeats's body was re-interred in Drumcliff churchyard in October 1948, the Irish nation, led by de Valera the Taoiseach, gathered round his fern-strewn graveside. The tension in this photograph is partly offset by the grave-digger and his spade, who in a curious way occupy centre stage. *Picture Post*, 9 October 1948.

E. J. Hobsbawm distinguishes two stages in the history of nationalism, one ethnic, the other civic. Civic nationalism, which owed much to the citizen state of the French Revolution, flourished in the period 1830–70. It operated a 'threshold principle', insisting that only nations with large populations and territory were entitled to form independent states. It was followed by an ethno-linguistic nationalism in which smaller groups, on the basis of ethnic and/or linguistic ties, laid claim to independence. Ethnic nationalism flourished in the period 1870–1914, and then resurfaced in the last decades of the twentieth century. According to Hobsbawm, the passage from civic-democratic to ethno-linguistic nationalism was marked by 'a sharp shift to the political right of nation and flag'.[27] Like Renan, Yeats was an ethnic rather than a civic nationalist. If he had spoken Irish he would have been doubly so. But, as he later acknowledged when tempted to vaunt the 'Irishry', Yeats was restrained by English: 'Then I remind myself that. . .I owe my soul to Shakespeare, to Spenser, and to Blake, perhaps to William Morris, and to the English language in which I think, speak, and write, that everything I love has come to me through English.'[28] Like Renan, Yeats was a 'tissue of contradictions', 'a member of the romantic school, protesting against romanticism'.[29] The idea of the good citizen, however, he attacked with the fervour of an ethnic nationalist, bracketing him with 'comfort and safety, and with vulgarity and insincerity'.[30] He admired Romantic Ireland, not its opposite, which he identified in 'September 1913' with the lower middle class, fumbling in a 'greasy till' adding 'the halfpence to the pence' (*VP* 289). What he valued in particular was strength of personality and individual heroism, or as Renan once remarked in his autobiography: 'I only care for characters of an absolute idealism' (p.113). Like Joyce, but for different reasons, his nationalism was never pure, therefore, and he would have had difficulty subscribing even to the 'simplest definition' of nationalism recently propounded by Perry Anderson (following Thomas Masaryk, the Czech national leader): 'any outlook that treats the nation as the highest political value'.[31]

Do Nations Have Navels?

Historical definitions of nationalism are still the subject of disagreement among the experts. In a recent eloquent summary, Anthony D. Smith inserts a frame around the topic:

> A single red line traverses the history of the modern world from the fall of the Bastille to the fall of the Berlin Wall . . . . The name of the red line is nationalism . . .. Historians may differ over the exact moment of nationalism's birth, but social scientists are clear: nationalism is a modern movement and ideology, which emerged in the latter half of the eighteenth century in Western Europe and America, and which, after its apogee in two world wars, is now beginning

to decline and give way to global forces which transcend the boundaries of nation-states.[32]

The neatness here commends itself, but not everything began in the eighteenth century. Irish claims to nationhood stem from a much longer history, and for Northern Republicans such claims did not come to an end in 1989. In a witty Tree-of-Jesse passage in his nineteenth-century historical novel *Glenanaar* (1902), Canon Sheehan underlines the essential unity of Irish history, governed in this case by the revenge motif:

> Cromwell begat massacres and burning; and massacres and burning begat reprisals; and reprisals begat Penal Laws; and Penal Laws begat insurrection; and insurrection begat the Union; and the Union begat outlawry; and outlawry begat Whiteboyism; and Whiteboyism begat informers and judicial murders; and judicial murders begat revenge.[33]

Like the Old Testament Jews, the Irish are tied to a patriarchal idea of history, and, whether the focus is on heroes or victims, engraved on their culture is the word 'continuity'. 'Keep the fires of the nation burning' was a phrase of Parnell, which was used as a motto by the *Spark*, a revolutionary newspaper in the years leading up to the Easter Rising. In *Ireland A Nation* (1919), Robert Lynd sketched in the background to Easter 1916 with four chapters on 'The Historical Thread'.[34] In the Irish context, the sense of nationhood is not so much discovered as stimulated by contact with oppression and prejudice. When asked to identify his nation, Shakespeare's Macmorris – his petulance a sign of latent nationalism – reflects in part the expected Elizabethan response, that the Irish fought for their own leaders, not for kings of England.[35] Such inconvenient attitudes are frequently overlooked by theoreticians of nationalism, but what is striking, for example, about an older generation reflecting on the Easter Rising is their frequent recourse to the issue of the harp's social inferiority. 'Those who had been bred in an atmosphere of social inferiority began to come into their own,' writes M. J. MacManus in his 1947 biography of de Valera.[36] Liam de Paor offers a similar observation: 'The self-contempt, which is apparent in so many Irish expressions of political and social ideas from the middle of the nineteenth century onwards, was suddenly checked.'[37] And Ernie O'Malley in a classic account of the War of Independence also speaks of 'self-respect', to which he adds the soldier's supplement: 'Only by fighting had Ireland ever gained its own self-respect.'[38] In this context we might also recall an observation made by Brinsley MacNamara in 1919 that Yeats was a poet 'of whom we should be so proud. . .because he is one who magnifies our nation in the world's eyes'.[39]

However, it *is* the case that the eighteenth century injected something special into Irish nationalism in two respects: one is the civic nationalism of the ruling

1950s Dublin, with Nelson still on his pillar, Clery's clock after midday, and the tricolour proudly flying above the GPO. O'Connell Street was still a place to park the car or hop on a brightly-coloured green double-decker bus. John Hinde's contribution to the modern view of Ireland, whether in terms of style or ideology, should not be overlooked. In the 1950s the English photographer-entrepreneur set up shop and added colour to the Irish landscape. On some of his cards there appears 'Greetings from Ireland'. The phrase is worth pondering for its layers of cultural appropriation. Courtesy of John Hinde.

group, the Protestant Ascendancy, and the other is the emerging ethnic nationalism associated with the Catholic dispossessed majority. According to the historian George O'Brien, in eighteenth-century Ireland there were two nations, 'the historic and the hidden', one associated with the Protestant Ascendancy, the other with Catholicism.[40] The modern face of Dublin, with its splendid Four Courts and Custom House, designed by James Gandon and overlooking the river, and its fine eighteenth-century squares and town-houses, was constructed in this period, and it gave expression to a civic pride worthy of the city that ranked only second to London in the kingdom. That it was based in part on dispossession of the majority population – the Penal Laws denied Catholics access to the professions, to education, and even to training their own clergy in Ireland – ensured that modern Irish nationalism was impelled more by dreams of the future than by the bricks and mortar of the present.

As for Anthony D. Smith's metaphor of birth, this is especially persuasive, as we have seen with Joyce's Bloom, in the Irish context. The subtitle of *1922*, Tom Garvin's important study of Irish nationalism, is 'The Birth of Irish Democracy'.[41] More recently, in his discussion of the Belfast Agreement, Rick Wilford quite naturally has recourse to 'Difficult Birth'.[42] Modern Ireland has witnessed at least two significant births. There was a short-lived birth in the eighteenth century with the Irish Parliament, which met on College Green in Dublin from 1782 until 1801, when the Act of Union returned Ireland to rule from London. Known to history as Grattan's Parliament, it was the inspiration largely of Irish Protestants, who took their cue in part from the American War of Independence and from the French Revolution and Tom Paine's *Rights of Man*. Outside Parliament, the birth was accompanied by a more militant form of nationalism, and in 1798, the Protestant-led United Irishmen under the leadership of Theobald Wolfe Tone took up arms to break the link with Britain. The uprising was suppressed, and, two years later, the Irish Parliament was abolished by the Act of Union. The second birth had a long gestation and it was delayed for over a century or more until, if we listen to Yeats, the Easter Rising of 1916 – not for nothing does Yeats's poem end on a famous birth-note, resonating against not only 1916 but also 1798.

What exactly was born at Easter 1916 was not at the time – or indeed since – very clear. Ray Ryan inserts two dates around his recent study of Irish and Scottish culture and nationhood '1966–2000', 1966 being the fiftieth anniversary of the Rising and the year which also witnessed the destruction of Nelson's Column in Dublin. In a curious 'reverse-swing' sentence, ironically designed to draw connections, he inadvertently reveals something of the confusion that continues to surround the Rising: 'When an attempt is made to cleanse the landscape of nationalism. . .it is hard not to view the process as the psychological equivalent of blowing up Nelson's Column: removing the visible indications of an oppressive past is no guarantee that liberty can mean liberation.'[43] In *The Two Irelands 1912–1939* (1998), the historian David Fitzpatrick divides his material chronologically into two halves and, as if in doubt, calls the first 'What Revolution? Ireland 1912–1922'.[44] Sean O'Casey, who refused to submerge his socialism under nationalism, remained sceptical: 'Things had changed, but not utterly; and no terrible beauty was to be born. Short Mass was still the favourite service, and Brian Boru's harp still bloomed on the bottles of beer.'[45] The denigration has continued. In Frank McGuinness's play *Observe the Sons of Ulster Marching Towards the Somme* (1985), the Ulster Protestant McIlwaine dismisses the Rising as a post office robbery with spineless Fenians walking in to post a letter and kicking out all the female counter assistants: 'Disgrace to their sex, the whole bastarding lot of them, I say.'[46]

The more positive view is that when the Proclamation of the Republic was read out by Patrick Pearse on the steps of the General Post Office on Easter Monday

Robert Ballagh's engaging print, *In the Heart of Hibernian Metropolis* (1989), with a title taken from the opening to the 'Aeolus' episode of *Ulysses*. Ballagh has superimposed a lithographic print on a black-and-white photograph from the Lawrence Collection, and inserted the middle-aged Joyce and himself walking across the newly laid tramlines in turn-of-the-century Dublin. Courtesy of the artist.

1916, the event marked the birth of the Irish Republic. In answer to Ernest Gellner's unorthodox question about origins and the body politic – 'Do Nations Have Navels?' – the Irish nationalist could legitimately reply yes, its spot being identical to the General Post Office where, daily, the monarch's head was repeatedly stamped on.[47] Certainly, everything conspired to mark the occasion. The colour was appropriately green, the place a non-military building in the centre of Dublin, near Nelson's Column, in the heart of Joyce's Hibernian metropolis, the hub of the newly-laid tram system, and the time coincided with the most important feast in the Church's calendar. 'Surrection!' is Joyce's word for the event in *Finnegans Wake*; it is a play on insurrection and resurrection, and a reply in its own way to the headline in the *Connacht Tribune* on 25 April 1916 which read simply 'Is It Insurrection?'[48] 'Eireweeker to the wohld bludyn world' (*FW* 593:3). From Eire to the whole bloody world. Tellingly, the author of 'Easter 1916' did not avail himself of the Christian significance of the Rising but, for his famous collocation 'terrible beauty', took his cue from the Godless Nietzsche. The older Joyce, however, with his Catholic background intact, could see the liturgical significance of the Proclamation, which was indeed like the Pope's Easter message to the world, 'Urbi et Orbi' ('to the city of Rome and the world'), only this time the country was weaker, the city was bludyn (an anagram of Dublin), and the reception (Earwicker, the earwig) also weaker than when it was first heard on the airwaves, as it were, in 1916. He was also lucky in having another ready-made coincidence: *éirí* in Irish means 'rising'.

1890s: Winds of Change

To return to the 1890s, the clarion-call, the wake-up call, for modern Irish cultural nationalism was highlighted by Douglas Hyde in 'The Necessity for De-Anglicising Ireland' (1892), a famous essay that attacked the whole concept of hybridity:

> I have no hesitation at all in saying that every Irish-feeling Irishman, who hates the reproach of West-Britonism, should set himself to encourage the efforts which are being made to keep alive our once great national tongue. The losing of it is our greatest blow, and the sorest stroke that the rapid Anglicisation of Ireland has inflicted upon us. In order to de-Anglicise ourselves we must at once arrest the decay of the language . . . . We must arouse some spark of patriotic inspiration among the peasantry who still use the language and put an end to the shameful state of feeling . . . which makes young men and women blush and hang their heads when overheard speaking their own language.[49]

The wake-up call worked, for as Horace Plunkett concluded in his Preface to *Ireland in the New Century* (1904): 'Those who have known Ireland for the last dozen years cannot have failed to notice the advent of a wholly new spirit.'[50] Or as George Moore cuttingly suggested in conversation with Edward Martyn:

> 'Ninety-nine is the beginning of the Celtic Renaissance,' said Edward.
> 'I am glad to hear it; the Celt wants a renaissance, and badly; he has been going down in the world for the last two thousand years.'[51]

The year following Hyde's essay, an Irish-language organisation, the Gaelic League, was founded to foster the growth of the Irish language, and language classes were organised throughout the country. According to Hyde, the harp's distinctiveness resided in a series of cultural markers to which he was keen to see a return, such as Irish surnames, Irish first names, Irish place names, Irish traditional music, Gaelic football, Connemara home-spun tweed and Anglo-Irish literature rather than English books. What he feared most was a 'nation of imitators . . . alive only to second-hand assimilation' (p.160).

Language and culture provided the driving force behind claims to nation status. Hyde emphasised how the present could be transformed through active participation by the people. In 1894, Plunkett founded the Irish Agricultural Organisation Society, to enable small farmers to pool resources and to benefit from the establishment of creameries (one of the most distinctive features of Irish rural life in the twentieth century). It was a time for the practical imagination to flourish, for the spread of all things Celtic, for Celtic crafts, Celtic lettering and borders, for Irish books, and above all for completing a task pioneered, as Jeanne Sheehy reminds us, by antiquarians from the 1830s.[52] Yeats, the greatest poet Ireland has ever produced, the visionary with the dark dreaming eyes, not only helped found the Abbey Theatre in Dublin in 1904 but, as a Senator in the 1920s, also chaired the committee that decided on the design of Ireland's coinage.

If the nation for some was a practical venture, for others it remained essentially of the future. In 'Nationality or Cosmopolitanism', an essay that, according to Maurice Goldring, approximates to a manifesto of the Irish cultural renaissance, Yeats's friend George Russell provides another take on nationalism – an imagined community that Benedict Anderson might well have included in his influential study of the topic:

> Every Irishman forms some vague ideal of his country, born from his reading of history, or from contemporary politics, or from imaginative intuition; and this Ireland in the mind it is, not the actual Ireland, which kindles his enthusiasm. For this he works and makes sacrifices. . . . We are yet before our dawn. . . . We can see, however, as the ideal of Ireland grows from mind to mind, it tends to assume the character of a sacred land.[53]

It is clear that for the generation that created the modern Irish Revival, Ireland was both an idea and an ideal, awaiting the light of independence after the colonial dark. Appropriately, the suitably vague umbrella title for a 1901 collection of essays by Moore, Hyde, Russell, O'Grady, D. P. Moran, and Yeats, was *Ideals in Ireland*.

Everything, especially the past, pointed to the future. On their estates in the west of Ireland, Lady Gregory and Edward Martyn planned with Yeats and George Moore the establishment of what would become a national theatre. Every folktale collected by Yeats and Lady Gregory was further ammunition in the struggle for a separate identity. When Moore returned in 1901 to Dublin to live he painted the door of his house in Ely Place green, as if nationalism was now on the agenda, his own included. His collection of stories *The Untilled Field* (1903), whose title was taken from Shelley's revolutionary poem 'Sonnet: England in 1819', was Moore's contribution to the future, couched as a critique of the Irish present. George Russell compared the national spirit to 'a beautiful woman' who 'cannot or will not reveal itself wholly while a coarse presence is near, an unwelcome stranger in possession of the home'.[54] At Kilteragh, the house he had built at Foxrock near Dublin in 1906, Horace Plunkett entertained all the leading opinion-formers and social reformers from Britain, Ireland, and the United States, including his cousin the novelist Emily Lawless, Russell, Shaw, H. G. Wells, W. T. Stead, Lord Grey, the U.S. Commissioner for Forestry, Gifford Pinchot, and J. P. Mahaffy, the Provost of Trinity.[55] Even commemorations such as the 1798 centennial celebrations were in essence about the future, as indeed were 'retrospective' popular ballads such as Ethna Carbery's 1898 'Rody McCorley', whose stanzas were no doubt a comfort to those who died 'today' for 'Mother Ireland'.[56]

Carbery believed in 'thinkin' long', the title of a poem told from a female perspective about a young man who went away to fight for the 'soul of Ireland' (p.67). Memory and rehearsal were in the air, filling the heads of poets with dreams of battles and men of action. In the first poem of Yeats's *The Wind Among the Reeds* (1899), the invisible army of the *Sidhe* or fairies are gathering again, while in the apocalyptic poem 'The Valley of the Black Pig', 'unknown perishing armies beat about my head'.[57] As if to complement Yeats's 1890s swirling white-and-gold cover design, Carbery's *The Four Winds of Eirinn* (1902) carried a more focused Celtic lettering and motifs. But, as the martial lines of 'Rody McCorley' convey, the verse was no less forceful in its clamour for resolution outside of poetry. In 'Mo Chraoibhín Cnó' ('My cluster of nuts' or 'Brown-haired girl'), a poem which includes the line 'Oh! famine-wasted, fever-burnt, they faded like the snow', Ireland is addressed directly as both an invocation and a challenge:

A Sword of Light hath pierced the dark, our eyes have seen the star.
O Mother, leave the ways of sleep now days of promise are:
The rusty spears upon your walls are stirring to and fro,
In dreams they front uplifted shields – Then wake Mo Chraoibhín Cnó! (p.9)

Thus, even what appear to be fairly empty symbolic phrases had the potential in this period to become weapons in a (future) war. 'Sword of Light', translated into Irish as *An Claidheamh Soluis*, was the title of the Gaelic League newspaper founded in 1899 and edited by Eoin MacNeill and, later, by Patrick Pearse. Constantly, throughout Carbery's volume, what is displayed is a form of political rallying, from the Dedication to the Gaelic League of Argentina, to the phrase at the end of 'Shiela Ní Gara', how 'the hour is drawing near', to the lament for the Irish emigrant in 'The Passing of the Gael', which ends with the line 'Oh! Kathaleen Ní Houlihan, your way's a thorny way!' (p.110). If such forms of expression seem less persuasive now, that is in part because political independence was followed almost immediately by civil war and in part because, after the demise of 'the 1860s generation', it became increasingly unfashionable to address Ireland in such symbolic terms.[58]

English As We Speak It in Ireland

Checking himself as if to confirm his first impression, Broadbent in *John Bull's Other Island* imagines that Haffigan speaks in the true brogue: 'But he spoke – he behaved just like an Irishman.' To which Doyle, in one of the most apposite speeches in the play, replies:

> Like an Irishman!! Man alive, don't you know that all this top-of-the-morning and broth-of-a-boy and more-power-to-your-elbow business is got up in England to fool you, like the Albert Hall concerts of Irish music? No Irishman ever talks like that in Ireland, or ever did, or ever will.[59]

Part of the achievement of cultural nationalism in Ireland has been to fill the stage with authentic Irish voices, so that today Doyle's venom seems slightly misplaced, if only because the Broadbents of this world have largely disappeared. If elsewhere in postcolonial literature, the Empire Writes Back – an expression designed to characterise the way colonised, or formerly colonised, people have written about the struggle for redress, to get their own back, as it were, on the colonial power – in Ireland the issue takes on a different character, of the Empire Talking Back, and this is especially true of Irish drama.

'Back' is the key word with both Wilde and Shaw, whose one-liners reverberate around the stage and out into the night sky. 'As far as the piano is concerned, sentiment is my forte. I keep science for Life.' So Algernon observes at the beginning of *The Importance of Being Earnest* (1895), where the double meaning of 'forte' – as both strength and loudness – and the opposition between science and Life with a capital letter anticipate two key devices in the play, namely doubling and contrast or similarity and difference. 'The truth is rarely pure and never simple. Modern life would be very tedious if it were either, and modern literature a complete impossibility!'[60] Here is talk spilling over from afternoon tea in London studios and drawing rooms, polished and elegant, designed as much to impress as to carry a social message. The dialogue keeps running as if it were a non-stop performance, banishing all doubt or embarrassment or depth of character, for to adopt a recent remark by Hugo Hamilton: 'In Ireland the words never touch the ground.'[61] Drop the 'a' and you have the name Ernest, keep the 'a' and you have the combination of moral attribute and the contemporary gay scene where, in 1895, 'earnest' was slang for 'gay'. Let the audience determine where to place the significance, whether it's Worthing, where Wilde wrote the play which, presumably, gave Wilde the idea of calling Jack or John by this name, or bunburying, which covers a multitude of sins for the more conventional Algernon or the more deviant Ernest.

By all accounts, Yeats was Wilde's equal as a conversationalist, but he needed the assistance of Lady Gregory to mould his dialogue into something which could pass

Wilde understood modernity better than most, but even he was no match for today's Madison Avenue. From *The Listener*, 22 May 1986.

for natural speech on the stage. On a famous occasion, when he was wintering with Ezra Pound at Stone Cottage in Sussex during the Great War, the American poet thought he heard the wind blowing down the chimney but then realised it was 'Uncle William' upstairs composing 'that had made a great Peeeeacock/in the proide of his oiye'.[62] Yeats was compelled, as he tells us in one of his retrospective essays, to *hammer* his thoughts into unity;[63] they rarely came like leaves on a tree. He enjoyed more success with poetry than stage dialogue, for his lyrical impulse there found its natural outlet where the emotional charge is held down or embedded in syntactic structures which are closer to written than to spoken English. In recalling the mood of the years 1892–1902, Yeats chose for his title 'Dramatis Personae', as if indeed everyone was playing a part. In a revealing sentence comparing his own 'sensuous, concrete, rhythmical' mind with George Moore's, which was 'argumentative, abstract, diagrammatic', he explained: 'In later years, through much knowledge of the stage, through the exfoliation of my own style, I learnt that occasional prosaic words gave the impression of an active man speaking.'[64]

Wilde, for Yeats, was the active man, a judgment which seems a little surprising today, but then Yeats understood better than most commentators Wilde's personality and formative Irish background. 'We are too poetical to be poets,' Wilde told Yeats in the late 1880s. 'We are a nation of brilliant failures, but we are the greatest talkers since the Greeks.'[65] In Robert Sherard's *The Life of Oscar Wilde* (1906), the remark is prefaced by this observation: 'Speaking of the Irish, he once said, referring to himself, in that self-accusing way which was one of the pathetic traits of his character . . .'[66] For Yeats, it is not so much a personal as a national trait on display here; he commented that Wilde, 'commended and dispraised himself during dinner by attributing characteristics like his own to his country . . .'. Wilde's remark struck a chord with Yeats who, in the early 1920s (when he composed 'Four Years 1887–1891'), was constructing a system in which to situate historical periods, personality types, and exemplary individuals. But, interestingly, when he compiled *A Vision* (1925; 1937), the Irish dimension tends to be lost in the much larger cycles of Western history, and Wilde appears at Phase Nineteen, along with Byron, where the Will manifests itself as Assertive Man and the Body of Fate as enforced failure of action.[67]

The attempt to bring apparently unconnected subjects into the same field of play – as here with the Irish and the Greeks, who were failures in action but great talkers, or with character and action, the personal and the national, aptitude and writing, art and life, or sincerity and the doctrine of the mask – is what distinguishes both Wilde and Yeats. If Wilde had lived into middle age and had been asked to systematise his thoughts, scattered as they are amid a thousand aphorisms, his whimsical instinct would probably have got the better of him. When *Salome* ran into problems with the Censor in 1892 on the grounds that it introduced Biblical characters, Wilde declared in an interview that he would settle in France: 'I am not English. I am Irish – which is quite another thing.'[68] It is this spirit of whimsy which resurfaced when Samuel Beckett was asked by a French interviewer if he were English: 'Au contraire' was his answer. Many commentators infer that Beckett is defining Irishness by what wasn't English, but I think it isn't so much the contrast that is on display here, as Wilde's 'quite another thing'. As if unwilling to play the hybrid game, Wilde and Beckett are defining themselves not by the idea of a conventional opposite but by something wholly different. The 'contraire' is thus closer to contrary (as in awkward). On the other hand, because he was governed by systems of contrast which worked against the exercise of free will, the single-minded Yeats never approached such a position. For Yeats, the Irish, like Berkeley, are not-English, but this is not Wilde's 'quite another thing'.

In the sucking stone sequence in Beckett's novel *Molloy* (1954), Molloy at the seaside is deeply perplexed by a logistical/mathematical/philosophical problem about how to suck in turn sixteen different stones, which are distributed equally in the four pockets of his greatcoat, without sucking any of them twice. After two

Jack MacGowran was one of Beckett's favourite actors. Claddagh record sleeve.

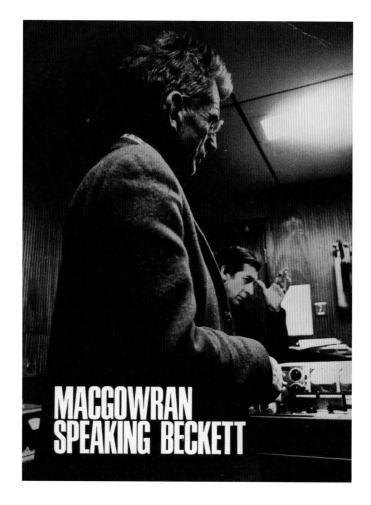

MACGOWRAN SPEAKING BECKETT

thousand words of deliberation as he seeks a solution, he confesses: 'But deep down I didn't give a tinker's curse', throwing away all the stones but one, which he then proceeds to switch from one pocket to another before either losing it, throwing it away or swallowing it.[69] Behind everything Beckett wrote is the stance, attitude and identity embodied in his 'au contraire'. When stop-searched he has an answer, just as historically, when questioned by the gentry and those in authority, the Irish country people knew how to answer back by recourse to the unexpected. Beckett's Irish voice – a feature of the 2004 Albery Theatre production of *Endgame* with the English actors Michael Gambon and Lee Evans as Hamm and Clov – constantly intrudes into his writings.[70] In his reference to 'tinker's curse', he switches to an informal register. Elsewhere in this sequence, Molloy reaches a temporary solution which he describes as 'sound', an overused word in Ireland, which expresses approval for a person or an action but which is given a new lease of life by Beckett.

Ireland's cockpit, where the project to rewrite the way English was spoken in Ireland assumed particular intensity, first in the plays of Synge and, later, in those of O'Casey. The original interior of the Abbey Theatre with balcony and hooks for hanging coats. Taken in 1942 during the interval of a performance of O'Casey's *The Plough and the Stars*. *Picture Post*, 11 April 1942.

Beckett's language is always more than simple texture or local colouring, and not infrequently it seems to belong to a form of slippage, an Irish sense of defiance that can be seen as underlying all his work.

By the time Beckett put pen to paper, the English reader had been dislodged from the shoulder of the Irish writer. This, above all else, was the great historical achievement of the Revival, from the 1890s to the 1920s. That it wasn't effected all at once is evident from Somerville and Ross's humorous portraits of Irish speech in the stories of *Some Experiences of an Irish R. M.* (1899), where substituting 'i' for 'e' in words such as 'devil' and 'tent' or an apostrophe for the 'g' in words ending in '–ing', or inserting 'h' into words such as 'porter', 'true' and 'drive', or adding phrases, such as 'says I to meself', and spelling words as they might be pronounced, such as 'obstackles' – all convey the attitude that Irish country people were still fun to listen to and to ridicule. The breakthrough came with Douglas Hyde's transla-

Left: The Saville Theatre on Shaftesbury Avenue played host in 1937 to O'Casey's *Juno and the Paycock*, starring the great Abbey Theatre actresses, Sarah Allgood as Mrs Boyle and Maire O'Neill as Mrs Madigan.

Right: A young-looking Sean O'Casey with receding hair, which was used in the same programme at the same time.

tions of the love songs of Connaught, which paved the way for the Kiltartanese dialect of Lady Gregory and the speech of Synge's plays, which was 'as fully flavoured as a nut or apple'.[71] It was then possible for 'home-grown' writers such as Padraic Colum and George Fitzmaurice to provide a double-take on the deprivation of their fellow-countrymen without the need to humour or defend, and, in Fitzmaurice's case, in the kind of heightened language we associate with Synge. A telling phrase from the opening scene of his play *The Dandy Dolls* (1914) encapsulates a whole moment, providing, in addition, one of the most suggestive leads into the work of Martin McDonagh. A stranger enters a cottage asking for the man of the house, and, when informed by Cauth Carmody that her husband is 'engaged', he replies: 'What sort of talk is that in a cabin black with soot?'[72] As for Beckett, when Hamm, groping for his toy dog, declares 'Our revels now are ended', we are reminded of the Empire talking back across the centuries and also of modern Irish writers completing the task begun by Shakespeare, even daring to speak on behalf of a wider humanity.

From Gael to Gall

As is evident from P. W. Joyce's classic study *English as We Speak it in Ireland* (1910), Gaelic speech patterns ensured a new life in the borrowed but then naturalised language of the group once identified with, or as, the English stranger.[73] Lady Gregory learnt the language of her servants and tradespeople on her estate at Coole Park in County Galway, while Synge, upstairs in the cottage on the Aran Islands where he was staying, fixed his ear to the floor to eavesdrop on the talk and rhythms of his hosts. The people were sovereign and at their feet the masters paid homage. In retrospect, it can be discerned that it was historically necessary for this intermediate phase in the process of decolonisation to take the shape it did, where, to adopt a vocabulary derived from Marx and Bourdieu, the accumulation of cultural capital is related to the emergence of bourgeois Ireland and, at the same time, to the dispossession of the poor.[74] In the beautifully rendered translation of ancient myths in *Cuchulain of Muirthemne* (1902) and in her one-act plays for the Abbey celebrating aspects of rural life, Lady Gregory showed her Protestant class how to wrap themselves in the new flag of Irish nationalism. Adding dignity to Ireland is how she expressed it, and she did have something to add, for this is not the comic, knockabout, irresponsible world of the Anglo-Irish in decline, as depicted in Molly Keane's entertaining *Good Behaviour* (1981). Rather, it concerns a small group from the landed classes and Protestant middle class who knew instinctively that, if it was to retain anything of its status or influence, it had to abandon its class position, identify with the land of its birth, and go over to the other side, as it were. In this she was following 'The Fenian Unionist', Standish James O'Grady, who, after abandoning his role as an apologist for the gentry in the 1880s for an All-Ireland position in the late-1890s, had blazed a spectacular trail, joining myth and history, to ensure that Cuchulain became the central mythological figure for Yeats's generation, and earning for himself the epithet of 'father of the Revival'.[75]

Anthony D. Smith attempts to position nationalism within a larger historical frame, but again the Irish context refuses to perform as it should. In the aftermath of the Easter Rising, Winston Churchill, in a wildly optimistic comment, 'expressed the sanguine view that the Irish Question was nearing a settlement', a comment that would still be wildly optimistic if uttered today, nearly a century later.[76] Out of sync, Irish nationalists were forced to think long, situating their actions within a cycle of history much broader than the present. It was not uncommon in the early 1970s in Belfast to hear an older Catholic generation, with portraits of the United Irishman Wolfe Tone and of Robert Emmet's Speech from the Dock secreted about the house, refer to Westminster as the 'Imperial Parliament'. In this regard, modern theoreticians of nationalism are but catching up with what their subjects have long held. At the same time, focusing on the larger frame can exaggerate the truth. Thus

D. George Boyce makes much of the Catholicism of the leaders of the Easter Rising and how in the nineteenth century the national ideal had passed hands from Protestant to Catholic: 'For nationalist and Catholic Ireland found that at last it could stand on its own feet.'[77] It's a common enough view, shared, for example, by the Bloom-like figure Mr Mack in Jamie O'Neill's historical novel *At Swim, Two Boys* (2001), when he enthuses – oblivious of the repeated 'stands' or 'risings' taking place between his son and male lovers – that it 'was indeed a Catholic rising and therefore a blessed one too.'[78] But all this needs careful handling, and the suspicion forms that Boyce, for example, is party to another agenda.

Fictional accounts and documentary records present a complicated picture of the relationship between Catholicism and the Rising. In Iris Murdoch's *The Red and the Green* (1965), the Sinn Féin supporter Pat – the author presumably has Pearse in mind – 'was not one of those who made their Catholicism into nationalism',[79] while in *A Star Called Henry* (1999) – a novel which focuses in part on the influence of the Christian Brothers on the Rising – the Citizen Army protagonist reacts strongly when he witnesses his fellow revolutionaries in the GPO on their knees saying the rosary, adding in characteristic Roddy Doyle fashion: 'What sort of a country were we going to create. If we were attacked now, we were fucked. I didn't want to die in a monastery.'[80] Interestingly, according to Kathleen Clarke, the priest who attended her husband after his arrest 'wanted him to say he was sorry for what he had done'.[81] Holiness and patriotism were clearly linked in Pearse's mind, but, as the Jesuit scholar Francis Shaw in a controversial essay argued, 'this equation of the patriot with Christ is in conflict with the whole Christian tradition',[82] a view which in turn has prompted a heated exchange.[83]

In the years following the Rising, as can be observed in the 1930s (see Chapter 7), the Church did increasingly identify it as a 'godly struggle'.[84] As David Fitzpatrick notices: '[T]he new rulers blatantly identified Catholic with national values.'[85] Such a move chimed with a divided Ireland then in the ascendancy. In his St Patrick's Day broadcast to the United States in 1935, de Valera, ignoring the feelings of the Protestant Irish, declared: 'Since the coming of St Patrick . . . Ireland has been a Christian and a Catholic nation.'[86] On the other side of the border, ignoring his Catholic minority, James Craig, the Ulster Prime Minister, was asserting in similarly blunt fashion: 'We are a Protestant Parliament and a Protestant State.'[87] De Valera's view stands in marked contrast to the generous vision of John O'Leary, the Fenian mentor of Yeats and Maud Gonne.[88] O'Leary believed 'our doctrine' was 'no priests in politics':

> Lying newspapers are for ever trying to connect . . . Catholicity and Nationality . . . . But the claim is too patently false. . . . Nine-tenths of the leading patriots for the last century have been Protestant. . . . Who thinks the worse as Irishmen of Tone, Davis, or Mitchel. . .because they were not Christians? The main

thing to all us is, whether a man be Irish or not, and not whether he be Catholic, Protestant, or Pagan.[89]

According to D. George Boyce, 'Catholic nationalism was characterised by a confused rhetoric about allegiance, but its thrust on the ground, especially from the Land War (1879–82) onwards, emphasised an exclusive Irish loyalty.'[90] Four pages earlier, he notices the irony 'that a union designed to give security to Irish Protestants afforded instead a United Kingdom platform for Catholic grievances and a means to moderate the supposed guarantees to Protestants' (p.5). The larger frame here looks uncomfortably like a commentary on the state of the Union in today's Northern Ireland, where for some Unionists nationalism is identified simply as a matter of grievances. Terence Brown provides a more sensitive reading. To survive as a caste or a class, the Protestant Anglo-Irish needed to counter the view that they were 'the alien culture of a garrison society'. In writers such as O'Grady, George Russell, Yeats and Lady Gregory, they 'sought to popularise a view of Irish identity that might soften the stark outlines of politics, class and sectarianism in the benign glow of culture'.[91]

The literary historian and postcolonial critic, especially when the spotlight is cultural nationalism, are frequently forced to move back and forth between the frame and the canvas. 'Easter 1916', the subject of the next chapter, belongs to several overlapping stories – Yeats's position in Ireland, the relationship between 'Easter 1916' and the Easter Rising, the response of cultural nationalism to militant nationalism, the colonial encounter between Britain and Ireland, and the place of the poem in subsequent developments within nationalism. Attending to each of these stories returns Yeats to the circumstances of history, exposes the foundations of his thinking, and raises questions about the power and authority of his verse. Joep Leerssen speaks of assessing 'the specificity of the traffic around the specific and somehow special genre of imaginative literature'.[92] In the light of Boyce and Brown, we might well discern some denominational traffic around the word 'them' in the first line of Yeats's poem on the subject, 'I have met them at close of day'. Yeats seems to be referring not just to the leaders, which is a conventional reading, but also to the fact that they were (devious, plotting) Catholics and a subject of conversation, therefore, at his (non-Catholic) club. The interpretation can alter our sense of the poem and serve to highlight how hybridity, if subjected to detailed historical or textual criticism, is invariably more than a verbal counter in the Irish context.

1920s: Then It Was All Over

In the 1890s the future beckoned, but in 1923 the present was all that was left to engross the imagination. In the nineteenth century 'A Nation Once Again' was sung with gusto. But after the bloody birth and the establishment of an independent Ireland in the years 1916–23, who but militant Northern Republicans two generations later could any longer be so sanguine about the future? As Russell wrote in 1923 at the end of a Civil War that had torn families apart:

> The champions of physical force have, I am sure without intent, poisoned the soul of Ireland. All that was exquisite and lovable is dying. They have squandered a spirit created by poets, scholars and patriots of a different order, spending the treasure lavishly, as militarists in all lands do, thinking little of what they squander save that it gives a transitory gilding to their propaganda. With what terrible images have they not populated the Irish soul as substitutes for that lovable life![93]

In January 1923, the same month Kilteragh was burnt to the ground by Republicans, and the same month in which Yeats seriously thought of permanently severing his links with Ireland,[94] Victor Pritchett, then a young English journalist, crossed to Dublin to report on the Civil War. Four decades later, in an inspired portrait of the city (accompanied by Evelyn Hofer's now-period photographs from the 1960s), he compared the atmosphere post-1916 with post-1923:

> Then it was all over. Hunger and exhaustion defeated the rebels, but the defeat turned into a triumph. The British executed the leaders and sent others to life imprisonment. The gallows and the prison have always been the shrines of Irish freedom. It would be inaccurate to say all southern Ireland was now united, for Sinn Féin had a large number of enemies, but Ireland had woken up from its Victorian sleep.
>   In the years between 1918 and 1923 Dublin saw the worst kind of warfare – guerilla warfare in terms of assassination and bomb throwing, secret sentences, executions, murders at night. There was a curfew, Auxiliary police and the detestable Black and Tans patrolled the streets. . . . By 1921, Dubliners were exhausted and on the point of nervous breakdown; family or sectarian hatreds had reached an intolerable pitch and brutal muddle on the British side began to be matched by hysteria and jealousy among the Sinn Féin leaders. Differences which were metaphysical became violent, because the habit of violence had grown. The Four Courts were occupied and bombarded; in the course of this the Irish suffered a loss which was hardly noticed at the time but the humiliation of which has been lasting: the loss of their archives. As always, revolution consumed its own children. Leader after leader was killed. Many of them felt – what one of them told me – that retribution would fall upon them for their own blood guilt. . . . Among the younger people – in 1923 – there was a strong feeling that the extreme side was the more honourable; extremism and lawlessness having a traditional prestige.[95]

Michael Collins addressing a crowd. It was this shot that Liam Neeson reproduced in Neil Jordan's film *Michael Collins* (1990), a film that in the controversy it aroused showed how Collins continues to address a crowd in Ireland.

1916 was a defeat, but it ushered in the new Ireland. By 1921, Ireland – or at least twenty-six of its thirty-two counties – was independent of Britain. But, with the descent into Civil War in 1922–3, the hopes and aspirations of a generation turned sour, and following the death of Michael Collins at thirty-one in 1922, it was all over, at least in one respect. In the mortuary in Dublin, Sir John Lavery painted the last portrait of Collins. The tribute is full of tenderness and composure, with the tricolour, the crucifix, the army uniform, the mystery that played about his mouth, and the simple, if slightly strained, caption 'Love of Ireland' staring out from the canvas. At the same time, it affords a fitting accompaniment to Lavery's portrait *Cathleen Ni Houlihan*, with the harp, the lakes and mountains for background, and the large eyes and beautifully sensuous lips of his wife-model Hazel Lavery looking for ever into the future. The stillness in both portraits conveys more an aspiration than a resolution, for as Lavery later observed: 'I felt then and still feel, that on that night the Irish slew the Irish, that the Irish killed Ireland as a force for good and greatness in the world of to-day, when every horror is committed in the name of nationalism.'[96]

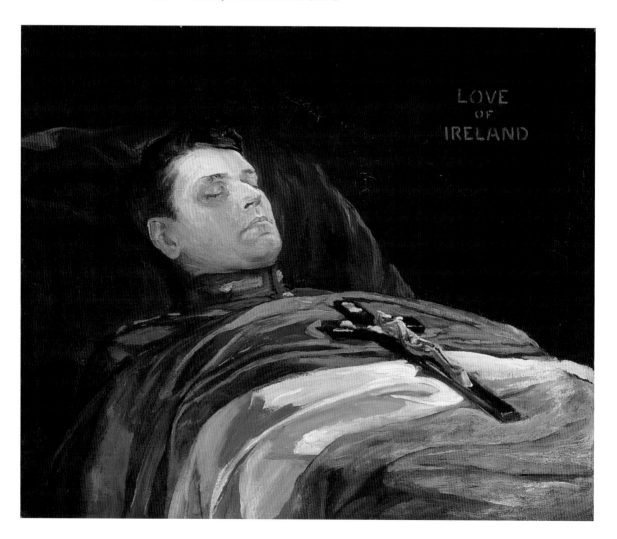

John Lavery's tribute to Collins painted before he was entombed for ever. By courtesy of Felix Rosenstiel's Widow & Son Ltd, London on behalf of the Estate of John Lavery and Dublin City Gallery The Hugh Lane.

What Russell, Lavery and others perceived was that the war for the harp's soul continued on the ideological front long after the guns were silent. According to the Irish historian George O'Brien, writing in the 1930s, the 1921 Treaty had closed the door of the cupboard marked 'The Irish Question', but 'the skeleton is still within'.[97] As Sebastian Barry's play *The Steward of Christendom* (1995) or Neil Jordan's film *Michael Collins* (1999) or, indeed, the affectionate sequence in Heaney's 'The Loose Box' from *Electric Light* (2001) testify, the issue of Collins, his place in Irish history, and the fondness with which he is still remembered, has been a constant across the generations, as if the harp couldn't let go of the colonial encounter. The closing lines of Denis Devlin's fine 1956 elegy, where Collins achieves an identity with his country, capture something of the enigma of the man:

How sometimes death magnifies him who dies,
And some, though mortal, have achieved their race.[98]

Let me touch on one of the many examples of what happened in the 1920s to the young Douglas Hyde's ambition regarding de-anglicisation. In a textbook on Ireland aimed at secondary schools and published by Cambridge University Press in 1922, the section on Literature begins: 'We confine our attention in this section to the native literature, in the Irish language. The works of Anglo-Irish writers, using English as their medium, do not here concern us.'[99] It's a painful remark, a deliberate exclusion of the great work of the Revival in the name of Irish Ireland, the irony especially marked both because the book was published in England and because the following year Yeats was awarded the Nobel Prize for Literature. The policy of exclusion was continued by D. P. Moran's disciple Daniel Corkery, who posited that the Irish national being was composed of 'three great forces': the religious consciousness of the people, Irish nationalism, and the land.[100] The only positive gloss that can be put on this is that Ireland needed time before it could again open its door to the world, for as Thomas McGreevy pleaded at the time: 'British imperialism has to leave us Irish alone before we can let England alone, before we can cease to be, at least defensively, nationalist.'[101] The Irish-language poet Máire Cruise O'Brien, looking back on that period in her autobiography, is not given to excuses, calling Corkery 'boorish': 'Puritans make virtue impossible; Corkery was doing this for Irish as a European language.'[102] The narrowing down, however, prompted a reaction. On reading Corkery's *The Hidden Ireland* (1924), the Irish-language poet Seán Ó Riordáin tetchily observed: 'I'm neither Christian nor Gael, Irish nor English. I don't go to Mass or the theatre. That's my life. Perhaps Prof. Ó Corcora is right. Lack of tradition. Too much ego.'[103]

Elsewhere in the 1920s, the satirical monthly *Dublin Opinion* continued to mock the achievements of nationalism. In February 1923, at the height of the Civil War, its front cover (by Arthur Booth) depicted 'The Four Horsemen', consisting of an iron-clad, medieval figure of mad Civil War, the bloated Profiteer smoking a cigar, a bald-headed Taxation with a monocle, and an exhausted figure on an exhausted nag with a placard reading 'Unemployment'. In 1925, under the umbrella title 'The Blatherskite Bequest: A Recent Notable Addition to Our National Museum', the magazine included sketches of the bullet-riddled 'Skull of Patriot', 'Dogs to which the country is going', and the pen with which Mr de Valera refused to sign Document No 1.[104] The subsequent issue featured a sketch of the tall, lean, humourless figure of de Valera, his head pushing through the 'Humorous Journal' in the subtitle, and at the bottom of the page the charge 'High Treason'. Then, in April 1928, an attack was mounted on Ernest Blythe, Minister of Finance, with a cartoon of him tightening a hand-press marked 'Budget, 1928'. Inside the press are a group of helpless taxpayers being squeezed, and underneath is the caption 'A Nation Wince Again'. From once to wince, the emergence of the Irish Free State was not so much the birth as the 'berth' of a nation.

Concluding Remarks

'Cultural nationalism' is a useful umbrella term, but, as we have observed, it has a complicated history and groundwork, largely because of the colonial encounter. Virtually no Irish writer, from Jonathan Swift to John Banville, sings from the same hymn-sheet. There is, of course, a chorus which can be heard singing at times in unison as in the 1890s, but, in spite of the cul-de-sac represented by the Civil War, what is worth stressing are the different voices, some oppositional, others muffled and indistinct, which belong to the development of cultural nationalism. Douglas Hyde, for instance, advocated the de-anglicisation of Ireland, but resigned from the Gaelic League when it took a political turn, while Yeats thought in sepa-ratist terms, but never learnt his national language and all the time wrote in English. Moreover, we shouldn't forget that some voices in certain of their works resist incorporation into something called 'Irish cultural nationalism'. This is par-ticularly so with someone like William Orpen, who is justly regarded as a leading modern Irish artist, but whose most remarkable series of sketches – *An Onlooker in France 1917–1919* (1921) – grew out of a British Government commission to act as a Great War artist. Interestingly, the first building to be completed after the destruction of O'Connell Street during the Easter Rising was Clery's department store, which was modelled on Selfridges in London, itself designed by the American architect Daniel Burnham in the modern Chicago manner.[105] Of the fig-ures mentioned in this chapter, Standish O'Grady, George Moore, Horace Plunkett, John Eglinton (W. K. Magee), George Russell (whom many contempo-raries considered 'the greatest man Ireland has produced since Parnell')[106] – all for one reason or another abandoned Ireland for England, but the ideals of cultural nationalism lived on, and from their exiled states in Devon and Paris, O'Casey, Joyce and Beckett breathed new life into the matter of Ireland.

Let me end with the figure of Fred Ryan (1874–1913), whose voice has never been entirely drowned out by the prevailing nationalist rhetoric. While not a major figure in the cultural history of modern Ireland, he shouldn't be neglected by those interested in altering their view of the relationship between culture and politics. In an ambitious survey, *Ireland and Empire* (2000), Stephen Howe man-ages to neglect Ryan: 'Early Irish nationalists hardly ever identified their situation or cause with that of other, non-European subject peoples in the British Empire or beyond.'[107] When Ryan died, his friend Frank Sheehy-Skeffington, the pro-feminist pacifist who was later murdered by a British Army captain during Easter 1916 (he had been trying to arrange a meeting to prevent looting), lamented: 'The school of Irish democratic Nationalists that includes Wolfe Tone, Fintan Lalor, and Michael

Davitt, has lost its ablest representative.'[108] More recently, Terry Eagleton has argued that, 'Those who try prematurely to live by culture in the present fail to grasp the necessary conditions for "culture" becoming available to all, and among these for Ryan are the cultural nationalists.'[109]

Ryan took an early interest in combining drama and nationalist politics and in the 1890s he joined the Celtic Literary Society. In 1898, he moved to the Fays' company, the Ormonde Dramatic Society, and then became the first Secretary of the Irish National Theatre Society when it was formed in 1902, with Yeats as President. Ryan was the first Secretary of the Abbey Theatre and is the author of an Ibsenesque play *The Laying of the Foundations*, one of the 'lost' plays of the Abbey. After 1904, his campaigning journalism took the upper hand, fuelled in part by a disillusionment with the theatre. By 1906 Ryan was 'disgusted with the whole thing. Said he had enough of it and did not intend to join any company. The bickering was awful when he was secretary.'[110] In 1904–5, he co-edited with John Eglinton, *Dana: An Irish Magazine of Independent Thought*, in 1905, he contributed articles to Tom Kettle's the *Nationist*, and in 1907 founded *National Democrat*, a penny monthly that ran for seven issues. He also contributed to *New Age* when it was edited by John M. Robertson. Towards the end of 1907 he was asked by William Maloney to become assistant editor of the *Egyptian Standard* in Cairo, a post he occupied until that newspaper collapsed in 1909. He then returned to Dublin, but two years later, when Wilfrid Blunt founded *Egypt* in London, Ryan was asked to become its editor. In 1913, just as a revolutionary decade was about to begin, he suddenly died, and was buried in the Franciscan Monastery Churchyard in Crawley in Sussex, a long way from Dublin and Ireland, having spent four of his last years abroad, devoted to the cause not of Irish but of Egyptian nationalism.[111]

In a letter Ryan wrote in July 1908 from Cairo to Frank Sheehy-Skeffington he advised his friend 'to take a good long rest, read no newspapers, & let humanity & its problems in Ireland & elsewhere go hang', and continued:

> I confess to having shed some of my enthusiasm for the Egyptian cause at the spectacle I see around me every day, of petty vanity & hopeless incompetence. But I correct myself by reflecting that perhaps it is only what an observant Egypt[ian] might have thought had he been planted in Dublin in the years after the Parnell split & been able, from behind the scenes, to observe Healy, O'Brien, Redmond & the rest with the paint off. However don't say that to Kettle who is a daily subject of comment in the Egyptian Press now – French, English & Arabic – & whose 'mystic' enthusiasm it is necessary to preserve as an asset. The truth, of course, is that, however incompetent the Egyptian leaders may now be, the English bureaucrats are hypocritical exploiters. Whilst as for the future of the Egyptian cause it is safe. The younger men who are more & more going to Europe will bring back method & sense, whilst Moustafa's impulse persists in

the national memory. He is already a sort of blend of Wolfe Tone, Emmet & Davis. The *mythus* is developing rapidly. And in the Egyptians' circumstances it is something to have a figure, even if he is a bit legendary, like that.[112]

Ryan's attempt to see Egyptian nationalism in Irish terms and vice versa marks him out from those of his generation whose view of nationalism never got beyond the borders of Ireland. Like Connolly (and to some extent Casement), Ryan had an internationalist (not to be confused with a cosmopolitan) perspective, for which he was prepared to campaign abroad, ever conscious that the struggle of the harp against the crown at this period was on a worldwide scale. Unlike Lady Gregory, Yeats, and Joyce, the comparison he drew for Ireland was not with the chosen people, the Jews, but with the Arab world as represented by Egypt. His attempt to forge a joint discussion was not successful at the time, and few shared his view of Ireland. But as we continue to make sense of the force of cultural nationalism in Ireland, we perhaps should not forget the clear-thinking 'fraidrine' as his name appears in *Ulysses* (9:1081–4), the principled, Kropotkin-inspired radical who lent two pieces of silver to the penniless artist on the eve of his departure for Europe in October 1904:

> [B]y 'Ireland' I do not mean any 'literary' or mystic entity or any 'nationality' divorced from the real life of the people. By Ireland I mean the peasants in the fields, the workers in the factories, the teachers in the schools, the professors in the colleges, and all others who labour in Ireland and desire to make this people a great people, an intellectual people, a noble people. But in building up that people we must, I submit, keep our eyes fixed on the permanent standards of right and wrong, of good politics and bad, and less and less on the mere ebb and flow of national impulse.[113]

PART TWO

FIELDS OF PLAY

Chapter 5

Yeats's Reveries on the Easter Rising

. . . a preparation for something that never happens.
– W. B. Yeats, *Reveries Over Childhood and Youth* (1916)

The hearts of creators groping for the foundations.
– Kathleen Coyle, *Piccadilly* (1923)

And thought before I had done
Of a mocking tale or a gibe
To please a companion
Around the fire at the club.
– W. B. Yeats, 'Easter 1916'

Reveries Over Childhood and Youth

On Christmas Day 1914, sixteen months before the Easter Rising, Yeats completed the Preface to the first volume of his autobiographies, *Reveries Over Childhood and Youth*. In a slippery sentence, complete with his characteristic rhetorical – as opposed to grammatical – punctuation, he defended himself from accusations often levelled against those engaged in writing their life story: 'I have changed nothing to my knowledge; and yet it must be I have changed many things without my knowledge; for I am writing after many years and have consulted neither friend nor letter nor old newspaper and describe what comes oftenest into my memory.'[1] With shifts in logic across semi-colons and conjunctions, the statement is a curious judgment on the book he has just finished.

Yeats defines the process of writing an autobiography in terms of knowledge rather than discovery. He admits at the outset to the possibility of error, but, as he is quick to explain, errors wouldn't be deliberate (and certainly not 'portals of discovery' [*U* 9:229] as they were for Stephen Dedalus). His memory is dominated by what comes most often into his head, and he infers that this is typical of the way

Opposite page
Detail of masked druid-like musicians in *The Dreaming of the Bones* (1917).

'What fingers first began/Music of a lost kingdom?' Three masked druid-like musicians in *The Dreaming of the Bones* (1917), holding their instruments like weapons. Set among the stones in County Clare, Yeats's play constitutes a profound meditation on the Easter Rising against the extraordinary background of the Norman invasion of Ireland, the betrayal by Diarmuid and Dervogilla, the idea of forgiveness and the role of the dead dreaming back. Abbey Theatre production, taken from *Holiday*, December 1949.

memory, which frequently hovers at the edge of consciousness, works. More curious is the way knowledge and memory, past and present, conscious and unconscious, truth and change, are all yoked together by three semi-colons, by the least secure punctuation marker in English grammar. Here is clubman Yeats at his consummate ease spinning together a series of connections that the reader, who is forced into a position of amateur sleuth or professional shrink, is obliged to disentangle if the original story is to be got right.

Yeats is an untrustworthy narrator of his own life, given to the glamour of 'half-read wisdom' rather than to attending to the more prosaic grey truth. The phrase 'yet it must be' raises but then closes off a question: why the obligation? Is it Yeats's awareness of psychology and the workings of the mind, the way the mind censors material that it cannot admit? Is it that as a matter of course he gets things wrong, that memory is an untrustworthy agency? Is it because he recognises the horizons of his own ideological thinking, first as a Protestant in a largely Catholic country and later as an Irishman in England? We are not informed. Other questions, such as why he didn't consult outside sources to confirm or qualify the picture he presents, prompt themselves. He might also have invoked Goethe's characterisation of autobiography as a mixture of truth and poetry, or Ernest Renan's view in his autobiography that, 'What one says of oneself is always poetical'.[2] For in such ways he could have bolstered his own position and deflected some of the imagined criticism.

As it happened, in the original manuscript, Yeats wrote: 'I have changed nothing to my knowledge & yet it must be writing after so many years that I have changed many things without my knowledge.' He then inserted: 'for I have consulted neither friend, nor letter, nor old newspaper but written from my habitual memories'.[3] In the manuscript, there were no semi-colons, and the phrase 'what comes oftenest into my memory' began life as 'habitual memories', where habit is transmuted into the flow of sensations, less amenable to conscious influence and, more tellingly, originating elsewhere. 'Reveries' is the first word in his title, not 'Recollections' or even 'Memoirs'. The mind is at rest, the machine put to sleep, storing, rather than switched off. Things float into the mind, fragments which subsequently have to be connected. This is the nearest Yeats gets to St Augustine's 'great storehouse of memory'.[4] That Yeats was altering things can be observed most graphically in the sentence about not changing things. This is the norm in writing, for it is doubtful if anyone writing their life, whether before or after Freud, can legitimately claim to have altered nothing. Patterns in experience manifest themselves after the event, rarely at the time; so there has to be, as Coleridge discovered about writing verse, a shaping of the imagination, never simply a recording or a recalling. But the idea of transcribing what happened governs Yeats's thinking at this point, even to the extent of his mistakenly calling his manuscript a 'Biography'.

What is surprising is how little he altered the account between the extant manuscript, the typescript and final publication in 1916. But this adds a certain piquancy to the actual changes that are then made. In a tender passage about his mother in the middle of Section 5, Yeats toned down a stark sentence which read 'She did not read books or look at pictures'.[5] Presumably he had second thoughts about this observation and cut the reference to her not looking at pictures. Yes, she listened to stories of fisherfolk while living in Howth and Sligo, but she never read books, something which, while regrettable, can be revealed. But, for an artistic family, it must have been hurtful that she never looked at paintings. In the manuscript version, Section 7 opens with two scenes, one of Yeats at school imagining himself as famous, 'proud as a March cock', the other of the shame brought on the family by an impecunious cousin who fled to London to escape the law in Ireland. The two scenes act as companions, one a glimpse of fame amid his peers, the hero in the ascendancy, the other of shame in the family, the hero's rise threatened by circumstance. But in the manuscript version, there is a third scene concerning a relation who appeared on the doorstep while they were living at Bedford Park in London, who had escaped from an institution where she had been locked up 'for some temporary fit of madness'.[6] This passage is deleted from the published version, perhaps because it would alter the neat symmetry of the hero's expected rise and possible fall, but more probably because it was too damaging to the family, a family that contained financial misfits, mental instability, and a father who failed to provide for them.

If the process of composition is revealing, so too is the narrative itself. Yeats chooses to conclude the story of his childhood and youth with an enigma: 'It is not that I have accomplished too few of my plans, for I am not ambitious; but when I think of all the books I have read, and of the wise words I have heard spoken, and of the anxiety I have given to parents and grandparents, and of the hopes I have had, all life weighed in the scales of my own life seems to me a preparation for something that never happens' (pp.212–3). That he was not ambitious is clearly absurd; his boyhood dreams of heroic status vis-à-vis his peers is testimony in that direction. George Russell, the mystic friend of his youth, famously remarked: 'The boy in the book might have become a grocer as well as a poet.'[7] But the remark was made only because the friend of his youth had not become a grocer. As for Yeats's plans, these included the reshaping of Irish culture after the fall of Parnell in 1890 – again, no mean ambition, and no mean achievement, either. As for nothing happening, this too is undermined by the narrative he has just recounted; the Sligo Protestant who became an Irish nationalist. A tradition exists of reading *Reveries* in terms of Yeats's relationship with his family, and in particular his grandfather and his father, and the final sentence chimes with such an approach. But there is another traumatised, anxious narrative that can also be felt, and this relates more directly to Yeats and the wider field of cultural nationalism, together with the colonial encounter between Britain and Ireland.

In an intriguing paragraph in Section 1, Yeats runs together a series of distinct memories or sensations from his childhood: the voice of conscience and moments of crisis; running up a Union Jack at night in his garden and one morning finding the flag on the ground and knotted, responsibility for which, from listening to the servants, he attributes to the fairies; the occasion when he was told he saw a supernatural bird in the corner of a room; a premonition in his sleep of the wreck of his grandfather's steamer, a wreck that actually occurred with the loss of eight men; his grandfather's later memories and recourse to the passage about the wreck of St Paul when asked to read at family prayers. It is hard to determine the governing principle here, unless it is an early attempt by Yeats to say something about the beginnings of his identity with Ireland. On the one side is ranged his Protestant upbringing: family prayers and readings from the Bible (a Catholic family would be saying the rosary at this time); a moral upbringing in which he is tormented by the voice of conscience; and a political presence identified with Britain. On the other side are the fairies, who impishly lower the flag of allegiance; Catholic servants who murmur non-rational but persuasive things in his ear; and premonitions which belong to the world of the paranormal outside the control and influence of the rational Victorian mind.

Early in life, largely through shocks of one kind or another, Yeats came to understand that his national identity was composed of competing layers. The Imperial capital – not Dublin or Paris, as it was for Joyce and Synge – was crucial in developing his general awareness of difference. As a young boy, he enjoyed listening to the rhymes of Orangemen recited by a stable boy and to stories told by servants, stories that, when remembered in London, brought back tearful memories of Sligo. On one side of the colonial divide was Sligo; on the other London. Passing the drinking fountain at Holland Park in London, he recalls Sligo and longs for a 'sod of earth', which he connects with the 'old race instinct'. The flag he ran up as a boy is discovered at the bottom of the flagstaff 'touching the grass'; touching, that is, not so much the earth as Irish Ireland. At the Godolphin School in Hammersmith he is called names for being Irish; identified by others as Irish, he learns in turn not to identify with Cressy and Agincourt and the heroes of English history. Equally, as if she had been reading a description of Lord Clonbrony in Edgeworth's *The Absentee* (1812), one of his aunts declares: 'You are going to London. Here you are somebody. There you will be nobody at all' (p.46).[8] In London, Yeats is the colonised subject; in Ireland he should be the coloniser, but he learns – largely through his father and later through O'Leary – that his identity lies elsewhere than in representing the crown in Ireland. In a valuable essay, significantly entitled 'W. B. Yeats as Third World Paradigm', Edwin Thumboo extends this line of argument by noticing the parallels between Yeats and Shakespeare's Ariel: 'As an Ariel figure, he partook of both the *impulse of rule* and the *impulse of freedom* from that rule. Tensions created by this "duality" were felt, variously understood and resolved by all colonial subjects. Yeats gradually discovered, adjusted, made, chose, balanced his allegiances.'[9] All the people he knew in Sligo despised nationalists and Catholics alike. It was convenient for Yeats that they also despised England, for such an attitude allowed scope for an ideological position which sought a unity between Catholic and Protestant against a threat perceived now as external.

Bringing together the two halves – not Britain and Ireland, but Protestant and Catholic Ireland – is how Yeats formulates the ideology of 'undivided inheritance' in Section 29 of *Reveries*. Catholics, he explains, lacked the good taste, household courtesy and decency of Protestant Ireland, and Protestants thought of nothing except getting on. Catholics had history on their side, albeit a history of defeat, with memories in particular of the siege of Limerick in 1690; on his side, he had geography and landscape and social importance, mountain and lake, his grandfather and ships. From that union would come a retreat from provincialism and a more exacting form of criticism, 'an European pose' (pp.199–200). Yeats is here aligning his own personal identity with Ireland's cultural identity, seeing both as being divided into two halves, in his own case, of Ireland and England, and in the case of Ireland of Catholicism and Protestantism. And in a suggestive image, which anticipates his response to the Easter Rising, he compares the emerging Ireland to 'soft wax': 'I began to plot and scheme how one might seal with the right image the soft wax before it began to harden' (p.199).

In one sense, no one in the revolutionary years of 1916–23 could have been better positioned than Yeats to observe events unfolding in Ireland, for in advancing a new cultural identity he could have been commenting on, or indeed advancing, his own position. In another sense, no one could have been more outside of things. Nowhere in *Reveries* do we have a portrait of Yeats feeling at home either in London or Sligo. School, he tells us, was 'an obscene, bullying place', a commonly held view of the English public school system. After being chased off an estate in South London by a gamekeeper, he suddenly realises 'I was a stranger there'. In Sligo he is fearful of his father and of his grandfather, of the harsh word and of the book thrown at him for being a slow learner. He deletes from the manuscript an overblown sentence about how 'I was spreading out my life and becoming marvellous to myself'.[10] Pain, anxiety and fear are the emotions most often on display. He blunders, gets found out, is useless at games, and spends his time in pursuits typical of a lonely boy, such as hunting moths, riding his pony, or discovering which birds are first to sing in the morning. In Sligo he roams the countryside looking up – or perhaps we should say looking for – his family; his Middleton cousins at Castle Durgan, or his great-uncle Mat at Rathbrougham. Only in intimate company is he self-possessed. His father reads to him a passage from Thoreau's *Walden* and he imagines living like Thoreau on the island of Innisfree, free from bodily desire and women. Hamlet is one of his models, as is Shelley's Alastor. 'The great event of a boy's life,' he enigmatically tells us, 'is the awakening of sex.' And this is followed by some absurd description about jumping naked over sticks laid upon two chairs and enjoying his nakedness. When his mother suffers a stroke she spends the rest of her days 'feeding the birds at a London window' – in 'perfect happiness', Yeats adds, either seemingly oblivious to, or deliberately conscious of, the pain in that glazed expression. From his grandfather's memories and from his father's repeated attempts to establish himself as an artist to his mother's final divorce from reality, there is a locked-in quality about the subjects of *Reveries* and no one is more confined than the narrator himself. Soft wax is rarely an appropriate description we can apply to Yeats's forceful personality, but he was in his childhood and youth subject to the hardening process, and one aspect of this concerned his family. Eventually, at precisely the time he embarks on this, the first volume of his autobiography, he discovers that he has virtually no family left in Sligo.

'Easter 1916'

In one of the early sections of *Reveries,* Yeats tracked his ancestry back to the eighteenth century and, not surprisingly, he discovered a mixed estate. One of his great-uncles had chased the United Irishmen in the 1790s, and his great-grandfather had been a friend of Robert Emmett, leader of the failed Rising in 1803. But, with the miniatures in front of him of soldiers, lawyers and Castle officials, what most intrigues the poet is a sense of belonging: 'I am delighted with all that joins my life to those who had power in Ireland' (p.35). Rebels were few in the family; in 1916, what did the boy who had run up the Union Jack in his garden in Sligo make of the rebels who took over the General Post Office in Dublin and hoisted a green flag with the words 'Irish Republic' blazoned for all the world to see?

Only a short distance in time and thought-process separates the sentences beginning 'I am delighted' and 'I have met them', for 'Easter 1916' is in part a continuation of a meditation begun in *Reveries.* As in *Reveries,* on display throughout 'Easter 1916' are two concerns – the nature of heroism and the issue of Irish provincialism – and a mode of enquiry closer to reflection than analysis. In *Reveries,* Yeats confused his grandfather with God and, like Hamlet, struggled to overcome the influence of his father. The 1916 rebels renewed his interest in heroism (which had been channelled in the years leading up to the Rising through Irish myths) and brought into play not the passive issue of authority but the active challenge by his fellow-countrymen to history. For the generation that produced the Revival, provincialism was always a possible, or indeed likely, fate that confronted the present – hence the surprisingly vitriolic remark by James Connolly in November 1914 when he spoke of how the Irish would be 'a diseased remnant of a once great people' if no resistance was shown to the Great War, or the reference to saving 'the soul of Ireland' in Thomas MacDonagh's last address, where he contrasted the rebels with the 'inert mass' of the Irish people, 'drugged and degenerate'.[11] While several removes from revolution and not sharing in the rebels' intensity, *Reveries* does provide a recollection of nineteenth-century Ireland that is essentially provincial. By contrast, the green that Ireland wears in 'Easter 1916', represents the triumph over such provincialism. As for the kind of enquiry, there is a meditative quality about both *Reveries* and 'Easter 1916', as if Yeats is attempting to capture the mind at work, processing, weighing things up, but not necessarily coming to a firm conclusion. Paragraphs in *Reveries* – reminiscent of his stories in *The Celtic Twilight* (1893) – work more by association than by organisation according to topic sentence. Divided into separate stanzas that focus on particular facets of the Rising, 'Easter 1916' is more coherent. But in both texts Yeats is the observer making sense of a world that is changing before his eyes, searching out the enigmatic phrase that will lift the narrative into elegiac mode.

Reading 'Easter 1916' is more complex, not only because of its density but also because each line and phrase seems to contain a buried target, which may not always be conscious on Yeats's part. What adds to the burden of interpretation is the number of such targets, targets which cannot be easily gathered under a simple heading. There is clearly a balancing of allegiances, as Edwin Thumboo suggests. However, as in *Reveries*, narrative and discourse are not so much at variance as in need of some higher principle of integration. Yeats's other 1916 poems are in this respect less problematic. 'Sixteen Dead Men' runs along the same track throughout, while 'The Rose Tree' has the simplicity of a ballad. All approaches to 'Easter 1916' issue in a slightly different poem. As noted in the previous chapter, there is a degree of traffic around 'them' in the first line which can affect our reading. In the context of *Reveries*, and more specifically its last sentence, 'Easter 1916' resembles a poem about life as a preparation for a meaningful death or, more poignantly, about death as an interruption in the preparation for life. The poem injects a note of urgency into such an idea and gathers to itself all the contemporary talk about sacrifice and Pearse's message to the pupils in his care about Cuchulain and how 'better is short life with honour than long life with dishonour'.[12] Mention of rebels and flags in the autobiography provides an approach to the poem that highlights the colonial encounter and Yeats's competing identities. In *Reveries*, Yeats uses his family to illustrate his purchase on Irish history, while in 'Easter 1916', it is his acquaintance with the rebels that revives such a purchase.

Frequently the task of the critic is to read between the lines, but in the case of 'Easter 1916' we also need to respect the eddies and currents that carry the poem forward and hold it back, and in this regard the recently constructed narrative of Yeats's life shouldn't be overlooked. It would be helpful if there existed extant drafts of the poem – presumably these were shown to Maud Gonne – for then we could discern more sharply what was in fact between the lines. As it is, we are forced to rely on various symptomatic or patterned readings, in which we draw on the usual arsenal – history and ideology, audience and contexts, hybridity and postcolonial theory. In attending to the various shifts in the poem, it is worth recalling that we are in the presence of some key tensions, not only in Yeats but also in the wider culture. In this sense, we cannot afford to neglect the afterlife of 'Easter 1916', a poem that has created its own series of responses, especially in the area of gender and nationalism.

Troubling the Living Stream

As in *Reveries*, it is the speckled response that attracts Yeats. He seems incapable of writing an uncomplicated elegy as is to be found in, say, Father P. O'Neill's popular ballad 'The Foggy Dew'.[13] In comparison with 'The Foggy Dew', 'Easter 1916' is a troubled and troubling poem. The half-rhymes and eye-rhymes seem designed to thwart harmony: thought-lout, turn-born, road-cloud, stream-brim, dive-live, name-come, death-faith. By contrast, there is a reassuring quality to the internal rhyme scheme in 'The Foggy Dew', and rhymes such as hum-drum, bell-swell, keep-sleep and fled-dead suggest that everything chimes, that the national liberation struggle had a successful outcome: 'For slavery fled, O glorious dead', and so on. There is nothing to interrupt the narrative flow, either. Absent Irishmen in British uniforms are quickly absorbed into the song. Those who fell in the Great War were fighting the wrong fight; if they had fought with de Valera (significantly not mentioned by Yeats),[14] they would now have hallowed graves in Ireland. The author is deliberately absent, more like a traditional singer of tales than a modern poet: he came and saw and went, and now he kneels and prays. By contrast, at the centre of 'Easter 1916' is the author and the author's psychology, and his reading of the event.

In the opening lines, Yeats reveals he was personally acquainted with the insurgents. In 'Salutation', the poem that immediately precedes 'Easter 1916' in *Nineteen-Sixteen*, the 1935 commemorative anthology, George Russell declares, 'Here's to you men I never met'.[15] Yeats, on the other hand, had met them. 'I have met them', not 'I have seen them' or 'I have come across them', or even the informal reminiscing of 'We used to cross paths'. 'I have met them', where in the tense of the verb the link is established between past and present, a present much closer to the executions in May than September 25 1916, the date inserted at the end of the poem. Yeats met them, 'met' being the only full stress in the first four words of the poem, and he stopped to talk with them coming home from work, work in offices in grey eighteenth-century houses, former homes of the Ascendancy.

As if to insist on his social status, and conscious that he is among 'an audience, in part alien and unsympathetic', Yeats adopts the style of the Ascendancy with them. He is the public figure, who recalls, now that the action is over, their 'vivid faces', faces, that is, of 'poets and schoolmasters' as he explained to his English friend, the artist Will Rothenstein, 'idealists, unfit for practical affairs'.[16] After sitting at desks and counters in offices and shops all day, an environment which, according to Yeats in 1901, 'had created a new class and a new art without breeding and without ancestry',[17] they bear not the Blakean London marks of weakness, but excitement at the thought of Dublin rebellion. Yeats is the stately protagonist – not Benjamin's flâneur or Joyce's advertising agent who is ever ready to meet whoever. Ireland's national poet had met the flushed insurgents. The author of *Cathleen ni Houlihan*, who in February 1907 had faced down the angry audiences at the Abbey Theatre over Synge's *Playboy*, the keeper of the flame of cultural nationalism and former member of the underground Irish Republican Brotherhood, he had 'met them', and, perhaps, had privately 'fretted somewhat that he had not been consulted'.[18] Such an extraordinary view he had conveyed to William Rothenstein at his country house in Gloucestershire at the time of the Rising. In contrast to the direct and meaningful action of taking up arms against the British, the insurgents had merely exchanged 'polite meaningless words' (*VP* 392) with Yeats.

Yeats's interest is focused almost exclusively on the inner landscape of the insurgents, on their transformation, and on the transformation of Ireland as a result of their transformation. Unlike the War of Independence (1919–21), which was to a large extent a guerrilla war fought in the countryside, the Easter Rising, as vividly illustrated in the BBC production of Ronan Bennett's *Rebel Heart* (2001), was fought out in the streets of Dublin. Buildings such as the General Post Office, the City Hall, the College of Surgeons overlooking St Stephen's Green, the South Dublin Union, Jacob's Biscuit Factory, Westland Row Station (now Connolly Station) were occupied by the insurgents and the face of the city made vivid, changed forever. If the Abbey Theatre constituted the arena for cultural politics, the streets were at the intersection of private dreams and military action. Joyce insisted on topographical accuracy and believed the city of Dublin, if it were ever destroyed, could be rebuilt from the portrait contained in *Ulysses*. Yeats's city is one step removed from the streets, already part of a conversation at a club. We obtain very little idea of a military engagement or of the 'scene of desolation', a phrase that recurs in the records of contemporaries.[19] In 'No Second Troy', he refers to the way Maud Gonne 'hurled the little streets upon the great' (*VP* 256), but not one shell is heard in 'Easter 1916'. On the other hand, whatever Joyce was up to, after 1916, as Yeats's poem reminds us, Ireland would never be the same again.

The eighteenth century, like a former mask, hangs over the city and the poem: both the city and the insurgents are products of that great period when modern Dublin was laid out as a city and when modern Irish nationalism was born. But there is an ironic sense of contrast in Yeats's choice of that century; the effect would not be the same if we substituted the century of the Famine. The great period is past, symbolised by the change of occupancy in the great townhouses of the gentry, which have now been taken over by 'counter or desk'. In his sights seems to be the aspiring lower middle class, not the Catholic middle class or O'Casey's impoverished Dubliners, who occupied the townhouses as tenement-dwellers. The underlying focus seems to be the conspiratorial moment when the ground for the Rising was being laid. Yeats would have been familiar with the drilling in the streets of Dublin by the Irish Volunteers and the Irish Citizen Army, and he must have known that Augustine Birrell, the Chief Secretary of Ireland, was heavily criticised by the Commission of Inquiry set up to investigate the circumstances surrounding the Rising for not preventing such seditious acts. But the aspect that intrigued Yeats was the relationship between conspiracy and insurgency. According to one recent commentator, 'The 1916 conspirators made determined efforts to confine knowledge of their plans to as few people as possible.'[20] Yeats was not consulted, but that didn't prevent him from reasoning that the streets were party to a conspiracy only detectable to a few at the time.

In *Reveries*, history unfolds; in 'Easter 1916' history is on the point of being transformed. In 1900, one of Yeats's mentors, Standish O'Grady, had predicted that

'Spells and enchantments of a kind so potent are not to be shaken off by word, no matter how eloquent. They will and can only be removed by shocks!'[21] No one, least of all Yeats, could have expected that the Great Enchantment would be overturned sixteen years later in such a dramatic fashion. It is the close of day; we seem to be at the end of something; it is not just the tills and offices closing but something more profound, not the endgame but perhaps the end of a chapter or era in historical terms. At the same time, any action is overshadowed by the past, and only revival is possible therefore. Not newness, but revival. Night will follow, but it will not be understood in terms of day and night. 'Not night but death.' The cultural nationalist in Yeats is here seeking for the line of continuity, but he is thwarted by his ingrained belief in the condition of motley that he imagines is the defining condition of modern unromantic colonial Ireland after 'September 1913'.

Cultural Versus Political Nationalism

'Easter 1916' is a poem about the encounter between cultural nationalism and militant nationalism. In this regard, it is hard to visualise Yeats encountering the rebels in the street. In the Folio edition of *W. B. Yeats: Selected Poems* (1998), which is accompanied by a series of paintings by his brother, Jack B. Yeats, the opening four lines of the poem are juxtaposed alongside *Lingering Sun, O'Connell Bridge* (1927). In the foreground of the canvas are some five figures, three walking in one direction over the bridge and two in the other direction. The figures are fairly indistinct, individualised but not yet symbolic. The woman on the right, the centre of light and the most intriguing figure in the painting, looks as if she is wrapped in a shawl; the woman on the left, who is looking at us, is more fashionably dressed in 1920s style and seems more at ease with herself. Of the other three figures, one has a bobbed hairstyle, is walking with head down and is about to pass two well-dressed men sporting ties and hats. One of the men, the darker figure, is talking animatedly to the other. Behind the figures stretch the Liffey and the banks of the river, lit up by patches of light, reminiscent more of the Left bank of the Seine than the grubby Dublin quayside. Indistinct buildings merge into each other and taper off into the lingering arching light in the background. The contrast with the opening of 'Easter 1916' could not be more pronounced. Jack B. Yeats's Dublin is Sligo transposed to the east coast. If the scene is inviting, it is because of the natural world that beckons. The poet, on the other hand, shapes up as if to concentrate on the relationship between figures and a landscape, but the focus shifts because his interest, characteristically, lies elsewhere. Even the natural world of horses plashing and moor-hens diving is already part of a symbolic order, folded into the psychology and motivation of the insurgents and into an enquiry into how history comes to be made.

Contemporaries – and Yeats is no exception – found it difficult to interpret the Rising. Some understood it to be part of a German plot against England. The

Map of Dublin with key sites marked. Suddenly the city was being looked at through the eyes of the military strategist, with the river as a highway for gunboats. *The Sphere*, 6 May 1916.

Sphere, a London-based weekly aimed at an upper middle-class readership, immediately castigated the rebels as 'the enemy':

The armed rising in Dublin began on Easter Monday with the capture of the Post Office in Sackville Street and the City Hall on the south bank of the Liffey. The Post Office lies to the west of Liberty Hall. A party of Sinn Fein volunteers arrived here at midday, and immediately began to erect barricades on the ground floor. All the telegraph connections were destroyed, and communication with England was thus practically impossible; the green flag of the 'Irish Republic' was run up over the building, and remained until the ruined building was recaptured by the loyal forces. The City Hall and the offices of The Evening Mail on the south bank were captured at the same time, and a short time later the first shots with the military were exchanged.

The Four Courts, on the banks of the Liffey, half-a-mile from Sackville Street, formed the second position occupied by the Sinn Feiners on the north side of the river. The buildings were deserted at the time they were captured. On the south side of the river, at St. Stephen's Green, the Sinn Feiners turned out the public and proceeded to dig themselves in. On Tuesday and Wednesday, however, machine-guns posted on buildings overlooking the Green riddled the enemy and made their position here practically untenable.[22]

The report, entitled 'The Sinn Fein Revolt In Dublin: Scenes in the City During the Struggle with British Forces', was accompanied by a map of the city with the main battle sites indicated, and it was preceded by a full-page article on 'The Great European War: Week by Week'. For nationalists, 'England's difficulty is Ireland's opportunity', but to many, both in Ireland and in Britain, the Rising constituted an act of betrayal. Indeed, for Unionist Ulster, the proximity of the

1. PATRICK H. PEARSE.
2. THE O'RAHILLY.
3. EAMON CEANNT.
4. THOMAS J. CLARKE.
5. THOMAS MACDONAGH (in uniform).
6. JAMES CONNOLLY.
7. THOMAS MACDONAGH (in civilian dress).
8. SEAN MACDERMOTT.

The Leaders of the Rising wreathed in shamrock, as they appeared in *The Voice of Ireland* (1924).

Rising and the Battle of the Somme meant the two would be for ever united, 'the former the epitome of treachery, the other the price of loyalty'.[23] What the Rising did, however, share with the Great War was sacrifice and military manoeuvring. In the *Sphere* account, the capture of certain buildings across the city is described as if this was some military action in Flanders, and the action is explained to its readers in suitably military terms – 'subsidiary operations', 'the enemy', and so on.

In the context of the great battles fought during the Great War, the Rising must have been genuinely puzzling to the outside world. But for neutrals, sympathisers and detractors alike, one of the intriguing questions was motive. It did seem hopeless, capturing the GPO, running up a flag, then finding their position was 'practically untenable'. The *Sphere* highlights the military action but seeks to learn the plans behind the Rising. The report seems to imply that the capture of the GPO was perhaps designed to cut communications with England. Interestingly, the symbolic gesture is missed – that the Rising was intended not so much to cut the physical communications as to break the political connection with Britain.

The puzzle has to some extent continued. We know that, with the outbreak of the Great War, Tom Clarke and others within the Irish Republican Brotherhood had determined on a military Rising, that in 1916 schematic plans for a Rising in Dublin were drawn up by Joseph Plunkett, that, with the help of Roger Casement, German arms were to be landed off the west coast, and that the original day selected for the Rising in Dublin was Easter Sunday. According to C. Desmond Greaves, while actual plans have not survived, there seem to have been two components of the strategy: a general rising linked with the German arms, which were to have been distributed north to Athenry and south to Cork, and an ensuing immobilisation of the British forces; and, secondly, a specific Rising in Dublin.[24] In a well-researched recent study of the Rising, Michael Foy and Brian Barton provide ballast to this argument. The German navy was to have prevented cross-channel troop reinforcements, the Rising in the West was to have been more solid, with a shipment of arms landing at Fenit in County Kerry, and the encirclement of the Dublin insurgents was to have trapped the British forces between the city centre and the provincial Volunteers streaming in from the outskirts: 'In that event the

Liberty Hall, headquarters of James Connolly's Irish Citizen Army, with defiant motto for all the world to see.

Rising was envisaged as ending with the capitulation of the British Army leadership not of the Provisional Government.'[25] Not everything fits this account, not least the pervasive sense of blood sacrifice among the insurgents, that failure would lead to triumph. But as a theory it offers a counter to the view that the Rising was a passive affair, designed to end in surrender. Indeed, Pearse in the GPO remained optimistic that a German U-Boat would soon appear in Dublin Bay. And it chimes with a comment made by Tom Clarke to his widow before his execution, that the rebels hoped to hold out for four or five months, during which time 'the Irish in America would be roused and would force the American government to come to their assistance'.[26]

Whether consciously or unconsciously, Yeats seems to have absorbed something of the public confusion about the Rising and he positions himself between the insurgents and the chattering classes of the time. Ignoring the issue of military plans, he instead concentrates on the contrast between the streets and the rebels' motivation, and then within that on the fork that divides idle dreaming from conscious determination, and then within that on the charge of fanaticism that can be levelled against the dreamer of revolutionary action:

> We know their dream; enough
> To know they dreamed and are dead; (*VP* 394)

Whatever their plans were, it's enough for us to know they entertained or were possessed by a dream – this seems to be the burden of these lines, a counter to the argument Yeats must have heard at the time that their plans were amateurish or easily thwarted. In his notes to *Responsibilities* (1916), dated July 1916, at the end of a paragraph about Romantic Ireland being dead and gone, Yeats had tellingly observed: 'The late Dublin Rebellion, whatever one can say of its wisdom, will long be remembered for its heroism.'[27] It was not, therefore, as a Catholic parish priest in County Meath had suggested, 'a feeble attempt . . . to establish a toy Republic'.[28]

Significantly, when Yeats and his fellow-poets speak of the Rising, the word they repeatedly have recourse to is not 'plans' but 'dreams', a word that would be out of place in newspaper accounts of military action.[29] At one level, the encounter in 'Easter 1916' between cultural and militant nationalism is re-enacted for us as a study in motivation, which is itself subject to a sceptical reading. In Kathleen Coyle's novel *Piccadilly* (1923), there is a reference to 'the hands of bandits' of the Irish insurgents who possessed 'the hearts of creators groping for the foundations' 'deeper than filthy politics'. But, later in the novel, Coyle also includes a thought missing from 'Easter 1916', an observation relevant to the discourse below about gender and nationalism, how 'men find solace in action'.[30] Yeats's stress is different. As is apparent in the punctuation which mirrors throughout the shifts and insertions of the argument of the poem, dreams are opposed to action but not to solace, or indeed solidarity, in action. We know their dream because they took to the streets and the semi-colon which follows separates as much as it joins, acts as a pause as if there were a fork in the road. We know their dream and how foolish their actions were – this is one response to their dream, but it is one Yeats, while allowing it to surface, stops dead in its tracks: 'enough/To know they dreamed and are dead'.

'In dreams begins responsibility' (*VP* 269) is the opening to Yeats's 1914 volume *Responsibilities*. The subject of *Reveries* is nothing if not the stuff of dreams. So it would be almost impossible for Yeats not to respond to the dreams of the insurgents. In this regard, the rebels contradict the final sentence of *Reveries*, for they had prepared for something that did happen. It is dreams – but not the 'terror of a dream', as one newspaper reported[31] – which connect public events with the private thoughts of individuals. The emphasis is not on their ideas, for Yeats could discern, as could a later commentator such as Liam de Paor, that the rebels' ideas 'were little known and were for the most part not especially profound'.[32] Without dreams, however, without the (Fichtean) dignity which dreams conferred on the rebels, the Rising would have been a mere comedy, a side-show with plans and military action worthy of a short write-up in the pages of the *Sphere*. They were not, therefore, 'extreme nationalists' as Niall Ferguson describes them in *Empire* (2003), and if they were, there would have been no 'Easter 1916'.[33] Characteristically, as if to underline the significance of dreams – not the madness that besets the Irish as Father Keegan laments in *John Bull's Other Island*, nor Renan's view of Celtic civilisation which had worn itself out in taking dreams for realities[34] – Yeats insists on twinning dreaming with death: they dreamed and are dead. And in death they at once outflank their critics and strike a blow against the whole contemporary order, an order in which their position is deemed 'untenable' by ideologues for the crown.

As in *Reveries*, 'Easter 1916' reveals something of the tension in Yeats between opposing loyalties, where the image of the school-as-site-of-struggle gives way to that of the club-as-refuge:

> And thought before I had done
> Of a mocking tale or a gibe
> To please a companion
> Around the fire at the club. (*VP* 392)

Yeats was a lifelong clubman. In Dublin he was a founder-member of the Arts Club (launched in 1907) and joined the Stephen's Green Club in 1914, from which he resigned in 1923 to join the Kildare Street Club;[35] and in London, after twenty years at the Savile, he was invited in 1937 to become a member of the prestigious Athenaeum Club. In May 1916, the same month that witnessed the executions, he applied for membership to the Savile Club on Piccadilly in London, a male-only club noted for conversation – and we shouldn't overlook that it was Rothenstein's brother, Albert Rutherston, who acted as his sponsor. The following January he was formally accepted into a club that included among its members W. E. Henley, Edmund Gosse, Thomas Hardy, and Max Beerbohm. As he told Lady Gregory, it was just the right club for him, for there he could talk in the silence and the fires were warm, while at his previous club he had no one to talk to and it was cold.[36]

It was natural for Yeats to turn to clubs when composing 'Easter 1916', for clubs served his need for companionship, status and distance from (the) people. The kind of club he joined or frequented tells us much about the man. It goes without saying that he would not have joined the Malahide Golf Club that Brian Inglis describes in his opening chapter 'Our Set' in *West Briton* (1962), a club designed for Anglo-Irish Protestants.[37] As *Reveries* makes plain, Yeats had no intention of writing about 'our set', for the pressures he felt were at once more individual and, as if he aspired to the status of an organic intellectual in the Gramscian sense, more attuned to the consequences both of and for 'our set'. Equally, his lifestyle was not circumscribed by endless rounds of golf or, at least at one level, by fear of the new Ireland taking over. In his background and education, Yeats had altered the fit between class position and class horizon, becoming in the process more alone and less representative in his understanding of the relations between Britain and Ireland. 'London and Dublin' is how he defined his schooling for a 1916 biographical dictionary – not a more prestigious but narrowly defined collocation such as English public school and Oxbridge college.[38]

In some respects it would be neat and proper if the club referred to in 'Easter 1916' fell clearly within the orbit of Anglo-Ireland, as did the Kildare Street Club. This club, which admitted senior resident magistrates and serving English officers (so long as they were above the rank of major), was home to Irish landlords and Ascendancy families, and its committee, in the words of Mark Bence-Jones, constituted 'the innermost enclave of Ascendancy Ireland'.[39] To Nora Robertson, author of the aptly named *Crowned Harp* (1960), the Kildare Street Club was 'the symbol of what was unchangeable and absolute', a club which L. P. Curtis Jr. groups with the Shelbourne, the Sackville Street Club, and the Royal Dublin Society as lying at the convergence of 'the social routes of Anglo-Ireland'.[40] The snooty 'gibe' referred to in the poem would then be Yeats siding with the mocking Unionist or English viewpoint against the native Irish (who were up in arms again). But Yeats in 1916 was not a member of this club – which did not preclude him having lunch there – and one suspects he would have found its anti-nationalist atmosphere stifling.

In *A Commentary on the Collected Poems of W. B. Yeats* (1968), A. Norman Jeffares claimed the club reference was 'probably the Arts Club', but in his 1988 biography of Yeats, he quietly altered this to the Stephen's Green Club.[41] I think the change is right. This particular club, which grew out of the Union Club in 1840, stood for 'middle class liberalism and home rule by parliamentary procedures', attracting 'Irish liberals of parliamentary reforming outlook'.[42] The character of the club was essentially social, not political, and was geared towards the professional and business classes of Dublin, whose favourite pastimes were billiards and squash. In the club's records there is only one mention of Easter 1916, and this was to the 'Sinn Fein Rising' not to the more negative-sounding 'rebellion'.[43] In 1914, however, the club raised funds for the Prince of Wales' National Relief Fund Committee, and some of its members, including the Secretary, saw active service. In 1916 this was the kind of club (Home Rulers for the most part, but not militant unionists) where Yeats would be free to tell in confidence 'a mocking tale or a gibe', and it was here that Yeats stayed on his return to Dublin from abroad in the first week of June and from where he applied for a police pass to get about the city.[44]

By contrast, the Arts Club combined 'the unusual advantages of a social club, open to both ladies and gentlemen, with features of special interest to workers in Art, in Music, and in Literature',[45] counting among its members Ellie Duncan, Jack B. Yeats, Percy French, Constance Markievicz and her husband, Conor O'Brien, Maurice Joy and Padraic Colum (and, later, Yeats's wife George, and Thomas McGreevy). In a memoir of that period, Page Dickinson recalls that Yeats 'was, in the intellectual sense, the father of the Arts Club. He attended its dinners and discussions pretty regularly when in Dublin'.[46] It would be difficult to imagine Yeats telling a gibe about the insurgents in this particular club, which was one of the few clubs to admit women and which in 1911 had approached Maud Gonne to join.[47] It's not impossible, but if Yeats did have this club in mind, or partly in his mind, then the reference to beauty in the phrase 'terrible beauty' would perhaps carry some of this association, implying that the rebels, like the members of the Arts Club, were also engaged in an aesthetic venture.[48]

Having separated out all these clubs, my own view is that Yeats probably had all of them somewhere in his mind when he made the single reference in the poem: the Kildare Street Club and the image of 'unchangeable' Anglo-Ireland, which was then in retreat and undergoing a crisis of identity brought on by the Great War; the United Arts Club, which gathered together the new-found enthusiasm of a small group of Irish Protestants for the revival of arts and Gaelic culture, an enthusiasm that Robertson describes with particular insight in a chapter suitably entitled 'The Pen and the Sword';[49] the Stephen's Green Club and the middle-class 'whigs on the green'; and, finally, perhaps, the Savile Club he hoped to join in London, where he would need to defend the Irish rebels against a more open English hostility.

With Maud Gonne, an exponent of political nationalism, Yeats had shared his thoughts about the Rising and he no doubt turned over in his mind some of the phrases in her letters to him, such as: 'tragic dignity'; 'I do not think their heroique sacrifice has been in vain'; and the deaths of the leaders she described as 'full of beauty and romance'.[50] But it is with companions at the club he chooses to rehearse his argument:

For England may keep faith
For all that is done and said. (*VP* 394)

When the Great War began, all bills at Westmin-ster were suspended, including the Third Home Rule Bill of 1913, which was then in its final stages. So the suggestion in these lines is that at the end of the war the British Government might grant Home Rule, but Yeats takes care not to presume. The possibility of that happening is finely balanced in the auxiliary verb 'may'. For England *may* keep faith, but may not; it depends on how the word is stressed. In his 'Speech from the Dock', made in June 1916, Roger Casement, for whom Home Rule was a right, not a concession, dismissed British promises as empty, a view shared by Yeats's American friend John Quinn, and perhaps it was these comments the poet had in mind.[51] The phrase 'keep faith' brings the actions of the British Government into the same moral universe as those of the rebels, who also have kept faith in their ideals. In this poem about fundamental changes, the position of the poet, too, has changed. At first Yeats, the Ariel figure, is tempted to identify with the haughty English view of the Rising; this gives way to the realisation that green is now the fashion, and the poem ends with the nationalist poet implicitly taking Britain to task in its policy towards Home Rule, but then admitting a rider. If you agree to do something then you are under an obligation; on the other hand, your contractual obligations might be terminated if the other party does or says something that is deemed outrageous. Yeats, the intermediary, is aware of the threat and in the line 'For all that is done and said' seems willing to rehearse an argument that could count against the rebels.

Yeats the cultural nationalist omits any reference to the particular actions of the militant nationalists, or, indeed, to the centres of action. But, like George Russell, he is intrigued by the names of the leaders, names which quickly acquired symbolic status when the British embarked on a policy of execution. Pearse, MacDonagh, and Connolly are mentioned by name in Russell's elegy 'Salutation', a poem that also contains the lines 'Here's to you, Connolly, my man,/Who cast the last torch on the pile'. In 'Easter 1916', Yeats is more ambivalent. The insurgents are referred to without names in the second stanza and by names in the last. Constance Markievicz (née Gore-Booth) was heir to the estate at Lissadell near Sligo, the Big House that Yeats as a boy associated with beauty and privilege.

Yeats believed that 'England may keep faith,' but the exclusion of Ulster from a united Ireland was being discussed again in Irish newspapers in June 1916. Report in the Dublin *Evening Herald*, 5 June 1916, the week Yeats was in Dublin.

HOME RULE?

The Question of Ulster Exclusion

DUBLIN PARLIAMENT

Meeting of Ulster Unionist Council To-Morrow

In political circles in Dublin to-day it was freely stated that "the Home Rule question was settled." The new scheme of Government, which seems acceptable to the leaders of the Irish Party, provides for the exclusion of six counties.

It is stated that a guarantee has been given that if any Ulster county wishes to come under the Dublin Parliament within two years after the conclusion of the war it can do so.

These terms are to be discussed by representatives of both parties. The Irish question will be considered in all its bearings at a special meeting of the Ulster Unionist Council in Belfast to-morrow, at which Lord Londonderry, Lord Lansdowne, Sir Edward Carson, Captain Craig, and other prominent members are expected to be present.

To-day a prominent Nationalist, speaking with some authority, states that the following basis of a settlement "had been practically agreed upon" by both Nationalists and Unionists:—

The immediate establishment of an Irish Parliament in Dublin.

The appointment of an Executive by that Parliament, the Lord Lieutenant to represent the King in Ireland as heretofore, his appointment to be one outside party considerations.

The six counties of Ulster, namely, Antrim, Down, Armagh, Tyrone, Londonderry (including Derry City), and Fermanagh, to be excluded from the operations of the Dublin Parliament; Donegal, Cavan, and Monaghan, the three remaining counties of Ulster, to come under the Home Rule Parliament with the rest of Ireland.

All the Ulster counties to have the option if they so desire of coming under the Dublin Parliament.

Arrangements to be made by which legislation introduced by the Dublin Parliament may, with the consent of the representatives of the excluded counties, be applied to the whole country equally.

Periodical conferences in connection with such legislation to be held between representatives of the excluded counties and representatives of the Irish Government in Dublin.

The excluded counties to remain under the control of the Imperial Parliament until such time as they, of their own wish, come under the Irish Parliament.

The present Irish representation to be maintained at Westminster for the time being, and probably until the end of the war.

Generous financial provision to be made for the settling of the Irish Parliament.

The settlement terms to be presented to Parliament immediately after the reassembling of Parliament in the form of an amending Bill by consent to present Home Rule Act.

Markievicz and her sister Eva had abandoned their birthright and taken up the cause of Irish nationalism, in the case of Markievicz, and of the English working class, in the case of Eva. The phrase 'ignorant good will' seems to be a patronising reference to Markievicz's running soup-kitchens for working-class families during the 1913 Dublin Lock-Out.

Pearse (to Yeats's ear his surname rhymes with verse, a fact that adds yet more dignity to the rebel) was the leader of the Rising, a visionary thinker and the founder of St Enda's School in Rathfarnham, where classes were held in Irish. Yeats's gibe about Pearse riding 'our wingèd horse' is in keeping with loading the scales against the insurgents at this point in the poem, and it seems unlikely that it marks a swerve away from a powerful influence. In point of fact, their paths frequently crossed: at a meeting held in 1910 under the auspices of the Gaelic League, Pearse proposed a vote of thanks to Yeats for his talk on 'The Theatre and Ireland', and the two had shared the same platform in 1914 to commemorate the nineteenth-century cultural nationalist Thomas Davis. However, Joan Towey Mitchell has argued convincingly for a degree of Pearse's influence in the poem, especially in the mother naming her child, citing the lines from Pearse's poem 'The Mother' – 'But I will speak their names to my own heart/In the long nights' – and the dream of impossible things in 'The Fool'.[52]

MacDonagh escapes the poet's disdain. A university lecturer, MacDonagh start led his students by placing a large revolver on the lectern and declaring: 'Ireland can only win freedom by force'.[53] His critical monograph *Literature in Ireland* (1916) was devoted in part to the hybridity of Irish writing in English and the extent to which Gaelic rhythms informed Irish verse in English (including Yeats's work). In a thought that belongs to the poem's counter-argument, Yeats could discern that 'He might have won fame in the end'.

John MacBride, 'that vainglorious lout', was Yeats's rival for the affection of Maud Gonne. Their marriage in 1903 proved unsuccessful and Yeats was told the inside story of MacBride's womanising and abusing, which he confided to Lady Gregory in a series of disturbing letters in 1905.[54] As it happened, the death of MacBride meant that his Catholic wife was then free to remarry, a situation that Yeats was keen to capitalise on in the summer of 1916 when he travelled to her house in Normandy. But none of this surfaces in the poem, even though he seems to have composed or completed the poem while at her house in September.[55] MacBride rhymes with 'died', a rhyme that rebounds rather than resonates, as if this is all that needs to be said at this juncture. Nothing is made by Yeats of the public position of MacBride – the Boer War veteran who returned to Dublin an anti-British hero – nor of the comic aspect of his joining the Rising after coming to Dublin to attend a wedding.

In the final stanza Yeats adds to the list the name of Connolly, who died not knowing whether his actions would be understood by those who believed socialism and nationalism should be kept separate. In June 1897, Connolly was with

Maud Gonne and Yeats on an anti-Jubilee demonstration that turned into a riot, and Connolly and Gonne shared political platforms against the Boer War, but it's not known if Yeats met Connolly subsequently.[56] Significantly, nothing is said in the poem about the gruesome manner in which Connolly met his death, that is, tied to a chair on account of injuries sustained during the Rising and shot by a firing squad in the ironically named Mountjoy Jail.

Gender and Nationalism

In the list of names Constance Markievicz is the odd one out, for she avoided execution on account of her gender, and her name is omitted by Yeats from the final stanza. But neither Markievicz nor the issue of gender and nationalism could be so easily removed from the poem. 'On a Political Prisoner', composed in January 1919, contrasts the little patience she knew as a child with the confinement she now enjoyed in Holloway Prison. In *Michael Robartes and the Dancer* (1920), the poem marks the end of a series that begins with 'Easter 1916', 'Sixteen Dead Men', and 'The Rose Tree', and, significantly, it is positioned in the middle of a volume that also includes, in the second half, 'The Second Coming' and 'A Prayer for My Daughter'. Yeats was a 'Constance-watcher', and, in October 1927, after her death, he again returned to '[t]hat woman' in his beautiful elegy entitled 'In Memory of Eva Gore-Booth and Con Markievicz':

> The light of evening, Lissadell,
> Great windows open to the south,
> Two girls in silk kimonos, both
> Beautiful, one a gazelle. (*VP* 475)

These opening lines recall Yeats's childhood and youth, his nervous sensibility filtered now through other forms of displacement. Yeats reflects the unease of Merville, the Pollexfen family house in Sligo, looking up to the great estate of Lissadell on the outskirts of Sligo. It is money made in trade; they are 'merchant people of the town', in awe of landed wealth. When he stayed at Lissadell in 1894, Yeats imagined an amorous relationship with Markievicz but realised that 'this house would never accept so penniless a suitor'.[57] Looking beautiful, wearing exotic clothes, riding to harriers, avoiding argument – Yeats's views on upper-class women also reflect in no small measure his middle-class background.

If Yeats was interested in deepening the political basis of cultural nationalism, he possessed in Markievicz not only a powerful addition to the theme of transformation but another meaning to the phrase 'terrible beauty'. It was indeed terrible – in the sense of breaking convention – that a beautiful woman should deliberately refuse to live out a male sexual fantasy and step out of a canvas filled with gazelles.

Studio portrait of Constance Markievicz. Writing from jail in July 1919 to her sister, Markievicz noted how, 'it was a common sneer in England at one time that we could not talk of Ireland in Plain English. It was always "Kathleen ni Houlihan" or some other unpronounceable name, and her "four green fields" gave great offence too. Now I like all that.' There's something profoundly ironic in the thought that the modern romantic, given to identity politics, hated 'the modern curt style'.

Markievicz's biographer in the 1960s is more reticent and doesn't enquire into Yeats's ideological position: '[N]o amount of the sterner virtues displayed by both Constance and Maud Gonne could reconcile the poet to their politics.'[58] In a famous studio portrait photo of her in the uniform of Connolly's Citizen Army, dressed in green from boot to slouch hat with feathers, Markievicz holds a revolver in both hands, her delicate looks at odds with the gesture she is making. Her femininity cuts both ways: not only does it soften aggression but it also undermines the pacifist role assigned to women in patriarchal societies. She linked herself at the time with women in the Irish Volunteers' Cumann na mBan (League of Women), who avoided fashionable clothes and who, according to C. S. Andrews, refused to wear make-up.[59] As second-in-command to Michael Malin, Chief of Staff of the Irish Citizen Army, Markievicz saw action and was possibly involved in killing an unarmed policeman, PC Lahiff.[60] It was her green bedspread, with gold paint touched up with mustard, which flew over the GPO as the flag of the new republic. Not content to remain in the kind of ancillary role typically reserved for women, such as messenger, nurse or stretcher bearer, she helped defend the College of Surgeons on St Stephen's Green. According to a young Cumann na mBan member at the time, Markievicz, who taught members how to clean revolvers, was 'the living embodiment of Kathleen Ni Houlihan'.[61] And when she surrendered, as the Dublin papers at the time noted, she kissed her revolver before handing it over.[62]

In *Cathleen ni Houlihan*, whose call to arms anticipates the Easter Rising, Yeats had assigned Maud Gonne to that symbolic role, but in 'Easter 1916' such a thought is studiously avoided, in part because of a reluctance to align or join together the two leading female exponents of political nationalism, Gonne and Markievicz. According to Roy Foster, the poem is situated between Lady Gregory and Gonne, the women who played host to Yeats when the poem was being com-

IN DUBLIN G.P.O.

LADY PRISONER'S EXPERIENCE.

A lady visitor to Dublin who, without knowing that the Sinn Feiners were in possession of the building, sought refuge in the G.P.O. from street disturbance on Easter Monday, and was detained until the following Friday night, states that she waited on and cooked for the prisoners—3 officers, 24 privates, one policeman and a girl—who were given the best of everything. There was abundance of food of every kind—meat, vegetables, etc. Once the lady cooked dinner for the Sinn Feiners, of whom, she asserts, there were not at any time more than 150. The officers and girls had couches to rest on; the others, Volunteers included, had to snatch their occasional hour or two of rest on the board floor. Three priests came and heard confessions, except in the case of the officers and two of the soldiers, who were Protestants.

Cooking for the Sinn Feiners. *The Irish Independent*, 11 May 1916.

posed, Gonne in the summer and Gregory towards the end. Foster goes further and argues that Gonne stands at its centre 'all the more so, as the values of uncompromising, "advanced", Anglophobic nationalism which she had always personified had been spectacularly embodied by the 1916 martyrs'.[63] Lady Gregory, the cultural nationalist, helped to moderate Gonne's passionate, 'abstract' values, and when he inserted '25 September' at the end of the poem, Yeats also might well have added 'Coole Park'. That Yeats was ambivalent in his attitudes toward Markievicz can also be discerned in a far from fluent early draft of the poem: 'That woman at while would be shrill/In aimless argument;/Had ignorant goodwill;/All that she got she spent.'[64] Foster stresses the tension in the poem between Lady Gregory and Maud Gonne, but the biographical details lend support to the wider argument being pursued here, for the issue of gender and nationalism in the poem remains unresolved by the poet who insisted on viewing women as, in the words of Eva Gore-Booth's biographer, 'inspirational but not inspired'.[65]

The terms of the debate, however, have an authority that still need addressing. In a justly celebrated pamphlet, *From Cathleen to Anorexia* (1990), Edna Longley argues that Yeats, in such poems after 1916 as 'On a Political Prisoner' and 'A Prayer for My Daughter', 'broke the icon his poetry had gilded. That is, he questioned Cathleen as then incarnated by Constance Markievicz and Maud Gonne MacBride'.[66] At one point, after noticing that Cathleen-Anorexia encourages women to join male death-cults, Longley cites the lines from 'Easter 1916' 'Too long a sacrifice/Can make a stone of the heart' and comments on the contrast between the stone and the 'living stream': 'Surely the chill, the stone, the self-destructiveness at the heart of Irish nationalism shows up in its abuse of women and their gifts of life'.[67] For Longley, feminism and the physical force tradition in Ireland is 'self-evidently a contradiction in terms', and, enlisting Yeats on her side, she quotes his views on femininity ('natural kindness', 'courtesy', 'rootedness') as opposed to what she sees as the 'ideological rigidity' of 'dogmatic nationalism'. According to Longley, Yeats may have been patriarchal in the female qualities he values, but 'at least he replaces the aisling of nationalist male fantasy with a model for the Irish future that draws on (some of) women's own qualities'. This is perhaps the least satisfactory part of her argument. 'Women's own qualities' has a dangerously essentialist ring about it and Longley doesn't address the key issue, that valorising the so-called female virtues of pacifism, sensitivity, and the quality of nurturing *may* establish a more humane ethics in opposition to the brutally masculinist, but can do so only by risking an identification with patriarchal views of women.

While it is right to share her concern for peace and mature dialogue, 'Easter 1916' is not a particularly reliable prop – and neither, for that matter, to take a contrary tack, are political melodramas from the period, such as P. J. Bourke's *For the Land She Loved* (1915).[68] Yeats does not write that a sacrifice *does* but that a sacrifice *can* make a stone of the heart, and he rhymes 'sacrifice' with 'suffice'; that is, he positions the concept within an argument about strategy. Equally, the symbol of the stone is essentially ambivalent, commitment to a cause being both admirable and destructive. There is something uncomfortable about 'Easter 1916', not only in its admiration for heroism and in its unresolved flirting with those who took part – which includes women – but also in its belief that commitment to a cause is double-edged. On reciting the poem by the shore at Colleville in Normandy, not surprisingly, Yeats implored Maud Gonne 'to forget the stone and its inner fire for the flashing, changing joy of life'.[69] In 'Say a Prayer', Seán Ó Tuama, meditating at the graveside of young men who gave their lives in the 1920s fighting for a republic, asserts (rather chillingly) that it is 'against all nature to deny homage/to that violence'.[70] Yeats doesn't go this far, but, equally, Yeats was not a liberal humanist and he had little time for Ulster Unionism.

As is evident, both in *Reveries* and in 'Easter 1916', Yeats, the sensitive son and spurned lover, encountered problems in erasing women:

O when may it suffice?
That is Heaven's part, our part
To murmur name upon name,
As a mother names her child
When sleep at last has come
On limbs that had run wild. (*VP* 394)

Finding a position inside and then outside the struggle was, ironically, Yeats's historic task as a cultural nationalist. The figure of the mother afforded Yeats an opportunity, the mother here naming her child on the point of sleep at close of day. That Yeats should compare his own activity as a poet to that of a mother is revealing if slightly puzzling (for, in spite of what Joan Towey Mitchell argues, it is more than a borrowed image from Pearse). A mother does not name her child at such moments. A mother might murmur the name of her child: 'Dear Patrick, dear Patrick, dear Patrick, sleep now, child.' But this is not technically naming. Naming belongs with numbering in this poem. As if they are already being assigned to some roster or register, the rebels are named and numbered by Yeats. Both activities define a relationship and imply in this case some form of possession, if not ownership. Yeats is here the mother, cross-gendered, morally not condemning but accepting, and giving dignity to the actions of the leaders. He murmurs, rather than recites, their names, murmur being a word full of emotion in Yeats's verse, a word associated, as in *The Wanderings of Oisin* (1889), with sadness, disappointment and depth of feeling. It is not the murmur of dissent but the badge of the tribe, as in the low murmuring of servants, for example, talking about the flag in his childhood memory. 'Easter 1916' is an act of recuperation, a performative utterance, but only the rebels' names and their dreams – not their lives – can now be recuperated. Typographically, Yeats does this by means of a dash, a break or rhetorical flourish, dead now, no conclusion, the future unknown: 'I write it out in a verse –'

Concluding Remarks

In an influential study, David Lloyd argues that 'Easter 1916' 'concerns the foundation of a nation'.[71] But when he wrote the poem, it is doubtful if Yeats imagined his object was such. There is certainly no sense of Wordsworthian bliss at being alive at such a moment in history. The tone, rather than the subject-matter, affords us a surer guide, and this is best captured in the open-ended question asked around the fire at the club: 'Was it needless death after all?' It is interesting to speculate on how the poem would have been received if Yeats had published it in 1916. On the first anniversary of the Rising in 1917, a performance of *Cathleen ni Houlihan* at the Abbey was considered 'a seasonable play these times':

It is rather satisfying to sit in an audience, in part alien and unsympathetic, and to hear that the cause of all her miseries was 'too many strangers in the house'; that red cheeks would be pale cheeks for her sake . . . that those who hearkened to her call would never die; and that surely in the end she would regain her four green fields. For the first time in its history probably, the play was interrupted with applause.[72]

By a strange irony, after the Rising Yeats is welcomed back into the fold of the nation. How much more would he have been welcomed if he had not delayed until October 1920 before publishing a poem about the nationalist forces transforming Irish history?[73]

'When will it suffice?' Although it is not often asked – and it is significant that it isn't by Longley – it is always a legitimate question in anti-colonial struggles: how much suffering, whether on one side or both sides, is needed before self-determination is conceded? And, if God has any role in this, then the next clause is also legitimate: 'That is Heaven's part'. Yeats side-steps the issue, for the question properly belongs to the realm of politics. But when Yeats composed the poem, the outcome was indeed uncertain. He suspected that Irish history had been changed utterly and that not a rough beast but something terrible – but not necessarily tragic – had been born. At the end of his historical novel *Trinity* (1976), the Jewish-American writer Leon Uris gives this a more upbeat twist: 'It was on Easter Monday of 1916 that a terrible beauty was born by a declaration of independence.'[74]

'Easter 1916' offers a contemporary reading of the Easter Rising, and Yeats changed nothing between its first private printing in late 1916 and its appearance in the *New Statesman* in October 1920.[75] The rebels are coming out of eighteenth-century houses. It is a first coming, not yet part of a series, or indeed an example of 'The Second Coming'. Not then a 'rough beast', nor an example of Gonne's tragic dignity, but the more nuanced 'terrible beauty'. The insurgents are on the stage of history – in one sense at least – for the first time. Compare this with the viewpoint that overhangs the BBC production of Ronan Bennett's *Rebel Heart* (2001), when defeat begins to face the rebels in Northumberland Street:

Ernie Coyne: Do you think we ever had a chance?
Volunteer: Realistically? No.
Ernie: Then why did we do it?
Volunteer: If we hadn't risen the British would never have let us have the Republic.
Ernie: They won't give it to us now that we have.
Volunteer: They will if we fight again. As long as we make a better job of it next time.

Running through *Rebel Heart* is the tune of 'The Foggy Dew'. It is a way of recalling the line of continuity and signalling that all the subsequent events from the War of Independence in 1919–21 until the Civil War in 1922–3 belong to the same story that was initiated by the Easter Rising. As with *Cathleen Ni Houlihan*, 'Easter 1916' was composed without such hindsight, but, when he positioned himself at the centre of the poem between I and them and noticed the stone in the stream, it would be interesting to know if Yeats knew he was about to strike one of the longest notes in modern Irish culture.

Chapter 6

BEYOND A BOUNDARY: JAMES JOYCE AND CRICKET

But cricket was no mere game.
– Peter Walsh in *Mrs Dalloway* (1925)

pick, pack, pock, puck
– *A Portrait of the Artist as a Young Man* (1916)

So Pat's a cricket fan, is he?
– Devereux in *The Crying Game* (1992)

A Useful Bat

At the time when he first met the English artist Frank Budgen in Zurich in 1918, Joyce was in dispute with Henry Carr, a member of the British Consulate, over the latter's fee for performing in *The Importance of Being Earnest*. Budgen recalled the meeting, and how the suspicious Joyce was happily reassured by Budgen's likeness to an English cricketer:

'And what good reason had you for coming to the conclusion that I wasn't a spy?'

'Because you looked like an English cricketer out of the W. G. Grace period. Yes, Arthur Shrewsbury. He was a great bat, but an awkward-looking tradesman at the wicket.'[1]

In point of fact, the resemblance is not very pronounced, and it is also doubtful if Joyce ever had occasion to watch Shrewsbury bat, not that that would have stopped him assuming expertise or familiarity from his reading. What the Budgen story serves to illustrate, apart from Budgen's good grace, is Joyce's familiarity with the world of cricket and his association of Englishness with cricket. With Budgen, he went on to form a close friendship. Carr, on the other hand, emerged from his

Opposite page
Detail of Chevallier Tayler's sketch of W. G. Grace.

Sketch of Arthur Shrewsbury from a photo by Hawkins, Brighton. From W. G. Grace, *Cricket* (1891).

encounter with Joyce suitably battered and diminished in stature; in the 'Circe' episode of *Ulysses* he appears as a private in the British Army, threatening to 'wring the neck of any fucker says a word against my fucking king' (*U* 15:4597–8).

Like his father and Parnell, his other childhood hero, Joyce was a lover of the game of cricket. Parnell was an enthusiast as a child and a captain of his eleven, and in later life, Kitty O'Shea had a private pitch laid out for him in a two-acre field when he was living with her at Eltham in Surrey.[2] Stanislaus Joyce recalls his brother's early life as a sportsman:

He disliked football but liked cricket, and though too young to be even in the junior eleven, he promised to be a useful bat. He still took an interest in the game when he was at Belvedere, and eagerly studied the feats of Ranji and Fry, Trumper and Spofforth. I remember having to bowl for him for perhaps an hour at a time in our back garden in Richmond Street.[3]

Unlike football or hurling, which under the influence of the Gaelic Athletic Association tended to be 'clannish',[4] cricket offered Joyce a test of wits against an individual opponent, pitting the batsman against the bowler (as Fergus discovers in *The Crying Game*), and offering the necessary isolation in which the artist's conscience could be forged or strengthened.

At Clongowes Wood school, where Joyce was a boarder between the ages of six and nine, cricket enjoyed a special position in the curriculum, being played from Easter until mid-June and then again for three weeks in September. But it was, for all that, a modern game, arriving in its modern form at Clongowes Wood only in 1850:

Of the primitive species, long known as 'Stonyhurst Cricket', something has been said before; it survives still under the name of 'stump cricket', and is to be seen in the transition time of the year, between St. Patrick's Day and Easter. The 'fifties' saw a great development in this respect. Much attention was paid to personal equipment by the players, and at one time the 'tall hat' was obligatory on the leading performers with bat and ball. The first match played against a visiting team was in June, 1861, when the Clongowes XI defeated a team from Trinity College. It is said that the injunction to each batsman as he left the tent was 'On no account lift your bat out of the block hole'.[5]

In *A Portrait of the Artist as a Young Man* we read how the fellows 'were practising long shies [a throw from the outfield, for example, not a ball bowled by a bowler] and bowling lobs and slow twisters [breaks, or spins with the ball once it bounces]'.[6] The terms are designed to evoke not only a schoolboy's interest in cricket but also a different era. Lob-bowling was eventually outlawed in 1921, while shies and twisters fell out of use from the lexicon of the modern game.[7] Practice, we might also note, was integral to the game, and here, too, Clongowes shone, enjoying a succession of high-profile professional coaches, mostly from Nottinghamshire.

Joyce and his Jesuit schools (Belvedere was the day-school in Dublin he attended for his secondary education, a school also run by the Jesuits) shared in the growing popularity of the game throughout Britain and Ireland during the reign of Queen Victoria, when membership of the MCC (Marylebone Cricket Club, the headquarters of cricket) increased ten-fold from 465 in 1843 to 4,197 in 1897. Ranjitsinhji (Ranji) devotes over fifty pages to public school cricket, with sections on all the leading English (but not Irish) schools, including Eton, Harrow, Rugby, and Haileybury. Clongowes was the Eton of Catholic Ireland. The charge made by Joyce's brother Stanislaus against the Jesuits, a charge that in one sense could not be levelled against Joyce himself, was that they merely aped the English model. Joyce's two passions in life, according to Stanislaus, were father and fatherland.[8] Cricket was an English, not an Irish game, but just as he came to realise in his late teens that heaven was not his 'expectation', so too he recognised there were problems in defining his 'nation'.[9] Cricket in Ireland was always a minority game, but, as the author of a standard work in the 1950s once cautioned, 'it would be hard to say what this minority consists of'.[10] In *At Swim, Two Boys* (2001), cricket is associated with 'Castle' Catholics and is mocked by the nationalist MP Thomas Kettle in his caricature of the English: 'Play up, play up and play the game. Lauded game of cricket. Load of rot.'[11] This wasn't Joyce's view of the game. If Joyce had been a narrow-minded nationalist like the Citizen in *Ulysses* or a high-minded nationalist like Kettle, he might have viewed cricket as a 'shoneen' game, a foreigners' game, ripe for satire. But cricket clearly extended the range of Joyce's sympathies, and this was not so much to do with including Britain as excluding the view that the Irish were to be defined by reference to Britain. There is a famous photograph of Joyce as a student among the Jesuits taken in the grounds of Newman House on St Stephen's Green in Dublin. It is a relaxed pose, with the fourteen 'players' arranged

Joyce as an undergraduate at Newman House. Still a team-player. Joyce, hands in pockets, is second from left on the back row. In front of him is George Clancy, who plays Davin in *A Portrait*. Coincidentally, the years around 1904 were, according to the historian of the game W. P. Hone, the peak period of Irish cricket. Courtesy of the Beinecke Rare Book and Manuscript Library, Yale.

around the trunk of a sturdy tree, much the same as you might find in a cricket photo of the time such as the 1899 Oxford XI reproduced in C. B. Fry's *The Book of Cricket* (1899). With his 'jesuit bark and bitter bite' (*FW* 182:36), Joyce brought the whole hybrid culture along with him from his past. Nothing was lost, neither his religion nor his love of cricket, for Joyce defined himself by reference not so much to what he had lost but to what he could use.

That Joyce retained an early enthusiasm for the game in the inter-war period can be judged from a paragraph in *Finnegans Wake*, where Luke describes in graphic terms a sexual encounter between the parents before they are disturbed by a cock crowing. For the sake of economy, I have indicated the names of cricketers by putting them in bold, while cricketing terms are italicised. Among other phrases associated with cricket that can be discerned in the paragraph are Empsyeas (MCC); the Ashes (the name of the trophy match between England and Australia); test match (a match between national sides); Wisden (cricket's annual book of words); and gentlemen versus players.[12]

Kickakick. She had to kick a laugh. At her old *stick-in-the-block*. The way he was *slogging* his paunch about, *elbiduubled*, *meet oft mate on*, like hale King Willow, the robberer. **Cain**maker's mace and waxened capapee. But the **tarrant**'s **brand** on his hottoweyt brow. At half past **quick** in the morning. And her lamp was all askew and a **trumbl**y wick-in-her, **ringeysingey**. She had to **spofforth**, she had to kicker, too thick of the wick of her pixy's loomph, *wide* lickering **jessup** the smooky shiminey. And her **duff**ed *coverpoint* of a *wickedy batter*, whenever she *druv* behind her *stumps* for a **tyddlesly** wink through his **tunnilclefft** bagslops after the rising *bounder*'s *yorkers*, as he **studd** and **stoddard** and **trutted** and **trumpered**, to see had **lordherry's blackham**'s red bobby **abbel**s, it tickled her *innings* to consort *pitch* at kicksolock in the morm. Tipatonguing him on in her pigeony linguish, with a flick at the *bails* for lubrication, to scorch her faster, faster. Ye hek, ye hok, ye hucky **hiremonger**! Magrath he's my pegger, he is, for bricking up all my old kent road. He'll *win your toss, flog* your old tom's *bowling* and I darr ye, barracky**buller**, to *break his duck*! He's posh. I *lob* him. We're **parr**ing all Oogster till the empsyseas run *googlie*. *Declare* to ashes and teste his *metch*! Three for two will do for me and he for thee and she for you. Goeasyosey, for the **grace** of the fields, or hooley **pooley**, cuppy, we'll both be *bye* and by *caught in the slips* for fear he'd tyre and burst his **dunlop**s and waken her bornybarnies making his boobybabies. The game old **merrimynn**, *square to leg*, with his **lolleywide** towelhat and his **hobbs**y socks and his wisden's bosse and his norsery pinafore and his gentleman's grip and his playaboy's plunge and his flannelly feelyfooling, treading her hump and hambledown like a *maiden* wellheld, *oval*led over, with her *crease* where the *pads* of her punishments ought to be by womanish rights when, keek, the hen in the doran's shantyqueer began in a kikkery key to laugh it off, yeigh, yeigh, neigh, neigh, the way she was *wuck* to doodledoo by her gallows bird (*how's that?* **Noball**, he *carries his bat*!) *nine hundred and dirty too not out*, at all times long past conquering cock of the morgans. (*FW* 583.26–584.25)

If we extracted one figure from the list to comment on, it would be W. G. Grace, 'grace of the fields', the Grand Old Man of English Cricket, who is here linked with the popular singer of the inter-war years, Gracie Fields. With his burly figure, sense of rootedness, and prodigious batting prowess, the bearded Grace is like a figure out of the writings of Richard Jefferies or Edward Thomas. He shares the same world as Thomas's 'Lob' (itself a cricketing term): 'An old man's face, by life and weather cut/And coloured, – rough, brown, sweet as any nut, – A land face, sea-blue-eyed . . .',[13] reflecting all that the English imagine was best about nineteenth-century England – rural England, that is, of lanes and village greens. He is the man who represented his county (Gloucestershire) but not the county set, undemonstrative yet determined to win, a plain-speaking man who let his batting speak for him and, when it didn't, was prepared to resort to guile and determination, as when, out for a duck (without scoring), he insisted on remaining at the crease: 'Don't be silly. They've come to see me bat, not you umpire.'[14] Like a character out of *Tom Brown's Schooldays* but without the fuss and bother and moralising of that classic boys' novel, if he didn't exist, Grace would have had to be invented. Among the stories told about him, one concerns the window in the Kildare Street Club,

Grace and 'Crack' Group of 'Gentlemen Players'. The Esq. marks each a player but not a gentleman. Ten years before Joyce was born, the game still retained its lack of polish and professionalism. *The Graphic*, 12 August 1871.

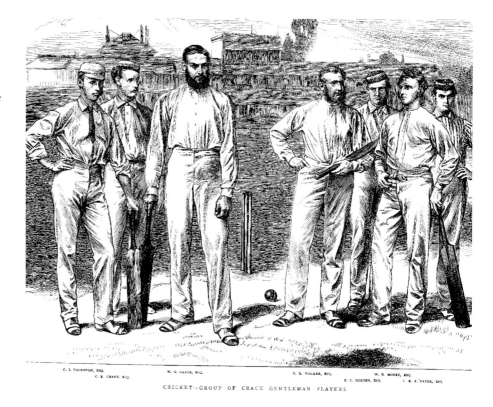

C. I. THORNTON, ESQ.   C. E. GREEN, ESQ.   W. G. GRACE, ESQ.   F. E. WALKER, ESQ.   W. R. MONEY, ESQ.   F. C. COBDEN, ESQ.   F. E. E. FRYER, ESQ.

CRICKET—GROUP OF CRACK GENTLEMAN PLAYERS

which he is said to have broken while batting across the road at Trinity College Dublin.[15] When playing against the Stephen's Green Club in 1902, he won the toss by calling 'woman', the coin having two such figures on its opposing sides in Britannia and Queen Victoria.[16] He himself played the part: 'I am a player pure and simple'.[17] W. G. – the initials alone are enough to distinguish him. And if he is slightly buried in the paragraph above in a welter of other associations, W. G. has already been identified with the main HCE protagonist of *Finnegans Wake* in a passage in the opening chapter which begins, 'Now be aisy, good Mr Finnimore, sir. And take your laysure like a god on pension' (24.16–17) and which ends, 'who was the batter could better Your Grace?' (25.35–6). Addressed to W. G., the question is rhetorical, but there's nothing rhetorical about the upper-case initial letters, for Grace is not unlike a bishop. In fact he assumes a higher rank, because W. G., who continued batting until he was sixty, was indeed like a god on pension. And more, because accused of being a 'Cumberer [destroyer] of Lord's Holy Ground' (71.34), the most famous cricket ground in the world, he was well able to defend himself 'at the wicket in support of his words' (72.28). The identification of Grace with HCE receives further support in one of his signs, the sigla ⫲, which looks uncannily like three stumps with two bails, the wicket in cricket.[18]

Chevallier Tayler's sketch of W. G. Grace, taken from *The Empire's Cricketers* (1905). Courtesy of the Trustees of the National Library of Scotland.

Excess, a refusal to stop when the point is made, is the name of the game when it comes to Joyce. James Atherton exaggerates Joyce's satire in this passage from *Finnegans Wake* – on the English public-school system, on the English conception of a cricketer as 'a clean-living upright gentleman', and so on.[19] This is to circumscribe the passage unduly, assigning Joyce to the (minor) role of Irish tormentor of the English. Reverse the vehicle and tenor of the extended metaphor, and it could be argued that the object of Joyce's satire is the sex act, a comment which seems equally misplaced. At the same time, we shouldn't forget that cricketing manuals, such as Ranji's section on Position in Batting, were full of innuendo, just waiting for the schoolboy Joyce to mock:

> A player should take up the position which is most natural and convenient to him. At the same time, I think many players have somewhat spoiled their styles by assuming positions which do not fit in with the requirements of the game. It is a good thing for a boy to be shown some of the subsequent positions he will have to assume before being allowed to contract the habit of standing in some particular way. For obviously the best position to assume while waiting for the ball is that one from which the body can pass with the greatest ease into the positions required by the various strokes. The most popular way of standing, and the one most generally adopted by good players, is to place the right foot a few inches inside the popping-crease, with the left just outside it, pointing slightly in the direction of the bowler. The bat is held with the left hand gripping it at the top, and the right hand almost immediately underneath it. The bat is grounded in the block-hole, which is usually made close to the toe of the right foot. The bend of the body in standing thus should be as slight as possible.[20]

As the many phrases full of double meanings such as 'a flick at the bails for lubrication', 'bricking up all my old kent road' and 'flannelly feelyfooling' suggest, Joyce might well have had such a passage in mind when he compiled his cricketing paragraph. And for good measure, Ranji, the 'Black Prince of Cricket', who owned an Irish castle at Ballynahinch in County Galway and who represented English athletes at the Tailteann Games in 1924, had class: 'He's posh. I lob him.' That is, light not heavy satire.

Cricket in *A Portrait of the Artist as a Young Man*

There is a sentence in *Stephen Hero* on the subject of language that is pertinent to a discussion on Joyce and cricket: 'He kept repeating them to himself till they lost all instantaneous meaning for him and became wonderful vocables.'[21] In *A Portrait*, to describe the noise of leather on willow, of cricket ball on cricket bat, Joyce writes 'pick, pack, pock, puck'. This is a good example of the 'wonderful vocables' that had attracted the young Stephen Dedalus. Joyce was evidently delighted with the series, for the tune can be heard constantly in *Finnegans Wake* in phrases such as 'Jenny Wren: pick, peck. Johnny Post: pack, puck.' (278:12–13) or 'Amick amack amock in a mucktub' (358:21–2). The fragment that constitutes *Stephen Hero* contains no reference to cricket, but in *A Portrait* cricket has an honoured place, not simply as a background presence or a portrait in sepia, but more importantly as a carrier in the opening chapter of the narrative itself.

The phrase, in part or as a complete sequence, appears four times in the first chapter. On the first occasion, the fellows in the playground are discussing the boys who absconded from school. At first it is thought the boys had been drinking altar wine in the sacristy, but then they learn from Athy that they had been caught 'smugging' with Simon Moonan and Tusker Boyle (smugging is presumably a form of homosexual activity).[22] The previous day, Stephen had been knocked over on the cinder track by an athlete and had had his glasses broken, and as a consequence the fellows looked a size bigger to the short-sighted Stephen. Football in the playground had finished and the cricket season was upon them:

> And all over the playgrounds they were playing rounders and bowling twisters and lobs. And from here and from there came the sounds of the cricketbats through the soft grey air. They said: pick, pack, pock, puck: like drops of water in a fountain slowly falling in the brimming bowl. (p.41)

'Pick, pack, pock, puck' functions in a number of ways at this juncture in the narrative. First, it alerts us to Stephen's growing sense of distance between himself and the world. In the earlier part of this chapter Stephen imagines he's on the train heading home at the end of term, his mind going in and out of the tunnel, veering between opposites, such as, term/holidays, and reality/fantasy. The discordant note is continued in the strange sequence of four plucked notes 'pick, pack, pock, puck'. Secondly, the sequence captures a rite of passage, a moment when the adult world is entering Stephen's consciousness without it being fully understood, a moment linked with a decline in the authority structures governing his world. To the young boy who has previously admired the boys in 'higher line', smugging and stealing wine from the sacristy come as a shock. With the loss of his glasses, the fellows seem bigger even as their power is in the process of being weakened. Thirdly, the sounds, which trip off the tongue, ironically constitute an interruption in the narrative discourse and insist on their being heard or noticed. What the sounds convey is not only a change of season from football to cricket but, more significantly, that the normal pattern of school life has been disrupted by some gross misdemeanour, resulting in the flogging or expulsion of the boys concerned.

A little later, as Stephen listens to the fellows debating the course of events and the consequences, Joyce repeats the sounds. The talk turns to rebellion as the fellows realise they might all be punished for the misdemeanour. 'All the fellows were silent. The air was very silent and you could hear the cricketbats but more slowly than before: pick, pock' (p.44). As they continue to deliberate, the narrative swings round again to Stephen's perspective: 'In the silence of the soft grey air he heard the cricketbats from here and from there: pock' (p.45). There then follows the classroom scene where Stephen is punished for not doing his exercises on account of not having his glasses. If this were *Tom Brown's Schooldays*, or, closer to home, the Irish novelist George A. Birmingham's *The Inviolable Sanctuary* (1912), Stephen's moment of triumph would be on the playing field, in Birmingham's case on the cricket pitch at Haileybury. Instead, Joyce focuses on Stephen's courageous visit to the Rector and the latter's admission that he would have a word with the Prefect of Studies. Immediately, Stephen makes for the playground where he is hoisted up among the fellows, who cheer for Fr Conmee, 'the decentest rector that was ever in Clongowes'. The playground symbolises the secular space free for the most part from clerical control, the freedom of the English secular game outdoors serving as a contrast to Catholic authority indoors. The secular triumph is muted, the cheers die away, and silence returns. Joyce could have ended the chapter with Stephen's submission again to authority and with kind thoughts for Fr Dolan, towards whom he did not want to feel 'proud'. Instead, we have two paragraphs, the first about the smell of evening in the air and the fields in the country, deployed here as another distancing device and reinforcing Stephen's isolation from his immediate space-time environment. And the second, the last paragraph, which returns to cricket again:

> The fellows were practising long shies and bowling lobs and slow twisters. In the soft grey silence he could hear the bump of balls: and from here and from there through the quiet air the sound of the cricket bats: pick, pack, pock, puck: like drops of water in a fountain falling softly in the brimming bowl. (p.59)

Why, we may well ask ourselves, is so much prominence given to the sounds of leather on willow? It clearly denotes more than simply the passage of time, though it does register that in a striking way, and this particular aspect is memorably captured in Sean O'Mordha's documentary film about Joyce, *Is There One Who Understands Me?* (1982). Moreover, there's nothing ironic about its effect here, unlike say the Pok!, spelt without a 'c', that punctuates 'Ivy Day in the Committee Room'. In that story from *Dubliners*, as the stoppers on the Guinness bottles are released with heat from the fire, we infer this is a comment on the sterility of Irish politics after the fall of Parnell. But here Joyce seems to be implying that sounds are more than simply an accompaniment, that they actually register some profound moment of change, that the noises off, like the sound of the bow being released in Chekhov's *The Cherry Orchard* (1904), come to symbolise the break-up

Cricket at Clongowes Wood in 1924. The cricket fields had doubled in size since Joyce's days, old king cricket remaining – in spite of Easter 1916 – the preferred summer game for Ireland's future elite (with tennis a close second). From *The Clongownian*, June 1924. Courtesy of Clongowes Wood College.

of childhood or way of life and a point of no return. But it's done in such a way that we are reminded not so much of a boys' adventure story as of a mind at the beginning of a journey, in Joyce's case a journey that would take him to exile, outside the confines of the Church and out of reach of the solidarity afforded by a boys' boarding-school education. In switching from the symbol of physical sounds to the metaphor of water dropping into a fountain, Joyce conveys an impression of profound changes under way, but he also insists on something else. The fountain is brimming with water and therefore any water added will automatically spill over. Only so much time can fill up the state of childhood before the adult world encroaches; only so much injustice or history, in the case of Ireland, can be endured before a spilling over occurs.

Cricket and the Colonial Encounter

In some respects, the oddest thing about Joyce's choice of cricket in the opening chapter of *A Portrait* is that its Englishness is downplayed. Yet given the house system and the competition between the two houses of York and Lancaster, it might be thought that Joyce would continue with this theme of Englishness, especially when the issue of Irish identity is given so much prominence in the Christmas Dinner scene, for example, or in the description of the colours of Dante's brushes that the novel begins with, one for Parnell, leader of the Irish Parliamentary Party, and the other for Michael Davitt, leader of the Land League in the 1880s. But this is in keeping with Joyce's method of working, a method of suggestion and implication rather than of outline and thesis. As Pound once quipped about Joyce, he 'carefully avoids telling you a lot that you don't want to know'.[23] So everything counts; each drop that falls into the brimming bowl, especially if it is concerned with Englishness, should be collected.[24]

In a classic statement about cricket published in the year of the Great Exhibition in 1851, James Pycroft observed:

> The game of cricket, philosophically considered, is a standing panegyric on the English character: none but an orderly and sensible race of people would so amuse themselves. It calls into requisition all the cardinal virtues some moralist would say. As with the Grecian games of old, the player must be sober and temperate. Patience, fortitude, and self-denial, the various bumps of order, obedience, and good humour, are indispensable. For intellectual virtues we want judgment, decision, and the organ of concentrativeness – every faculty in the free use of all its limbs – and every idea in constant air and exercise. Poor, rickety, and stunted wits will never serve: the widest shoulders are of little use without a head upon them: the cricketer wants wits down to his fingers' ends. As to physical qualifications, we require not only the volatile spirits of the Irishman *Rampant*, nor the phlegmatic caution of the Scotchman *Couchant*, but we want the English combination of the two; though, with good generalship, cricket is a game for Britons generally: the three nations would mix not better in a regiment than an eleven; especially if the Hibernian were trained in London, and taught to enjoy something better than what has been termed his supreme felicity, 'Otium cum dig-*gin-taties*'.[25]

The passage is a good example of the kind of national stereotyping that was touched on in Chapter 2. According to Pycroft, the Irish are not *otium cum dignitatis*, do not, that is, enjoy their leisure with dignity, but do so by digging potatoes; it's an image of the feckless and idle Irish. As for cricket, this is 'essentially Anglo-Saxon', the word deriving from *cricce* or 'crooked stick' in Anglo-Saxon (actually, the word probably derives from French *criquet*, a diminutive of Old Flemish *Krick*, meaning 'stick', the game having arrived in England with the Normans). Pycroft compounds matters:

> Foreigners have rarely, very rarely imitated us. The English, settlers and residents everywhere play; but of no single cricket club have we ever heard dieted either with frogs, sour crout, or macaroni. But how remarkable that cricket is not naturalised in Ireland! The fact is very striking that it follows the course rather of ale than whiskey.[26]

The similarity between Pycroft's views and those of a near-contemporary, Matthew Arnold, on Irish character in *On the Study of Celtic Literature* (1867) is striking. The

English are characterised by Arnold as steady-going, and the Celts as quick but in need of patience, 'sentimental, – *always ready to react against the despotism of fact*'.[27] The English, God's chosen race, manage to combine the extremes, and hence their success. Pycroft's use of the word 'temperate' is telling. To claim the temperate region dates from the Renaissance and suggests how a much older ideology was put to work in the Victorian period, when the English became 'settlers and residents everywhere' round the globe. Everywhere the imperialists went, they played their game, not with an eye to converting the natives but to serve as a reminder of their village greens back home, 'a corner of a foreign field', to cite the Rupert Brooke-inspired title to Guha's Indian history of a British sport.[28] From today's perspective, knowing what we do about the end of Empire and the limited English success at the game in the modern period, such views seem faintly ridiculous, but they do serve as a reminder of the background against which Joyce's generation had to kick.

In 1917, the year after the publication of *A Portrait*, an Irish weekly, the *Irishman*, carried an article about cricket at Joyce's old school, Belvedere:

> When one looks over the photographs of football and cricket teams, one is immediately struck by the fact that when Irishmen copy the English they occupy the relative position of electroplate to solid silver. When Irishmen devote themselves to Irish pastimes, they are dignified. Traditions are broken down with difficulty and English games are hard to eradicate; but with the fine spirit that is now growing among Dublin boys in common with all the youth of Ireland, there is every reason to hope for the much desired national reform in our Irish Colleges. Belvedere has a great chance.[29]

Joyce's use of cricket constitutes an act of refusal and defiance; a refusal to toe the nationalist line and an act of defiance against the English imperialist who sought to wrap a flag around the game. As it transpired, it wasn't until the 1950s that Ireland enjoyed a soccer victory over England. As for cricket, this is still played at Belvedere, but the game in Ireland is awaiting a Babe Ruth, Christy Ring, or Roy of the Rovers to take off.[30]

Cricket in Ireland in the nineteenth century never became a national game and if 'An Encounter' is anything to go by, it was associated in the Dublin area with Protestantism. In that story, the boys are chased by some ragged girls who assume that, because Mahony wears the silver badge of a cricket club, they are swaddlers. In the 'Lotus Eaters' episode of *Ulysses*, cricket, along with other modern Homeric equivalents such as letters, Holy Communion, and cigarettes, should afford a break on the journey of life. Bloom (who in fact betrays only a limited knowledge of the game) enjoys the heavenly weather on Bloomsday but registers a qualification: 'If life was always like that. Cricket weather. Sit around under sunshades. Over after over. They can't play it here' (*U* 5.558–9). This seems a bit harsh. Engulfed by the advance of nationalism, cricket was perhaps too closely identified with the coloniser, an argument not lost on the Gaelic Athletic Association, which insisted on the Irish playing Irish sports such as hurling and Gaelic football. Equally, there weren't enough schools teaching the game and those that did were not the breeding ground when the struggle for independence entered its vital phase in 1916–23. In his use of cricket, Joyce reflects all these hesitations and hybrid attitudes. For Yeats, Ireland was a little room that created fanatic hearts, but for Joyce the impulse to assert the claims of difference in the colonial encounter, the demarcation dispute, between Britain and Ireland, needed tempering. You might want to kick it, kickakick, but cricket was like the language he used, the language of the oppressor but also the vehicle of self-expression, the weapon for writing back, and a key to an important source of aesthetic pleasure, a stick-in-the-block.

If Joyce had assigned a subtitle to the various sections of the first chapter of *A Portrait*, he might have called the last section 'Beyond a Boundary'. If he had done so, he would have anticipated an account of West Indian cricket with that title by the Marxist activist and intellectual, C. L. R. James. Beyond the boundary of school is the direction *A Portrait* is heading in at the end of the first chapter; the 'pick pack pock puck' is time passing but also future time, not just back but also forward. We can, in addition, discern in the pattern of sounds the 'starting points of a connected pattern', as James defines his own first stirrings of an independent spirit on the island of Trinidad in the period before 1914.[31] Puritanism and cricket were

Learie Constantine in the nets. From Constantine's *Cricket in the Sun* (1946).

James' inheritance, and both were associated in his mind with the England of 'Shakespeare and Milton, of Thackeray and Dickens, of Hobbs and Rhodes' (p.38).[32] What he picked up from his study of English literature was that the novel was 'an instrument of reform', the title of one of his assignments at school. The empire was writing back. At one stage in *Beyond a Boundary*, referring to the English habit of sweeping things under the carpet, James deploys Arnold's phrase 'sweetness and light' to expose English hypocrisy (p.116). More telling is when he writes: 'I haven't the slightest doubt that the clash of race, caste and class did not retard but stimulated West Indian cricket' (p.72).

The instinct of the oppressed was to score a century at Lord's or the Oval. In the figure of Learie Constantine (1902–71), West Indian cricket entered the world stage as an equal. According to James, echoing a phrase of T. S. Eliot about Yeats: 'He belongs to that distinguished company of men who, through cricket, influenced the history of their time' (p.105). And the company he's here referring to included Grace, Fry, Ranjitsinhji, Lord Hawke, Sir Pelham Warner and Donald Bradman. Constantine graced the inter-war years. His career in England began with the professional, working-class form of cricket, playing Lancashire League cricket for Nelson, a rung or two below the gentlemen versus players kind of cricket but not unlike the Southern origins of the game in the eighteenth century. The counter-experience paid off. When James joined him in Nelson in 1932, the Trinidad intellectual found his politics deepened by the simplicity of Constantine's

1945 Dominions side, with Captain Constantine the only black face among a sea of colonial whites.

manner and by his quietly expressed opinions – as when he remarked of his English hosts: 'They are no better than we'(p.116).

Cricket in the West Indies belongs to the movement for independence. It furnished one of the most powerful mediums for expression and was used to good effect, being a form of cultural politics, or politics by another means. It was, as James suggests, both within the oval and beyond a boundary. The first victory by the West Indies over England was at Lord's in 1950, with a side where the captain, assistant manager and scorer were all white. Thereafter, the rise of black players reflected the growing assertion of indigenous native peoples over the white coloniser. After Constantine, West Indian cricket never looked back, and until the 1990s the West Indians were always at or near the top of world cricket. The 1940s and 1950s produced the three Ws (Worrell, Weekes, and Walcott), and then came the era of Garfield Sobers, 'a symbol', according to Hilary Beckles, 'of what the independence movement was all about'.[33] Under Sobers' leadership in the 1960s, for the first time in their history, the West Indies dominated world cricket. Success continued into the next generation with Clive Lloyd and Vivian Richards, but after 1994 West Indies cricket entered a period of steep decline. In his two-volume history, *The Development of West Indies Cricket*, Beckles subtitles the first volume 'The Age of Nationalism', and the second 'The Age of Globalization'. The remarkably talented Brian Lara, the first batsman to hit more than four hundred runs in a single innings in a test match, represents the second, an era driven less by nationalism and the idea of village culture and more by 'a retreating "nation-building" nationalism'.[34] Globalisation, another word for crisis in the West Indies, has helped ensure that myths are divorced from reality and that the 'twenty-first century is going to be a brand new ball game' (p.108).

In one sense we are a long way from Joyce and Ireland, and yet from another angle the colours of the same club seem to be on display. *Beyond a Boundary*, published in 1963, is a postcolonial text that looks back on the transition from colonialism to independence. *A Portrait* is a colonial text that anticipates the overthrow of colonialism in Ireland. 'They are no better than we' is the anti-colonial or decolonising banner under which both texts march. 'Pick, pack, pock, puck' – hear the sounds of the language, the wonderful vocables, the IOU in three of the four English vowels, the plosives so dangerously close to the fricatives, but hear also the collapse of British rule in Ireland and don't neglect to notice in the soft grey air the lingering attachment to the pleasures, not all of which were innocent, once enjoyed by Joyce on the playing fields of late-Victorian Ireland.

Postscript: *The Crying Game*

Neil Jordan's film *The Crying Game* (1992) forms a natural backstop to this discussion of Joyce and cricket. Cricket constitutes part of the film's essential discourse and, as it did with Joyce, the game seems to have broadened the range of Jordan's sympathies. 'And that is cricket, hon,' the off-duty black English soldier Jody declares in triumph as, with his trusty right-throwing arm, he wins a teddy bear for Jude at the funfair. Born in Antigua, where 'cricket's the black man's game', as he informs Fergus, Jody emigrated with his family to Tottenham when he was two, only to discover that in England, cricket's 'a toffs' game'. Fergus, his captor, advances the claims of hurling, the fastest game in the world. Jody's attempt to establish a common ground, whether in sport or in shared feelings of exclusion, leads in turn to the midway observation: 'So when you come to shoot me, Paddy, remember you're getting rid of a shit-hot bowler.'

From Jody's pocket Fergus lifts out two snapshots; one is of Dil, his transvestite 'girlfriend', and the other is of Jody sporting a cricket jumper. It is this photo of Jody that comes to haunt Fergus as the film switches to London and his involvement with Dil. On entering her flat, Fergus sees the same photo, and after love-making he sees Jody running at him in whites, ready to bowl. So intrigued is Fergus by cricket that on a building site (which looks out onto a cricket pitch) where he is temporarily employed, he begins imitating the actions of a batsman and is caught by his boss:

Deveroux: So Pat's a cricket fan, is he?
Fergus: I'm not Pat. It's Jim.
Deveroux: Yes, well I don't actually give a fuck whether it's Jim, Pat or Mick so long as you remember you're not at Lords. All right?

As for Dil, cricket also plays a part in her identity. After her hair is cut by Fergus to turn her into a man, she begins wearing Jody's cricket jumper, a sign at once of her increasing desperation and of her gender confusion.

The Crying Game begins with a familiar IRA hostage situation, and creates the impression that its primary focus will be the colonial encounter and the education of the heart. That aspect is certainly there, especially in the contrast between Fergus and his uptight commander Peter and the cold-hearted operative, the blond/brunette Jude. When Fergus is tracked down after absconding to London, Peter turns round in the car to stub out a cigarette on his hand: 'I don't like getting fucking emotional.' It's a line that has some resonance in a film that is all about getting emotional, and, inevitably, Jude and Peter get left behind as the emotional centre of the film intensifies. After kisses come sighs, then goodbye, in the lyrics to 'The Crying Game', the song that the desperately lonely Dil sings at the Metro. Elsewhere we hear 'When a Man Loves a Woman', 'Live for Today', 'I Only Want to Be with You', 'The White Cliffs of Dover', and 'Stand by Your Man'. Here is the familiar Jordan terrain, the landscape of desire as part of a fallen world where emotions find their deepest expression and entanglement (and humour) in the hackneyed lyrics of well-known popular songs.

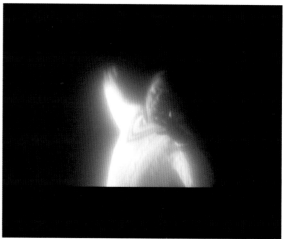

When he's making love to Dil, Fergus can't get the shit-hot bowler out of his head. Jody, played by Forest Whitaker, in Neil Jordan's film *The Crying Game.* Courtesy: Neil Jordan.

The opening shot is reminiscent of Malcolm Lowry's 'Mexican' novel *Under the Volcano* (1947), whose twenty-four-hour structure, stream of consciousness and reflections on the meaning of love, owe much to *Ulysses*. Under the railway viaduct across the water the moving camera is fixed on a funfair and a Ferris wheel revolving, and at once, amid the shouts of the North, we have an image of fortune both in life and love. The viaduct – the highway in Lowry – leads to destination, the funfair to destiny. Symbols partake of reality, reality activates a symbolic universe. The principle governing the triangular relationship between Fergus, Dil, and Jody also belongs to older forms of narrative: once the victim – in this case Fergus – has stepped onto the medieval wheel of fortune, the exit-point cannot be determined. In both Lowry's novel and Jordan's film, characters are living under a volcano that is both public and private. Like Geoffrey Firmin, the British Consul, Jody is in one sense the Englishman abroad, while Yvonne is the spurned lover defeated by Geoffrey's alcoholism, and Hugh, like Fergus, is the man of action in retreat, his thoughts haunted by the defeat of the Spanish Loyalists at the battle of the Ebro in 1938. As in the film, the novel explores the various permutations between the three, especially noticeable in Fergus' anxiety about usurping Jody's position in relation to Dil. Geoffrey is convinced that *no se puede vivir sin amar*; that it's impossible to live without love, precisely the strained tune that Dil also sings. In the public domain there is the threat of war or a simmering war, which will eventually catch up with all the characters; in private, relationships are subject to the same uncertainty and explosive potential. Little things also indicate the film's debt to this highly cinematic novel, not least the bar culture. Dil's favourite drink is Mexican margarita; tequila and mescal are the preferred drinks in *Under the Volcano*. El Farolito (The Lighthouse) is the name of the cantina that marks the end of the Consul's journey, at once a place of hope and the end of the road. In *The Crying Game*, The Metro offers solidarity for Dil and fond memories for Jody.

The only reference to cricket in *Under the Volcano* is when the drunken Geoffrey sees a cricket in a bathroom together with a scorpion, the insect that provides an important image in the film as part of the riddle involving the frog. 'It's not in your nature to let me go,' Jody tells Fergus, meaning the IRA. It's the scorpion's nature to kill. But as his hood is uncovered, Jody can see that kindness is in Fergus's nature. In prison, Fergus, under pressure to explain why he covered up for Dil, confesses enigmatically that it's in his nature. Nature, or, what amounts to the same thing here, kindness or fellow-feeling, is also central to *Under the Volcano*. In chapter 8, the first section of the novel to be written, Hugh instinctively responds to the plight of the dying *pelado*, the landless peasant, whom they see by the roadside on their way to the bull-fight. Geoffrey expresses caution, but by the end of the novel the *pelado* has become for the Consul *compañero* or 'comrade', a term of endearment and solidarity, the final point of connection with a humanity denied him through guilt, alcohol, and disappointment in love.

When approached by fascist thugs in El Farolito, the Consul, who is at first thought to be an *americano*, says his name is William Blackstone, the Englishman who in the 1630s went to live among the Indian tribes in the Narragansett region of Rhode Island to find relief from the encroachment of colonial civilisation. *The Crying Game* is also about identity, the struggle for identity, the struggle to escape identity, especially the identity carelessly or cruelly imposed by others, the struggle in the case of Fergus, as Patrick McGee puts it, towards 'the identity of nonidentity'.[35] The possibility of going native is not as fully developed as it is in Lowry's novel, but Dil crosses boundaries, as does Fergus, both by way of response to Dil's transvestism and also in his own withdrawal from republicanism. Names and naming are also important. Dil could be male or female, and Jody spelt Jodie is female. Fergus is also Jim or Jimmy, a necessary concealment; as a way of putting him down or goading him, he is also called Pat, Paddy, or Mick, and he is mistaken by Dil for a Scot. As with naming, so with identity. Jody, played by the American actor Forest Whitaker, is a black British soldier, who identifies not so much with Imperialism abroad as with North London and Antigua. Dil, who is called 'a wee black chick' by a jealous Jude, is a man dressed as a woman who, when teased by Fergus about her lack of female parts, replies 'Details, baby, details'. When her long, limp penis is finally revealed, the whole film comes into sharp relief as a film about identity. Black/white, blond/brunette, male/female, meat/penis, Ireland/England, cricket/hurling, scorpion/frog – race, gender, the colonial encounter, even riddles, are all here projected onto the big screen. In the cave of the Cyclops, Joyce undermines notions of fixed identity, but only in 'Circe', the night-town episode, when all the characters in the dream reappear, does he come close to what is being attempted here in *The Crying Game*.

With Joyce and C. L. R. James behind him, Jordan seized on a brilliant idea to enforce his point – the black cricketer. If Jody had been white, the discourse on cricket would have counted for little. An American reviewer, oblivious to all that cricket represents in the Caribbean, claims that Jody's 'love of cricket cannot conceal the history of racist oppression that he represents'.[36] But this is to ignore the complex seeing that Jordan is attempting in the film, for, as Elizabeth Butler Cullingford rightly concedes, cricket is 'the film's most complex visual metaphor'.[37] Interestingly, the badge Jody wears is his cricket jumper; we never see him in his uniform. On duty in the North, Jody is called 'nigger' to his face; he is the victim, in other words, of a different colonial encounter. That he is a member of the British Army also needs noticing, but this is Jordan's point: Jody is black, from Antigua, loves cricket, is a transvestite's boyfriend and has been sent to Northern Ireland as part of his duties. Each of these constituents represents one marker in his identity, and to execute him for one of these is to do injustice to the others. The temptation is to 'kickakick', but in essence the message of the film – which it has to be admitted is not particularly earth-shattering – seems to be this: identity belongs to several overlapping discourses and now – now in the early 1990s when the film was made and when there was a change of heart among republicans, but also now in the Yeatsian sense of 'now and in time to be' – is a time not for the hardening of prejudice but for the exploration of tolerance, hybridity, and the enjoyment of grace and difference.

PART THREE

CHANGING PERSPECTIVES

Chapter 7

IRELAND IN THE 1930S

Ourselves alone!
– Louis MacNeice, *Autumn Journal* (1938)

Anywhere. Out of Ireland . . . . There's no space here.
– Sean O'Faolain, *Come Back to Erin* (1940)

The whole psychology of civilisation went wrong on her.
– Kathleen Coyle, *A Flock of Birds* (1930)

De Valera's Ireland

In a letter to his English friend Olivia Shakespear in October 1922, Yeats wrote: 'Perhaps there is nothing so dangerous to a modern state, when politics takes the place of theology, as a bunch of martyrs. A bunch of martyrs (1916) were the bomb and we are living in the explosion.'[1] Move on ten years, de Valera is in power, the explosions have stopped, and Ireland is coming to terms with its revolutionary past and its new-found state. Suddenly, after years when the colonial encounter was the driving force in Irish life, old patterns of engagement and response were drained of much of their meaning, while the new patterns that emerged, such as, in the political arena, Cosgrave's pro-Treaty political party Cumann na nGaedheal (which later became Fine Gael) or de Valera's anti-Treaty Fianna Fáil (founded in 1926), would always retain something of their frozen Civil War character. Contradictions abounded. Ireland was a Free State but, given censorship, emigration and no divorce, it was uncertain what exactly the adjective was describing. The position of women, as the old campaigner Hanna Sheehy-Skeffington lamented, was 'much worse at all points' in 1936 than it was in 1916.[2] Economically, the symbol that captured the new independent Ireland was the hydro-electric scheme at Shannon, which opened in 1929. In the same year Sean Keating completed *Night's Candles Are Burnt Out*, an unnerving commemorative

Opposite page
Detail of *Dublin Opinion*, Christmas 1937 issue.

painting expressing at once the hopes and the fears of a generation. Candles were in fact superseded, but many families west of the Shannon remained without electricity until the 1950s and 1960s.

'To judge by the landscape alone,' the narrator observes in Patrick McGinley's uncharacteristically sober novel *The Lost Soldier's Song* (1994), 'the destruction was absurdly in excess of the scale of operations. It had been a war in which the combatants recognised no rules and no limits of self-degradation, because neither had any respect for the other.'[3] The Civil War put paid to de Valera's 'four glorious years' from 1917 to 1921, when Southern Ireland was united politically and militarily in engaging the British. In the early 1930s, on the outskirts of country towns, the burnt-out remains of RIC (Royal Irish Constabulary) barracks, accompanied by fading graffiti reading 'De Valera', was a common sight.[4] However, having opposed the Treaty in 1921, as a result of which Joyce's 'devil era' (*FW* 473:8) had been ushered in, de Valera came to power in the general election of 1932 and went on to establish Fianna Fáil as the major political party in twentieth-century Ireland. Terence de Vere White, who had been brought up among those who felt let down when the tricolour replaced the Union Jack in 1921, reluctantly conceded that 'it is de Valera and de Valera alone who overshadows the life of my generation.'[5]

The radio broadcast he made to the nation on St Patrick's Day 1943 provided an insight into de Valera's Gaelic League-inspired vision, even as it gifted excellent copy to his critics:

> That Ireland which we have dreamed of would be the home of a people who valued material wealth only as the basis of right living, of a people who were satisfied with frugal comfort and devoted their leisure to the things of the spirit – a land whose countryside would be bright with cosy homesteads, whose fields and villages would be joyous with the sounds of industry, with the romping of sturdy children, the contests of athletic youths and the laughter of comely maidens, whose firesides would be forums for the wisdom of serene old age. It would, in a word, be the home of a people living the life that God desires man should live.[6]

The ideal of an independent Ireland 'as self-contained and as self-supporting as possible'[7] was at once cultural, economic and religious, but in practice such an ideal could be achieved only at a cost – arguably to all three. Sean O'Faolain makes the telling observation about the backward look of Ireland's future, how de Valera 'has no time for the prospect unless it is implicit in the retrospect.'[8] As it happened, 'frugal comfort' met with some support from the small farmer, typified by the incident recalled by O'Faolain when an old woman went into a cross-roads shop to buy some canned food only to be told by the shopkeeper of a price increase on

De Valera as Prince Charming winning the hand of Miss Eire. *Dublin Opinion*, Christmas 1937 issue. Twenty years earlier in the *Dublin Evening Mail*, 6 May 1916, a columnist remarked, 'I had not heard of De Valera before though it seems to me that his name is something less than racy of the soil'.

account of de Valera. 'Now will you vote for him?' 'I'd vote for him,' replied the old woman, 'if I was to starve!'(p.172).

At the centre of de Valera's Ireland was a remote figure whose otherworldliness was both admirable and costly, both of this age in terms of its nationalistic perspective and of another age in terms of its detached monastic ideal. White refers to

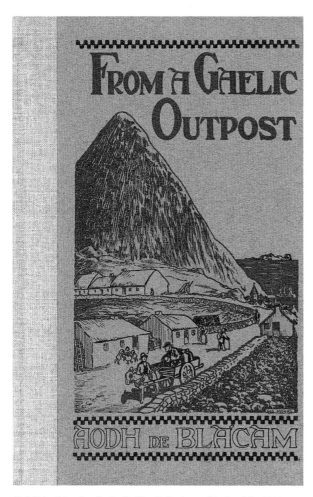

Published by the Catholic Truth Society of Ireland in 1921, the title of this book, with its ironic echoes of outpost of the empire, captures the turn inward in the culture. Even the terrible winters in the West are defended by the author as 'wild and blustrous, but not excessively hard'. The enchanting cover design, with its Paul Henry look, is by George Monks.

de Valera as a 'prelatic figure',[9] a description that also fits Sean O'Sullivan's portrait *An Taioseach, Eamon de Valera* (1943), which now hangs in Áras An Uachtaráin in Dublin. Although he enjoyed a Spanish surname and was saved from execution in 1916 on account of his American family connections, the County Limerick maths school-teacher insisted that the blood running through his veins contained not a drop of Jewish blood. Not that the blood was particularly Irish either; according to O'Faolain, 'A levee at the President's establishment . . . is as about as cheerful as a wake.'[10] But, ironically, the figure who did his utmost to disrupt the course of modern Irish history when he refused to sign the Treaty negotiated by Arthur Griffith with Lloyd George was the same individual who, when he came to power, provided in his person a sense of continuity and purpose.

A complex figure, de Valera's effect on the history of modern Ireland can be felt not only in the opposition he aroused but also in the support he received, in particular from the Church. It helped that his views chimed with thinking Catholics, who saw Catholic social theory in the 1930s gather momentum in part from the stimulus afforded by the Papal Encyclical *Quadragesimo Anno* (1931). Seeking to reorganise society along Christian lines through an emphasis on Vocationalism (the representation of vocational groupings), Catholic social theory argued that Ireland was a sound country, given to neither capitalism nor communism.[11] As with de Valera himself, such special pleading proved fatally attractive to its adherents, who fell under the illusion that Ireland – Pádraic Pearse's 'little world in herself'[12] – was morally (and therefore intellectually) superior to the rest of the world, a world which had sunk under the weight of materialism or 'one or other of the –isms or –ologies which are contending for the mastery of men's minds'.[13] In retrospect, we might well conclude that one of the legacies of the colonial encounter was the freedom to look in the cracked mirror and not see distortion.

There was, however, a certain rightness in the ascetic de Valera rather than the worldly Collins inheriting Pearse's mantle. In his poem 'State Funeral' (1978), Thomas McCarthy refers to Valera's 'austere grandeur' and 'taut sadness', qualities that chimed more readily with the sombre post-Civil War mood.[14] We might also note how, in the 1930s, the movement backwards worked to ensure that the Easter Rising and not the Civil War was given priority when discussing the struggle for independence, a struggle that was draped in increasingly religious colours. In the pages of Father Senan's *Capuchin Annual*, Church and State began to peer at the past through the same lens. According to Alfred Dennis in his 1934 memoir of Pearse, '1916 ended the scandal of the open separation between the revolutionaries and their Church, which had existed since 1867.'[15] And the author adds: 'The brown-robed Capuchins and the other priests who comforted the last hours of the doomed men were the first to bridge the gap.' The alignment of Church and State continued, thereafter, in every major celebration of Easter 1916, most notably in 1966 and more recently in October 2001, when the last of the Volunteers executed in Mountjoy Jail in 1921 (who included Kevin Barry) were given full State honours, including a funeral Mass in the Pro-cathedral in Dublin. Significantly, after the re-interment service, the Capuchins were among the first to process out of the Cathedral.

Censorship and fear of the world/word helped define de Valera's Ireland. The Censorship of Publications came into force in 1929, and by 1936 more than five hundred books had been banned.[16] This was the period when the three main areas of moral concern – cinemas, publications and dance halls – were brought under statutory control.[17] The impact of censorship was long-lasting. When Julia Carlson, on behalf of Article 19, the International Centre on Censorship, came to interview contemporary Irish writers in the late 1980s, she was not short of victims. They included Benedict Kiely for *In a Harbour Green* (1949), *Honey Seems Bitter* (1952) and *There Was An Ancient House* (1955); John Broderick for *The Pilgrimage* (1961); John McGahern for *The Dark* (1965); Edna O'Brien for nearly all her 1960s novels, including *The Country Girls* (1960) and *Girls in their Married Bliss* (1964); and Brian Moore, whose first four novels, including *The Lonely Passion of Judith Hearne* (1955) and *The Luck of Ginger Coffey* (1960), were banned.[18] When Donald S. Connery compiled his chapter on what he termed 'The Troubled Arts' in his survey *The Irish* (1968), he devoted thirteen of the twenty-eight pages to the issue of censorship.[19] As a footnote – and it clearly isn't – perhaps the most remarkable aspect of modern Irish writing is that it has been produced in a State which for half a century had a policy of trying to silence its writers.

The attack continued on the image front. Sermons were preached warning against 'immodesty in dress', especially at the seaside.[20] The Censorship of Films Act (1923) was extended in 1930 to take in talkies, and here, too, the damage was at once invisible and plain to be seen. In the first forty years of censorship, some three thousand films were banned and eight thousand films cut.[21] Titles to some films were doctored, as with *I Want A Divorce* (1940) with not only its title changed but also its genre when it emerged as *The Tragedy of Divorce*. But the cinema proved popular in Ireland and in 1934–5 there were over eighteen million admissions, eleven million of which were in Dublin. Moral outrage, however, with predictable appeals to decency, the soul, and 'the traditional culture of our race', was a constant accompaniment. The 1938 issue of the *Capuchin Annual* carried a lengthy article by Gabriel Fallon, a leading Abbey Theatre actor, on 'Celluloid Menace'.[22] In it he objected to the carpeted floor, the plush seats, the semi-darkness, and the '*penetrative* brightness of the illuminated screen':

> Observe our young men, and more particularly, our young women, cinema-goers all. Watch the fashion of their clothes alter to the whim of their favourite film star. Notice the Clark Gable moustaches, the *coiffures à la Garbo*. Remember the Valentino side-locks. One would need to be as familiar as they are with the wardrobe or toilet of their celluloid idols to recognise half of them. Nevertheless you will agree that there is a distinct, unmistakable Hollywood 'touch' about many of our young city cinema-goers. Not very much harm in all this, you say. But hero and heroine worship of this kind has its dangerous side. The step from copying your cinema favourite's screen apparel to copying your cinema favourite's screen attitude (or off-screen attitude) towards life is a short step and a particularly precipitous one.[23]

Behaviourism, the dominant paradigm in the social sciences in the 1930s, was the Church's particular target. As it happened, the fear of conditioning, which was made in the name of religion, stemmed in this case from something closer to home, and it could be argued by the more cynically minded that the condemnation arose from the Church's own secular interests in the market-place, where it was involved in running dance-halls and other money-making ventures.

In spite of the newly constructed Dublin Airport, which was a symbol of a new openness to the world, de Valera's Ireland was a no-go island. In effect, it said no to Hollywood, no to Irish writers, no to English goods, no to the border, no to divorce (deemed unconstitutional in 1937), and no to contraception; and if you had no work then your best recourse was to catch the boat for Holyhead. The people voted accordingly, went to dream at the cinema, read salacious stories in English tabloids, and emigrated in huge numbers. They also took to listening to the radio, especially with the establishment of a central transmission station in Athlone in 1933. In 1930, some 26,000 homes had a radio licence, and by 1939 this figure had grown to over 166,000. The strength of the signal frequently wavered but people persevered with their tuning and the wireless quickly became part of family life in 1930s rural

Designed by Desmond Fitzgerald and completed in 1940, Dublin airport gave Ireland a rare modern look. This Aer Lingus postcard carried information about the airline's European destinations (London, Liverpool, Manchester, Glasgow, Paris and Amsterdam), but no mention yet of transatlantic operations.

Ireland. It was 'company', the word often heard in the late 1960s, when television entered the life of rural Ireland, and it was at the same time a point of contact with the world outside. Here was a new Ireland in the making, one that had the potential to reconfigure itself, undermine parochialism, and shake attitudes.[24]

Brian Friel's 'memory' play, *Dancing at Lughnasa* (1990), is an accurate evocation of that period. According to Michael, the first memory he recalls is the wireless set purchased in the summer of 1936: '– well, a sort of set; and it obsessed us'.[25] The two dances in the play – traditional and modern – are occasioned and brought together by the wireless, the first when the sisters, hearing a ceili band playing 'The Mason's Apron', go wild with excitement. The stage directions indicate that the 'almost recognisable dance is made grotesque' and worked into a 'parodic reel', as if traditional Ireland was temporarily breaking out of itself by some collective primitive fit (pp.21–2). The second occasion is when the strains of Cole Porter's song 'Anything Goes' (1934) are heard in the background on the radio, and soon Gerry is singing the words and inviting Maggie to dance: 'Good authors, too, who once knew better words/Now only use four-letter words/Writing prose,/Anything goes.' This is Friel's 'ethnological' view of de Valera's Ireland, in its own way a riposte to the puritanical vision and a gesture towards diversity, hybridity, and pluralism, a rewriting of de Valera's vision of 'the laughter of comely maidens', now romping round the kitchen, seduced by the new American songs about fast cars and going nude, and desperate for a bit of fun, 'dancing as if the very heart of life and all its hopes might be found in those assuaging notes . . . and hypnotic movements' (p.71).

In terms of culture, isolation had its benefits. W. H. Auden's taunt against the 1930s – that it was 'a low dishonest decade' – could not in truth be applied to Ireland. In the face of a history gone wrong, Irish writers in the 1930s embarked on a struggle either to find their own strategy of independence, or to acquire, in the slightly menacing phrase of Desmond O'Grady, 'an exit visa'.[26] The note one finds everywhere in the 1930s is not dishonesty but disenchantment, perhaps best expressed by the most alienated figure in modern Irish writing, Francis Stuart:

> I walk through those streets [of Dublin] that I once fought to defend, feeling a little like a stranger. And it was this spirit of smugness and deadness that we fought against and were defeated by. The spirit of liberal democracy. We fought to stop Ireland falling into the hands of publicans and shop-keepers, and she has fallen into their hands.[27]

Frank O'Connor's *Guests of the Nation* (1931) captured the other side of this mood of disenchantment; it is a short story full of guilt about the War of Independence, where the sympathy lies not with the Irish guards but with the English hostages. Artists and art critics also voiced their concern. 'Art Does Not Get A Chance in Ireland!' was the title of an impassioned plea by Sean Keating that appeared in the *Irish People* in February 1936. Thomas Bodkin, the Director of the National Gallery, went further and raised in striking fashion the whole issue of the harp without the crown: 'Thirteen years have now passed since the establishment of the Irish Free State, and we can scarcely yet claim to have produced anything which proves us to possess an art of our own.'[28]

The picture assumes a slightly different complexion with writers and literature, where a reassessment of Irish history had been proceeding apace. While history in terms of the past or the future could no longer be relied upon as a means of deliverance, history as subject-matter called out for treatment. Novelists such as O'Connor, Sean O'Faolain, Liam O'Flaherty, Kate O'Brien and Kathleen Coyle all felt obliged, at some stage of their career, to make sense of the present by reference to the past. In an effort to get beyond the restrictions of the colonial encounter and to feel again the pulse that led to Independence, they turned to the workings of history among the people – even when that was critical. In Norah Hoult's *Coming From The Fair* (1937), a novel that, with *Holy Ireland* (1935), reconstructs the period from Parnell to 1916, the protagonist, Charlie O'Neill, is set thinking about a future independent Ireland when he collides with a little old man on the streets of Dublin:

Walking on, he thought, maybe an old Fenian with his brain turned. Turned from too much brooding on the wrongs of Kathleen ni Houlihan. This city was as full of madmen and madwomen as a bloody lunatic asylum. It would be a queer thing if the country ever got its freedom, if it got the republic that the cracked Sinn Feiners were shouting about. Could anyone imagine Ireland without its wrongs? Those that had burst their hearts out would be finished and done for: the others would walk through a bleak world, an Ireland swept and garnished, without shadows, speaking Irish Gaelic as if they were Welshmen. Tommy Langdale was right: where politics came in, good temper went out. And weren't they very well as they were? Was there another place in the bloody world where a man like himself who had spent the golden sovereigns when he had them wasn't left too long without a Christian turning up and asking if he'd a mouth on him?[29]

Brooding on the wrongs of Kathleen ni Houlihan continued long after Independence, as did the wrongs themselves, and there was to be no Ireland 'without shadows'. The phrase is apt: it is a way of linking not only a past vision of the future but also an evocation of that future as present. It was an impossible or an unearthly dream, the daylight too strong or too pure to be absorbed, the dark, we might notice, absent. Speaking Gaelic was fine, Charlie thinks to himself, but, without a social agenda, there would still be a place for the poor in a Sinn Féin republic.

A theme that acquired particular prominence with the decline of the colonial encounter was the self at odds with society, a theme that was almost invariably couched in political terms. Returning to Ireland after a sixteen-year absence, one-time republican activist Matt Costello in Kate O'Brien's fine novel *Pray for the Wanderer* (1938) sighs: 'Could he live in De Valera's Ireland, where the artistic conscience is ignored – merely because, artist or not, he loved that Ireland, its lovely face, its trailing voice, its ribaldry and dignified sense of the wide spaciousness of time?'[30] The outsider proved an especially attractive figure for those who were on the losing side in the Civil War.[31] 'Do you never feel you're alone at night in an empty house where nothing comes back to you but the sound of your own voice?'[32] This is Devane speaking in one of the blackest moments from Frank O'Connor's novel, *Dutch Interior* (1940). In the wake of the colonial encounter the new interior landscape was one marked by isolation and the absence of reciprocity or dialogue. The tendency or temptation was twofold. One was to temper criticism, as is the case with the level-headed, soft-centred O'Connor. The other was to collapse the analysis of society into a problem of and for the individual, as is the case in much of O'Flaherty's contemporary fiction – *Famine* (1937) and *Land* (1946), being historical novels, are not wholly representative in this regard.

O'Faolain is more successful in handling the relationship between the individual and society. In *A Nest of Simple Folk* (1934), a novel that focuses on the nineteenth-

century background leading up to 1916, he traces the life of Leo Foxe Donnel from County Limerick to Rathkeale to Cork City, from 'The Country 1854–88', to 'The Town 1888–98', and eventually to 'The City 1898–1916'. In his post-Parnellite novel *Bird Alone* (1936) there is a similar attempt to align the individual and society, character and destiny, the people and history. Thus the protagonist, Corney Crone, is referred to as 'Third Person' as if he had ceased to be an individual and become a part of grammar, but we never forget the determining social and historical frameworks even when he is poetically compared to 'a heron without a mate in an expanse of grass' (p.137). O'Faolain is both a cultural critic and a historical novelist, and in this sombre novel he tracks the source of 1930s conservative Ireland back to the 1880s and 1890s, when the Church allied itself with the emerging bourgeoisie in attacking Parnell and in creating the 'dead years'. Through the voice of Corney's Fenian grandfather he points out that the Phoenix – bourgeois entrepreneurship such as ship-building, house-building, and tanneries – never rose from the ashes of Home Rule. This in turn constitutes the context for personal tragedies. Corney's friend Christy is imprisoned in England for Fenian activities, and Corney himself, responsible for getting his girlfriend Elsie pregnant, is ostracised by his family after Elsie, torn between Corney's view of their passion as pure and her own sense of sin, commits suicide. It falls to the foreman of his family's building firm to offer Corney some bleak advice:

> 'But, listen to me, boy. If you're not going to turn to and put your back into this business – take my tip and clear out. Clear out of it altogether. This is a tight little city, and a tidy, small little place, where them that knows how to do it can make good money, and them that doesn't know how to do it might as well be trying to sell crucifixes in Jerusalem.'[33]

O'Faolain takes the foreman's advice and in his ambitious 'condition-of-Ireland' novel *Come Back to Erin* (1940) explores, through the lens of a turbulent County Cork family, changing attitudes to Ireland from an American perspective. The year is 1936, and the 'old crowd', that is, the Anglo-Irish, have gone.[34] Frankie Hannafey is on the run from the authorities after the murder of a general; his brother St John, who emigrated over thirty years previously, is hoping to return to Ireland with his wife Bee; Leonard, another brother, is a priest in Queens; his aunt Nell is dying; his mentally unstable mother jumped into a river twenty years previously; and Michael, his other brother, in spite of a drink problem, is trying to keep the family together. Frankie is the revolutionary, a one-time hunger-striker, now living on into a time when de Valera is in government and committed to dismantling the IRA. Michael thinks Frankie is getting in the way, a mere nuisance (p.135). In turn, Frankie dreams of seeing America, but St John seeks to disillusion him: 'No, baby brother, nobody gives a damn about anything or anybody but himself in New

Opposite page
Dev, at the seaside with his ministers, primly points to the border. Meanwhile Europe is about to go to war. *Dublin Opinion*, August 1939.

Sean O'Faolain as a grand old man of Irish letters in the 1960s. Photo by Evelyn Hofer.

York, nobody believes you if you say you're poor, nobody but thinks you're lazy, and nobody will do a thing to educate the poor immigrants who can only work with their biceps' (p.152). When it comes to Ireland, the position is reversed, for St John has no defence against nostalgia: 'My God, Frankie, to live here. To end my days here, in a cottage like that one, Mickey, down beyond the river, with a stack of turf against one gable to break the wind, and a donkey and butt all to myself.' This merely strengthens Frankie's resolve to get out: 'Anywhere. Out of Ireland . . .. There's no space here' (pp.139–40).

Come Back to Erin is divided into three sections – 'In Ireland', 'In New York', and 'Ireland' – providing a structure which helps to foreground and hold in place the opposition between the present and the past, between Ireland and America, between two ways of living and two sets of ideology. The phrase 'Out of Ireland' carries a triple inflection: emigration, running away, and rejection. But once out of Ireland, the self is confronted with new dilemmas, which shape themselves in part in communal terms: how do emigrants live? What gives meaning to their lives? How does Ireland appear to someone who has lived most of his life abroad? O'Faolain's sympathies can be felt at each point, for, like contemporary playwrights Tom Murphy and Jimmy Murphy, he understands not the over-sentimental view advanced by Yeats about the fanatic heart but the hard, isolating, truth about emigration: that the call to 'Come Back to Erin' rings for ever sentimentally in the emigrant's ears, but that if the emigrant were to return it would be to a different country.

Like George Moore's story 'Home Sickness' (1903), *Come Back to Erin* affords a study in disillusionment. Purged as it is, in the words of Elizabeth Bowen, of 'cynicism and sentiment', it scores over Moore in its incision, its sense of a contemporary target, and its realistic texture.[35] With an eye formerly trained on the colonial encounter and its accompanying sense of marginalisation, O'Faolain is one of the few Irish writers to convey the immigrant's sense of New York, of being *in* but not *of* America. By comparison, the New York passages in Kate O'Brien's historical novel *Without My Cloak* (1931) seem second-hand and poorly realised, as if the

Ireland, newly declared a Republic, featured on the December 1949 issue of this American travel magazine. The children were deliberately depicted by the artist John Cullen Murphy as never having been to Ireland, while the woman and child are 'Irish-Irish folk'. In the foreground is a High Cross, the exotic Other in place for the American tourist.

1870s atmosphere could be evoked by the accumulation of the known historical facts, conventional comment, and occasional prejudice (Grant's presidency, John D. Rockefeller, talk all of money, no literature, architecture a 'hideous joke', the image of America as a child, 'the days before it were great and terrible and long and dangerous').[36] O'Faolain is more convincing and gives us a portrait of New York that acknowledges its buzz as well as its superficial attraction. The June heat, men in shirt-sleeves sucking ice-cream cones in a park beyond Wall Street, girls dawdling in their lunch-hour 'so lightly clad, stockings rolled below the knee, or barelegged, in frocks of such light material, shantung, commercial silk, that their limbs were moulded clearly' (p.149). Cork, too, seems to pick up on this excitement and is evoked with the genuine thrill of a returned emigrant: 'The southern air was washed and the sunlight a glare . . . a Continental look . . . the general cut of its jib, the blare of the ruthless sun, the shawled women, the multitude of spires, the obstinate age, and the malt smell of the laneways' (pp.373–4). If for some Irish emigrants America represented an escape from the colonial encounter, for O'Faolain it was less free, being part of a familiar, rather than a new, world. He notices at one point, for example, the effect of the American Depression on Irish hotels with the dwindling of emigration. We wait a long time, but we know it's coming, and O'Faolain doesn't disappoint: 'All this exile business,' Frankie declares, 'is buncombe' (p.217), or 'bunkum' as it's spelt in the English edition.

In poetry, the most damning critique of de Valera's Ireland – damning in the Irish context is not the same as damaging – appears in Louis MacNeice's *Autumn Journal* (1938). Unlike de Valera, the Belfast-born son of a Church of Ireland rector was 'banned for ever from the candles of the Irish poor'.[37] But not being part of the Catholic majority on the island of Ireland gave MacNeice access to a different kind of insight, an aspect that is underplayed by Declan Kiberd in his chapter on the poet's isolation in *Irish Classics* (2000).[38] MacNeice's take on the colonial encounter led him to explore not the reassuring dark but the pervading hollowness of Irish life. In the famous section on Ireland in *Autumn Journal* (1938), Arthur Griffith's Sinn Féin clarion-call to his successor, 'Ourselves Alone', is quoted by MacNeice, followed by an exclamation mark indicating in this instance not support but contempt for the new harp without the crown:

> Ourselves alone! Let the round tower stand aloof
>   In a world of bursting mortar!
> Let the school-children fumble their sums in a half-dead language;
>   Let the censor be busy on the books . . . (p.133)

In that first line, MacNeice could be describing de Valera himself, who was both 'aloof' and 'alone', isolated in his pride. The section closes with some of MacNeice's most despairing lines:

> She is both a bore and a bitch;
> Better close the horizon,
>> Send her no more fantasy, no more longings which
> Are under a fatal tariff.
>> For common sense is the vogue
> And she gives her children neither sense nor money
>> Who slouch around the world with a gesture and a brogue
> And a faggot of useless memories.

If Yeats lived in the explosion, MacNeice chose to live outside it. But he was in another sense inside the culture, for his critique of de Valera's Ireland is articulated in the language and imagery of the everyday world. It is the poetry of prose, words put together with unusual force. He rhymes 'vogue' with 'brogue', 'bitch' with the empty word 'which' (which then sounds like witch), collocates 'tariff' and 'fatal', 'faggot' and 'useless memories'. 'Slouch' waits for 'gesture' to pounce. The Irish language is 'half-dead', stronger in its indictment than simply 'dead'. The voice is sharp, caustic, bitter, and the mood is decisive, as if there were no room for further argument. 'Let the censor be busy on the books' drives home its point without fuss. Meanwhile, outside Ireland 'a world' is bursting.

No other Irish writer in the 1930s is this forceful. Yeats relies on an alternative vision of reality or is constantly caught in the act of getting down from his stilts. Beckett remains unsure about the grounds of his loss. In the lead-up to *The Great Hunger*, Patrick Kavanagh is still learning how to bark. At the same time, however, there is an irony here. Unless it's 'common sense', the vantage-point from which Citizen MacNeice launches his attack remains largely hidden. Battles are waged against censorship, against forcing children to learn Irish, against isolationism and against sentimentalism, and the armoury is pierced. But, to inject a slightly critical note, MacNeice tends to persuade us only while the line is in motion, or only later, when consciously recalled. The shock waves of a larger vision are rarely felt, unless it is, as Thomas McCarthy has recently suggested in a poem entitled 'Louis MacNeice in America', 'hope without faith'.[39]

Claustrophobia drove the Irish out of Ireland and forced those who remained to become watchers of the world from afar. By 1950 there were reports in Irish magazines that television in the United States was ousting the cinema as the main form of entertainment, while 'Stay at home and watch the screen' was a growing trend in Britain.[40] For a country with an enormous appetite for visual stimulation, who went to 'films that glorified everything Ireland pretends to despise', as Honor Tracy noticed in 1953, this must have increased not only frustration but also the sense of being left behind.[41] At the same time emigrants or visitors such as Tracy who returned to Ireland also became time-travellers between the crown and the harp, and they were often accompanied with suitably breezy comments: 'Nothing was

The watchers and the watched. Irish Mods. 1960s Ireland grew impatient with the Land of Youth and increasingly looked abroad for its icons and images. Courtesy of Evelyn Hofer.

changed: how pleasant!' (p.28). In such ways Ireland became that space between inside and outside, squeezed between competing pressures and conflicting emotions, both timeless and, as the appearance of ice-cream parlours in O'Connell Street in the early 1950s confirmed, on the way to becoming Americanised. If you left you could get on; if you returned you could measure the distance and either rejoice you left or rejoice you returned. If you stayed you became by turns the watcher and the watched, caught between dreams of escape and the feeling of being confined in something akin to an institution. For the writer, however, there was a bonus – the exploration of *transition* or the comparative viewpoint.[42] In 'Return from England' (1955), Austin Clarke, ever critical of the narrowness of Irish life, wondered how could he have known 'That I would sleep in England/Still, lie awake at home?'[43] In the Addenda to Beckett's novel *Watt* (1953), there is a curious but revealing sentence: 'for all the good that frequent departures out of Ireland had done him, he might just as well have stayed there'.[44] This is almost certainly untrue in Beckett's case, but it does remind us of the compulsive checking on exchange rates among the Irish at home and abroad.

The Wild West Show

The eternal present or sameness offered a more direct route out of the colonial encounter. Sameness was in fact integral to, and a legacy of, the colonial encounter. When the colonial power ruled Ireland, it had sought sameness. That is what the Act of Union meant – same government, same legal system, same prison system, same currency, same red letter-boxes. After Independence, Ireland was the place where sameness could be enjoyed free from control by Westminster and free from the historical and economic forces then transforming Britain. All that was asked, as it were, was for Ireland to keep its rivers unpolluted and well-stocked. To insist on sameness, therefore, has always been an ideological move in the Irish context, whether the discussion is focused on market-forces, Swift's complaint against Irish coins being minted in Bristol, de Valera's Ireland, or the harp's complicity in its fate. With a little adjustment, sameness was a quality that could be turned into a commodity by the tourist board and into rich subject-matter by the anthropologist and film-maker alike. Another word for sameness in the 1930s is the West, for it was here that cultural difference could be felt most sharply.

In the nineteenth century it was still just possible to imagine the West as that region beyond 'the dark mutinous Shannon waves' as Joyce writes in 'The Dead'. In *Finnegans Wake* Joyce even imagined that '[T]he west shall shake the east awake' (*FW* 473:22–3). But with the transfer of land from landowner to tenant-farmer in the period between the 1880s and the early 1900s – precisely the period of the beginnings of the Revival – the West had been tamed and the land issue effectively divorced from the national question. Synge's brilliant moment passed without, in one sense, any shift in relations between centre and periphery, and it was left to a later commentator to offer a sobering if slightly harsh assessment of the subsequent history: 'The half century from the 1920s to the 1970s saw the disintegration of peasant society which was characteristic of the west. . . . The west today is like a sliced-up newsreel, the shots out of sequence, the images superimposed on each other.'[45] In retrospect, as Robert Ballagh rightly concedes, Keating's painting *Men of the West* (1915), with its three gunmen posing desultorily against an Irish tricolour, has more in common with the Wild West than with the West of Ireland.[46] For the individual, the effects could be devastating, if seldom voiced, but Máire Cruise O'Brien is one of the few writers to deploy the word 'schizophrenia' to characterise the gulf at this time between a home life in story-telling and Irish-speaking County Kerry on the one hand, and school in Dublin on the other.[47]

So the West was a site of contradiction, the place where nothing happens and the place where something happened. It comes as a shock to be reminded that the West wasn't always there, that it was effectively constructed between 1650 and 1840, when the limits of cultivation in the West rose from *c.*500 to *c.*900 feet, when the 'spade and the spud' conquered its contours and frontier.[48] When writers, artists and politicians engaged with the West, their minds were exercised not by history or deprivation or subsistence farming practices but more by the charmed lifestyle of the people. On the eve of the new free State, in a faith-based book ironically entitled *From a Gaelic Outpost* (1921), Aodh de Blacám mused 'The Gaeltacht is the living past.'[49] 'It is only in such places [as Achill Island] that one gets a glimpse of what Ireland may become again', Michael Collins had unnervingly observed in *The Path to Freedom* (1922).[50] Those who sought to depict the West in the 1930s tended to be either filmmakers, such as Robert Flaherty (*Man of*

The capturing of a living culture inevitably has something artificial or constrained about it. Seosamh Ó Dálaigh recording on an ediphone Cáit and Máire Ruiséal, Dún Chaoin, County Kerry 1942. Courtesy of the Department of Irish Folklore, University College Dublin.

Aran, 1934), ethnologists, such as Conrad Arensberg (*The Irish Countryman*, 1937), natural historians such as Robert Lloyd Praeger (*The Way That I Went*, 1937), or travel writers such as H. V. Morton (*In Search of Ireland*, 1930), Stephen Gwynn (*The Charm of Ireland*, 1934) or Michael Floyd (*The Face of Ireland*, 1937). Only occasionally, as in the fiction of Peadar O'Donnell, or in a painting such as Keating's tender *Slán Leat, a Athair* (Goodbye Father) (1935), do we hear – or rather overhear – the West speaking for itself.

Few betrayed the compromised nature of the pastoral vision.[51] Thus it was possible in the 1950s for an English outsider such as John Hinde not only to produce the famously garish postcards of Ireland, full of nostalgia, cottages, donkeys, bogs, and red-heads – 'symbols of a backward country' as the Irish Tourist Board, Bord Fáilte, had complained – but also to make the wonderfully outrageous claim that 'most landscapes in Ireland have no colour' and stand in need of 'colour corrections'.[52] On display in the 1930s is a collection of rural types (the countryman, man of Aran), or the embodiment of a search, a face, or charm, all of them aspects of a culture seen from outside, written often by outsiders for outsiders. Ironically, the real outsiders in rural Ireland were the itinerants, the travellers or 'tinkers' (a term of abuse still current today). But their story remained largely untold, and one of the few books in the 1930s to open a window onto their world was a dry academic enquiry into their language in a book which has the attractive title *The Secret Languages of Ireland* (1937).[53]

The appeal of the West was contrast. The painter Gerard Dillon, writing in 1951, was quite sure about his inspiration: 'Think of the West and the life lived there. Then think of my childhood and youth in the middle of industrial Belfast. Is not the West and the life there a great strange land of wonder to the visitor from the red brick city?'[54] Ulsterman Paul Henry was also attracted to the 'wild beauty of the landscape, of the colour and variety of the cloud formations, one of the especial glories of the West of Ireland'.[55] The interplay of light and objects which absorb and reflect light, of towering clouds and black mountains, of muted colours and white-washed gable ends, give to his paintings not only a distinctive look but also a pervading and attractive serenity, what Heaney calls 'the unspectacular excitement of his engagement with the subject'.[56] This is not the wide-angle panoramic left-to-right dramatic vision of the West, nor the 'dramatic death' that Jennifer Johnston speaks of in one of her novels about evenings in the West,[57] but the controlled upright shot where movement is captured and stilled at the same time.

Under the impetus partly of documentary realism and partly of an interest in a disappearing lifestyle, the West was given another make-over in the 1930s. The age of depicting traditional culture on the stage in Dublin was past – at least in the sense as understood by Yeats, Synge, and Lady Gregory. But there was still an appetite for doing something with that western alternative lifestyle, of recuperating its folds for posterity (as with the foundation of the Irish Folklore Commission in 1935), of memorialising its passing (as with the accounts by Peig Sayers, Muiris Ó Suilleabháin (Maurice O'Sullivan), and Tomás Ó Criomhthain (Thomas O'Crohan), the last generation of Blasket Islanders), or of using it to make a comment about modernity (as with Flaherty's documentary film, *Man of Aran*).[58]

Man of Aran (1934) is at the centre of several overlapping discourses, including visual anthropology, ethnology, documentary film-making, Grierson and the 1930s, the ethics of documentarists, and Robert Flaherty's career as a film-maker.[59] Surprisingly, analysis of the film's place in modern Irish culture has been less forthcoming, and the critical probing has tended to come from elsewhere. In the 1939 edition of the Irish Tourist Association guide to Ireland, the language used in praise of the film (sensational, epic, natives) betrays the kind of prejudice associated with an outside colonial power: 'Interest in the Aran Islands has recently been enormously stimulated by Mr Robert Flaherty's sensational picture – "Man of Aran". All the stories from this epic island story were "shot" on the islands, the actors being natives playing on Nature's own stage, with the Atlantic Ocean as a background.'[60] More properly, George Stoney's film *Man of Aran: How the Myth Was Made* (1978) questions the accuracy of the portrait of life on the Aran Isles and raises the ethical issue of the effect of the film on the islanders. According to Stoney, the film is 'the historic benchmark by which most older Islanders measure their existence'.[61] Islanders became 'island-conscious' and began wearing white woollen caps again.[62] As former film stars, neither 'Tiger' King, the father, nor Micilín Dillane, the boy, could continue living on Aran. There is also an issue with the storm scene, when islanders risked their lives putting out to sea to allow Flaherty to obtain some dramatic footage.[63] More recently, Tim Robinson has drawn attention to 'the politically ambiguous storms of *Man of Aran*' and to the reception the film received in Mussolini's Italy and Hitler's Germany.[64]

In the Irish context, Flaherty's *Man of Aran* belongs not so much with Wordsworthian Synge but with a body of work that includes most notably Darrell Figgis's novel *Children of Earth* (1918), where the forceful naturalism of Zola is joined to Hardy's sense of place. Synge's work lives in its language, a language which has a life seemingly of its own, not so much racy of the soil as racy without the soil, conscious of its beauty as well as its fascination for others. Only occasionally, as in Ben Barnes's Abbey Theatre 2004 production of *Playboy*, where the word 'lonesome' carries an unmistakeable Durkheimian resonance, is Synge given the interpretation his work can sustain and in fact deserves. In *Man of Aran* there is almost no dialogue and only occasionally do we hear snatches of conversation, as when Micilín asks the old man about the soil in the crevice: 'Much more down there, Pat?' To which the reply is: 'A couple of baskets more anyway.' The addition of 'anyway' is the one sparkle to delight the ear, the one unforced genuine word in the exchange. What also distinguishes Flaherty from Synge stems from his attitude

Man of Aran opened
on Broadway in
October 1934. When
the film opened in
Dublin in May 1934 it
was attended by de
Valera and members
of the Free State
Executive Council.

to the material, graphically displayed in the first stark caption thrown up onto the screen: 'The land upon which Man of Aran depends for his subsistence – potatoes – has not even soil!' The use of the exclamation mark is wholly foreign to Synge, the writer who, when leaving Inishmaan, movingly confessed: 'Am I not leaving [there] spiritual treasure unexplored whose presence is a great magnet to my soul? In this ocean alone is [there] not every symbol of the cosmos.'[65]

There is a narrative of sorts in *Man of Aran* – constructing a vegetable patch, catching fish by line or shark-fishing with harpoon, and surviving a storm in a currach – and a gesture towards characterisation, especially in the delightful movements of Micilín around his mother and in her facial expressions of concern towards her husband at sea. Frank Delaney has suggested that 'every picture told a story', but this is to confuse 'story' with 'drama': every picture is dramatic, but not every picture told a story.[66] Flaherty is prevented, as it were, by the exclamation mark, by the use of the word 'Man' in the title, from getting close to his material. The opening scene-setting chapter in *Children of Earth* resembles *Man of Aran* – the dramatic landscape with the Atlantic waves, the 'torn and tangled rocks', 'the howling wind', the headland, 'the grey ruining clouds', 'the waves pounding on the strand', the 'infinity of music in the roaring', 'the throbbing rhythms from the heart of Earth itself'.[67] In Figgis's novel, the power of climate and landscape everywhere confront the struggling poor. Figgis moves beyond the first chapter to produce, according to Ernie O'Malley, one of the best books about the West of Ireland.[68] Figgis shares a setting with Flaherty, but he has a story to tell, a story which, while

Opposite page
A tongue-in-cheek
comment on the
popularisation of the
West in the work of
the Blasket Island
writers. *Dublin
Opinion*, June 1933.

invoking the 'naked friendship of earth and sky', also shows individuals responding to disappointment in love and to the 'unseen tides' of history,

> of action and reaction of souls and conditions of souls, of psychological tension and interplay, of conflict of wills and intentions, of emotions and desires, fates and characters and determinations that met and contended ceaselessly, weaving a criss-cross pattern of life – unseen tides all of them, only to be discovered, yet to the attentive eye very clearly to be discovered, in the bodily erosions that they caused (pp.158, 167).

Figgis, who was imprisoned in England after the Easter Rising on account of his nationalist activities, possesses an attentive eye and with it comes an important discovery – that, away from the glare of the camera, people in the West are more than figures battling against a hostile environment and have passions that arise from relationships with each other, not with their environment. From within the culture the focus is on narrative; outside the culture it is on sameness, which is what the crown had also insisted on.

In many ways the most telling Irish critique of *Man of Aran* – aside from the remarkable work of the Blasket Island writers themselves – remains Denis Johnston's little-known satirical play, *Storm Song* (1935), which was first staged at the Gate Theatre in January 1934, four months before the film's release, with Hilton Edwards as the Hungarian-born cameraman Szilard, and Cyril Cusack in a cameo role as the Cockney Alf Quilt.[69] Szilard has come to the West to make a film for his studio boss Solberg about the 'struggle and real meaning' of island life, 'a memorial to your fathers and your fathers' fathers', but has been delayed from shooting a storm sequence by an anti-cyclone: 'Pah – call this the Atlantic! Bathwater – that's all it is.'[70] He has shot a huge amount of film and has been ordered to finish the project and return to London to edit it. But Szilard thinks moving pictures should be filmed as they happen and not falsified with a pair of scissors. Over the wireless the crew hear the weather forecast from London, promising a gale, and at 3 a.m. they begin shooting, photographing indoors the reflection in a large mirror of a gramophone resting on a stool.

'Don't you love the Atlantic? It's the only sea in the world. . . . People who live in towns never really understand that there is such a thing as weather, do they?' (p.105). Some of the dialogue is deliberately over the top, as if Johnston has Flaherty's film in mind. The final scene in the play takes place in the Majestic Cinema in London with a first-night showing of the film. This is a clever self-conscious touch by a playwright who delighted in mixed modes of presentation,[71] for even if such films as *Man of Aran* studiously avoid this kind of contamination, they are in fact made with the metropolitan box office in mind (the first screening of *Man of Aran* was in London in April 1934). If we hadn't already guessed it, we learn

that Szilard died that night at sea, his camera lashed to the mast of a hooker. Above the voices at the reception is heard, 'Such a pity he was drowned!' (p.127). And the play ends with the triumph of the studio over the filmmaker with the commissionaire calling out: 'Ladies and Gentlemen – Mr Absalom Solberg!'

The word that resonates through *Storm Song* is 'fake', precisely the word that Myles na Gopaleen (aka Brian Nolan) used in his blistering attack on the language of Synge in the column he wrote for the *Irish Times*: '[N]othing in the whole galaxy of fake is comparable with Synge . . . amusing clowns talking a sub-language of their own . . .. And now the curse has come upon us, because I have personally met in the streets of Ireland persons who are clearly out of Synge's plays.'[72] The issue of authenticity – the contrast with Lewis Grassic Gibbon's lyrical Scottish novel *Sunset Song* (1932) and the 'speak' of the Mearns is inviting in this regard – is

The endpapers of Myles na Gopaleen's *An Béial Bocht* (The Poor Mouth), first published by An Press Naisiunta in 1942, carried Séan O'Sullivan's satirical map of Ireland. The island is surrounded by An Doman Mór (The Big World), with foreigners and China to the north; Over There (Tar Lear) is America, and The Other Side (Odar Saigo) is Britain. It is an island dominated by Sligo Jail, given to poteen and cashing in money orders from Britain and the States, and where every point of the compass leads to the west. Orange people live in the north, while noble and gentle people occupy the grey sites of Blah Cliat (Dublin) and Cark (Cork).

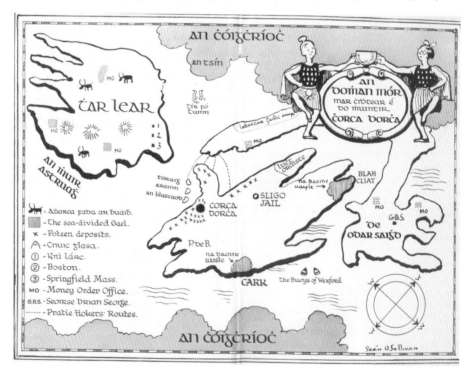

wrapped up in the colonial encounter. That encounter made the West economically extremely poor and, culturally, with the Revival, extremely attractive. It also heightened a concern with representation and cultural difference. After Independence, older attitudes continued as if the West was still a site for contention between the harp and the crown, but now it was fought over as if it belonged to the family (which was never in a sense the case with Revivalists such as Yeats and Synge). Myles na Gopaleen and his satire on The Plain People of Ireland notwithstanding, it has been almost impossible to draw a neat line between fake and authenticity when the West is under consideration, for that line is itself part of the problem. In this, the West both resembles and distinguishes itself from other characteristic 'rebound' effects identified in this book, such as the pleasure to be derived from an empty landscape, or Yeats's ambivalence with regard to English, or Joyce's 'kickakick'. The West is both Synge and McDonagh, both Keating's tender moment *Slán Leat, a Athair* (Goodbye Father) and a 'sliced-up newsreel', both Paul Henry and *Dublin Opinion*'s debunking cartoons about Henry. One of the legacies of the colonial encounter has been to produce a situation where it is at times uncertain whether the burden of an argument leads to a valuing or a devaluing of the West, so that today, even though it might still contain a residue of truth, to speak of the tragedy or the 'charm' of the West, especially in a period made ugly by the bungalow and the dormer window, can invite a blank response or raised eyebrows.

Recovering the Self

The language of authenticity in Ireland was the historical province of the Church, and it is for this reason above all others that an ongoing task for modern writers and dissidents alike, from George Tyrell and Forrest Reid to Austin Clarke and Edna O'Brien, has been to wrest the self from the Church.[73] In a parallel way, some writers in the 1930s undertook the task of extricating the self in the aftermath of the Civil War. Kathleen Coyle's technically ambitious female-centred novel *A Flock of Birds* (1930), the novel I focus on here, owes much to the emergence of the psychological novel in the 1920s, and it deserves to be better known since it furnishes a very different attempt to redefine identity in the wake of the colonial encounter, one that cannot be understood without a detailed attention to style and language.

Set in Ireland in 1918 during the Great War, *A Flock of Birds* focuses on how a mother copes with the period leading up to the execution of her son, who has been accused of a political murder he probably didn't commit. The novel begins with hats in a hat-shop, with a long opening paragraph in which Catherine, the mother, finds herself in thought moving away from her daughter, Kathleen, and from the way hats are tilted on the stands. Distinct echoes of Virginia Woolf's *Mrs Dalloway* and shopping in Bond Street can be heard, but then comes a note that anchors the story to a more violent history elsewhere:

> They became significant for Catherine of the whole meaning of life – headless. Headlong. She stood staring at them as if they mattered, as if they could stretch up on their steel necks and nod judgement to her soul. The judge had said: 'to be hanged by the neck until you are dead.' The hangman was waiting.[74]

The technique is to concentrate, not disperse, thought as is sometimes the case with Woolf or indeed with Matt Costello in *Pray for the Wanderer*, who looked to escape 'from the particular to the general'.[75] Because the focus is personal and the mind passive, the reader is forced to pay attention to both language and psychology – Coyle refuses the normal props of definite place and time, and neither the prison, nor the city, nor the circumstances of the killing are identified.[76] Catherine is trying desperately to absorb the fact that Christy, her son, is to be executed. The play on words with 'headless' followed by 'Headlong' as a one-word sentence ensures that her consciousness has a palpable presence from the outset as our guide to the events in the novel. Governing her consciousness is the twin emotion that carries the novel forward: a sense of inwardness and of detachment. She has recourse to none of the nationalist rhetoric then current, no reassuring image, either of a speech from the dock or of being part of the onward march of history. The pain constantly intrudes. What matters for Catherine is not the hats, and neither is it the cause for which her son is prepared to die. The hats come to signify 'the whole meaning of life', in that they are headless. The explanation or amplification is odd, the meaning of life here seen as the negation of life. Life without her son will become not just empty, a word she might have used, but headless. The idea continues in another unusual way through word association. 'Headlong' contains three possible meanings: one, that the path to execution is now set; two, that her son went headlong into his fate; and three, that his neck will indeed become long with hanging. Her thoughts are interspersed with the judge's sentence, a sentence which she feels to be a judgment on her own soul. And all the time the narrative is in suspense, the hangman is waiting.

A Flock of Birds – the title alludes to the way appearances can be deceptive, in that a black cloud in the sky can turn out to be a flock of birds – makes no squeals against nationalism or indeed against history. Joyce's phrase from *A Portrait of the Artist as a Young Man*, that Ireland is 'an old sow that eats her farrow', is alluded to on at least two occasions, more as a signpost than as part of a fully-fledged critique. Coyle sets her face against tragedy and at the same time she attempts to deconstruct the hierarchy of values that ranks sacrifice for the cause as supreme. She also avoids pitting the public against the private spheres, or history against the family. The most intense moment in the novel is Catherine's farewell meeting with Christy:

> She went down the carpeted stairs after the warder, across the prison yard to the corridor and staircase of stone that was already known to her. The clean sum-

mer sunlight lay in rays across the stone passages. All this, these walls, these stones, had been built by human hands. She was reminded of the stone of the Bastille in Paris which had been preserved and was now a Montsouris. Mice ran where thoughts had run in despair. Prisons were still there. The King is dead, long live the king. She kept her eyes down, on the warder's shiny heels and his narrow blue trousers-ends. She did not want to see Christy until he saw her nor surprise him – too much. It was when she came right up to his cell that she raised her eyes and looked. It was she who suffered the surprise. She was caught, but differently, as she had been caught by the picture of Mary. They had shaved him. They had shaved off his dark hair.

It pierced her with revelation, stabbed her as though she had come upon them weaving his shroud. Her throat was parched so that when he cried her name she would say nothing, only look at him as though, like Mary's son he lay on her knees . . .

Left: Kathleen Coyle's novel was first published by Jonathan Cape in 1930. Used by kind permission of The Random House Group Ltd.

Right: Katheen Coyle (1886–1952) as she appeared on the dustjacket for *To Hold Against Famine* (E. P. Dutton, 1942).

'I wasn't expecting you so early . . . Mother!'

She got her voice out: 'I came. I had to come before all the others.'

'Mother . . . don't mind . . .'

His eyes looked enormous and full of vision, reading her. She put her fingers against the grill, touching him: touching him with her consciousness beyond her finger-tips. 'Don't,' she pleaded quietly, 'tell me not to mind.' There was such a little time left. They must not waste it.

. . . He revealed himself: 'I used to talk about that, about religion to Cicely.'

A few weeks ago she would have had a sense of robbery. She would have been down on Cicely, suspicious.[77] She did not think of anything base now, he was accepting essentials. She gave him revelation for revelation. 'I think that, perhaps, we have been too reserved about religion. I was a child, Christy, at a time when the scientific mind was beginning to rise for a great flight. Anything that could be regarded as superstitious was scoffed at. Saints were on the same plane as wizards.'

'You believe in saints?'

'Yes, I do.'

There was another brief pause, out of which he said simply: 'I believe in God.'

. . . 'In the church this morning,' she said slowly, measuring her own meaning, 'I felt that we were not alone, that this, all this we are feeling now, has been felt, and suffered over and over. We belong . . . spiritually to a communion . . . the communion of saints, can you understand, Christy?'

He thought it out. 'I would call it God.' (pp.111–15)

The mother-and-son exit tableau, frequently, as here, overlaid with the Christian image of the pietà, is especially charged in the Irish context. But there is nothing sentimental in Coyle's treatment. By way of contrast with the world of feelings, Catherine notices the stone, an image that runs through the novel. Even while fastened on the warder's 'narrow blue trousers-ends', Catherine's thoughts carry her to the Bastille and to the mice which 'ran where thoughts had run in despair'. A lesser novelist would have made much of the comparison between the French Revolution and the coming Irish War of Independence, how from despair would come new hope, how the prisons would burst open and the Irish prisoners set free, and how the prisons themselves would eventually crumble and concede to the mice. But Coyle avoids such an obvious inference, as if the primary focus is on a rewriting of the conventional relationship between the individual-as-victim and society-as-determining, between, that is, in the Irish context, the harp and the crown.

The passage is rich in association, particularly word association. Christy's shaved head 'pierced her with revelation, stabbed her'. The use of the word 'stabbed' recalls the Latin motet *Stabat Mater*, where Mary the Mother stood at the foot of the Cross, 'stabbed' now replacing 'stood' for the piercing moment when the spear enters Christ's side. It is a moment of revelation. Again, Coyle refuses to play the propaganda novelist. In spite of his name, Christy is no saint, his mother tells him, no martyr, that is. The shaved head picks up on the image of the hats at the opening of the novel and on the 'clean' summer sunlight on the stones of the courtyard. But any reference to the croppy boys, to the United Irishmen in the 1790s who wore cropped heads as a mark of their republican identity, is passed over by Coyle. By contrast, religion has to be energised from within. The conventional notes are struck but their meaning needs to be felt on the pulse by the mother and son. 'I would call it God', Christy affirms, while offering thoughts is interpreted by his mother as prayer. Throughout, the attempt is to define a space that is meaningful for the participants. When the voice falters, emotion breaks through, breaking 'her completely out of every thought of her self, of her own feelings'.

The relationship in this passage between dialogue and narrative voice is expertly rendered, and all the time the words convey the novelist's attitude to her material: 'revelation' (precisely what her characters stumble upon in their use of language), 'consciousness beyond her finger-tips' (precisely what Coyle is attempting to articulate in this novel), 'measuring her own meaning' (a phrase that could with justice serve for all that this novel is seeking to define). Like Catherine, Coyle is given to waiting. She believes in patience, patience as a quality of observation, of heightening observation, understanding how a pause, as she puts it in an earlier novel, *The Widow's House* (1924), can become 'an evocation'.[78] Keep noticing the little things, the way words follow one another, often without necessarily being related to each other except by sound or look. The present is then capable of being redefined as 'more than present':

> The present became more than present, fraught, loaded, heavy as stone in the prison silence, the chained silence. Her patience became as chains to her, a weariness. The knowledge of men, young men like her son, shut up in solitariness with thoughts that ought not to be indulged in, because they could not avoid, under the special circumstances, over indulgence struck her as deliberate madness. The whole psychology of civilisation went wrong on her. It exaggerated everything and in this exaggeration men got killed. Battles, revolutions, war and peace and politics were means to the end of life, to death. She felt grey as the walls about her. (p.58)

In Kate O'Brien's *Pray for the Wanderer* (1938), Matt Costello is 'in flight from the present, in pursuit of a future'.[79] *A Flock of Birds* keeps rebounding on itself. We expect the phrase 'means to an end', but Coyle deliberately chooses to run it into the ground: war was a means to the end of life, to death that is. And it is young men shut up with their thoughts – thoughts which Catherine believes should not be indulged – who prompt her to conclude that the 'whole psychology of civilisation went wrong on her'. As in the earlier reference to 'the whole meaning of life', Catherine is given to exaggeration, precisely the word that appears in the next sentence. But Catherine is of the period when gestalt psychology was coming into vogue, when civilisation was thought to be in decline, and when putting the two together was a concern of thinkers from Reich to Freud. What makes her remark more arresting – apart from the application of the phrase 'exaggerated everything' to our post 9/11 world – is the conversational tone of 'went wrong on her', as if the novelist is anxious not to let Catherine sound pretentious.

Written even as the decade was getting under way, *A Flock of Birds* provides one of the most thoughtful critiques of 1930s Ireland. Not only is the sentence beginning 'The knowledge of men' not quite grammatical ('The knowledge of men . . . struck her as deliberate madness'), it is also ambiguous. The reader is unsure if it is men doing the knowing or if it is men who are the object of knowledge. Running through all the pages of the novel is the idea of knowledge as gender-based, how 'women had to think it all out for a very long time afterwards' (p.18). In the female protagonist Catherine, Coyle takes this further and presses the case for a centre independent of the public sphere of history and politics. But she does this without privileging the idea of family and home. Family love, she says at one point, was 'so profound that you had to hide it' (p.42). Under pressure there is no retreat into shopping or the home: heads become headless, the street a plain country. The novel also includes one of the few references to contraception in twentieth-century Irish fiction, and, again, it is filtered through a female consciousness: 'She had never been able to accept it and never would. There was something vulgar about it, like consciousness where no consciousness ought to be' (p.106).

The issue of gender is marked here. In magazines and journals from *Nationality* to *Our Irish Girls*, Irish women in the 1930s were frequently encouraged to play subordinate roles. 'The good maid and the good mistress each knows her place, and is careful not to overstep it.'[80] In a series of articles in *Nationality* entitled 'Mainly Feminine', women could learn about floor staining, cake making, uses for 'Chef' sauce, bridge without bickering, Irish chocolates, silk and satin raincoats, cycling and health, Irish piety, royalty and vice-royalty and the use of fresh fruit. In *Signpost: A Monthly Magazine for the Irish-Home-Circle*, girls could become model housekeepers if they observed how to clean saucepans, make coffee, and learn the uses of glycerine. The housekeeper held up for veneration was called Mary: 'She wrote no books, she painted no pictures, she thrilled no audience with her eloquence, she inaugurated no great reform. She spent her life in none of the brilliant spheres for which many of our girls sigh today. She simply lulled a little Babe on her breast.'[81] In ads, women were invited to support young men for the foreign missions, and in another section on 'Wonder' they were allowed to exercise a critical faculty with questions such as 'Does the Earth Ever Bump Into Anything?' 'Is There a Reason for Everything?' 'Why Does a Match Go Out When We Blow it?' and 'What Makes a Soap Bubble Rise and Fall?'[82] It is difficult to believe *A Flock of Birds* belongs to the same culture as such magazines, and yet in its depiction of Catherine (and Cicely, and Christy's sister Kathleen), Coyle is clearly making a point about women's independence and the need for self-reflection as both a weapon and a comfort. When Catherine notices a black cloud in the sky at the end of the novel, Christy's brother Valentine comforts her comfortless soul with the remark:

> 'It is going to rain.'
> A smile widened her mouth: and she gave him back madness:
> 'It is only a flock of birds.' (p.159)

In other novels, Coyle betrays a keen fascination with gender, place and identity outside Ireland. 'We have become like the earth we inhabit,' remarks the wise aunt Sonja at the end of Coyle's 'Viking' novel, *Liv* (1929). 'When we go south, into warmer lands, we lose something of ourselves.'[83] Liv, her niece, has to discover this for herself, travelling to the Paris of modern exiles before returning north to the mountains and fjords. The obverse – not the reverse, for the two are more closely allied – is on display in Coyle's 'East Anglian' novel *The Widow's House* (1924), where Annie Capgrave, the protagonist, notices how it is men who wander the earth 'seeking, seeking' but how women store up things in their hearts, adding: 'It would be a great mercy to her if she could fall back on her old passion for places'(p.60). Coyle's own passion for places, for here, not there, took her beyond the borders of her country and upbringing, and enlarged the territory of her sympathies and imagination. Annie herself is attracted to her lodger, Stephen Host, whose father was an archaeologist set on proving the Roman foundations to his village. With a map of Roman Britain in front of them, Stephen confides in her: 'They never really conquered us, you know, but we've got them in our blood' (p.59). In such moments we not only catch something of the Irish writer's concern with placing Britain, the imperial power that was itself once colonised, but also stumble on an important Coyle philosophical truth: 'And for the first time it occurred to her that history was just a name for the tidiness of the world' (p.61).

Coyle's English theme is continued in *The Skeleton* (1933), a novel set in Laverack, a village identified by the engagingly imprecise Coyle somewhere between Bishop's Stortford (in Essex) and Cheltenham (in Gloucestershire). After spending thirty years living in France, Mary Grace returns home, to be with her mother in her last years. The family skeleton, we learn, concerns the involvement of her brother in the murder of Thomas, her first husband, on the Alps, and the collusion between mother and daughter, who both know it was not an accident but share nothing of their secret until Mary Grace returns. Like *A Flock of Birds, The Skeleton*, too, is a novel about recuperation, how it 'was not the mistake that mattered, but how we dealt with it, and what it made of our characters'.[84] Thirty years previously, Mary Grace had run off with Thomas and later married him on discovering she was pregnant. On returning home, she rediscovers her affection for the English countryside: 'Nothing foreign had touched it. It had the sleepy contentment that has forgotten devastation. It knew the spade and plough and had forgotten the sword' (p.47). There is nothing indulgent about this even if it is close to a stereotype, for we read it as in part a description of Mary Grace herself and her own exiled state. That it is an outsider's view of English rural life can be accepted, and this constitutes something of its charm. However, the passage also signals an act of repossession, an attempt by the Derry novelist to redefine the relationship between the harp and the crown without the old animosity but never forgetting the skeleton within.

The French Husband (1932), a 'French-American' novel, opens with an echo of Eliot's *The Waste Land* (1922):

> The spring morning made Jane feel miserable. It was so full of all sorts of things, all sorts of desires. It made her feel that her young life was being wasted. . . . One never heard children's voices there as one heard them over at Sadie's when she stayed with the Princess.[85]

From a farming family in Vermont, American Jane is unhappily married to Lucien, 'the French husband' of the title, who's having an affair with a woman in Yugoslavia. For Jane, her sense of country is allied with her sense of countryside and she contrasts France unfavourably with her childhood in America, which was 'a wild garden to her, great wildernesses of lovely colours and surprises' (p.86). By contrast, Yugoslavia, with its wars and scars of combat, was a country with 'old forgotten memories' (p.86). The phrase is precise, not old memories but old forgotten memories, a phrase that seems singularly appropriate in the Balkan or Irish contexts, or indeed in the context of Jane's life. As with Mary Grace, Jane returns home to be with her dying parent, only to discover that the estate has been left to a neighbour. In this novel, memories are mixed with desire, stirred by association or contrast, and, in Jane's case, forced on her by her father's will, for, not being the beneficiary of a local habitation, it was then that she felt more American. As in her other novels, Coyle's twin themes are the recuperation of the self through suffering and the reshaping of the imperial world through consciousness. Jane is impressed by Sadie who, in journeying across Europe, 'had a habit of thanking God that the Romans had not discovered America' (p.86).

The theme of the recuperation of the self is continued by Coyle into the 1940s with her fascinating childhood autobiography, *The Magical Realm* (1943), as well as in *To Hold Against Famine* (1942), a sombre novel set in Paris during the Nazi occupation, which also deserves to be rescued from oblivion and neglect.[86] The fear in Paris under occupation that there would be a policy of systematic starvation provides the backdrop to the novel; hence the title, which implicitly asks what could sustain a person spiritually or emotionally against such a fate. As in *A Flock of Birds*, there is the same pattern of a mother and daughter awaiting news of, in this case, a missing son and brother and 'becoming stranger to each other' (p.16), and the same emphasis on men dying and women enduring, with men being 'more public than we are' (p.23). Characteristically, in keeping with a stress on internal states of mind and feeling, the rape of Marianne, the daughter, during a search of their flat by two Nazi officers is referred to only in passing, for the movement of the novel is in fact more public, namely to counter the view that the worst service to France at that critical time was to stay. Marianne has the opportunity of escaping across the Atlantic by marrying a neighbour who possesses an American passport, but she eventually declines flight and returns to Paris. 'Is there anything left that is private?' asks an exasperated Marianne at the beginning of this evocative novel, when 'all partings were menaced by eternity' (p.203), and in a sense, especially when parents and children were being torn asunder by the war, the conclusion we come to is that there is and there isn't. The one specific Irish reference is to the opening lines of 'The Second Coming', and we infer that Coyle, ever conscious of a missing generation, cites Yeats not only to deepen the sense of tragedy in the novel and to recall an earlier period of history which threatened to engulf both Ireland and Europe, but also to acknowledge that, while the centre cannot hold, the small flame of courage can.

The War Years and After

Criticism of de Valera's Ireland continued into the war years and beyond. His insistence on neutrality did not stop Irish writers, not least those already living abroad, from turning up in war-torn Europe.[87] Within ten days of the arrest of Joyce's Jewish secretary Paul Léon by the Nazis in Paris, Beckett joined the French Resistance.[88] In fleeing Vichy France in 1940, Joyce himself had difficulty persuading the Swiss immigration authorities that he was not Jewish. Denis Johnston became a BBC War Correspondent from 1942 until 1945, covering the North Africa campaign; later, he was among the first to reach Buchenwald Concentration Camp. Buchenwald unnerved Johnston and tore away the protective masks of the correspondent and dramatist, as an extract from his diary reveals: 'Oh, I have tried so long to fight against this conclusion, but now . . . all previous pronouncements become suspect too. Everything else falls into place and acquires a new meaning in the hideous light of Buchenwald.'[89] In the 1950s, Hubert Butler, in essays such as 'The Children of Drancy', sought to underline, as Zygmunt Baumann and others have done since, the connection between the civilised world and the camps.[90] But such falling into place was rare in a country sheltered from direct exposure to the Holocaust where, apparently, pro-German and pro-Nazi sentiments were common among the so-called 'West British'.[91]

Francis Stuart spent the war years in Berlin, seriously compromising himself with a series of German radio broadcasts favourable to the Nazis.[92] After the war, in two compelling guilt-laden novels, *The Pillar of Cloud* (1948) and *Redemption* (1949), 'Ireland's Haw-Haw', as he was described in *Picture Post* in April 1942, sought not forgiveness for the Prodigal Son but an acceptance of repugnance and an exploration of the line dividing goodness from evil. When Ezra, the protagonist of *Redemption*, returns from Germany to the 'duck-pond arguments' (p.36) of sleepy provincial Ireland after the war, he tells the local priest that 'life has been narrowed down and a wall built around it. But on the other side of the wall is the forest.'[93] Like D. H. Lawrence's protagonists, such as Birkin in Lawrence's *Women in Love* (1920), Stuart's protagonists are preachers with a message from beyond ordinary experience, but, as Dominic Malone admits in *The Pillar of Cloud*, a novel set in Berlin at the end of the war, 'it will take more than a prophet to save us'.[94]

An anti-bourgeois, rather than a socialist, Republican, for whom the hopes of a transformed tomorrow evaporated in the present, Stuart was animated, perhaps above all else, by officialdom and the kind of bureaucracy which he saw descend on Ireland after the Civil War and which he witnessed again in war-torn Europe in the form of an invisible violence. The evil-doers are always there but, as Dominic suggests, there is a double marvel: 'The marvel that such pure evil exists in the human heart, and the second marvel, which is actually a greater one, that there is such an unfathomable innocence in others' (p.218). Whether such insights absolve Stuart is for readers to decide. In 1996, Máire Cruise O'Brien launched a fierce attack on Stuart's election to the eminent position of Saoi (or sage) in Aosdána on account of his anti-Semitism.[95] This is not the place for a rerun of that dispute but let me just point to a very small detail that has impressed me. It is the word 'crucial', which is used in *The Pillar of Cloud* for perhaps the only time in modern literature in its original meaning of 'cross' (Latin 'crux', 'crucifix'). Under suspicion for visiting camps as a spy or agent, Dominic is being interrogated in a cellar by a Frenchman. In his defence he argues that he 'did not yet understand that the crucial events in Europe would take place where people suffered most in long-drawn-out despair – that is to say, especially in the prisons and prison-camps.' (p.45) The events in Europe were indeed 'crucial', 'crucial' meaning both 'central' and 'connected with the symbol of suffering'. In some respects, to my mind, it's enough: whatever nationalist or neutral Ireland has made of him since, Stuart is forever linked with the history of suffering, with the 'living symbol of the lurking violence' which Ezra, in a novel that constitutes an uneasy meditation on redemption, associates with the cross.[96]

Elsewhere, if less dramatically, Frank O'Connor, when asked by the BBC to record something at the time of the Blitz on St Stephen's Day 1940, was required to cross to London instead of relaying it from Dublin, since the Emergency Powers Act prevented anything from being broadcast in Ireland which openly favoured one side in the war. The result, 'An Irishman Looks at England', was a programme of encouragement for his English listeners, spoken with a directness fashioned in isolation: 'I know well that many of you are in great trouble . . . while here we have been having parties of mummers – "wren-boys", we call them – going about with blackened faces.'[97] Ewart Milne, who fought alongside Charles Donnelly in the Spanish Civil War, was more anguished, as if he couldn't put out of his mind the evil elsewhere in Europe. In 'Letter from Ireland' (1940), a poem addressed to people abroad, he provided perhaps the best defence against the charge of neutrality – the articulation of an inner unresolved turmoil and the acceptance that he 'cannot go beyond' his people. As he tramps the Wicklow hills amid a people 'always scratching nowhere', there are no war nerves, his country is quiet now, thinking about its lost state in the North: 'O yes it is calm here: calm as storm centre: here nothing crashes . . .'[98]

In the Protestant North, John Hewitt could hear the crashes but retained his characteristic calm. *No Rebel Word* (1948) – the title is suggestive – begins with the lines, 'I know the touch of things: the play of mind/upon the smooth and ragged surfaces.'[99] His native Antrim, the land of his Protestant colonial ancestors, is lovingly drawn, a place of refuge where one showery August day he 'walked clean out of Europe into peace' (p.22). Throughout this volume, distinct echoes of Edward Thomas before he enlisted in 1915 can be heard, as if a deeply felt way of life was again coming into contact with war in Europe. As Hewitt writes in 'Townland of Peace', 'Change is far away,/where a daft world gone shabby makes its war . . . from Poland to the Yangtse . . . but here's the age they've lost (pp.22–3). In his own province of Ulster, as Hewitt with his sure touch and fine conscience understood better than most of his contemporaries, there was another war brewing – the more familiar one between Catholic and Protestant. His own people, he confesses, occupy 'a fat country rich with bloom and fruit . . . bound to paved unerring roads and rooms/heavy with talk of politics and art' (p.11). But, even though he's 'as native in my thought as any here', Hewitt also seeks not some Aboriginal song line but 'a native mode' where he can become fluent in 'the graver English, lyric Irish tongue' (p.10). Such a thought in 'Not Alien Here' leads quite naturally to 'The Colony', a poem published in the *Bell* in 1953, and to the fate of his dispossessed fellow-Catholic Northerners, 'co-inhabitants' of a shared province who have all, Catholic and Protestant, been altered by labour, light and landscape.

In a novel of spying and intrigue such as *The Heat of the Day* (1949) and in more straightforward stories such as 'Mysterious Kôr' and 'The Demon Lover' (1945), Elizabeth Bowen – who was known to have provided information about Ireland to the British secret services – created some of the most vivid portraits of London in the war years. It is a city eerily like the great houses of the Anglo-Irish, exposed and vulnerable, where 'London looked like the moon's capital: shallow, cratered, extinct.'[100] When Mrs Drover returns to her shut-up house, vacated because of the bombing, she notices that in 'her once familiar street . . . an unfamiliar queerness has silted up; a cat wove itself in and out of the railings, but no human eye watched Mrs Drover's return' (p.82). For someone who had witnessed the destruction of the Big House in Ireland, such switching between the familiar and the unfamiliar – on the other side of the glass, seeing what's going on but unable to help it, as one of her characters puts it in 'Ivy Gripped the Steps' (p.146) – had become a force of habit, but it was an inheritance that gave the historian of her class a capacity not only to sympathise with those facing similar extremes but also not to lose sight of the world of love, the 'silted up' emotions, amid the craters. While Aidan Higgins's *Langrishe, Go Down* (1966) is a darkly probing, erotic Big House novel, where an Anglo-Irish family of spinsters plays host in the early 1930s to a German student who begins to disturb them with his opinions, in Bowen everything is muted and the burden of her argument is at once more diffuse and gripping.

Houses and places are evoked by Bowen as if they still retained the presence of their former owners. 'The particular secret of [a] place,' she writes in a later novel, *A World of Love* (1955), 'was that it was pre-inhabited.'[101] In September 1944, with 'the turn of the tide of war', when south coast towns, drained of vitality and soldiers after D Day and 'the Invasion victories', assumed 'a final air of defeat' (p.120), Gavin Doddington seeks out the vacation haunts and houses of his childhood in Southstone, which he hasn't seen since before the Great War. His aunt's still has ivy, 'the tomb-defying tenaciousness of memory' (p.150), feeding, as it were, on something inside the house, while the Admiral, who in 1912 had constantly warned against Germany, has had his house requisitioned by the military. Bowen is, like Coyle, a patient writer and she enforces her point at the end of the story, when Gavin's attempt to engage in conversation with an ATS woman who works there is met with an unconcerned 'I'd sooner live in a tomb', a moment made even more poignant when the woman notices how his 'features had been framed, long ago, for hope' (p.154). As with Lois in *The Last September* (1929), Gavin finds the tomb blocking his path to fulfilment, and he is left with no one to talk to, becoming part of what, in a later brilliant passage in *A World of Love*, Bowen would call 'another generation of the not-dead', the product, that is, of another world war, of 'unlived lives'.[102]

In post-war Ireland, writers continued their skirmishing against the claustrophobia in the culture. In little magazines such as the *Bell* (1940–54), *Envoy* (1949–51), and *Kavanagh's Weekly* (1952), renewed attempts were made to introduce a new sense of honesty into Irish life, but this was not a period for co-operative ventures. The photo that bests captures the literary scene at that time was taken on Sandymount Strand on Bloomsday 1954, the fiftieth anniversary of the date on

John Ryan, Anthony Cronin, Brian Nolan, Kavanagh (and a dentist named Tom Joyce). Bloomsday, 1954. Sandymount Strand.

which Joyce's *Ulysses* is set. It consists of John Ryan, editor of *Envoy* and author of *Remembering How We Stood* (1975), a valuable book of personal memories about this period, Anthony Cronin, the prolific writer and later biographer of Beckett, Brian Nolan, that generation's best satirist, Patrick Kavanagh (and a dentist named Tom Joyce). As a group portrait it fails miserably, with none of the participants showing much interest in anything but themselves as individuals. Their intention was to visit as many of the *Ulysses* sites as they could – starting at the Martello Tower in Sandycove, hiring broughams for the day and ending up in the centre of Dublin – and thus to pay homage to the writer who continued both to impress and to incite hostility. But what remains is largely a gesture, a working-through of conflicting emotions towards the penman who had himself mocked the pretensions of a previous would-be literary generation in the 'Scylla and Charybdis' episode when he observes, 'We are becoming important, it seems' (*U* 9:312–13).

Frustration is never far from the surface in these years, as if the conservative forces had become so entrenched that writers began to turn in on themselves.[103] 'A Bash in the Tunnel', an article that appeared in *Envoy* in April 1951, contains Nolan's unflattering portrait of Joyce, 'locked in the toilet of a locked [dining train] coach where he has no right to be, resentfully drinking somebody else's whiskey'.[104] Drinking became a feature of cultural life in Dublin, for this was the era of the literary pub when larger-than-life writers (and newspaper editors) held court. If the

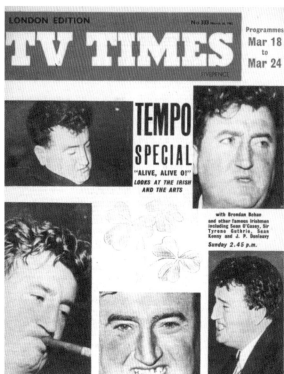

Left: 'Who the hell are you' was Kavanagh's abrupt greeting to a group of international scholars in Dublin for the first James Joyce Symposium in 1967. Here he is quietly supping in his snug in the Bailey. Courtesy of Evelyn Hofer.

Right: The many sides of Brendan Behan. In plays such as *The Hostage* (1958), produced at Theatre Royal, Stratford, East London by Joan Littlewood, Behan, through the force of his own personality, repeatedly broke through the British Establishment's 'cordon sanitaire' around Irish republicanism. In March 1962, ITV ran a programme on 'The Irish and the Arts', presented by Dominic Behan, which included interviews with Austin Clarke, O'Casey, Donleavy, O'Connor, Behan and Tyrone Guthrie.

age demanded anything it was to imbibe with Brendan Behan in McDaids, Kavanagh at the Bailey, or Bertie Smylie, the editor of the *Irish Times*, at the Palace and Pearl bars. Behan's talent, at its most controlled in *Borstal Boy* (1958), a memorable account of his imprisonment in England for IRA activities in 1939, found more lively expression in plays such as *The Quare Fellow* (1954) and *The Hostage* (1958), in which he could hit an audience with a mixture of deadly humour, sure-fire repartee, and songs you'd hear in a Dublin pub. Kavanagh, who was capable of producing highly lyrical verse such as 'On Raglan Road' (to the tune of 'The

Eamon Morrissey as The Brother, his one-man show based on the figure from Myles na Gopaleen's *Irish Times* column. Three Firs Hotel, Strabane, October 1985. Photo by Dan Harper.

Dawning of the Day'), could also descend in prose to pieces which were by turns angry, dyspeptic, and libellous. In *The Dalkey Archive* (1964) and *The Third Policeman* (1967), Flann O'Brien furnished his admirers with yet more examples of his ingenuity and humour. Meanwhile, Beckett, holed up in Paris, writing for posterity, was on his own with his fictional protagonist Malone – man alone – waiting to come into his own with *Waiting for Godot* (1954) and *Endgame* (1958).

Concluding Remarks

The image of the border dominates English culture in the 1930s, and it is frequently associated with the idea of Englishness. In Ireland, the border is politically sensitive but its check-points have been repeatedly ignored by writers. The border, then, never defined the limits of Irishness but in a perverse way, especially under the impact of emigration, extended them. Indeed, the 1930s was the decade when writers and filmmakers from the Irish Diaspora began to re-define and make inroads into the concept of Irishness.[105] John Ford's *The Informer* (1935) (based on O'Flaherty's 1925 novel of the same name), Spencer Tracy as the sympathetic Catholic priest Father Flanagan in *Boys Town* (1938), the films of James Cagney

" Darn it !   Paul Henry has been here already !"

Henry's images were soon everywhere. Cartoon in *Dublin Opinion.*

(often associated at the time with an Irish kind of lawlessness, a 'Mick' as the word appears in *Butterfield 8* (1934), John O'Hara's Irish-American novel about disintegration and New York café society), and, later, Maureen O'Hara as the red-headed Irish colleen in *The Quiet Man* (1952) all helped fix an image of Irishness for cinema audiences worldwide. This was the coming of age of the 'Hibernian Green on the Silver Screen'.[106] In addition, Irish-American and Irish-Australian writers and others began to establish themselves in the popular imagination with novels such as Henry Handel Richardson's Australian saga novel, *The Fortunes of Richard Mahony* (1930), Patrick Slater's Canadian novel, *The Yellow Briar* (1933), James T. Farrell's Chicago novel, *Studs Lonigan* (1935), Joseph F. Dinneen's *Ward Eight* (1936), the classic account of Tammany Hall politics in the 'Irish' city of Boston, and Miles Franklin's study of the Irish in the Australian outback in *All That Swagger* (1936). This is to say nothing of the most relentless exploration of Irishness or the dark written at this time, namely Eugene O'Neill's *Long Day's Journey into Night* (1956).[107] Here was a new way of conceiving Irishness, associated now not simply with place of origin but more with destination, orientation, images, cultural baggage, and psychological traces (and damage). When F. Scott Fitzgerald blames his Irishness for his intense self-consciousness, we know we are inside a different period of history where people not only consciously provide the contexts, whether ethnic or otherwise, to their own life-story but also begin to decide whether they want to inhabit such contexts.[108]

Inside the border, a new generation, born between 1896 and 1907, emerged without the showiness or the unity that marked the MacSpaunday (MacNeice, Spender, Auden, Cecil Day-Lewis) generation in Britain.[109] When all the responses are gathered together across the arts, it becomes clear that something significant happened both outside and inside Ireland in the 1930s. 'His writing is not *about* something; *it is that something itself.*'[110] Beckett's comment in 1929 on the language of the work in progress that became *Finnegans Wake* (1939) heralded this new change, as did Michael Scott's Shamrock Building at the New York World's Fair in 1939. Inspired by Le Corbusier, Scott's building projected not the weary-looking,

Celtic-inspired 'Eire' but a modern, independent 'Ireland'.[111] Although it lacked a certain urgency, the meaning of contemporary reality post-Independence was a preoccupation for those who came to maturity as writers, cultural thinkers, and artists at this time. Resistance to little Ireland or to bourgeois images of Ireland (Yeats, Stuart, Kernoff), a concern to position Ireland in the wider world (Micheal MacLiammoir, Milne, Thomas Bodkin, *Ireland To-Day* magazine), redefining the relationship between literature and the Church (Clarke, *The Capuchin Annual*), a continuing interest in formal experimentation (Joyce, Beckett, Flann O'Brien, Jellett, the furniture designer Eileen Gray), commitment to an alternative political reality (O'Casey, Charles Donnelly), rewriting the West of Ireland in social or materialist terms (Keating, Peadar O'Donnell), retrieving traditional culture (Maurice O'Sullivan, Peig Sayers, Irish Folklore Commission, Sam Henry), shaping personal visions (Blanaid Salkeld, Denis Devlin), a renewed interest in forms of social life outside of conventional politics (O'Connor, Kavanagh, McLaverty, Hewitt), attempts at understanding what went wrong in Irish history or at reconstructing the continuity of Irish life (O'Flaherty, Kate O'Brien, O'Faolain), reassessing the relationship between the private and the public spheres (Coyle, MacNeice), reconfiguring the power relationship between local, regional, and national (O'Faolain, Kate O'Brien) – all these concerns, as we have in part observed in this chapter, are indicative of a new direction whose impact is still being felt and waiting to be fully absorbed.

Dancing on the pier, Clogher Head, County Louth, 1935. Courtesy of the Department of Irish Folklore, University College Dublin.

DONMAR
WAREHOUSE

AT THOMAS NEAL'S

presents

ROUGH MAGIC
THEATRE COMPANY

AWARD WINNING
IRISH CLASSIC

PENTECOST
by
STEWART PARKER

Directed by
LYNNE PARKER
Set & Costumes by
BLAITHIN SHEERIN
Lighting by
STEPHEN McMANUS

Cast:
BRIAN DOHERTY
MICHELE FORBES
PAUL HICKEY
ELEANOR METHVEN
MORNA REGAN

PENTECOST

Chapter 8

Ireland in the 1980s

We're the only people on the face of the earth who want
the undivided truth.
– Kathleen Coyle, *Youth in the Saddle* (1927)

The body turns in, restless, on itself.
– Medbh McGuckian, 'Drawing Ballerinas' (2001)

Don't you fucking move. I'm warning you.
– Dinky in *Hush-a-Bye Baby* (1989)

The Same Renew

The 1930s and the 1980s are excellent gathering-points midway between the two halves of the century for providing contrasting portraits of Irish culture in the light of the colonial encounter. The emphasis in this chapter is on the North where the colonial encounter – nowhere more visible than on the RUC badge with the crown positioned above the harp – still produced considerable tension in the 1980s, but I want to begin in the South. 'That is no country for old men' – so opens Yeats's 1920s volume *The Tower* (1928), where the first word to be stressed is the first, in a line that contains a half-serious reply to all the young men then running the new Ireland. Five decades later, the young men have grown old, and Julia O'Faolain adds her own footnote to this history in a novel with the pointed title *No Country for Young Men* (1980).

At one stage in the novel, the seventy-five-year-old Judith, who has spent her life as a nun, confronts her brother-in-law, Owen O'Malley, a one-time IRA man and now successful politician, about the past:

> 'It's funny,' she said. 'When the fighting was on, even during the Civil War, we felt the future was ours. If the past was as bad as ours was, then we had to own

Opposite page
Detail of a poster for
Stewart Parker's
Pentecost (1987).

the future. It was our due, inevitable, do you remember, Owen? Ours!' She let her eyes shine out at him with irony. Judith was twenty-eight that year. She had recovered from years of almost catatonic silence. '*You got your future!*' She faced him down, emphasizing her point.

'I never wanted anything for myself.'

'Power?'

He made his impatient gesture.

'You're naive,' he said. 'We have no power. The economy is in an appalling state. We entered the Dáil in a spirit of sacrifice, to see what help we could provide. We've been called every name: "pitiless idealists", "turn-coats". . .'

'Well, you did turn your coats!'

'We couldn't leave the country to rot. We had to be practical, get our hands on the helm and steer it out of the doldrums.'

'How I hate politics!'

'You can afford to. That's your luxury.'[1]

In such altercations, direct echoes of O'Faolain's father's novel, *Come Back to Erin*, can be heard. Indeed, in terms of character, theme and discourse, the two novels afford striking similarities, particularly in the sifting and weighing up of the new State's achievements and in a distinctively Irish form of exasperation. The focus is the early 1920s, but the past is now the future, and the one question that at root matters to both novelists, a generation apart, is revolutionary idealism – not to be confused in the Irish context with revolutionary consciousness – the 'old bogy' (p.208) ever poised to reduce Ireland to the chaos that always threatened it in the 1930s.

After a period of passionate politics, the injunction or question bequeathed to a subsequent generation is not Jameson's 'always historicise' but 'Follow that!' or, more worryingly, 'How do you follow that?' And immediately, as if to complicate the response, Julia O'Faolain adds: 'How *did* you honour a grandfather who, having helped forge change through violence, ended his days guarding the outcome from any further change?' (p.44). In exploring the tensions in the family and their differing attitudes to the Civil War, the novel zeroes in on the part Judith played in the murder of the American fund-raiser Sparky Driscoll (whose disillusionment threatened future arms shipments and whose final words to Judith as she lunges at him with a knife are 'forget heroism'). In returning to the formation of the Irish State in the early 1920s, O'Faolain signals her intended message: that contemporary Ireland is still best understood by recourse to history and the colonial encounter. In updating her analysis she adds Freud and the return of the repressed, for, as Owen, a character not dissimilar to de Valera, remarks: 'In history, as in matter, nothing . . . is lost. It comes back in another form' (p.164).[2]

The focus of *No Country for Young Men* is the Republic. The context, however, is in part the North, so it would be difficult not to read into the 'old bogy' an allusion to the revival of republicanism and to its destabilising effects on the Republic. What O'Faolain's novel underlines is how the colonial encounter not only made it impossible to draw a line under history – to find freedom away from Jameson's injunction – but also had the potential to collapse different periods and different age-groups into each other. Thus, while old men, former revolutionaries, in the South were running the country, in the North young men were again taking up arms. This is a different view from the 'same renew' (*FW* 226:17), one of Joyce's most enigmatic ways of referring to the course of history, where, depending on what is emphasised, the stress falls either on sameness, or on repetition, or on newness, or on all three together. But what they both share, a role assigned them by the colonial encounter, is an attention to history as pattern, not history as design. The Joyce country was in some respects recognisably the same as in the 1920s and 1930s and given to repetition, closer, therefore, to farce than to tragedy. The 'devil era' was over, but politics in the South was still overshadowed by two political parties that had their origins in the Civil War, and the warring brothers Shem and Shaun, Catholic and Protestant, Nationalist and Unionist, Republican and Loyalist, were still on guard in the North. As for the sisters, they too experience, according to the ever-deflating Joyce, 'arch trouble' (*FW* 459:16), only now the immediate reference is not to politics but to breaking in new shoes.

O'Faolain strikes a cautionary note, but, in truth, as is particularly evident, for example, in the nine volumes of *The Crane Bag* (1977–85), Ireland in the 1980s, especially in the Republic, was in the process of putting space between itself and the past, and undergoing, if not renewal, then some kind of adjustment. The phrase used by two of those interviewed by Rosita Sweetman in *On Our Backs* (1979) is 'loosening up'.[3] Alen MacWeeney's photograph on the front cover of *Ireland: A Week in the Life of the Nation* (1986) shows two frilly turquoise dresses, worn by bridesmaids, hanging up to dry on two red and pink plastic hangers against a dry stone wall with a blurred view of Galway Bay in the background. The same shot is reproduced inside, with a companion photo of the old woman of the house with broom in hand standing in front of the whitewashed walls of her cottage on Inishmaan, the Aran Island where Synge stayed at the turn of the twentieth century. In the 1930s, the old woman would have been on the front cover, as was the case with *Picture Post* in July 1940, which carried an old man and child with rosary beads under the caption 'The Faith of Eire',[4] but in the 1980s it is a less flattering photo that occupies centre stage.[5] The new Ireland was declaring its hand: the wedding is over, no more sentimental views of poverty, no more illusions, tell it as it is.

Stagnation and how to energise the Irish economy and motivate the workforce was the theme running through *Ireland in the Year 2000* (1983), a Dublin-based conference that brought together demographers, social scientists, government planners and historians.[6] But in terms of literature and the arts, Ireland enjoyed a genuine renaissance, and this was true on both sides of the border. Perhaps the most spectacular 'event', both at the time and in retrospect, was Field Day. Founded in 1980, with the intention of making Derry and the North a vital centre for theatre and the arts, Field Day brought together, in a loose federation, leading figures whose work has continued to resonate both in Ireland and abroad: the playwright Brian Friel, the actor Stephen Rea, the writer and critic Seamus Deane, Seamus Heaney, whose *Field Work* (1979) had just been published, the poet and critic Tom Paulin, and the traditional singer, David Hammond. Also in the North, though less well-known, there appeared in 1981 the first issue of *Circa*, perhaps the liveliest arts magazine produced in Ireland in the twentieth century.[7]

In London in February–March 1980, as if confirming that something new was on the horizon, a festival with the umbrella title 'A Sense of Ireland' was staged to commemorate both the 'startling upsurge of creative activity in all areas of the arts' as well as the transformation then occurring in both parts of Ireland.[8] Here was the harp announcing itself again to the crown, a 'sense' being a gesture towards something unknown as well as a response to those in Britain who couldn't indeed make any sense of Ireland. Plays produced during the festival included Hugh Leonard's *A Life*, James Plunkett's *The Risen People*, and Peter Sheridan's *The Liberty Suit*. The visual arts were especially well-represented, with exhibition space devoted to conceptual art installations by Nigel Rolfe, Alanna O'Kelly, and Joan Aiken; modern Irish painting, print and sculpture by Patrick Scott, Patrick Collins, Barrie Cooke, and Robert Ballagh; photographic work by Tony Murray and Bill Kirk; and craft exhibitions, including weaving, patchwork, and Irish pipes.

The showcase for writers was similarly impressive, with readings by all the major poets, playwrights and fiction writers, including Liam O'Flaherty, Denis Johnston, Francis Stuart, John Montague, Richard Murphy and William Trevor. New writers, such as Neil Jordan, Aidan Mathews, Paul Muldoon, the Irish language poet Cathal Ó Searcaigh, and the highly talented Northern playwright Stewart Parker, also featured. Classics of 'Irish' film such as *Man of Aran, The Informer*, and Joseph Strick's *Ulysses* – grouped under 'outsider's view', an overly protective term and period marker – were also shown, as was the work of new filmmakers such as Cathal Black and Thaddeus O'Sullivan. There was excitement too – justified in the light of the films made over the next two decades – about the fact that the Irish Government was prepared to invest four million pounds in the development of an Irish film industry. The festival also included traditional music from The Chieftains, Tony McMahon, and Dolores Keane, contemporary Irish jazz performed by the Louis Stewart Quartet, as well as concerts by the RTÉ Symphony Orchestra and recitals by Bernadette Greevy and others. Not everything, however, contributed to the celebration of Ireland. As if the terms of the debate still owed something to the colonial encounter, the brochure announced a series of the seminars on the 'major issues affecting Ireland today', one of which was on 'The Future of the European Periphery'.

What is surprising is how little is made of cultural developments in histories of the time. In the ITV series *The Troubles*, broadcast in 1980–1, or in Robert Kee's BBC/RTÉ survey, *Ireland: A History* (1980), there is virtually no reference to writers.[9] Yet in many respects, the culture tells us far more than histories can about what was happening and what was stirring. South of the border – but the point still holds – in the appropriately named *Invisible Cities* (1988), Dermot Bolger, with the anonymity of Northside working-class Finglas in mind, complained that 'real news always happened off screen, ignored by most of the media who would not finally catch up until years later'.[10] In *Images of Belfast* (1981), Robert Johnstone not only decidedly answers the FAQ on the dust-jacket 'Is there life in Belfast?', but, more importantly, makes the necessary correction that 'our "men of violence" are as mysterious to me . . . as to any foreigner'.[11] 'Violence is terrible,' says Hark in the play-within-the-play in McGuinness's Brechtian *Carthaginians* (1988), 'but it pays well'.[12] These kinds of insight are missing from histories which assume there is nothing of recordable note between the violence of the streets and the corridors of power. As Henry Glassie, the American ethnographer and author of *Passing the Time in Ballymenone* (1982), wittily observed about his own practice and the object of his study: 'I was in Northern Ireland to create an ethnography that would avoid common error by facing the commonplace.'[13]

In the long run, what is happening in the culture – both when it belongs to a counter-culture or even when writers ignore the political – can offer forms of hope

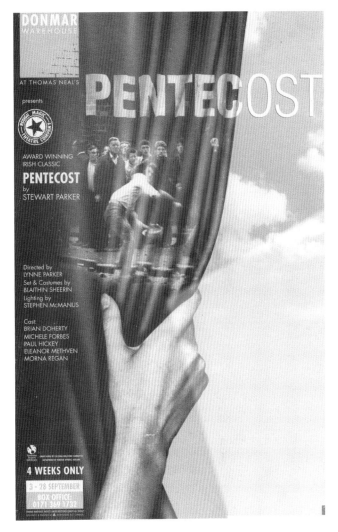

A poster for Stewart Parker's *Pentecost* (1987), a powerful play set in Belfast during the Loyalist Association of Workers strike in 1974. The play itself is bleaker than this 1996 poster suggests. There's little blue sky to be seen, and if anyone speaks in tongues it is not the stone-throwing loyalists but the characters on either side of the sectarian divide lamenting the sacrilege against life in 'this wee province of ours'. Parker's early death robbed the Troubles of their most eloquent tragedian.

in reshaping the future. Thus, no one coming away from seeing a performance of Brian Friel's *Faith Healer* (1980) or *Translations* (1980), or indeed from reading Seamus Deane's *Reading in the Dark* (1996), a novel that to my mind belongs to this dark period, or John Montague's *The Dead Kingdom* (1984), a collection of verse steeped in the 'the flowering absence' of the 1930s and in a 'forgotten/Northern landscape' where place names 'sigh/like a pressed melodeon', could think the contemporary is confined to what they read in newspaper head-lines.[14] Seasons change, lambs step out 'from last year as from an enclosure' but, as Michael Longley notices in his arresting poem 'Gorse Fires' (1991), while the fires are smoking, 'primroses burn/And celandines and white may and gorse flowers'.[15] Even the unpromising subject of an abstemious and saintly life, as in Thomas Kilroy's *Talbot's Box* (1979), can reveal a sharp insight into contemporary attitudes towards the body, as when the reformed alcoholic Matt Talbot exclaims at one point in the play in Dublin twang: 'Dear Gawd! I bind meself wid the bonds of this earth that I may know the weight o' the flesh; and learn to free meself from its bur-den.'[16] Culture always threatens to fill up the space left by the real, to intervene in our experience of the world, sometimes to confirm what we already knew, and sometimes to challenge or alter the known. Culture is never therefore a parallel universe or, as Brendan Murphy's remarkable collection of photographs in *Eyewitness* (2003) reminds us, a mirror-image of external reality, but is always involved in some kind of negotiation, intervention, confrontation, or encounter.[17]

Bodily Secrets

In 1966, Gay Byrne asked one of his guests on *The Late Late Show* to recall the colour of the nightie she was wearing on the night of her honeymoon. The ques-tion was seized on by outraged bishops and the chattering classes in Ireland.[18] By the 1980s, only a decade and a half later, however, there had been a climate change in Ireland as the culture turned to connect what was going on below the waist with what was happening above. In Christina Reid's play *Tea in a China Cup* (1983), when Beth and Theresa, on the verge of puberty, discuss what their respec-tive Belfast Protestant and Catholic parents have told them about menstruation, the words they repeat are 'curse' and 'troubles'.[19] Whether intended or otherwise by Reid, the last word resonates not only against the respectable world of china cups and straitened circumstances but also against the Troubles themselves. In poetry south of the border, embarrassment was also raising its head. Eithne Strong's long sally against what Kavanagh had identified in 1942 as the great hunger in Irish life is entitled quite simply *Flesh . . . the Greatest Sin* (1982). To Tom Regan, the schoolmaster, flesh is 'the betrayer', and likened to 'slopping in ditches, that meant knickers,/odours that frightened with the pull of temptation'.[20] 'Kill the flesh/that the soul can live' is the advice of Nance's parents, who repeatedly fix on her ugliness, until eventually she believes she is 'An ugly thing, me,/with a damned soul'.

Flesh . . . the Greatest Sin bears out what a contemporary American ethnologist discovered in her study of Brandon in County Kerry, that 'throughout all the records runs a strong current of sexual repression and personal ascetism – one that interferes not only with intimacy between the sexes, but with the nurturant and generative aspects of personality itself'.[21] In a country given over to weekly confessing, Nance has no one to confess to but herself. After a sexual incident with a boy of sixteen when she is only a girl, Nance faces the burden of telling an unsympathetic mother and encounters no relief in confession. She then spends her teenage years at a boarding school with nuns, who tell her nothing about the anus or the female 'hole/in stolen dirty stories', only how to 'forgo pleasure'. A spiritual phase follows, with yearnings for 'stigmata', at the end of which she is invited to become a nun. Imagining the future, Nance longs for 'pure mind' to unite men and women, a state where the epistemological 'pure' and religious 'purity' belong together. Inevitably, marriage leaves her 'frigid'. Through despair, she slowly discovers 'No short-cut/to discovery which was a movement/infinitesimally gradual', and in time the synthesis comes: 'it is essential to celebrate the deep interiority/of spiritual flesh in the eternal now'.

The sharpness with which the body is exposed in this poem is striking, and reminds us that the power of *Flesh . . . the Greatest Sin* stems from breaking taboos, from its forcing open the historic door of censorship. Kavanagh puts feelings into words, Strong puts the body into words, and while Kavanagh uses the traditional metaphor of 'worm' for penis, Strong calls the vagina, more crudely, a 'hole'. Against the traditional image of Irish womanhood and the role model of the Virgin Mary, Strong opposes the physical body, a body now divested of its comforting images in religion or myth, its sanctity in language, or its solidarity with others. In her sights is the harp's view of itself and the crossover or relationship between secrecy, disclosure, and ideology, between, to invoke a larger context, loss and struggle and censorship. Part of the exposure concerns Catholic Ireland, the Ireland that was driven underground by the Penal Laws in the eighteenth century, but now the stripping is one step removed from the crown and much closer to a more general trouble-spot in patriarchical society.

Maeve Kelly's feminist novel *Necessary Treasons* (1985) has a canvas as wide as the system of patriarchy it seeks to castigate. Throughout, Kelly insists on a series of connections or contrasts between working-class battered and deserted wives and middle-class professionals, between the taste for romantic literature aired on the radio and the brutal reality confronting such wives, between 'the lusty call of the flesh' and the sordid, mechanical repetition or violent sexual intercourse that constitutes marriage for many women, between a woman discovering the Messiah in Simone de Beauvoir's *The Second Sex* and men appreciating life's incongruities reading Joyce's

Ulysses, between the male domain of the Church, politics, and medicine, and the historical exclusion of women, between marching for peace in the North and campaigning for kidney machines in the local hospital in Limerick.[22] At one point, the hardened but defiant Eleanor is overwhelmed by society's female victims presenting at her surgery and wishes they would all rise up together and take to the streets. In an important insight particularly relevant to the discussion here, the narrator also notices that there was 'no great public expression of the anguish she listened to each day' (p.120). Here was another level of secrets finding articulation, not in the confessional but in the consciousness-raising women's groups and in the doctor's surgery. As its title suggests, *Necessary Treasons* constitutes a polemic against contemporary Ireland at a time when the battle of the sexes threw into sharp relief the alignment of Church and State, a time when dissent was looking around for company, and when injustice couldn't hope for too much from the upholders of patriarchy.

The most famous bodily secret to be exposed in the period under discussion was Micheal Farrell's *Madonna Irlanda* (1977), a painting which he impishly subtitled,

Micheal Farrell's *Madonna Irlanda* (1977), more indebted to Baudrillard than Boucher. Courtesy of Margaret Early and Dublin City Gallery The Hugh Lane.

along with quotation marks, '*or, The Very First Real Irish Political Picture*'. There are many ways to read this painting, the most immediate being alongside François Boucher's *The Blonde Odalisque* (1752), where the pink-and-white fleshy model is stretched out, legs splayed, front down on a sofa, her face childlike and expressionless. It was thought that Boucher's model was Louise O'Murphy, an Irish mistress to Louis XV, but in point of fact, as Farrell notes with some delight, she was a whore, and for that reason, 'She is my Mother Ireland. Why? Because she was a whore!'[23] In an early sketch by Farrell of another odalisque, this time using Boucher's *La Brune Odalisque* (1745), the model's head and bottom are turned more towards the viewer, and across her midriff, with hints of 'boucher' (butcher in French), is written the word 'Fourquarters'. *Madonna Irlanda* as we have it is more subtle in its effects. Farrell has placed a halo above the model's head, painted her as a piece of sculpture, but reddened her buttocks and made her face and body more sensuous. Boucher's classic portrait, with its heavy furniture, panelled wall, drapes, and footstool, is transformed by Farrell into the artist's studio with paint still flowing, a grotesque parody of Leonardo's Vitruvian Man, and a frame inserted as part of the painting, with a title stencilled in to resemble a Cubist painting by a Picasso or Braque. In what looks like a late addition, Farrell has painted a facial self-portrait in the top right-hand corner, complete with a French cigarette, descending out of the blue like the Holy Ghost, leering at his whore (from) behind.

Madonna, the Catholic-educated American icon who was named after the Blessed Virgin Mary, has destroyed some of the freshness of Farrell's critique. But *Madonna Irlanda* still delights in its consciously controversial image. Without the title, it would be less controversial: the male gaze given a little too obvious expression in a painting that reinterprets the world of classical portraiture for a modern audience. With the title, as if to emphasise the classic struggle between word and image, we are forced to pay attention to the more specific cultural effects. 'Mother Ireland' is here displayed through several overlapping perspectives: Spanish religious paintings of the Madonna and Child, classical French paintings of nudes, relics of other forms of Western art, orientalism, postmodernism, and the exile's mixed feelings for his native land. As for interpretation, this remains intriguingly open-ended. Is it a blistering attack on the whole concept of Irishness, the way it has prostituted itself to the outside world? Is it a descant on the colonial/male gaze, showing how Ireland, the colonised female, was abused by the male coloniser? Is it a 'metaphor for the country', a country, according to Farrell, 'still being screwed today'?[24] Is it an image of Ireland, taking our cue from O'Faolain, as a country for young men? Or is it that all religious images are now up for grabs, for secular exploitation? Whichever viewpoint we lean towards, we are reminded that there is something additional – and therefore excessive – about the concept of interpretation. Here, too, Farrell is deliberately provocative. However, while his republican sympathies are evident throughout his work, comparing Ireland to a whore was perhaps a dangerous move in a period when some Irish women were being abused by forces of the crown (and by their own partners).

In contrast, Robert Ballagh's painting *Inside Number 3* (1979) lends a more serene, less troubled or indeed furtive, perspective to the Irish nude at this time. Betty, his wife-model, is descending the staircase, only in this case – in contrast to Duchamp's original – it is a highly personal and revealing shot, caught by the eye of the painter-photographer, with a pair of crossed legs in the foreground adding to the male viewpoint. The title anticipates a voyeuristic disclosure of secrets, which in turn invites a matter-of-fact response: 'Oh, so this is what your wife looks like'. But, at the same time, the title is designed to ensure the canvas is also read against the banal, the serial, the anonymous. This is not yet the Age of the Catwalk, not yet the generation who've grown up, in the words of Dave Eggers, 'thinking of

Robert Ballagh's painting, *Inside Number 3* (1979). Courtesy of the artist.

ourselves in relation to the political-media-entertainment ephemera . . . for whom the idea of anonymity is existentially irrational'.[25] The fleshy model, with her big thighs, neat breasts, and natural look, dominates the painting, but the object of her attention, and therefore to some extent ours, is the opposite side of the room, where a television screen advertises the smiling face of a media personality and where the painting on the wall shows Delacroix's bare-breasted figure of *Liberty Leading the People* (1830), a painting that Ballagh used for his Easter 1916 commemorative postage stamp.

This is my home life, says the painter, and I have deliberately invited in the whole world to see it. 'If you're going to deal honestly with your own circumstance,' the political Ballagh once remarked, 'you must be part of it. You can't be on the outside looking in.'[26] This is where the sexual is part of the furniture, part of the world outside, part of images that are at once invasive and revolutionary, domestic and domesticated, 'high' and 'popular' culture, part of the black metal staircase, part of the bookshelves with books on Goya and other artists, the 1980s Habitat paper light-shade, the rubber plant, the shoe-lace, the curved, latticed ceiling, parquet flooring, the red brick wall, and the Fender sports bag. If the painting is 'Inside' then it belongs also to the outside world, not just by it being painted and displayed in galleries but also because a line cannot be drawn between the sacred space of the personal and the public space outside. This is all there is: inside is outside, outside is inside. Ballagh's attack is on secrecy, on what Sissela Bok has defined as 'intentional concealment', not on privacy.[27] Ironically, to extend Jean-Paul Sartre's discussion on seriality, what each of us does in our private lives links us serially to each other.[28] We create our own spaces, and enjoy our sexuality alone, but we also repeat what everyone else is doing. And in that sense the television screen, which every household has but which speaks to us *as if* we were being addressed individually, offers us a clue to the painting's deeper meanings. For his case study, Sartre takes the bus queue and the radio broadcast in the home to underline that alterity is always elsewhere, that in the queue I am the Other for others and they the Other for me, that the voice broadcasting ideologically reactionary views is unbearable precisely because it cannot be gainsaid and because it is being listened to by Others. For Ballagh, inside the home also contains its own version of alterity but, because it admits of reciprocity, remains less threatening than in Sartre's examples. We can go further: if Farrell's is the first Irish political picture then this is a close second, for what Ballagh asks us to consider is the relationship between human sexuality, the culture of consumption, and political freedom.

Aidan Mathews' engaging story, 'Lipstick on the Host' (1992), furnishes a related discussion on the theme of bodily secrets, taken this time from the more knowing 1990s. When the forty-one-year-old English teacher Meggie looks at herself in the mirror, she sees that her breasts 'were still beautiful; or, at least, they weren't poignant. They were perfectly womanly and matter-of-fact. . . . If there were a picture of them in the *Irish Times*, lots of people would write letters to the editor about decency and degradation. They would, actually.'[29] As the title suggests, there is not so much a contrast as traffic between the sacred and the secular, between the inane and the profound, the serious and the chatty. Where Molly Bloom has an elaborate sense of subterfuge as part of her construction of sexuality, Meggie thinks of her secrets in terms of the world of newspapers, capping such a train of thought with: 'They would, actually.' Invited out to dinner by Antony, a gynaecologist, Meggie is attracted by his hands and imagines herself as his patient, spraying the inside of her thigh with an atomizer and reading his Latin diplomas while his fingers slip inside, wondering all the while 'why his name didn't have a H in it' (pp. 240–1). Appropriately, in a story about access to the spiritual, at one point they discuss religion. The gynaecologist informs her of his lack of a supernatural – but not spiritual – sense, nature being super enough for him: 'The world is pretty phenomenal, when you think about it; and even more phenomenal when you don't' (p. 241).

With the aid of clichés in the language and a female consciousness almost wholly defined by the outside world, Mathews provides a humorous postmodernist meditation on the Kantian distinction between noumena and phenomena, where what can seem ordinary can suddenly partake of the profound. Joyce begins *Ulysses* with Mulligan mocking the opening of the Catholic Mass; Mathews focuses on a different encounter between the sacred and the secular, best summed up in the story's title, 'Lipstick on the Host'. Meggie isn't a mystery to herself or to the reader. As the narrator informs us, she thinks her soul is somewhere between her mouth and her anus. But the burden of Mathews' story seems to be that, in a country once given to censorship, displaying her secrets – or, what amounts to the same thing, having no secrets – is a necessary first step to salvation. Accompanying that display is the acceptance of the consumerism of popular culture, a pervasive Anglo-American consumerism that leaves almost no room for the harp and whose historicity is so precisely located that some of its terms will fox a younger generation of readers. These include: baby-gro, Milton, the sterilising fluid, Flymo, Baader Meinhoff, *Bonanza*, Emma Peel, Morris Minor, beehive hairstyle, styrofoam cup, Captain Peter Townsend, Golda Meir, Ghostbusters T-shirt, *Cosmo*, *Bella*, *She* and Trivial Pursuit. How a city and a country noted for its face-to-face community came to embrace and not recognise such alterity is a question not pursued by Mathews.

Overshadowing the stories of William Trevor, the Irish prose writer with the best claim to Joyce's mantle, there hangs a label not dissimilar to *Inside Number 3*. Whether the story is set in London, the home counties, Italy or provincial Ireland, the procedure is the same: this is a story about a person who lives behind a closed door and who has secrets that will be revealed. But there are no shocks, no Joycean epiphanies, only the slow growth of some kind of understanding or sympathy on the part of the character or reader. In *The News from Ireland* (1986), Trevor even manages to deflect the powerful presence of Joyce by impudently entitling one of his stories 'Two More Gallants', a fanciful story in which Corley's skivvy reappears in later life to disclose that Joyce got his story from her when she worked at a dentist's in North Frederick Street in Dublin. More is revealed in 'Bodily Secrets' when Mrs O'Neill, who is fifty-nine and the widow of a factory owner in a small town in Ireland, thinks of marrying the factory manager, Mr Agnew. At the club-house the talk is of *Dynasty*; at home she watches a Hollywood film about drug-running, dozes off and awakes to the sound of a priest with a Cork accent talking about the feast of Corpus Christi, the body of Christ. And then comes a paragraph about her body:

> In her bedroom she did something she had not done for ten years at least: before she slipped into her nightdress she paused in front of the long looking-glass of her wardrobe and surveyed her naked body. It was most certainly no longer her best feature, she said to herself, remembering it when she was a child, standing up in the bath to be dried. She remembered being naked at last in the bedroom of the International Hotel in Bray, and the awkward voluptuousness that had followed. The bearing of four children, her fondness for sweet things, the insidious nips of gin in the club-house – in combination they had taken a toll, making clothes as necessary as all that meticulous care with make-up and hair. The first time she'd been pregnant, with Cathal, she had looked at herself in this same looking-glass, assuring herself that the enormous swelling would simply go away, as indeed it had. But nothing would go away now. Flesh hung loosely, marked with pink imprints of straps or elastic. If she slimmed herself to the bone there would be scrawny, empty skin, loops and pockets, hollows as ugly as the bulges. She drew her nightdress over her head and a pattern of pink roses in right little bunches hid what she preferred not to see, transforming her again into a handsome woman.[30]

This is Trevor's gentle satire at its best. He allows Mrs O'Neill – an image, in her own way, of Ireland in middle age, sixty years after Independence – space for her bourgeois illusions, while not condemning her as a person. As she looks at herself in the mirror, Mrs O'Neill reads her body, and what she discovers is the value of clothes, and how her body is transformed by them. This is what her bodily secrets tell her, and it is something that Trevor insists on in his stories. Once the fire is spent, what then for the individual? In a world where sexual desire comes clothed in the culture of consumption, what hope for the individual to pursue or achieve wholeness or uniqueness?

In films in the North, the theme of bodily secrets was again to the fore in the 1980s, but was now linked more closely with the national question. From the opening image of male sperm swimming in water to the held shot of an egg being

Dinky and Goretti passing the statue of the Immaculate Conception in Margo Harkin's film *Hush-a-Bye Baby* (1989). On their return Dinky, having listened to Goretti disclosing her unwanted pregnancy, turns to the statue and, with an eye also on accounts in various parts of Ireland of moving statues, exclaims: 'Don't you fucking move. I'm warning you.' Courtesy of Margo Harkin.

broken into a mixing bowl, Margo Harkin's film *Hush-a-Bye Baby* (1989) deliberately highlights not only the physical but, more importantly, the confrontation between the physical and the ideological in Catholic Ireland. The story of an unwanted teenage pregnancy belongs to an earlier decade but here it is given a particular intensity because the colonial encounter – the film is set in Derry in 1984 in what Republicans sometimes call 'the North of Ireland', not, that is, in Northern Ireland. Goretti Friel's first response on revealing to her friend Dinky that she's pregnant is a desperate cry: 'Dear God, I want to die.' Goretti enjoys none of the official valuing of children in the culture and neither does she feel any of the responsibility that motherhood with its chores might bring. A recent film historian mistakenly claims that 'the film portrays a society run by a strong female network'.[31] Goretti's wish, quite simply, is to die, but the gods are unmoved. Dinky and Goretti pass a statue of the Virgin Mary in a country lane in the Donegal Gaeltacht. The film is set at a time when all over Ireland there were reports of moving statues, and, as if in response to such unreality, the down-to-earth, good-humoured Dinky speaks up for her friend: 'Don't you fucking move. I'm warning you.' Nature, too, is impervious to Goretti's supplication. The waves wash over the pebbles on the beach but for Goretti – whose namesake, Maria Goretti, preferred death to forced sexual intercourse, becoming, at the age of eleven, the Church's youngest saint – there is no cleansing to be had. She is surrounded by a culture and a religion which is quick both to censor and to abandon its children to isolation from the tribe. In her dreams Goretti is woken by flashes of her role model, the Virgin Mary, flashes which serve to recall the flipside of the words from Yeats's poem 'Among School Children', how 'images too break hearts' (*VP* 445). Walking across the estate, with the famous slogan 'YOU ARE NOW ENTERING FREE DERRY' painted on the wall behind her, she informs a friend that she can't join the school team. Conversely, when stopped by a foot patrol, Ciaran, her boyfriend, reminds his British master that *Tiocfadh Ár Lá*, ('Our day will come'), but, when he learns about Goretti's pregnancy after being 'lifted' by the military, his first response is telling: 'Does anyone know? . . . Fuck me. Don't you think I've enough shit as it is.'

The film exposes the cruelty in certain Irish attitudes to the 'fallen woman', attitudes that made it possible for the Sisters of Charity and other religious orders effectively to imprison the 'Magdalen Laundresses' (the 'Maggies' as they were called, who were unwed mothers, daughters of unwed mothers and prostitutes), without it coming to light until a television documentary exposed the practice in 1993.[32] Almost as soon as she embarks on her teenage years, Goretti discovers what a sanctimonious Church teaches, namely that sex and children belong together. When the local priest interrupts Goretti and Ciaran's lovemaking by knocking at the door 'to bless the house', he reminds us of a wider truth about the role of the Church; how, traditionally, it has sought to intervene between couples in their most private moments and how it has used the unmarried priest (and nun) for this purpose. Hence the satire of the classroom scene, when the girls have their gaze fixed on the priest's crotch and inner thighs while he is giving them a talk about the dignity of marriage. Houses are blessed and walls carry images of the Pope and the Sacred Heart, but Goretti is reduced to bringing on a miscarriage in the bath. What the film emphasises by such contrasts is that all the forms of mediation in Ireland, in particular the Church, the school and the family, are seemingly constructed to avoid both the body and discussion of the body.

Pat Murphy and John Davies' film *Maeve* (1981) offers an extended discourse on the relationship between Second Wave feminism, as represented by Maeve Sweeney (whose name carries echoes from Irish mythology of a strong queen and a mad king, one of whom is engaged with power and one of whom is in flight from the world), and traditional Irish Republicanism, as represented by her partner, Liam Doyle. Nothing is forgotten in the North, neither the IRA campaign in the early 1940s and 1950s, nor the pogroms in the 1920s and 1930s. Nights out, too, are also occasions for remembering: 'Brave Tom Williams, we salute you/And we never will forget' are lines from the song Maeve hears on her night out, Williams being the last Republican to be hanged in Belfast Prison.[33] But while the power of this kind of memorialising is acknowledged, with Maeve herself joining in the singing, another source of feeling is

When feminists attempted to import copies of *Spare Rib* into the Republic, the law was on hand. Report in *Hibernia*, 21 February 1980.

Feminist Faces Jail As Customs Seize 'Spare Rib'

By Darach MacDonald

AS CUSTOMS officers again stopped delivery of British feminist paper, *Spare Rib*, Irish feminist, Marie MacMahon faces a week in Mountjoy Prison on a charge of 'defacing public property', in February, 1977. Last week, she was informed by a sergeant from Donnybrook Garda Station that a warrant for her arrest had been issued. But when Ms MacMahon presented herself at the Garda Station as arranged on Monday morning, the warrant could not be located. She is now waiting for it to be served and her week in prison.

The conviction of Ms MacMahon arose from a public meeting in 1977 to protest over the banning of *Spare Rib*. She and others had posted notices of the meeting. Since then the 'Spare Rib'

ban has expired and, among other brushes with the law arising from her political activities, Ms MacMahon had charges of being a 'common prostitute' dropped. Most recently she has been involved in the campaign over feminists who face charges arising from their Women's Day protests outside Armagh Prison.

But while Marie MacMahon awaits the warrant summoning her to a week in Mountjoy, retailers of 'Spare Rib' have discovered that the 1977 issue is not dead. December issues of the magazine were seized by customs officials at the Sherriff Street postal sorting office 'pursuant to Section 42 of the Customs Consolidation Act, 1976, and sent to Division 2, Stamping Branch, Dublin Castle'. Though the Censorship (Continued on Page 7)

Marie MacMahon informs Garda Inspector Hurley of her intention to sell the banned 'Spare Rib' in February, 1977.

also accessed in *Maeve*. At the beginning of the film, Maeve returns to Belfast from London and on the flight has a brief conversation with an English archaeologist sitting beside her. Flying into Aldergrove Airport, she notices an ancient ring fort. On arrival, she wishes her travelling companion au revoir: 'Enjoy the megalithic sites.' The comment is slightly tongue-in-cheek, but at once it announces the major themes and contradictions dealt with by the film – coloniser versus colonised, English versus Irish, names and naming, past and present, history and topography, images and reality. Later on, there is a shot of Maeve as a child accompanying her father through the countryside, stopping to stare at a hill of the fairies, and the film ends at the Giant's Causeway, with a ranting Orangeman. Here are the 'bodily secrets' in the landscape of Northern Ireland, a link with a patriarchal past which has to be confronted if a new conscience and consciousness is to be forged.

The female body is a recurring motif in the film. After lovemaking, Maeve, wrapped in a blanket, and a naked Liam, sit by the fire with a glass of wine in hand. It's a consciously romantic scene. Liam thinks he's done enough to satisfy his partner, but Maeve, ever attentive to signs and patterns of discontinuity and inauthenticity, observes that, 'If someone were to write about this, the description would fit the magazines.' Later, in a discussion about his father's commitment to Republican ideals, Liam is insistent: 'It's not like it is with women you know. He can't extend himself through his body. It's only through his beliefs.' Maeve doesn't take up the challenge at this point, but the theme is continued in the next scene, without Liam. Róisín is taking a bath in the living room, talking with her sister Maeve about marriage, abortion, leaving home, and sisterhood. Róisín is wary of her sister's feminism, insisting that men are not the enemy. She climbs out of the bath-tub and covers herself with a towel. Maeve, who is naked at this point, replies that she is opposed to the idea of woman as sex object. It's a risky moment but central to a film where – as with *Hush-a-Bye Baby* – the physical confronts the ide-ological. The camera throws into relief the female body as object of the male (and female) gaze, speaking out against being a sex object. The body has a 'natural look', and in the still atmosphere, drained of movement and sexual arousal, the point is well-made. Pat Murphy, aware that the camera has a 'very cold eye', later confessed that with hindsight she would have shot the scene differently: 'It's as if every time women are looked at through a camera, they are making themselves available, they seem to be offering themselves to be looked at.'[34]

Predictably, Maeve's argument with Liam resurfaces, this time in the most highly charged scene in the film, in Clifton Graveyard. 'When you're denied power . . . the only form of protest you have is your body. Our struggle is for autonomy, for the control of our bodies.' Liam counters by alluding to the blanket men, but Maeve won't be contained or silenced by their sacrifice: 'Men's relationship to women is just like England's relationship to Ireland. You're in possession of us. You occupy us like an army.' This is too much for Liam: 'Women, you're like anarchists.' Maeve reserves to the last her most telling comment on Republicanism: 'I belong to a class that's oppressed whatever happens.'[35]

Like Anne Devlin's play *Ourselves Alone* (1986), *Maeve* is of its time, a striking attempt to involve Republicans and socialists in thinking about the position of women. If Pierre Bourdieu had developed his argument in *Masculine Domination* (2001) in relation to the film, he might have produced a more nuanced study. Much of what Bourdieu writes can be insightfully applied to the film: it is relevant to Maeve's education at the hands of nuns, her family and symbolic capital, male honour and the assertion of dominance, male domination of the public space, the 'symbolic' and physical violence against women, and even the dualism inscribed in bodies.[36] But the application becomes less convincing when there are *competing* claims to liberation, one sexual, the other political, and when an analogy is drawn, say, between England/men and Ireland/women. As for the male body wasting away on hunger strike and the severed bloody red hand – the Red Hand of Ulster – on constant display in the North, this, too, would complicate any argument not only about male domination in this period but also about the link between symbolic and physical violence.

How men like Liam – who fails, or would fail, to notice that men on hunger strike were indeed extending themselves through their bodies – could respond to the feminist challenge is deliberately left open or closed off in the film. At the same time, Liam isn't a macho figure in control of Maeve, and there is no struggle for mastery as there is in *Nora* (2000), Murphy's film about the early years in the relationship between Joyce and Nora Barnacle. Liam is already on the way to becoming fixed as an ex-boyfriend, and his power is accordingly diminished. In the abandoned space, Maeve seems to be applying arguments she's learned among her liberated friends in London, so that in her struggle for articulation not all of it rings true. 'Even writers have to use the same words as other people,' Nora taunts Joyce. Murphy's focus in the two films is trained on the area between self and non-self, between image and reality, between facing and not facing up to difficulties, between two opposing paths in life, but what emerges is not the clarity of a binary opposition but something less clear-cut.

Contrast this struggle for articulation with the famous mural facing the Falls Road that a visiting Canadian woman designed in 1983. In this mural, a young Cumann na mBan volunteer is flanked by two women also in arms, one from the Palestine Liberation Organisation, the other from the South West Africa People's Organisation. They are encircled by the female symbol and above their heads an automatic rifle is brandished. The caption reads 'SOLIDARITY BETWEEN WOMEN IN ARMED STRUGGLE'.[37] Murphy is more interested in the issue of vulnerability and women achieving power, not through armed conflict but through their bodies. Could the body become the ideological means for finding liberation, liberation from (male) republican politics, and liberation from the male writer as culture? And how could that be achieved? Both *Maeve* and *Nora* are gestures towards a future, one that we have already in part inherited in the case of *Nora*, while the other is still awaiting its answer.

Why was so much attention given to the female body in this period? The question is intriguing and invites several responses. One explanation is that gays and lesbians were beginning to come out, and RTÉ programmes such as the influential *The Late Late Show* were exploring these issues and changing attitudes in the process. Emma Donoghue, the lesbian novelist who came to prominence in the 1990s, recalls the thrill of surreptitiously reading, as a fourteen-year-old, Maura Richards' novel *Interlude* (1982), and in particular the lesbian scene between a saleswoman and a woman being fitted with a bra in a department store on Grafton Street in Dublin.[38] Another explanation, which is especially evident in the underlying tone of a novel such as *Necessary Treasons*, is that there was a renewed sense of urgency and defiance. In the two decades from the Pill Train in 1971, when women illegally imported forms of birth control on a train from Belfast to Dublin, to the 'X' case in 1992, what women did with their bodies had dramatically exposed and challenged the conservative forces at work in Irish society. As many as seven thousand women a year travelled to Britain for abortions, while countless others handed over illegitimate children to nuns and other adoption agencies.[39] The case of the fourteen-year-old rape victim, 'X', who received an injunction in the Dublin High Court in 1992 preventing her from going to Britain for an abortion, under-lined the fact that the crisis was about more than reproductive rights and that it involved a whole section of the ideological state apparatus. The women's liberation movement was slow to take off in Ireland, and when it did it was inevitably preoc-cupied with contraception, abortion, and divorce, but it clearly wanted more, not least to engage its male counterparts in Republican and socialist circles.[40] As Ursula Barry has rightly suggested in reflections on the 1980s struggles: 'Making a separa-tion between sexual pleasure and reproduction has been an immense achievement by the movement for reproductive rights.'[41] While the self-regarding Joyce in the early 1900s had advocated 'copulation without population', this new generation had campaigned for something akin, but now from the viewpoint of women, with the emphasis falling on control over their bodies rather than simply on sexual pleasure (though that was clearly implied).

The argument against women's liberation that angered Rosita Sweetman, an argument with echoes of 'Labour must wait' from the period 1916–21, came from left-wing males: 'Women must wait until after the revolution they say.'[42] The work of Pat Murphy, Margot Harkin, Eithne Strong and Maeve Kelly betrayed years of accumulated frustration that women such as Rosita Sweetman had to endure in previous decades. In the freshness and the rawness of their arguments and in the position they assign the reader or viewer, it is as if they had little to build on, only the determination of individuals to resist, and in so doing find a voice. Ranged against them was the Catholic Church, the most powerful ideological force (and comfort) in Ireland. When Pope John Paul II visited Ireland in September 1979 he said Mass in the Phoenix Park in Dublin for an audience of a million people, a gathering thought to have been the largest in the country's history. In advocating control of their bodies, women were on a direct collision course with the Church and, to some extent, with popular opinion. The newspaper stories that emerged in the 1980s were often grotesque, as in 1984, when Anne Lovett, a young unmarried woman from County Longford, died alone giving birth at a grotto dedicated to the Virgin Mary, graphically pushing, in the words of Paula Meehan, 'her secret out into the night'.[43] In sexual matters, every family did its best to protect its bodily secrets: unwanted pregnancies were terminated abroad, supplies of contraception were smuggled in from the North, and wives were unceremoniously deserted. Hence, in *Flesh . . . The Greatest Sin*, Nance's struggle is for her soul as much as for her body. Even the liberated sisters in *Maeve* fight shy of divulging to their mother their sexual exploits.

Part of the pressure on women to concentrate on the body came from abroad, and involved a realignment with the position of women elsewhere in Britain, con-tinental Europe and North America. This was also the period when, according to Jane Gallop in *Around 1981* (1992), the wars in the American academy over feminism and poststructuralism were at their most intense.[44] In Ireland, a double movement can be detected. Ireland was like everywhere else, but on the other hand, with megalithic sites constantly on view, Ireland was indeed different. At the same time, with the presence of the British Army on the streets of Belfast, it was difficult to deny that, as a Frenchman once quipped, Ireland was an island behind an island. Maeve's struggle is both peculiar to Northern Ireland and part of the wider movement within Ireland at this time for articulation. Nance's struggle is representative of a wider struggle in Ireland, North and South of the border, to find an accommodation with the body against the censorship of the mind. Just as in the political arena the spotlight has constantly oscillated between the South and the North (with Southern politics dominating in the first quarter of the twentieth century, and Northern politics in the last quarter), so in the area of culture and politics the issue of women has shifted back and forth, one minute seen in cultural, and the next in political terms. Thus, Nance's predicament would remain even if abortion, contraception and divorce were readily available in Ireland, while Maeve's struggle would continue – and probably intensify – even if the unification of Ireland were achieved.

The 1980s was not a revolutionary period but it was a time given to extremes. Kathleen Coyle, writing a generation or more earlier, declined such extremes, whether in political or personal terms. 'We're the only people on the face of the

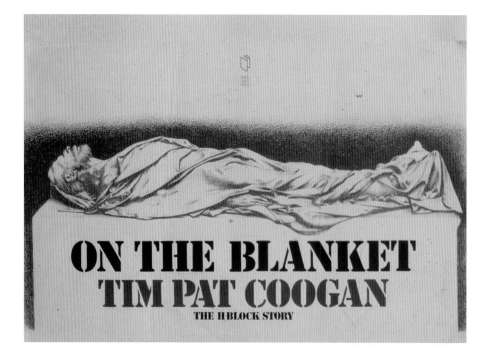

Ballagh's controversial cover for Tim Pat Coogan's book published by Ward River in 1980. Too much dignity for anti-republicans. Courtesy of the artist.

earth who want the undivided truth,' declares a character in *Youth in the Saddle* (1927), her novel which makes a plea for the acceptance of political differences.[45] For Mrs Lutrell, in Coyle's 'Scottish' novel *Who Dwell With Wonder* (1940), the body is important, but, she wonders, once the sex instinct has been satisfied, what then? It's a common enough observation, but the subsequent thought was rarely pursued by a later generation passionate about anything which fell short of self-fulfilment: 'We were only completely happy . . . in those circumstances in which we were not aware that we had bodies.'[46] By contrast, Hark's question to the gay Dido in Frank McGuinness's play *Carthaginians* (1988) – arguably the most threatening line to emerge in that decade, and one that threatens the whole prospect of a linear narrative – has a modern, in-your-face look: 'Does your cock want a united Ireland?'[47] As for the Republican movement itself (to whom the question is first and foremost addressed), ever since the emergence of the Provisional IRA in the early 1970s, very few new ideas beyond military strategy and communitarian politics had been generated. Of all the books in the IRA's H-Blocks library, James Connolly commanded pride of place, and it wasn't until the collapse of Soviet-style communism in 1989 that a different kind of thinking began to emerge. Until then, the staple diet had been inspirational (Fanon, Castro's speeches, Nicaragua), Irish history (Tone, Lalor, Collins, O'Malley), cultural (Dickens, Rupert Brooke), and philosophical (A. J. Ayer, John Rawls).[48] Even the hunger strikes – the action of last resort – seem to have originated among the prisoners rather than from the Republican leadership.[49] But, ironically, because it couldn't have been foreseen in advance, it was through the body that a bridge back to politics was constructed. The body as a symbol of utter negation pleading before the bar of international opinion was unanswerable. It was an action without words but it spoke a language understood by millions. In his enthusiasm to see significance everywhere, Allen Feldman, in his absorbing study *Formations of Violence* (1991), overstates the case: 'The Hunger Strike can be seen as the ultimate resymbolisation of the Republican movement. It erased the imputed stigma of criminality and founded their violence on a new origin myth.'[50] The heated discussion in Anne Devlin's television play *The Long March*, shown by the BBC in 1984, qualifies such a view, and acts as a reminder that something was being forced on sections of the nationalist community. As the disillusioned 1969 civil rights marcher Helen puts it at the end of the play, 'If you use force to get your support, you'll always have to use force to keep it.'[51]

Killallwho

The 1980s is close enough to recall, and yet far enough away, to allow for perspective. The hunger strikes ensured that this was, arguably, the blackest period in modern Irish history. Attempts at negotiated solutions, such as the Sunningdale Agreement in 1973 and the power-sharing Executive in 1974, had come and gone,

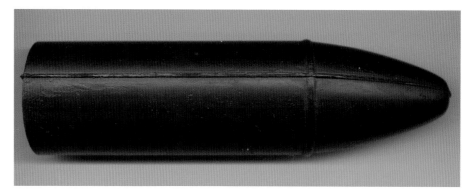

In the early years of the Troubles the British Army used rubber bullets like this to control hostile crowds. If it weren't for their deadly power, the six-inch bullets, complete with sheaths for firing, could have been the playthings of a sexologist. At another level they represented an act of sexual frustration, a version of the colonial encounter, or more precisely an example of killallwho. This particular bullet was recovered from the streets of Belfast in the weeks after Bloody Sunday in 1972.

and it would take the slow-learners and the hardliners over twenty years until the Belfast Agreement in 1998 to settle on terms not dissimilar to those earlier attempts.[52] 'By the summer of 1980,' wrote the authors of the ITV series *The Troubles*, 'the deadlock in Northern Ireland looks no nearer to resolution. . . . Sunningdale and the political initiatives that have followed it clearly spell out the intractable nature of the problem.' And 'deadlock' was the word they chose to characterise the whole period from 1972 to 1980.[53] In Edward Bennett's *Ascendancy* (1982), a film set amid the sectarian Troubles in Belfast in 1920, the very last words spoken by Connie Wintour, the Big House's traumatised daughter, are: 'One thought overwhelms me: that this horror goes on and on for ever.' And immediately the film cuts to the last scene, where, with its echo of the 1981 hunger strikes, she is force-fed by her nurse and doctor. The titles to some of the Troubles fiction that appeared at this time also attest to the period's bleakness (and ghoulish appeal): *City War, Bitter Orange, In Guilt and in Glory, Rag Shadows, Touch the Devil, Time Bomb, Kiss and Kill, A Certain State of Mind, Blood Sisters.*[54] Robert Kee's *Ireland* (1980) contains a photograph of six British soldiers, arms drawn, riot shields in place, charging down a street past two women in doorways. The horror on the face of one of the women chimes with Kee's understated caption: 'Is it dangerous to look too closely into Irish history?'[55] The BBC and the IBA (Independent Broadcasting Association) clearly thought so, for between 1972 and 1979 they permitted only eight interviews with the military wings of Irish republicanism.[56]

In retrospect, from the vantage-point of a new century, few can doubt that, with the establishment of a Scottish Parliament and a Welsh Assembly, Northern

Ireland would miss out on its own form of independence.[57] At the time, however, with a Tory majority in the House of Commons showing no signs of accommodating an increasingly alienated nationalist community or Republican movement, the Troubles looked set to continue – possibly for ever. Unduly optimistic, Bernadette Devlin McAliskey, watching the first big hunger demonstration in Anderstown in October 1980, scented a revival of the 1968–9 civil rights movement.[58] But who could be optimistic when one of the leading players had been writing his life on 'sheets of toilet paper with biro refills in a small filthy cell covered with excrement'[59] or when women in Armagh Jail, also on no-wash protest, were spending their exercise time during menstruation 'furtively hitching their sanitary towels into place out of view of the TV monitors'?[60] It's against this background that we should read Richard Hamilton's painting *The Citizen* (1982–3), for, with his haunting deep-set eyes and noble bearing, the blanket man who stares at us out of the canvas resembles a Christ figure seemingly unaffected by the excremental vision on the wall behind him.

What was happening was closer on all sides to what Padraig O'Malley has called 'the politics of despair'.[61] Mrs Thatcher thought the IRA 'had dealt their last card'[62] and she even entertained the fanciful notion of resettling Belfast Catholics and redrawing the Border 'to make it more defensible'.[63] By 1980, a decade or so into 'the Troubles' – a term redolent of the Civil War in the 1920s and a same-renew comfort of sorts, therefore – 2,297 people had been killed or murdered (out of a total of 3,601 for the years 1968–98).[64] Of these, 1,291 were civilian deaths. In statistical terms the worst years were 1971–6 when 1,843 people in total died, well above the average of 120 deaths a year over the thirty-year period. After 1982 the number began to decline.[65] But the cumulative effect of years of bloodshed forced people to look to hope rather than to reason for a resolution to the conflict. The one group to benefit from the hunger strikes, a gesture which a recent historian has described as 'the first significant step towards substantial "Republicanisation"',[66] was Sinn Féin, who within a year had won their first Assembly elections for twenty years and who then turned their attention increasingly toward the ballot-box. As John Hume wryly observed: 'It's quite clear they haven't dealt their last card. The Prime Minister dealt them a full hand, which they've been using ever since.'[67]

To insiders, many of the deaths were understandable, since many of the bullets had a name on them, 'fingered/at teabreak, shot inside their home', as John Montague puts it in his ironically entitled poem 'Red Branch (a Blessing)'.[68] But to outsiders it all seemed to invite a wringing of the hands, a response that the Southerner Joyce had half-anticipated in the first chapter of *Finnegans Wake*, when, after the Fall, the world descended into a state of 'wills gen wonts', followed by 'Arms appeal with larms' and then the more sinister 'Killykillkilly' (*FW* 4:1–8) and 'killallwho' (*FW* 15:11). 'Killallwho' calls to mind the wider use of *kill-*

(church) in Irish place names, as in Killaloe (the Church of St Dalua, an ancient Episcopal see in County Clare); in Boazio's 1599 map of Ireland, *kill* is translated as 'parishe', a word impossible to do without in thinking about Irish culture. But here the word is converted by Joyce into straightforward English, namely 'killing'. Contained within the other syllables, 'allwho' is 'hallow', as in All Hallows, all saints. In 'killallwho', seemingly anyone who moves or who happens to be different is a target for someone. This was Joyce's attack on the 'devil era', a mentality that produced the Civil War, an event that nearly claimed the lives of his family on a visit to Galway in 1923, and it was a Civil War waiting to break out again in some other part of Ireland. At the end of all the wars and 'the first peace of illiterative porthery in all the flamend floody flatuous world' (*FW* 23:9–10), we encounter not peace or poetry but only a stale modern headline, 'Angry scenes at Stormount' (*FW* 28:22). In a later chapter, 'the boarder incident prerepeated itself' (*FW* 81:32–3), where the verb, devoid of human agency, captures precisely a mixture of exasperation and resignation. In a 'disunited kingdom' (*FW* 188:16), allegiance is both vital and potentially lethal, and a recurring motif in *Finnegans Wake* is that of the warring brothers Shem and Shaun, the dissident and the conformist, the republican and the unionist, warring over 'Irrland's split little pea' (*FW* 171:6). Joyce had the good fortune to remain a contemporary of the Troubles and, in rounding on both sides, he shows the uncomfortably close union – in accents from the period of Parnell – between political positions: 'unhesitent in his unionism and yet a pigotted nationalist' (*FW* 133:14–15).[69]

Staring death in the face has been a feature of life in Northern Ireland. This has been especially so for those first on the scene after an explosion or a murder, as with the RUC officer recalling the Good Friday bombs in July 1972:

> The first thing that caught my eye was the torso of a human being . . . it was recognisable as a human torso because the clothes had been blown off and you could actually see parts of the human anatomy. One of the victims was a soldier I'd known personally. He'd had his arms and legs blown off and some of his body had been blown through the railings. One of the most horrendous memories for me was seeing a head stuck to a wall.[70]

For such people, and for critics and historians, visual artists and writers alike, how to gain a purchase on contemporary violence has frequently come down to a question not of intimacy but of distance. In Jennifer Johnston's novel *The Railway Station Man* (1984), Helen's artistic canvas and the Englishman Roger's reconstruction of a disused railway station are studied forms of retreat from the world, as well, as in Helen's case, a means of discovering her 'textured self'.[71] She likes to live 'on the edge of things', 'not lonely . . . just alone' (p.113), and she is surprised to find a new love in her life. But neither she nor Roger can prevent the explosion which overshadows the novel and which is the occasion of his death. 'As in a fugue the shattering glass recurs and recurs, punctuates the rhythm of my life,' thinks Helen in the coda to the novel, a novel that begins in Derry with news that her husband has been accidentally killed by a terrorist when visiting a pupil whose father was in the RUC.

Putting out of mind or recalling to mind are different activities, but in a sense both are intent on distance, in that one aims to destroy the image, while the other aims to release the image from its ground zero, as it were. 'Drawing Ballerinas' is Medbh McGuckian's deliberately wayward title for the volume of verse she published in 2001. It is a title taken from Matisse, who once remarked he survived the worst years of the Second World War by drawing ballerinas.[72] Poets such as Michael Longley and Seamus Heaney turn more directly to classical or Irish mythology. In the 1970s Heaney himself moved south, away from his native province, first to Wicklow and then to Sandymount (and then for one semester a year to Harvard). But, whether north or south of the border, Yeats's 'little room' has never stopped following him. In a poem such as 'Funeral Rites' from his most political volume *North* (1975), Heaney makes no secret of his debt to the final lines of Yeats's poem about rites, 'Prayer for My Daughter' ('How but in custom and in ceremony/Are innocence and beauty born?' [*VP* 406]):

> Now as news comes in
> Of each neighbourly murder
> We pine for ceremony,
> Customary rhythms[73]

For Heaney, rites are the bonds with community; they are how, at an Irish country funeral, the 'purring family cars/nose into line'. This is not the iconoclastic Yeats in a poem such as 'Meditations in Time of Civil War', turning 'towards my chamber, caught/In the cold snows of a dream', but, rather, the parishioner-poet responding to the way 'the whole country tunes/to the muffled drumming/of ten thousand engines'.

'Whatever You Say Say Nothing' was Heaney's uncharacteristically tight-lipped advice about 'The famous/Northern reticence' in the poem of that name, and it was mistakenly taken by some as the gospel according to Seamus.[74] In truth, in the face of repeated atrocities and attempts at making peace, Heaney has been more optimistic:

> But then, once in a lifetime
> The longed-for tidal wave
> Of justice can rise up,
> And hope and history rhyme.[75]

Heaney the family man relaxing at home in Sandycove, October 1985. Courtesy of Dan Harper.

For those tempted to question Heaney's commitment to his people, it is worth recalling that 'Whatever You Say Say Nothing' was first published in *The Listener* on 14 October 1971, two months after the introduction of internment, and carried a news-like subtitle '– Seamus Heaney gives his views on the Irish thing', which included a reference to 'the jacobites among us'.[76] *North* resonates against the contemporary Troubles and Heaney constantly reminds us not so much that 'his Derry is always with him' in the cutting words of Conor Cruise O'Brien (implying a regrettable clinging to the sectarian divide), as that his childhood is contemporary, too.[77] Thus, in 'A Constable Calls', he furnishes a telling portrait of Unionism as a system of oppression, where what catches the child's eye is the revolver butt, the belt, the boot, and the tick of the bicycle departing.

Heaney on the Irish thing. The photo records Catholics in Belfast, under attack from Protestant gangs, being forced to evacuate their homes. *The Listener*, 14 October 1971.

Whatever you say, say nothing —Seamus Heaney gives his views on the Irish thing

1.

I'm writing just after an encounter
with an English journalist in search of ' views
on the Irish thing '. I'm back in winter
quarters where bad news is no longer news,

where media-men and stringers sniff and point,
where zoom lenses and Uhers and coiled leads
litter the hotels. The times are out of joint
but I incline as much to rosary beads

as to the jottings and analyses
of leader writers or those marvellous men
who've scribbled down the long campaign from gas
to gelignite, whose day begins at ten,

who proved upon their pulses ' escalate ',
' backlash ' and ' crack down ', ' the Provisional wing ',
' polarisation ' and ' long-standing hate '.
Yet I live here, I live here too, I sing,

expertly civil-tongued with civil neighbours
on the high wires of first wireless reports,
sucking the fake taste, the stony flavours
of those sanctioned, old, elaborate retorts:

' Oh, it's disgraceful, surely, I agree,'
' Where's it going to end? ' ' It's getting worse,'
' They're murderers,' ' Internment, understandably . . . '
The ' voice of sanity ' is getting hoarse.

2.

Men die at hand. In blasted street and home
the gelignite's a common sound effect:
as the man said when Celtic won, ' the Pope of Rome
's a happy man this night.' His flock suspect

in their deepest heart of hearts the heretic
has come at last to heel and to the stake
We tremble near the flames but want no truck
with the actual firing. We're on the make

In November 1969, at the start of the Troubles, Heaney, as if writing about himself, drafted a tribute to John Hume:

> His understanding of the community is his understanding of himself. His ambition to set Derry's house in order is altruistic and whole because it is obviously the extension of an inner achievement of tolerance and concern. To call him a spokesman for the minority is only one way of putting it. He is the best consciousness of a submerged population group, the questing compass-needle of another hidden Ireland. Speaking a lucid language of sociology and politics with untrammelled conscience, he comprehends bitterness and negation of Derry without being possessed by it. By a generous effort of imagination, he has let any bad blood he may have harboured and thereby earned the right and the skill to diagnose bad blood in the community.[78]

Heaney, too, saw – or sees – himself as the consciousness of a submerged population group. The phrase 'submerged population group' is O'Connor's, coined to characterise and explain the emergence of the short story; how the short story as a form belongs with those marginalised by history; and how England produced the novel while Czarist Russia, modern America and modern Ireland were attracted to outlawed figures.[79] In 1969, Northern Irish Catholics were such a submerged population group that there was effectively a conspiracy of silence preventing anyone in Britain knowing what their lives were like under Unionist control.[80] Hence the importance that invariably attaches itself to the word 'news' in Heaney's writing: since 1969, Northern Ireland has become the news. Catholics weren't yet outlaws but many felt keenly the need for a civil rights movement. Heaney's early work predates the Troubles, and in many respects his whole career, including his most political volume, *North*, is foreshadowed in this tribute, a 'questing compass-needle of another hidden Ireland'.

In terms of a larger picture where history and landscape meet, Heaney's verse constitutes a counter to the emptiness of the Famine and the negation of the colonial encounter. Stocked with pagan wells, farmhouse kitchens, flour and bread making, folded sheets and fishing, his world is full of Corkery's hidden Ireland, of the 'underlife' of the earth and language, of bogs and Beowulf.[81] His preferred literary furrow has been Patrick Kavanagh and the line back to Francis Ledwidge and Thomas Hardy.[82] In his recent collection *Electric Light* (2001), he rewrites, with the relish of a disciple, in a poem entitled 'The Loose Bag', the threshing scene in Hardy's *Tess of the d'Urbervilles* (1891). Reading the scene as a child 'magnified' his soul, 'magnified' here recalling on the one hand the Marian Canticle 'Magnificat' (my soul does *magnificat*, magnify, esteem highly, the Lord, a word also used by Devlin, as we saw in Chapter 3, in his tribute to Michael Collins), and on the other hand prompting the thought that reading Hardy 'enlarged' his soul. Appropriately,

Kavanagh, too, is mentioned in the poem, as Heaney describes how, in an old recording, the poet had declared that 'in any talk about/The properties of land' there's 'health and worth'.[83] In reading the pastoral hinterland that constitutes Heaney's verse, we rarely forget the ambivalence associated with Yeats's 'little room'. For Heaney not only manages to extend the range of our sympathies, he has also shown by his example – a key concept for Heaney – not so much how the personal relates to the political and vice versa, but rather how to conduct oneself in public. Like Hume, he refuses to indulge the bitterness of his (former) minority status, or indeed to dig with both feet, since we are always conscious of his nationalist sympathies.[84] In this sense he shares with the Greek Chorus in *The Cure at Troy* (1990) the 'hope for a great sea-change/On the far side of revenge'.[85]

One suspects Heaney has rarely been distracted by the hype imagined for him as Yeats's successor. Unlike Yeats, he eschews the performative utterance or the ponderous pronouncement; instead, head down, he comes at his material with a degree of humility rarely observed in his lofty exemplar. Also unlike Yeats, he knows his place. To return to the phrase above, the 'neighbourly murder' has a reassuring tone and acts as a counter not so much to the sectarian divide as to the whole idea of murder as heroic or demonic. Murder, too, belongs to some rite, powerful in its own way, but at the same time not quite stitched into the customary rhythms of the country. In 'Lives', a poem by Mahon that is dedicated to Heaney, the poet begins with the image of a torc of gold and the conceit of being buried for two thousand years in the earth before assuming various other identities, such as a Navaho rug and a tongue of bark in Africa until he becomes an anthropologist with a credit card.[86] The poem is double-edged, a comment by Mahon both on his own predicament as a contemporary pulse-taker and on the familiar stance adopted by Heaney.[87] The contrast between the two poets is instructive. Heaney is not unlike an anthropologist – though one without a credit card, an image which marks the crossover in the poem from Heaney to Mahon – but he is an anthropologist who operates from within the culture. He doesn't shy away from the sectarian truth, that sectarian murder is in a class of its own, and that in areas along the border many of the murders were indeed 'neighbourly'.[88] Heaney carried a sense of neighbourliness with him from childhood, and in moving South never lost this all-encompassing emotion. When he went back to the North to attend funerals, old memories were stirred, and it was natural for the Northern European writer to invoke Gunnar in his burial mound from Scandinavian mythology. Closer to home, he also noticed the naturalness and the force not only of neighbourly murder but also of the far side of revenge.[89]

Under pressure himself, Heaney invariably leaves room for the reader to respond to the Troubles. By contrast, Padraic Fiacc is less polite, spurns distance, and impatiently fills the page with material that belongs by right to the streets. In a profoundly disturbing sequence of poems employing the prayers and liturgy of the Mass and published under the title *Missa Terribilis* (1986), Fiacc takes up his hand-held camera and turns on those who would doctor or ignore the news. In 'Crucifixus', the victim of a sectarian murder is identified with the crucified Christ.

I

Dandering home from work at mid
-night, they tripped him up on a ramp,
Asked him if he were a 'Catholic' . . .

A wee bit soft in the head he was,
The last person in the world you'd want
To hurt: His arms and legs, broken,

His genitals roasted with a ship
-yard worker's blowlamp.

II

In all the stories that the Christian Brothers
Tell you of Christ He never screamed
Like this. Surely this is not the way

To show a 'manly bearing' —
Screaming for them to *'Please Stop!'*
And then, later, like screaming for death!

When they made Him wash the stab
Wounds at the sink, they kept on
Hammering Him with the pick

-axe handle, then they pulled
Christ's trousers down, threatening to
'cut off His balls!' Poor boy Christ, for when

They finally got round to finishing Him off
By shooting Him in the back of the head,

'The poor Fenian fucker was already dead!'[90]

Patrick Joseph O'Connor (aka Padraic Fiacc) at home in Belfast with Brian Keenan, 1984. Courtesy of John Minihan.

Even when juxtaposed with reports of the Shankill Butchers, a loyalist murder gang that operated in Belfast in the mid-1970s, there is something profoundly shocking about this poem.[91] With dashes at the beginning of lines and 'He' and 'Him' capitalised, the layout on the page, more charged here than in Ciaran Carson's 'Belfast Confetti' (1987), bears all the stab marks of the victim. As if to allow the word space for greater effect, the 'stab' on one line dangles before it finds its completion in 'wounds' on the next line. The quotation-marks around Catholic are enough to mark him out, a sign for others filled with sectarian hatred: he isn't a Catholic but a 'Catholic'. Or, as Allen Feldman chillingly observes, 'Mutilation is . . . the physical erasure of individuality as a deviation from an ethnic construct.'[92]

Fiacc sketches in enough of the context: 'dandering', a Scottish-English word with homely associations, the shipyards in Belfast, which were dominated by Protestant workers, the Catholic poor, who were educated by Christian Brothers who themselves had a reputation for discipline. But all this is relegated to the back-ground – as is discourse about the 'crisis of masculinity' – as we hear the young man's cry through the italics and the exclamation mark: *'Please Stop!'* And what did he think as he was being tortured, that he wasn't prepared for this by his schooling at the hands of the Christian Brothers, that he wasn't manly enough, that he would scream for death? Fiacc is as merciless as the killers. Step by step, as Graham Reid also does in his harrowing play *Dorothy* (1980), he stages for us the nightmare – the cruelty of his torturers hacking away at his limbs, setting a

A detail from Rita Duffy's *Segregation* (1989) was used to promote Ciaran Carson's book of verse, published by Bloodaxe in 1990. Carson's Belfast is battle hardened, its streets named after other imperial ventures in the Crimea and Sevastopol, but, as he says about the streets in the new Belfast in 'Exile' (2003), 'it is/as much/as I can do/to save/even one/from oblivion'. Courtesy of Bloodaxe.

Opposite page
Dermot Seymour's *The Queen's own Scottish Borderers Observe the King of Jews Appearing behind Seán McGuigan's Sheep on the Fourth Sunday after Epiphany* (1988), the paint thick with symbols. Courtesy of Michael O'Brollochan and Kevin Kavanagh Gallery.

blowlamp to his genitals, the threats to 'cut off His balls', the use of a pickaxe to hammer him, and then the final move, which proved unnecessary. The poem's last sentence could not be bettered, the voice of someone, perhaps one of the torturers, recounting the incident, the flourish deliberately not quite secure in its effect.

'Crucifixus' resembles a tableau on the Stations of the Cross: we stop to meditate on one aspect of Christ's final journey, and for a minute it reminds us of what Christ might have thought on His own journey. The identity here is different from that on display in Dermot Seymour's *The Queen's own Scottish Borderers Observe the King of Jews Appearing behind Seán McGuigan's Sheep on the Fourth Sunday after Epiphany* (1988). In Seymour's highly symbolic and ironic oil painting, the crucified Christ hangs between army turrets in an Ulster drumlin landscape with menacing army helicopters hovering overhead and with a blood-stained sheep, its face turned towards the viewer, dominating the foreground. In Fiacc's poem, the young man is not Christ; if he were there would be a case for his beatification as a martyr for his religion. The comparison thus works up to a point but cannot be pressed further, since identity needs distance. No side has a monopoly on the execution of vicious murder, and while the liturgy of the Mass, the *Missa Terribilis*, is more appropriate to deploy with a Catholic than a Protestant as victim, we cannot forget its one-sidedness.

This is Fiacc's strength, to shock by the immediacy and to shock by the analogy. There is nothing 'neighbourly' about Fiacc. His work is not balanced, but neither, in some respects, was the poetry of the Great War. For this is how the Troubles are seen by Fiacc; not as anaemic, but as full-blooded war. At least that

is one line of interpretation, for Fiacc, aware of the quotation-marks that mark someone out as a target, also provides another perspective, which is not full-blooded war but something closer to the common humanity of no-man's land, which itself is a version of the colonial encounter. As the bombs ignite in 'Introit', 'Soldiers shake like flowers/Crying "Christ!" and "Fuck!"'.[93] In 'Explosion', bombs make the British soldier 'one of us', 'vulnerable', 'As Irish as the perpetrator/victim', but in 'Enemy Encounter', the British soldier is seen as an enemy: 'He is young enough to be my weenie/bopper daughter's boyfriend.' And he sees himself through the soldier's glass eyes looking past him: 'I am an Irishman, and he is afraid/That I have come to kill him' (pp.33 and 35).

Troubles Fiction

'Stiff' to refer to a political assassination, 'scone' or 'coup' to shoot someone in the head, 'fixer' the M15 rifle used by the Provisional IRA, 'touch up' a beating, 'bangling' to describe smuggling using the anus, 'peacelines' to refer to the erection of walls between communities – as the entry into popular speech of an often sinister new vocabulary suggests, Irish culture is never slow in closing the gap between language and experience.[94] Contemporary novelists in Northern Ireland have also not been short of time to reflect on the 'killallwho' issue. As is apparent from James Simmons's moving poem 'Claudy' (1974) or Carson's 'Blink' (2003), a poem which plays terribly on the word 'whereabouts', or from numerous accounts in *Lost Lives* (1999) by David McKittrick et al., the bomb that casually interrupts innocent lives seems to be especially outrageous.[95] The bomb explosion in chapter 11 of Robert McLiam Wilson's *Eureka Street* (1996) is, as Laura Pelaschiar suggests, among the most devastating in Troubles fiction, and it is a judgment with which few will disagree.[96] In terms of inspiration and technique, Wilson's chapter is indebted to the 'Wandering Rocks' episode from Joyce's *Ulysses*, for, as Joyce in his more plebeian moments recognised, everyone in the city has a story to tell, not just the main characters. In *Eureka Street*, Rosemary Daye takes to the streets for the last time, puts chewing gum into her mouth as part of an anti-smoking regime, pops into her favourite shop on Royal Avenue, keeps checking herself in the shop-windows and in the looks of male passersby, cuts down Queen's Arcade, and into a small sandwich shop on Fountain Street to buy something for lunch. Then come the explosion and the instant deaths of Rosemary and of the man who was holding the door open for her: 'She turned to murmur some thanks and stopped existing.'[97] Wilson needed the build-up to this moment, one that is immediately followed by a description of her injuries: 'Her left arm was torn off by the sheeted glass and most of her head and face destroyed by the twisted mass of a metal tray.' The scene recalls F. E. McWilliam's *Women of Belfast*, a series of bronze statues of women caught for ever by the bomb at the Abercorn Bar in March 1972 in the act of performing 'a ballet of death'.[98] But Wilson doesn't forget the other fifteen victims, who also 'had a story', a phrase that the novelist/narrator takes care to repeat. 'To sum them up is pointless . . .. They all had stories. But they weren't short stories. They should each have been novels . . . eight hundred pages or more.'[99] Tellingly, in the previous chapter, the city is presented as a whole, rising and falling like music, as at night 'one thing', the 'daytime jumble . . . unified' (pp.212–13). After the explosion the lens is withdrawn and the narrative becomes more sombre, as if the city had discovered its shame.

The nineteenth-century realist novel relied for part of its cohesion on extended organic metaphors, such as webs and nets or windows and mirrors. Such metaphors were increasingly abandoned, and in the 1930s, as in the work of Christopher Isherwood, George Orwell and John Sommerfield,[100] novelists imagined society not as an inclusive or unified whole but as a mutually exclusive set of different social groups and classes best understood through other (cinematic) techniques such as juxtaposition and cross-section. In his search for his native province in *Fat Lad* (1992), Glenn Patterson signals another departure to imagining a society by recourse to an acrostic – Fermanagh, Antrim, Tyrone, Londonderry, Armagh, Down. In *Burning Your Own* (1988), one of his characters, as if appearing in a William Faulkner novel, asks: 'I mean why did we have to get born here? Here of all places . . .'[101] In *Fat Lad*, Drew Linden's detachment from place accompanies him from the start as the Ex-Pat steps off the plane after eight years away. His homecoming is also marked by a return to his childhood memories and in particular to the early 1970s and to an incident in which a sniper's bullet arrives unannounced in a neighbour's house. In one of the most memorable sentences in modern Irish writing, the course of the bullet is described in detail by Patterson:

In the early hours of the morning of the second Saturday in August 1971, a sniper operating from the darkened window of a terraced house in an estate on the foothills of the Antrim Plateau discharged a rifle for the second and last time in his life, sending a single high-velocity bullet flashing down into the Lagan valley, evading the soft exposed parts of a platoon of soldiers pinned down behind a hedge a block away, evading chimney-pots, treetops, road signs, traffic lights, advertising hoardings, lampposts, church spires, flagpoles (an inordinate number of church spires and flagpoles), and all make and manner of buildings besides, till, closing in on the darkened window of another house on another estate two miles to the south-east, it drilled a perfect hot-poker hole in the glass, puncturing with ease the roll blind, the drapes, the kitchen's boast door, and the chipboard wall of the larder, where it entered and exited in turn a box of Kellogg's cornflakes, a packet of Polson's cornflour, a packet of Atora suet, a box each of Whitworth's sultanas and raisins, a tin of Campbell's cream of tomato soup; entered, finally, a full bag of Tate & Lyle sugar (annihilating the craggy sugar-cube gladiator), but, encountering solid brick on the far side, did not exit and came instead to a stunned halt in the granular belly of the bag.[102]

This is a *pathetic* image of Northern Ireland, brought into sharp focus by the potentially deadly path of a bullet whistling down the Lagan valley. Given the absence of other means of communication between the two sides, there is something misplaced about one estate talking to another two miles away by means of a bullet which lands in a larder full of staples that would have been identical in the cupboards of both working-class estates. It is as if the trajectory itself – cleverly associated with Drew's own feelings of guilt that he was responsible for his family staying in that area – has been requisitioned, like the acrostic title, to do the work that organic metaphors or the technique of cross-section did in the past. The public and the private worlds, the physical and the social, the domestic and the civic, are here imagined as connected or connecting by the novelist. But this, we realise, is only in the imagination, for the bullet is designed to tear communities apart, not join them together. That the bullet halts in the granular belly of the bag of sugar also offers us another image of Patterson's deflationary art, that, as Drew's sister Anna suggests, at the heart of the matter there was no heart of the matter (p.248). As a footnote, we can also observe the same rebounding vision at work in Patterson's *That Which Was* (2004) when we are told that 'North Belfast has peace lines in public parks'.[103]

Patterson's search in fiction for his native province provides a rich seam for those interested in the latest phase of the colonial encounter. He told an interviewer in 1995 that fictional representations of Northern Ireland appeared to have got stuck about 1972.[104] Of all Northern writers, Patterson is most alert to the issue of defining the contemporary. The powerful theme of teenage gangs getting caught up in sectarian violence is explored in *Burning Your Own*, which explains how people who came from everywhere in the North – including Ardoyne, Sandy Row, the Falls, and Shankill, as well as Lisburn, Strabane and Derry – could produce on the eve of the Troubles in 1969 a mentality which effectively burnt their own. 'In the beginning . . . was the dump' is how that novel begins. In *The International* (1999), in an attempt to discover an Eden before the Fall or the city's old self, Patterson returns to the days before the Troubles to the inaugural meeting of the Civil Rights Association in January 1967. *Fat Lad* is contemporary but, as if to emphasise a different kind of distance, the protagonist arrives home from work in England before the events of the narrative unfold. The image of the protagonist's granny's goldfish runs through the opening chapter of *Fat Lad*, and the chapter closes with a reference to the fish's nose and tail being so close together in the bowl 'it was almost able to eat its own shit'. One commentator interprets this image as an example of 'exhausted symbolism', but I would read this slightly differently.[105]

Patterson never strays far from his roots. The potential for tragedy, for symbols, is always present but is somehow declined by Patterson. Drew inhabits the same prosaic world as the reader. In Dublin he buys *Hot Press* (the music magazine); in Belfast, he hears someone shooting dead a policeman, five hundred yards away: '– That's fucking shooting. It fucking is. It's fucking shooting' (p.208). Patterson stresses a different take on the colonial encounter, one bent on lowering the temperature and on establishing points of contact which are at once independent of sectarianism but yet contained within it. One of the most disturbing remarks in *That Which Was* (2004), a novel steeped in the guilt of the Troubles, is what might be heard in ordinary conversation: 'You never know to look at anybody the things they might have done.'[106]

Elsewhere in Troubles fiction, as indeed in a contemporary film such as *The Crying Game* (1992), distance and intimacy are locked in a deadly embrace. Such an observation also yields a literal truth, for, as Allen Feldman points out, 'runbacks' – the retreat from incident to safe house – normally took no longer than five minutes by car, to which he adds that the combination of safe house, washhouse, and runback

Benedict Kiely, the most urbane voice on Irish radio in the second half of the twentieth century. Courtesy of John Minihan.

'signalled the emerging sacrificial patterning of violence'.[107] Jennifer Johnston's novel *Shadow on Our Skin* (1977) explores the relationship between a Catholic boy, Joe Logan, who is on the edge of being drawn into sectarian violence, and his Protestant teacher, Kathleen, who befriends him. In Bernard MacLaverty's novel *Cal* (1983), the protagonist waits in the getaway car while the gunman knocks at the door and fires at the husband of the woman with whom Cal later falls in love and from whom he conceals his role in the murder. In *Proxopera* (1977), a novel which recalls Frank O'Connor's *Guests of the Nation* (1931), Benedict Kiely takes up the hostage situation but he betrays an uncertain tone, as if he couldn't face too much intimacy with the hostage-takers. By contrast, *Nothing Happens in Carmincross* (1985) is a remarkable novel that allows scope for Kiely's leisurely prose and for his feelings concerning the 'acceptable face of Ulster', his native province, to find their true broad redemptive outlet.[108] Eugene McCabe's trilogy *Christ in the Fields* (1993), which is reminiscent of Reid's television play *McCabe's*

Wall (1985), is set along the border in farming country, and reveals another dimension to the play of distance and intimacy. At the end of Reid's play, one in a series that went under the title *Ties of Blood*, Sean, memorably played by J. G. Devlin, hands over money to a hood to kill his daughter because she is seeing a Welsh corporal. In McCabe's *Heritage* (1978), there is a shocking sectarian revenge murder in a farmyard when a Catholic neighbour, Willie Reilly, is found 'humped across a bag of dairy nuts, sprawled as though copulating in an obscene posture of death, mouth and eyes open, tongue out'.[109] Danny Morrison's highly charged novel *The Wrong Man* (1997), set during the hunger strikes, tackles the theme that has long haunted the Irish imagination, namely that of betrayal and the informer.

Such writing pays homage in a sense to two pervasive images, one of a festering wound, the result, according to R. H. Tawney, of a failure in Ireland since the seventeenth century to assimilate, the other of the 'narrow ground', which Walter Scott advanced nearly two centuries ago.[110] But the relationship between history and the novel arguably needs another twist. Underlying some critical accounts seems to be the belief or the claim that history is a wound and that the novel is a kind of bandage or balm or ointment ready to retrieve, in the words of Eve Patten, 'the *condition humaine* from a complex, impersonal reality'.[111] There is merit in such a view, but the best Troubles fiction writers are those who complicate the picture and, in the words of a recent commentator, 'challenge the received forms of "Troubles" narrative'.[112]

In this context, humour also needs careful handling. 'Did you hear the forecast, Dan?' asks one of the characters in Colin Bateman's comedy thriller *Divorcing Jack* (1995). 'Cloudy . . . with widespread terrorism', comes the reply.[113] *Cycle of Violence* (1995), also by Bateman, is about a reporter who rides a mountain bike round the city to report on courts and killings. The title is based on a pun. When Miller fails to return to the office after a drinking spree, the bike becomes part of the 'Endless Cycle of Violence'. 'It's getting into the bombing season again,' remarks Miller's old Belfast editor, while in the provincial town of Crossmaheart (a word that conjures up not only a child's vow 'cross-my-heart-and-swear-to-die' but also the Republican border town and stronghold of Crossmaglen), 'They liked their bombs home-grown.'[114] After the bombs come 'bomb damage sales' and 'a booming trade, so to speak' (p.159). The word 'manslaughter' intrigues the narrator: 'Man's laughter. So apt' (p.161). While there is a liberating irreverence about such humour – it works particularly well at the level of one-liners – it risks a patronising move, a playing to the gallery of those who are surprised to discover that people from the North have a sense of humour. What can be wearing is that *Cycle of Violence*, with its flatlander's view of life, late-night drinking, office banter, and talk of casual sex, is a young man's novel, written by and for people under a certain age. The problem with a knowing style is that it is not far removed from cliché and the commonplace. The Protestant pub, the Ulster Arms, was half empty. 'Or was it half full?'

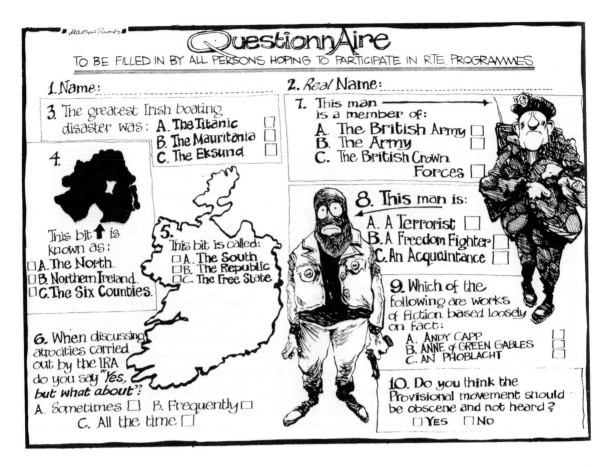

The Catholic pub in Crossmaheart had 'the same aura of barely suppressed violence, the same whiff of desperation brought on by poverty laced with alcoholism' (pp.115–16).

By contrast, in Martyn Turner's satirical cartoons, published in the *Irish Times* and *Fortnight*, the humour is inextricably joined to the serious intent.[115] The closing moment of Glenn Patterson's *The International* (1999) is designed to prevent a sentimental response: 'We're powerful people for remembering here, I hope that's one thing we don't forget.'[116] In the writings of John Morrow, humour is closer to popular speech, allowing space for the two communities to air their grievances without a creeping sentimentality. In spite of its title, Morrow's *Northern Myths* (1979) is as hard-headed as it comes (unless that, too, is one of the myths on display). 'The Bishop's Game', from a piece entitled 'Place: Belfast/Time: 1984/Scene: The Only Pub', recalls Myles Na Gopaleen's column in the *Irish Times* in the 1940s. Set out like a game of chess, the Bishop's Game is a metaphor for Republican tactics, giving advice on how to win moral approval for murdering soldiers. 'Move

The Troubles produced some excellent satire, none better than Martyn Turner's cartoons in the *Irish Times*. Courtesy of Martyn Turner one: blow up any Prod pub on a Saturday night. Move two: angry Prods blow up a Taig pub the next Saturday night.'[117] Morrow then traces ten moves to check mate, beginning with appeals to the Bishop, shooting of a 'sodger at a road check – or two if you're lucky', politicians at Westminster under pressure who force the Army to withdraw, and, finally, victory for Republicans who've made it look as if it's 'all somebody else's fault! So you can start again at Move One. . . .'

Narrate or describe was the famous ideological alternative proposed by Georg Lukács; the realist writer, such as Tolstoy, narrated or told a story, but the naturalist writer, such as Zola, merely described.[118] One linked the novelist to the progressive tradition of European realism, the other to a loss of values or an inability to distinguish values. In a strange way, reading Bateman and other contemporary Troubles fiction writers recalls Lukács and, as we saw in the discussion on *Man of Aran*, a previous but by no means sealed argument between aesthetics and politics. Aspects of the Troubles lend themselves to the conventions of the thriller, and Eoin McNamee, to name but one writer, has made in *Resurrection Man* (1994) – based on the Shankill Butchers – compelling use of the gangster movie against an urban landscape that is at once essentially Irish and, for some deluded characters such as Victor Kelly, John Wayne country. McNamee manages to distance the hard scenes of knife-cutting and torture with comments that are reminiscent of the 1950s TV series *Dragnet* or thriller writers such as Raymond Chandler from the 1940s: 'The city itself has withdrawn into its placenames . . . In its names alone the city holds commerce with itself, a furtive levying of tariffs in the shadow.'[119] The clinical description of butchery and the thriller writer's perspective work in tandem to disturb the reader, but in the case of *Resurrection Man* the thriller writer's dream prevents the narrative from being heard above the description. When Victor shaves his father towards the end of the novel the scene is riveting, but there is also something overcharged about it, as if the author was unsure whether his purpose was excitement or explanation.[120] Similarly, in *The Ultras* (2004), his novel exploring what happened to the British Army informer Robert Nairac, the 'best' moment is the murder of the Miami Show Band. When the ex-Sergeant investigator Blair Agnew explains his attraction to Nairac's story, McNamee could be referring to himself and, again, it concerns not a wider vision but rather the circumstances of Nairac's death, a death which may have taken place in a factory mincer: 'It meant there was a newness to the crime, a modernity to it. The amorality and existential vacancy to it.'[121]

There is a remarkable passage in David Park's novel *Stone Kingdoms* (1996) that describes the funeral scene in March 1988 when a Protestant gunman opened fire on the mourners at Milltown cemetery outside Belfast. The moment, perhaps one of the most memorable to have come out of the Troubles, was well-captured at the time by television cameras, but what the novelist does is to treat the scene not as background but as integral to the discourse of the novel:

Two days after Michael Stone attacks the mourners at the funeral of the IRA unit shot in Gibraltar I pass a paint-daubed wall. 'It only takes one Stone to kill three Taigs', it says. Soon the same celebratory slogan I see everywhere and suddenly it feels as if we are spiralling out of control, no longer just some monotonous side-show, each new burst of savagery reaching out to taint any life it chooses. The whole city tenses, the tight little lines of streets I pass each day, spokes on a wheel which rolls inexorably towards its fate. As always it is unspoken, but you feel it in your stomach, see it in the eyes of the policeman who checks your licence, hear it in the staff-room conversations which avoid its every mention. And always the hovering helicopter, watching, waiting, the sound of its engine throbbing at first like a migraine, then gradually absorbed into the consciousness until it is no longer heard.[122]

It takes time for the novelist, as Patterson also reminds us in *That Which Was* (2004), to handle atrocity. The temptation is to write a novel that deliberately avoids striking a moral note in its descriptions of torture and sectarian killings. It takes a writer such as David Park who – like Martin Waring, the museum curator, in his recent novel *Swallowing the Sun* (2004) – is given to looking rather than touching, to do something more and recycle the moment for posterity.

If Ireland's imagination in the 1930s was dominated in part by the West, it was the North which took centre stage in the 1980s. The colonial encounter ensured the issue concerned not so much a regional identity (as might be the case elsewhere with, say, the West Country or the North of England) as a political identity. The West in the 1930s was dominated by views from outside the region and there were few voices heard from within the region itself. In effect, the West wasn't a regional issue but a word given to a concept which, as I argued, was essentially contestable and which was associated with de Valera's Ireland, with stereotyping by outsiders and with the legacy of the colonial encounter. Hence the importance of the word 'fake' and the idea of recuperation. In contrast, when we turn to the 1980s, fake has given way to legitimacy and the outsider's view to the insider's perspective, where the struggle is on to be heard either inside or outside the violence. The sharpness of the response is testimony to the sharpness of the colonial encounter and a reminder that the endgame in Ireland still has some life in it. Equally, the colonial encounter, far from driving a wedge between the Republic and the North, has brought into closer alignment the destiny of these two parts of Ireland in a way that was never the case with the West, so that while the sleepy West never threatened to destabilise Ireland, the cock of the North has.

The Liffey

SWORDS

LEIXLIP

LUCAN

PALMERSTON

DUBLIN

RAH

CHAPELIZOD

CELBRIDGE

STRAFFAN

SOURCE OF LIFFEY

MILLTOW

KINGS

CLANE

SALLINS

Liffey

NAAS

KIPPURE

BLESSINGTON

R. Liffey

NEWBRIDGE

BALLYMORE

BALLYNULTAGH

KILCULLEN

BALLYKNOCKAN

showing the Principal
towns through & near
which it flows

Chapter 9

CONCLUSION

The fact is, we Irish are the most international people on God's earth.
– Kathleen Coyle, *Youth in the Saddle* (1927)

I used to think I was real because I came from here.
– Tom Murphy, *The Wake* (1998)

What was it all for? The whole thing was a cod.
– John McGahern, *Amongst Women* (1990)

Distant Music or Unfinished Business?

For the African American poet Michael S. Harper, 'History is your own heartbeat', while for Francis Mulhern, adapting a line of Louis Althusser, 'The present lasts a long time'.[1] Where the contemporary begins and ends is always, but especially in the Irish context, given the colonial encounter, an intriguing question. Joyce, author of the modern Odysseus, knew better than most that patterns recur – hence the power of 'the same renew' or 'riverrun', the suggestive lower-case word that launches *Finnegans Wake.* Contemporary Ireland – more so from the perspective of Dublin – runs on like a river, at times underground, the sea ever beckoning, the clouds ceaselessly discharging on moorland in the Wicklow Mountains, where all of Joyce's rivers have their source. Ireland – more so from the North – is a country that presents a standing rebuke to Heraclitus's view that you can't step into the same river twice. Sameness has been a continuing theme throughout this book, but sameness, as we have seen, is a problem term and should not be confused, at least not entirely, with repetition or, indeed, with that Wakean word, recirculation. Martin McDonagh is not Synge, but his plays have produced arguments in Ireland not dissimilar to those heard at the time of the *Playboy* riots in 1907. Loss and darkness continue to exercise Irish writers, as do the rite of passage from child-hood to adolescence and, for historical novelists such as Jennifer Johnston in *This*

Opposite page
Detail of a Bournville Cadbury's 'reward' card, showing the course of Joyce's Anna Livia.

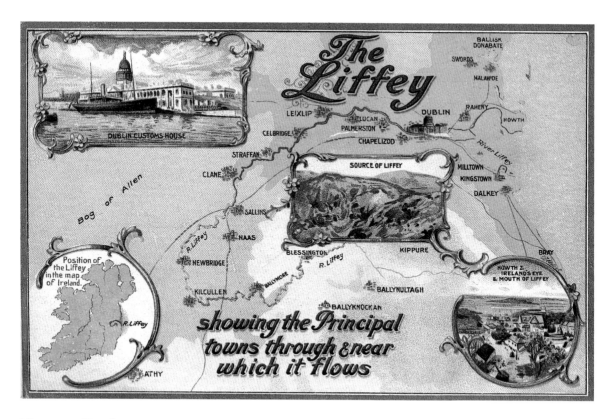

The course of Joyce's Anna Livia. A Bournville Cadbury's 'reward' card, printed when Dun Laoghaire was still known as Kingstown.

Is Not a Novel (2002), the revolutionary decade from 1913 to 1923. In his sequence of verse *The Pen Shop* (1997), which is reminiscent of 'Nightwalker', his poem from the 1960s, Thomas Kinsella, echoing the style of the 'Lotus-Eaters' episode of *Ulysses*, picks his way through the streets of Dublin, passing the sites associated with nationalist and colonial Ireland and ending up in a pen shop for a black refill (itself a suggestive image of postcolonialism and the afterlife of literature).[2] So there are still familiar seams being worked by contemporary Irish writers, and all the while there is a pressure on cultural critics and literary historians to determine whether the colonial legacy has resulted in unfinished business or (simply) the distant music that Gretta Conroy hears on the stairs in 'The Dead'.

John Banville, author of the aptly named *The Book of Evidence* (1989), is a writer's writer, for whom Ireland represents distant music rather than unfinished business.[3] His chosen topics reflect a desire to be taken seriously as a serious writer, and as a European writer, but not necessarily as an Irish writer. Three recent novels, *The Untouchable* (1997), *Eclipse* (2000) and *Shroud* (2002) are at once polished and impenetrable, each with a label attached, *per ardua ad astra* ('through struggle to the stars'). An aloof figure, a part of whom seems to have known from the outset that he would enjoy a career as a novelist, Banville remains the most focused and the most deliberative novelist currently writing in Ireland. The colonial encounter is not his focus, but, like Central Europe, it is never far away. His position is not unlike that articulated by a character in Kathleen Coyle's novel *Youth in the Saddle* (1927): 'The fact is, we Irish are the most international people on God's earth. That's our trouble. We hated belonging to the English, we don't belong to ourselves, we're Europeans. The English took us out of Europe!'⁴ As Banville's *Birchwood* (1973), his Big House 'Irish' novel that contains references to the Famine, suggests, the political unconscious of his fiction stems from a sense of loss rather than from the onward march of the nation. Almost with a sense of perversity, he sets *The Sea* (2005) in the village of Ballyless in the town of Ballymore. When asked to defend himself against the charge that he's not an Irish writer, Banville replies: 'I wouldn't regard this criticism unless I could see how it works. Because if you write in Hiberno-English and you're an Irish writer . . . what's the subject?'⁵

John Banville and Edna Longley at the Frankfurt Book Fair, October 1996. Courtesy of John Minihan.

For Banville, the freedom from an obsession with Irishness has meant the freedom to explore another form of authenticity, as if a new life could be forged in writing. There is a striking coincidence between Banville's subject matter and his way of telling a story. On the opening page of *Eclipse*, the protagonist finds he is being watched by a figure he takes to be his wife: 'I felt diminished briefly, an incidental in that gaze'.⁶ The use of 'diminished' and 'incidental' (here as a noun) is a wake-up call to the reader to pay attention, for, as was suggested in Chapter 2, there are words in a Banville novel that many readers will encounter for the first time, at least with that particular inflection. How a character formulates his or her predicament – and Banville's choice of title is also relevant here – becomes therefore as telling as what s/he is attempting to express. Banville's preference for first-person narratives means that the stress falls naturally on mental processes and on a modernist concern with consciousness and states of mind. Equally, like a latter-day George Eliot, Banville's work is punctuated with phrases that resonate as much against the world outside the novel as against characters inside the novel: 'I do believe that at these times our thinking is thought for us' (the duplicitous Axel is confronting Cass, who is dying of cancer, but yet manages to stop us in our tracks),[7] or 'There are occasions when one catches memory at work' (*Eclipse*, p.84). And, throughout, it is as if the sound has been turned down and all we see is the picture, for Banville's novels are surrounded by the profound postcolonial silence from which they in fact issue.

Anthony Blunt, the 1930s spy who became Curator of Queen Elizabeth's art collection, is the subject of *The Untouchable*. In what we might see as a take on the colonial encounter, Banville invents an Irish past for Victor Maskell, his Blunt-like figure, who, unlike the 'unspeakable' Wilde, remained outside the courts, untouched, that is.[8] Banville also makes much of Blunt's friendship with MacNeice. The two were pupils at Marlborough and later travelled to Spain in 1936. The sixth section in *Autumn Journal* beginning 'And I remember Spain/At Easter ripe as an egg for revolt and ruin'[9] is evoked by Banville in a remarkable paragraph that sheds light both on his fictionalising procedures and on his attitude towards the afterlife of literature or cultural belatedness. 'There were wall-posters, the hammer and sickle on every street corner, and violent-looking young men in red shirts whose flat, weathered features and evasive glances reminded me of the tinkers who in my childhood used to go about Carrickdrum selling tin cans and leaky saucepans.'[10] MacNeice refers to 'the surly or the worried or the haunted faces/With writings on the walls –/Hammer and sickle . . . .' Banville wants the reader to be reminded of this passage in MacNeice, but his object is not pastiche or imitation or parody or quotation or indeed background, for this is the language of the past folded again into the new, where the new is sufficiently itself as not to be overwhelmed by its original. It is Blunt in Spain looking at the same things as MacNeice but with different eyes, seeing not 'haunted' but 'evasive' faces. Once the debt is established, the novelist can then add the Irish local colour and the kind of conventional image that an upper-middle-class figure like Blunt might imagine in retrospect.[11]

Eclipse, the story of a 'thinking man's thespian' (p.12), is ideally suited to the exploration of characteristic obsessions in Banville's work – consciousness, authenticity, playacting or role playing, memory, and the self through time. Such obsessions carry the barely disguised hallmark of a postcolonial discourse. Like his protagonist, Alex, Banville broods on words and constantly hears the soliloquies or dramatic monologues of figures from the past, such as Hamlet or T. S. Eliot's Prufrock or Gerontion. At times there is exaggeration, or what can amount to the same thing, namely indulgence, as when Alex declares: 'There is no present, the past is random, and only the future is fixed' (p.77). Banville is sufficiently removed from his characters to allow room for doubt as to whether he himself believes such remarks, but he is nothing if not profound or well-schooled, as when Alex asks, 'what makes for presence if not absence?' (p.46). At other times, Alex recalls the narrator in Ford Madox Ford's *The Good Soldier* (1915), a novel the interpretation of which depends on the reliability or otherwise of the main protagonist. But whatever judgment we come to about Dowell, we are pretty sure that Alex is not psychologically deranged, only that he is 'never off the stage' (p.140) and therefore that he is given to forms of displacement and psychological manoeuvring.

Shroud (2002) takes up the story of Alex's unbalanced daughter, Cass, the research student who foregoes to use the knowledge she has to expose the Nazi past of the Paul de Man figure Axel Vander (the play on Alex and Axel is presumably intentional). Again, Banville manages to have his cake and eat it. There are whole passages in which the author could be describing his own work, as in a paragraph where Axel reflects on his essays on Rilke, Kleist and Kafka: 'a master of compelling inventiveness . . . an alchemist of word and image' (where 'inventiveness' and 'alchemist' carry a certain ambivalence), 'passages of ecstatic intensity . . . world-drunk lyricist' (the risk Banville runs), 'desperate and inconsolable' (Banville is out on his own), and then the most enigmatic of all sentences to conclude the paragraph: 'What troubles me only is the thought of all I might have done had I been simply – if such a thing may be said to be simple – myself' (p.62). It is in the nature of things that Banville's fiction will always shelter under a mask of his own making, but he has a strengthening quality we might associate with Joseph Conrad, only now the moral universe is more closely allied with a decidedly postmodernist interest in identity and epistemological doubt. As for Irishness, try a different question seems to be Banville's advice, but we would be wrong to follow such advice.

One response to the unchanging nature of Irish life, or – as it has sometimes been perceived – to the dead hand of the past, has been to stress the idea of an afterlife, not in the traditional meaning of what comes after death but in the sense of cultural belatedness or of living on in the shadow of the past. How this is connected with the colonial encounter, or whether this is a symptom of that encounter, remain intriguing questions. Running through Derek Mahon's *Collected Poems* (1999)[12] – arguably the most engaging and unified of all recent collections by an Irish poet – from his best-known poem 'A Disused Shed in Co Wexford' to the painful 'Dawn at St Patrick's' (about being hospitalised in Swift's asylum) and later moving sequences in *The Hudson Letter* (1995) and *The Yellow Book* (1997), there is this 'shadowy' quality, and invariably it is something which poses a threat or challenge to life as lived 'in here or out there' (p.171). As his predecessor Austin Clarke also discovered from his experience in St Patrick's – 'The Mansion of Forgetfulness/Swift gave us for a jest' – it takes only a little adjustment for 'in here' and 'out there' to be mapped onto the mind and body.[13] Even descriptive phrases such as 'a late flame flickering' (p.190) in 'Global Village', or 'Left-over echoes of the night before' (p.109) in 'Rock Echoes', or 'an afterlife/Of dead leaves' (p.60) in 'Leaves', have a capacity to wither or disturb (though less so, as with the first example, if we are reminded of Matthew Arnold and the Victorian loss of

A high window on the world. John Lavery's *Daylight Raid from my Studio Window, 7 July 1917*. Courtesy of Gallery Press.

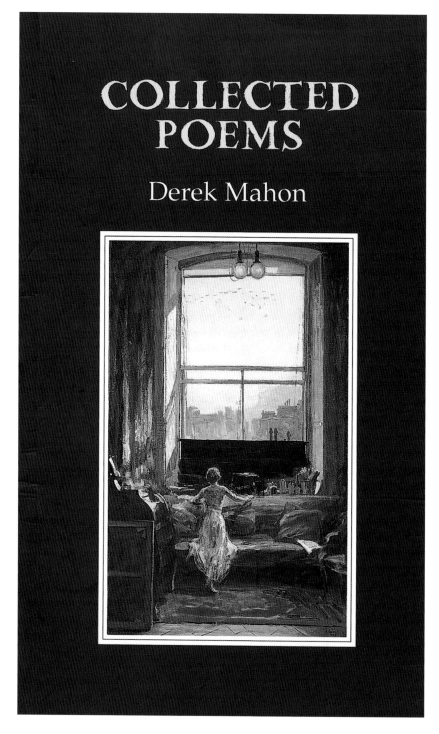

faith). When Mahon confesses in 'Ovid in Tomis' that 'The Muse is somewhere/Else' (p.161), he could be expressing his own thoughts, for his verse is indeed about elsewhere. Any 'Rage for Order', the title of a poem that is closer to home in that it addresses the Troubles, occurs within an 'unstructurable sea' (p.47), an adjective and a collocation which betoken elsewhere. Even what is most pressing is expressed through the prism of elsewhere, as when in 'Camus in Ulster' Mahon declares he 'never imagined the plague to come' (p.99). With *Collected Poems* in front of us, it becomes clear that the work of this Irish Protestant 'make-believe existentialist' staring at 'the clouds of unknowing' (p.170) constitutes a sustained meditation on the vacuum that exists at the heart of the universe, where stars are perhaps no more than 'glittering dust' (p.161), where (anonymous) space threatens to dissolve (familiar) place, and where the past offers a quarry but little comfort.

'A Disused Shed in Co Wexford' was written before the recent Troubles and during a decade when there was a renewed attempt at economic co-operation between the Irish Government and Stormont. Mahon's primary focus seems to be on bringing together a disparate trio of sites (Peruvian mines, the concentration camp at Treblinka, and Pompeii) which he imagines – imagines, that is, not the mage-like Yeatsian 'conjures up' – are inhabited by former spirits who cry out 'Save us, save us'. Such a thought would be unexceptional if left there, but what makes the poem resonate is the connection Mahon draws with a disused shed in the quiet backwater of the south east of Ireland, where the spirits 'have been waiting for us . . . since civil war days' (p.89). The association works in an odd way, for what at first appears deliberately strained somehow also looks of a piece, as if history is always ready to unfreeze or to re-surface in the most unlikely of places. Some readers have been tempted to read the poem in terms of Mahon's prescience or his awareness that fissures in the North were about to open up again. Tom Paulin goes further: 'Among other historical subjects, Mahon's poem, which dates from early in the 'Troubles', gives a voice to the victims of political violence – violence which a substantial section of Ulster Unionism is trying to ensure continues.'[14] But this is to tie the poem to a wrong kind of history, for it is much more about listening to the past and allowing room for the mute or inarticulate voices of those abandoned by history to be heard again. Mahon understands the depth of the colonial encounter, and how the spirits have been waiting for the light, but not necessarily waiting to be avenged.

The two poems preceding 'A Disused Shed in Co. Wexford' anticipate and amplify the theme of the afterlife. In 'The Banished Gods', Mahon adjusts his telescope, drawing back from history to focus on the banished gods on the Greek island of Paros who 'sit out the centuries' spinning out a reverie of a 'world without cars, computers,/Or nuclear skies' (p.86). In 'A Refusal to Mourn', he returns to Ireland and to an old man living alone in a country farmhouse having survived his wife and now with only a clock's tick to fill the silence and the long evenings. In time he will be buried and in yet more time the name on his gravestone will fade and the stone itself will be transformed to mud. Here the afterlife – the fate that awaits us all – threatens to nullify human endeavour and encourage depression. The poet's recourse, his turn back or rescue from such a way of thinking, is via an essentially Stoic idea, how 'the secret bred in the bone . . . survives in other times' (p.88). What such poems reveal is a loss of attachment to the nine-to-five world and a retreat into the self of the small hours (when many of Mahon's poems seem to have been composed).

There are few places in Mahon's verse that don't carry the look of the afterlife. In an early poem, 'Ecclesiastes', he confesses: 'God, you could grow to love it' (p.35). He is thinking of Belfast, a city that can be accepted only in retrospect (itself a form of afterlife). In 'Glengormley', the attachment to place comes without an emotional entanglement: 'By/Necessity, if not choice, I live here too' (p.14). Seemingly, only thus, by a process of reflection hanging on a string of single-syllable words, could he develop a liking for his native province. In 'Going Home', a poem dedicated to John Hewitt, the author of the line 'We are not native here or anywhere' (quoted in Chapter 7), Mahon finds comfort in the echo 'As if I belonged here too' (p.95), a phrase in which each word carries its own form of displacement but which, when take as a whole, enforces the connection with one of Mahon's predecessors. However, it is because of his radical dis-ease with bourgeois life, with the '"family values" brigade' (p.200), that he is attracted, on the one hand, to the homeless in New York, for he has been there – 'in detox' (p.208), too – and, on the other hand, to scenes, as with Oates's moment of sacrifice in 'Antarctica', which connect the ridiculous with the sublime: 'I am just going outside and may be some time' (p.166). Instead of the wishful thinking that Yeats undertakes in 'Prayer for My Daughter', Mahon stares straight into the postmodern condition, writing from the edge, with a pained heart and without stilts. In his verse letters to his daughter and son (*Collected Poems* is dedicated to them), from whom he is now separated, he acknowledges his debt to the great man but wishes for 'not innocence and ceremony/exactly, but a more complicated grace':

> I've had neither the authority nor the opportunity
> to tell you about the things you need to know,
> as your mother will: how not to rely on looks
> only, but on acquired skills and the wisdom found in books –
> up to a point of course . . . (p.201)

That last phrase adds a double qualification, a lessening of the tension, but the effect is to intensify the plight of the poet for the reader. In the poet's own life he too shares with his themes the fate of an afterlife, only in this case it is the realisation that he, in New York, has been 'five time-zones' away from his children growing up in London, that leading a parallel life when it comes to children is indeed not only elsewhere but a form of afterlife.

Paul Muldoon's *Moy Sand and Gravel* (2002), which won the Pulitzer Prize for Poetry, affords another distinctive perspective on the legacy of the colonial encounter and the afterlife of literature.[15] In the long sequence that concludes the volume, 'At the Sign of the Black Horse, September 1999', Muldoon – like Yeats, a father again at a similarly late age of around fifty – consciously deploys lines from 'Prayer for My Daughter' to apply to his own son, Asher, who too sleeps 'half hid/under the cradle hood' (p.77). As his name in Hebrew suggests, Asher is blessed, an example to his father of Yeats's 'radical innocence', an idea co-opted with peculiar force here (even if it comes across as strangely out of place). The context of the poem is the aftermath of Hurricane Floyd in 1999, when the Delaware and Raritan Canal – beside which Muldoon now lives with his Jewish wife – broke its bank. Into the afterlife of the canal flowed street and other signs which usually surround our lives with advice, exhortation, warning, and in this case, because they are detached from context, inanity. Such signs are cleverly deployed by Muldoon to punctuate the onward flow of the poem: 'No Turn/On Red', 'Please Secure Your Own Oxygen Mask/Before Attending to Children'. 'Please Use The Hammer To Break/The Glass.' In this characteristically densely worked sequence, which gathers together all the themes of this finely wrought and intricate volume, Muldoon, as if to put down roots in the New World, carries out a priestly act of consecration whereby the discontinuous is made continuous, the past present, and the guilty goy 'shriven' (p.78). This is not Yeats pacing the battlements on his Tower at Ballylee but rather a poet finding a different accommodation with the world. As if indicative also of the distance he has travelled from his roots, the poet's spelling has been Americanised by his publishers (as in 'rumored' and 'plowing') and there is even a reference to 'fixing' a meal (p.75), but, despite this, Muldoon's imagination is anchored – more than Yeats's was – to the world of his childhood and youth. Hence his title is not 'Sand and Gravel' but *Moy Sand and Gravel*, an acknowledgement of distant music and of a local habitation where his construction as a person and poet began and continues. Everywhere in this volume he is alert to the fate of his countrymen on what for them was always the other side. He refers to the Irish navvies who built the canal in the 1830s as 'the groundbreaking Irish navvies' where the physical takes proper precedence over the metaphorical, and in their 'keen and kvetch' he imagines them as both Irish and Jewish. In 'The Loaf', a memorable poem about installing a dimmer switch into the wall of his ancient house, it is the same navvies he recalls. This time, in touching the texture of the original wall with its horse-hair matted into the clay for strengthening, all his hybrid senses are excited and he imagines hearing the clink of the spades and shovels.

Muldoon is an expert at reconfiguring or bringing into active alignment the past and present. In the light of the discussion in Chapter 3 about the Great Famine and the Holocaust, it is worth recording that 'At the Sign of the Black Horse, September 1999' is one of the few poems in modern Irish writing to include Auschwitz in its frame of reference. In *Moy Sand and Gravel* roads lead to Auschwitz and from Auschwitz – but perhaps, it has to be admitted, only because of the poet's newly acquired family connections and his voyage out again in mid-life. In his exploration of the construction or deconstruction of identity, Muldoon as a poet repeatedly discovers that 'the stone's in the midst of all', only in his case it is words, not revolutionary commitment, as it was for Yeats in 'Easter 1916', which have this lapidary, punning quality. But Muldoon's extraordinary capacity to read the signs in the culture, a culture that both does and does not recognise borders, gives him the power to disturb. The 'bourne' in an earlier poem gives way to 'boreen', an image of life's boundary, reward or final destination being reached via the homely Irish word for country lane, 'boreen'. As the flood carries along with it 'piles of hair, spectacle frames, bootees and brogans' (p.97) it throws together the fates of his new-born child, the Irish schlemiels who built the canal, and his new Jewish family, survivors of the camps and massacres in Europe.

On a determinedly lighter note, the word 'as' recurs in Muldoon's verse and it is fitting that in this volume he constructs a whole poem under this umbrella title. 'As dutch treat gives way to french leave/and spanish fly gives way to Viagra . . . I give way to you.' Alignment, coincidence or association – work at it, the super-subtle Muldoon seems to say. Always in his sights is not so much iconicity as relationship, the movement from I the poet to you the reader. At times, as with the image of the dimmer switch, Muldoon enforces his point in characteristic fashion with a deflat-ing end-rhyme – 'it seems I've scratched a two-hundred-year-old itch' (p.47). The dimmer switch, however, resonates long after the poem has been put down as an image of Muldoon's semi-detached relationship with the present and past, where 'dimmer' gestures towards a favourite mode (that of adjustment) and where 'switch' signals a key rhetorical procedure.

That Muldoon is a difficult poet needs little insisting on, but we would be wrong not to feel the pressure behind this volume. The response of the boy in 'The Misfits' to uncomplimentary, racy remarks about a gay ex-priest, such as how he had 'no lead/in his pencil', is both amusing and genuine: 'I think you've all been misled' (p.10). In 'Unapproved Road', the young boy in a car with his uncle is stopped at a border customs post. It is 1956, during the bombing campaign in the North, and a time when de Valera was considering re-introduction of internment in the South. The future poet notices in the customs officer 'another black-coated, long fellow' (p.4). The misfit Muldoon, 'the Goy from the Moy', is a poet fascinated by linguistic contamination and word association, but frequently, when he doubles back on himself, he is intent on questioning or ironising known identities and exploring the 'unapproved roads' that straddle the border, whether that is seen in political, sexual, cultural, historical, linguistic or religious terms. The customs officer, with the Irish derivation of his local village in mind, believed his ancestors drove their sheep all the way from Africa, knowing no frontier. Here is another image of the afterlife, where the past offers itself as a prospect of the future, the bourne in the boreen, where, after all the marking out of territory between the harp and the crown, perhaps now is the time for relinquishing 'fastness' in favour of 'no fixed abode'.

Despite the backdrop to his work in the classics, the Great War and the contemporary Troubles, the Irish poet most at home in the world is Michael Longley. A deeply religious poet, his purchase on this world shines through everything he writes. Even his prayers have a sensuous quality, as in 'Burren Prayer', whose opening line weaves together flowers, embroidery, and a female-centred traditional culture: 'Gentians and lady's bedstraw embroider her frock.'[16] In 'A Prayer', an exquisite four-line poem lamenting the desecration of churches in Ireland, he prays that rain will pour into the font and snow fall on the altar because 'no snow flake ever falls in the wrong place' (p.17). His characteristic way of dealing with the Troubles is via a finely observed view of nature, a necessary distance which yet manages to bring us closer to the possibility of redemption. 'My nature writing', he has recently suggested, 'is my most political.'[17] In poems such as 'Ceasefire' and 'The War Graves', he brilliantly illustrates the continuing truth, the unfinished business, of Wilfred Owen's remark that 'the poetry is in the pity'. The encounter between Achilles and Priam forms the vehicle of his poem about the IRA ceasefire in 1994; the tenor concerns the need for forgiveness by and towards those with blood on their hands: 'I get down on my knees and do what must be done/And kiss Achilles' hand, the killer of my son.'[18] In 'The War Graves', a poem on the Great War that makes no specific reference to his native province, Longley returns to the primary scene of modern history for Ulster Protestants, a scene that forever binds their fate with that of Britain and the Commonwealth. More importantly, Longley reminds us that poems about the Great War by the children of those who participated (Ted Hughes is another example) still have the power to strike home as if their authors, too, shared with Owen and Charles Sorley and Edward Thomas, poets mentioned by name in this poem, something of the same need to bear witness. As is shown in 'The headstones wipe out the horizon like a blizzard', Longley's lines are visually alive and devastating, and never far away from his feet are the flowers of survival or redemption. He ends the poem at Owen's grave, where, with his companion – his poetry is nothing if not social – he picks from a nettle bed 'One celandine each, the flower that outwits winter' (p.23).

For some writers in the North, the Troubles cleared the air; for others, such as Medbh McGuckian, the dust has taken longer to settle. In *Drawing Ballerinas* (2001), there is a kind of distillation as she reflects more systematically on the personal tragedies that went under the name 'the Troubles'. In the title poem, written to commemorate the death of a schoolfriend in the Abercorn Café explosion in 1972, McGuckian manages to combine a tender portrait with a characteristic interest in difficulty as a means of communication. The insertion of 'restless' into the line 'The body turns in, restless, on itself' acts as a pause or caesura, restores dignity to the victim and focuses our attention on the line of verse and on the line of the poem.[19] At the moment of the explosion the body is indeed restless but on turning over 'reveals opposing versions of itself', 'lips that half-belong to a face'. In a poem such as this, we eventually arrive, after all the shocking descriptions of violence, in the last chapter, at the gate that marks the departure point and the destination of the Troubles, for what did the Troubles demonstrate if not only (a) that the human body is vulnerable and does and does not exist detached from the person, and (b) that sectarianism reveals opposing versions of itself? In retrospect, it becomes clear that McGuckian's verse owes more to the Troubles than at first meets the eye, and that she is involved in wresting meaning from ground zero or the blindingly obvious. 'In every language it is already/past midnight,' she declares enigmatically in 'Crumlin Road Courthouse' and by way of explanation she continues: 'all they give us/in the way of sunlight is a log/veiled by the fire it feeds'(p.59). She could be describing or justifying her own practice as a poet, where clearings are few and far between and where any gesture towards Plato's Ideal Forms is met by a language that veils, or by metaphors or analogies which insist on incorporation even as they delight in resisting such a move. In contrast with Muldoon, there is no more uncertain or angst-inducing word in her verse than 'as'.

On display throughout Brendan Kennelly's poetry are remnants of the colonial encounter. The sense of the afterlife – also to be observed in the end-of-world lyrics of Bono – tends to find expression as a heightened engagement with the here and now. There is a telling remark in the Preface to *The Book of Judas* (1991): 'Half-heartedness is a slow, banal killer.'[20] 'Explode' is what his correspondent The Bomb does best (p.302) and this, too, is Kennelly's high energy trademark, but with a difference. From *Cromwell* (1987) to *The Book of Judas* to 'A Black-and-Tan' in *Begin* (1999), Kennelly is intent on exploring objects of opprobrium, whether specifically in Irish society or more generally in Western culture. Giving a voice to Judas or Hitler or Cromwell (who was hated above all others for his military exploits in Ireland) or to the British soldier who belonged to the unit that terrorised Irish rural communities in the War of Independence, is a politically or religiously charged move, which relies in part on the Christian distinction between hating the sin and loving the sinner. At times, because no more evil will issue from a particular source, he can afford to be indulgent, as with the trolley-bus driver he worked with in London in 1957, who recounted his time in Ireland: 'The blokes were out for our skins/but the birds opened up in style.'[21] Kennelly, an adept at seeking out

Ready for the world outside, Brendan Kennelly in his papermill at Trinity, 1997. Courtesy of John Minihan.

'the dark realities of the heart' as he puts it in 'Limerick Train' (*Begin*, p.79), was 'somewhat surprised to find/how much I liked Will Flint/and his Black-and-Tan talk/warming my heart and mind' (p.68).

More characteristic is the alignment of discourses between history and contemporary attitudes and behaviour. Judas picks blackberries in Connemara with Hitler and impishly suggests a link between his companion's blindness, vitality, and love of perfection and the man with a thesis about poetry or the gospels. 'He's glad he's seen the light. . . . He has a thesis to prove' (*Book of Judas*, p.319). Kennelly is here continuing a complaint made by Patrick Kavanagh in 'Who Killed James Joyce?' that the academy often serves to negate the life of literature. Kennelly's comparison is deliberately far-fetched and yet there is merit in not confining Hitler to history. Judas is a more formidable figure, for betrayal is woven into the fabric of Western culture, making reversal one of the most beguiling rhetorical tropes: 'Don't make my lie your truth, my truth your lie' (p.279). As ever, Kennelly goes off-campus, as it were, to amplify the theme: Judas, the unfaithful husband, pays lip-service, while, 'so long as he doesn't tell me' (p.213), his wife finds she can cope. Occasionally, as in 'Limerick Train', a poem that first appeared in *Real Ireland* (1984), a book of photographs by Liam Blake with text by Kennelly, the contemporary is confronted without any personae or theatricality. While travelling home from Dublin to Kerry across a land now devoid of gods and heroes, Kennelly notices a man in a field like an effigy, lifting a hand to salute only to disappear 'drowned in distant anonymity' (p.78). It's an image of the fast-disappearing Irish countryman frozen by the camera in time, waving emptily at the future. The reflective turn deepens with 'We have travelled far', where 'far' comes to signify no longer the landscape but history, 'the land's uncertainty'. The anger that sustained a previous generation is now dead, 'power in hand' is now in the hands of those with 'power in pocket', while ruined castles are 'witnesses to all we've squandered and spent'. The poem ends on a familiar note – the need to 'cherish, and reject, the dead', where the commas suggest an insertion, a conscious choice, between cherish and reject. But the most intriguing idea in the poem is reserved for a question about Ireland's afterlife post-Independence:

> Who, I wonder, fully
> Understands the imminent predicament,
> Sprung from rooted suffering and folly?

It is not a *tragic* predicament or even a tragedy but an 'imminent predicament', a slightly awkward phrase where the final syllable in each word undercuts any potentially portentous statement; 'folly' is a similarly deflecting word. And yet, Kennelly manages to express not the abyss but the predicament that is now beginning to face a country with (a) history no longer straightforwardly on its side.

The playwright Tom Murphy continues to disturb the calm of Irish life. *The Wake* (1998) – another suggestive image of the afterlife, of Irish life after Independence – works the same seam as *Confessions on a Homecoming* (1983). After years away, Vera, the black sheep of the family, has returned from New York (where she has been working as a prostitute) to pay her respects to her grandmother and to sort out the family hotel left her some time before by her mother. She takes up with an old flame, the dissolute Finbar, who was abused by the Christian Brothers while in a children's home, and the two are soon joined by her brother-in-law Henry, a disillusioned, alcoholic, drop-out lawyer. The rest of the family, who hadn't informed Vera of her grandmother's death, are determined to block the auction of the hotel. That is the groundwork of the play, but the play's discourse centres on another form of dissolution, the dissolving of images and in particular of Vera's *awakening* to her fate. While her family are in one sense dead, given over to busy, bourgeois, money-making concerns and to protecting 'the Catholic ethos in this country', Vera no longer belongs anywhere, neither in Ireland nor the States. Repeatedly and involuntarily, she uses 'Ah-haa!', a sign of her waking up to reality, but then towards the end of the play she poignantly discovers that the real is itself an illusion: 'I used to think I was real because I came from here.'[22] When all the family come together and, as if to 'redeem something of their innocence' (p.93), start singing and reciting the old songs such as 'The Lily of Killarney', 'My Little Grey Home in the West', and Mangan's poem, 'Vision of Connacht', Murphy twists the knife on the whole culture. The final scene, a coda to the play, takes place in the cemetery, where Vera meets up again with Mrs Conneeley, a widow tending her husband's unmarked grave. When Mrs Conneeley concedes that the graveyard is getting crowded, we sense the remark is more than merely casual. Vera, meanwhile, Murphy tells us, is overcome with '[g]rief for her grandmother, for the family she perhaps never had, and for herself and her fear at this, her first acceptance of her isolation' (p.106).

One writer who appears in both the poetry and drama sections of the women's edition of the *Field Day Anthology of Irish Writing* (2002) is Paula Meehan.[23] Her poetry has received wide and proper recognition but here I want to touch on two of her plays, *Mrs Sweeney* (1997) and *Cell* (2000). In terms of unfinished business, these plays remind us of Fred Ryan's critique of nationalism in the 1900s, providing, as they do, a terrible record of life for those excluded from the wealth created by the Celtic Tiger or 'this tiger bastard' as it's called in Jimmy Murphy's play *The Kings of the Kilburn High Road* (2000).[24] Behind Meehan can be heard Tom Murphy and O'Casey, 1960s kitchen-sink dramatists and 1970s and 1980s feminist theatre, but the energy comes from elsewhere. Meehan deliberately turns her back on the picture postcard view of Ireland and holds a mirror up to nature, nature now seeking not so much expression as relief from drudgery. On display is a combination of working-class female oppression and a distinctively Irish form of exile in Catholic Ireland, exile, that is, from the good life and any sense of heaven on earth. In *Mrs Sweeney*, a play set in a run-down Dublin estate which begins with a messy burglary and the destruction of Mr Sweeney's racing-pigeons, there is a poignant moment at the end of the first Act when Lil Sweeney recalls the words of the prayer 'Hail Holy Queen', a prayer which includes phrases such as 'poor banished children of Eve' and 'after this our exile'.[25] Religion is distant music and priests are of little practical help, being but part of a male world defeated by circumstance or inaction. Dead pigeons are named after figures from Ireland's heroic past, such as Theobald Wolfe Tone and James Connolly, figures who have become but a symbolic heap of feathers on the floor to be poked at with tongs. Sweeney himself carries the name of the king in Irish mythology who, driven mad by the

Paula Meehan at home with the world. Courtesy of John Minihan.

noise of battle, fled to the woods, only in this case the modern counterpart, who was once going to change the world, retreats under the furniture, never to recover his sanity. Relief for Lil comes from alcohol, neighbours, quick repartee and fragments of songs, and she turns repeatedly to a photo of her daughter, Chrissie, who died of AIDS. In Meehan's world, unlike Yeats's, there never was a time when one could speak of romantic Ireland.

Cell, a play about four (non-political) women prisoners, is, as the title suggests, even more confined and even more Hobbesian, the setting being an unmodernised modern prison cell with only a window offering a view on the world. 'Sure isn't it a terrible world out there?' Delo, the prison supplier and bully, remarks about the prevalence of drugs beyond the prison walls.[26] Because of the irony and deception, the remark is noticed by the audience but calls for a different kind of response than simple assent. Yes, it is terrible out there but the theatre needs to address it – this seems to be part of Meehan's uncompromising message, and her work engages, like Jimmy Murphy's, with deprivation, exclusion, and oppression. As with the other writers of the poor mentioned in the Introduction, Meehan's concerns – concerns shared by Ursula Rani Sarma in plays such as *Touched* (2000) and *Blue* (2002) – are with those who are trapped or defined by circumstance, hardened yet vulnerable; those who didn't make it through. The abject world of *Cell* is a reminder that negation for Irish writers does not always come with the resonance that we find in, say, Beckett's writing. According to Hamm there may be no more nature, but repetition in Beckett is invariably shown as double-edged, both stultifying and reassuring. In *Waiting for Godot*, nothing, as someone once quipped, happens twice; in *Endgame*, in answer to Hamm's inquiry about the weather, Clov replies 'As usual'. By contrast, for playwrights with working-class roots such as Murphy and Meehan, the bleak stage is indeed bleak, as if there were no half-way houses to arrest the descent into hell, as if the Famine or an Ireland without either the harp or the crown beckoned. When Laurence, a male prostitute, enters the dimly-lit stage in Conor McPherson's unsettling domestic play *Shining City* (2004), which is set in contemporary Dublin, he gives the appearance of someone walking in off the streets, a reminder to the audience of another kind of drama more real than the theatre itself. Equally, to escape the ghosts of the failed relationships which haunt them, widower John and his gay counsellor Ian crave physical contact, only to discover that reality lies elsewhere. When, at the end of McPherson's play, Ian, an abject future ahead of him, declares that 'we know nothing', John, abjection now behind him, concurs in a worn-out yet heartfelt line that still has some power in it: 'We're just barely fucking hanging in there, really, aren't we?'[27]

As we have seen, McGuckian pursues one line of enquiry, where language follows experience, but there are other ways of conceiving that relationship. Anne Devlin's *After Easter* (1994), a play about Pentecost, is a reminder that, while in the beginning there may have been the Word, with the descent of the Holy Ghost, language becomes associated not so much with logocentricity and origin as with the expression of diverse, scattered, and, in Gretta Flynn's case, unhinged voices. *After Easter* – the echo of Easter 1916 and of Stewart Parker's play *Pentecost* (1987) is presumably intended – British soldiers still patrol the streets in the North and the banshee is still heard by Gretta on her visit to Belfast from her home in Oxford, where she is a psychiatric patient. England v Ireland, exile v home, mental illness v visionary or religious experience – Devlin's play provides a *moving* critique of the colonial encounter, where the emphasis falls on character and betrayal within a Catholic family. Gretta's atheistic father retains his left-wing beliefs to the end, her mother tempers her beliefs so as not to risk losing contracts for the family outfitters, Manus, Gretta's younger brother, bristles when tackled by British soldiers, her sister Helen is a successful commercial artist living in London, another sister, Aoife, a teacher with five children, has never left the North, while her cousin, Elish, is a nun and Prioress of her convent. Because it's played out in the context of family, it is also a generational play, largely centred on women in their thirties reflecting on their own lives and on those of their parents. Measuring difference is at the heart of the play, particularly the difference between living in England and Ireland. In reply to Aoife's observation that Gretta's ghost might be English, Helen, the worldly success, is touchy: 'does everything have to have a nationality?'[28] The deeper reaches of the play, as in the beautiful children's story that marks the closing scene, or in the enigmatic expressions that pierce the play's ordinary texture, suggest otherwise. With 'Harvest Home' for a brief musical accompaniment, *After Easter* is a richly allusive play that challenges an audience to make sense of it in its own terms while never forgetting that at its centre is not so much a family as a tribe. As ever, Devlin never strays far from her roots and has few equals as a commentator on her own people. One sentence that reverberates long after the play has ended is Gretta's comment to Paul, a Catholic policeman: 'We have the faith of the killers and the guilt of the spared' (p.55).

One consequence of the colonial encounter was a fierce censorship, which, as I suggested in Chapter 7, was in part the harp's attempt to block the worldview of the coloniser. As if they still believe in the absolute autonomy of the body, contemporary Irish writers continue to delight in breaking taboos. The loosening up that was ushered in by the 1980s has continued apace, even at a time when sex abuse cases and priests involved in paedophilia were coming to light. In a recent poem, 'The Tantric Master', Meehan sings in praise of the male body through the voice of an Indian aspirant, homing in on 'his noble and magical wand. He do good/business throughout the night with it.'[29] Anne Enright's novel *The Pleasure of Eliza Lynch* (2002) welcomes the reader to the new Ireland with a frankness that would have been unthinkable or unprintable a generation ago: 'Francisco Solano López put his penis inside Eliza Lynch on a lovely spring day in Paris, in 1854. . . . In the spring of 1854, no imagination was needed as Francisco Solano López pushed his penis into Eliza Lynch and pulled it back again, twenty times in all.'[30] To describe this as an historical novel is as misleading as implying that 'no imagination was needed', for Enright has absorbed, on the one hand, all the playfulness of the Latin-American novel and the *jouissance* of Barthes's *The Pleasure of the Text* (1976)[31] and, on the other hand, all the memory of a culture which had traditionally excluded women from sexual pleasure.

For many writers, struggle is no longer part of the contemporary scene as it was for Edna O'Brien and John McGahern's generation in the 1960s – unless it is the struggle to be noticed (which needs to be distinguished from the struggle to be heard). In a world in which almost anything can be said, serious writers now operate without prescribed boundaries and have to relearn the rules of the game. A poet such as Paul Durcan, as is evident from my remarks in Chapter 2, seems to have absorbed this from the start, and he has gone about his business delightfully refusing to play any recognisable game except his own – unless that game has to do with the new discourse on masculinity. In *Cries of an Irish Caveman* (2001), a volume that includes a series of poems in which the persona shifts from human (male) to cow (female), he connects the word 'testicle' with 'testify'. 'The Lady Testifies' (the poem's title) that men are for ever speaking of breasts and wonders if he is 'environmentally testicular'.[32] He, meanwhile, is standing out in the fields, conscious she is watching his 'rod' hanging 'hopelessly down'. 'I am not my testicles,' he protests, to which she replies, 'You are nothing but your testicles', adding that, while upstairs she may have breasts, downstairs she is so much more.

The verse of Cathal Ó Searcaigh breaks new ground not only in its frank reporting from the front-line of gay experience but also in its serious co-opting of the freedom banner, not from the Irish tradition but from the American Beats (Kerouac, Ginsberg, Corso and Ferlinghetti are mentioned by name throughout his verse). A century after Wilde, there is still a love that dare not speak its name, but now it takes a slightly different form. Writing about one of his lovers in 'Ceann Dubh Dílís' ('My Blackhaired Love'), Ó Searcaigh spends little time weighing the scales: 'I'd deny the Gospels for your sake.'[33] What is also impressive is his evocation of life among Irish labourers in London, life that continues to be affected by historical stereotypes dating back to a time when the harp was under the crown. To his credit, Ó Searcaigh is a redskin of Irish literature and has nothing of the paleface about him. 'I see them here, my brothers, the stock of hill and shore:/their granite faces, their hard "heron" stroll,/as out of place here as limpets in concrete.'[34] There are few writers discussed in this book who could speak so directly about *mo bhráithre* ('my brothers'). Behind him are the Donegal Gaeltacht and the 'small parishes of hypocrisy' (p.155), where the word 'hypocrisy' suggests a criticism of his background, but this is precisely the world that has given Ó Searcaigh a language and a voice. Elsewhere, in Whitmanesque fashion, he lays bear his feelings, the need to 'wrap my days in joy' (p.157), and when his approaches to boys or young men are not reciprocated he finds consolation in his American books and 'in a star-spangled blanket of sky' (p.159).

With lines taken from Whitman for an epigraph and constant references to Wilde throughout, Jamie O'Neill's ambitious historical novel about the Easter Rising, *At Swim, Two Boys* (2001), also foregrounds the gay theme. While *Ulysses* begins at Sandycove with the phallus of the Martello Tower and the Forty Foot – where male nude bathing has been enjoyed for generations and where Buck Mulligan throws out an invitation to a moody Stephen – in O'Neill's novel, the male space takes precedence throughout, with swimming at once acting as an intertextual marker, a device for narrative cohesion, and as a setting for the scene of seduction, first between the two boys – lower-middle-class Jim and working-class Doyler – and, later, for the upper-middle-class dilettante, Anthony MacMurrough. Set in the year leading up to the Easter Rising, *At Swim, Two Boys* rewrites both Irish history and the afterlife of Irish history, and it does so in terms that not only recall the late Victorian and Edwardian era of outdoor pursuits (this was the period when Baden Powell founded the boy scouts and Constance Markievicz the Fianna, and when Standish O'Grady and Yeats celebrated the exploits of the boy hero Cuchulain) but, more importantly, in terms which call attention to the real boys' story which somehow got omitted in the making of modern Ireland. In 'The Statues', Yeats wondered if Cuchulain stalked through the Post Office with Pearse, but O'Neill concentrates on the idea of a rising as ushered in by Pearse's boys (Pearse founded a school at Rathfarnham in 1909). Jim joins the struggle for independence not for blood sacrifice or heroic action but because of Doyler: 'It's silly, I know. But that's how I feel' (p.435). And MacMurrough confirms this view: 'Not courage, but a kind of love, a bonding of disparate souls to the one company.' (p.445). When Doyler admits the rebellion went off 'half-cock' (p.615), the pun is there to be noticed, for this is an extraordinarily physical novel, where metaphors have the habit of being supplanted by the body and where the sexual theme has the potential of giving way to the political, as when MacMurrough, in discussion with Doyler, insists that he wasn't watching the two boys at swim 'so much as waiting my turn' (p.281). Waiting my turn is in one sense precisely the mood leading up to Easter 1916, and as we look back on the events in the novel we can discern that characters such as MacMurrough did indeed move from watching to action, which is precisely, in some respects, the major discourse or trajectory of the novel.[35]

From this brief snapshot of a selection of contemporary writing – and I have said nothing about the cultural greening of Britain, about which Rosa González and others have written so perceptively – it can be discerned that the colonial encounter continues to leave its mark.[36] Sebastian Barry's plays *The Steward of Christendom* (1995) and *Our Lady of Sligo* (1998) are brave attempts, a generation or two later, to recuperate the voices of those compromised by their identity with the crown, especially those who worked for the Dublin Metropolitan Police before Independence. Following Friel, who pioneered for later Irish playwrights the powerful use of dramatic monologues, Barry has shown that speech on the stage can intervene directly in how history has been written. The one reservation is less that his plays are propaganda and more that the lyrical quality has become detached from its social base and transformed into something else, an act of homage, perhaps, to his family roots. In consequence, as a commentary on the colonial encounter – and the contrast with *The Force of Change* (2000), Gary Mitchell's play about the fragmentation inside Northern Unionism post-1998, is striking – the plays look not so much reactionary as stunning and beguiling oddities. In time, that may change, but what Barry's work does underline is that the legacy of colonial encounter still has some unexpected twists and turns and that, as at the time of the Revival, there is no single colonial/postcolonial banner under which contemporary Irish writers choose to march.

John McGahern: A Parting Glass

Few modern Irish writers have understood better than John McGahern that 'there is nothing more difficult to seize than the day'.[37] Only through time, to borrow St Augustine's metaphor, can the food of the present be committed to the stomach of memory for later use by the mind.[38] From the deliberately pointed symbol of the watch in 'The Gold Watch' (1986) to the play on the concept of return in *Amongst Women* (1990) to the turn of the seasons in *That They May Face the Rising Sun* (2002), McGahern has produced a sustained engagement with a theme which, quite simply, won't go away for him. Whether he has himself seized the day and provided a lasting portrait of contemporary Ireland in the wake of the colonial encounter is for posterity to decide. He is, however, more deceptive and original than he at first appears. In *Amongst Women* he writes: 'Nothing but the years changed in Great Meadow' (p.168). But in McGahern's world everything is subject to change, not least to change through repetition – the seasons come and go, sharp Christmas morning frosts return, as if from nowhere the masked wren-boys appear again on St Stephen's Day, weddings are celebrated and brides installed in new houses, bodies are laid out, telephone poles erected, televisions bought and English programmes watched, meadows mowed and hay saved, evening rosary said, faith lost, moods initiated, feuds ended. An expert at registering change, whether in the natural world or in people, McGahern relies for the most part on the iterative mode where things gather meaning with repetition and where the larger frame of ritual, or the seasons, or family history, informs or obtrudes. The lesson he constantly imparts is that of the Irish proverb: *Is maith an scéalaí an aimsir* ('time is a good storyteller'). In his last two novels, a passage of dialogue near the beginning is reproduced towards the end, as if everything needs a second showing, just to remind the reader that under the impact of familiarity the world does indeed look different. But such a gesture towards a self-reflexive mode of narration is in general avoided by McGahern, who insists on everything – with the possible exception of the title to his recent novel – being integrated.[39]

In *That They May Face the Rising Sun*, McGahern's great theme can be heard on the lips of Joe's wife Kate Ruttledge: 'The past and present are all the same in the mind. . . . They are just pictures.'[40] This is the nearest McGahern gets to a philosophical position, for he is most at ease exploring character and environment in a farming community. There is a memorable scene of a Shorthorn cow calving in the corner of a spruce plantation above the lake. McGahern avoids the primitivist fascination shown by Liam O'Flaherty in his short story 'A Cow's Death' (1926), and instead concentrates on the varied details of an unfolding picture. Joe Ruttledge has just returned from taking a neighbour, Patrick Ryan, to visit his brother Edmund, who's dying in hospital. As he thanked Ruttledge for coming to visit him, Edmund 'reached back to an old tradition of courtesy' (p.48). Patrick is different. They stop off on their way home for a drink ('I never left this town yet without leaving them money'), meet a crowd of football supporters ('Their frigger of a team had lost'), and talk desultorily about success and failure in life. Then into the conversation Patrick inserts a somewhat impertinent question: 'Do you miss not having children?' Ruttledge doesn't take offence: 'You can't miss what you've never had' (p.52). After dropping him off, Ruttledge returns home.

Everything in McGahern is subject not only to change but also to the law of narration. The narrator doesn't tell us if Patrick lacks his brother's courtesy or is garrulous because of learning of his brother's fate or if Ruttledge is slightly taken aback by the enquiry. We infer all three, especially the last: when Ruttledge is changing clothes at home he suddenly remembers 'that he had completely forgotten to look at the Shorthorn' (p.52). In ways that recall an oral tradition of storytelling, where forward momentum is not always easy to discern amid the teller's pauses, *That They May Face the Rising Sun* is a risky narrative told without chapter headings. The cow is eventually found. She has been in labour for some time. Ruttledge's talkative neighbour, Jamesie, is on the scene. Feeling for the calf, he makes a comment as if unconscious of its oddness: 'The calf is coming right. She's making no headway though' (p.53). A jack is needed to help pull out the calf. Kate puts aside what she was doing and gets 'warm water, soap, disinfectant, a towel', and whispers to Jamesie: '[I]t's great that you're here.' Jamesie's thoughts are on the way the cow is helping by pushing, then the calf appears, 'covered', the narrator tells us, 'in the gleaming placenta'. 'Careful not to stand in her way,' Jamesie cautions Kate. 'You never can tell.' And the next sentence is given over by the novelist to the cow's perspective: 'The Shorthorn's whole attention was fixed on her calf as if it were her first calf all over again, the beginning of the world' (p.54).

John McGahern, October 1985, ever conscious of the music of a lost kingdom. Courtesy of Dan Harper.

McGahern's work is full of such precious moments, which act as reminders – on display throughout this book – that culture, through such writing, is capable of renewing itself from within. The uncompromising quality in McGahern's case needs stressing. Even as a way of life is disappearing from the Irish countryside (by 2010, it is estimated, the numbers working the land will halve from the present 80,000 to 40,000), McGahern is hitting the brake pedal. Not yet, he seems to be saying. Listen to the voice of the people and observe their take on things, their shaping imagination, their frequently unexpected exchanges of conversation.[41] 'You see nothing at home,' complains Jamesie, only to have Ruttledge reply: 'You see the birds and the sky and the tracks of the animals' (p.140). In *A Year's Turning* (1996), which in other respects is an enjoyable diary kept by the journalist and nat-uralist Michael Viney at his 'remote' cottage in County Mayo, there is a description of a heron taking off in December: 'It lifts its wings like Otto Klemperer at the rostrum and lets itself be snatched aloft.'[42] McGahern never succumbs to such strained comparisons, but seeks instead a lower register, where writing is seen not as an added extra but as adequate to its material.

There is nothing prim or inhibited about McGahern, a writer whose second novel, *The Dark* (1965), was banned in Ireland because of its use of the f-word and its inclusion of a scene describing a boy masturbating.[43] In *That They May Face the Rising Sun*, crudeness comes in the outlandish shape of John Quinn, a wom-aniser who cannot live with or without women. His first wife, he tells Ruttledge, 'died under me after bringing eight children into the world' (p.22), and during the course of the novel the 'Gentleman Farmer with Lakeside Residence' manages to secure another bride, apparently from the Knock Marriage Bureau – which prompts the immediate thought among the locals: '[Y]ou'd think the priests and nuns would have something better to do than running a bucking shop' (p.119). At the wedding day party, the couple disappear for a while upstairs, and we are treated to a similarly racy remark, this time made by the simple Bill Evans, 'She'll get the rod' (p.168), a comment that receives an immediate and enthusiastic response from Jamesie's wife, Mary. After the week's wedding celebrations, Quinn's wife leaves him. 'Gone. Out the gap. Gone!' is how the news is relayed by Jamesie, who recalls the whole episode in suitably choice language. Quinn had revealed his new wife 'tasted like a ripe plum picked from the tree', to which the 'newsy', attuned Jamesie adds: 'I'd give good money to know what the plum thought' (p.176).

McGahern swings by this irreverent corner of Irish rural life, which has never been short of a rich non-PC vocabulary, but he is not delayed by it. There is another world outside rural Ireland across the water that awaits his attention. England, now the fallen crown, is associated with: 'alphabetical' (p.79), a set way of doing things; *Blind Date* on TV, an 'eejity' programme Jamesie 'goes wild for' (p.189); and a place of exile for their son Johnny. After falling in love with Anna

Mulvey while acting in Synge's *Playboy of the Western World*, Johnny shoots his pointer and red setter and follows her to England. Her interests lie elsewhere, disappointment in love follows, and Johnny ends up working as a cleaner at Ford's in Dagenham. Reality is McGahern's touchstone, not tragedy or comedy but something less structured or resolved, and what I think Paul Durcan is alluding to in his enigmatic two-line poem 'Reading McGahern': 'the open endings of my days'.[44] After watching the two rehearsing and acting out the great love scene between Christy and Pegeen, Mary knows which is more real: '[T]erribly old eejity stuff. . . . Especially when you compare it to what was happening under your eyes' (p.97). Even the great lines of Synge's play can sound less than the real thing in McGahern's hands.

Equally, while reality is close to realism it is not to be confused with it. In *I Could Read the Sky* (1997), Timothy O'Grady's wrenching novel about the Irish labourer in England, P.J., who has worked in England for seventeen years, is asked by the newly-arrived emigrant in the Lincolnshire potato fields: 'What's it like?' (meaning what's it like living in England.). P. J., looking out of the window at the night sky, turns, puts out the lantern, and replies: 'It's like you're trying to talk to somebody out of a deep black hole.'[45] The remark is telling, encompassing as it does the plight of the rural emigrant, forced by economics to leave an impoverished countryside and work the land of the former coloniser. McGahern, as if conscious both of such loss and of his own limitations as a writer, keeps his concentration on Ireland, so that he includes, but is never overwhelmed by, the plight of the emigrant. After all, the returning emigrant brings to the Moran household not only sadness but also 'the bracing breath of the outside'.[46]

In his autobiography, Hugh Maxton suggests that, 'Memory and the past tense are implacably opposed to each other. When we try to join them together, usually it is pain that verifies their tension.'[47] This isn't quite true for McGahern except in one respect. McGahern has a long memory and the backdrop to his work is the War of Independence. In *Amongst Women*, Moran, who had been part of a flying column, makes a comment that recalls the fiction of Sean O'Faolain and Frank O'Connor in the 1930s: 'Things were never so simple and clear again' (p.6). Moran's generation were 'bound together', McGahern remarks in a recent interview, 'by something bigger than themselves. And then normal life restored itself and the Church and the medical profession got power. And, if anything, the country got poorer.'[48] If Yeats imagined he was living in the explosion in the early 1920s, McGahern is doubly conscious not only that he is living in the aftermath of that explosion but also that history turned sour:

> 'What did we get for it? A country, if you'd believe them. Some of our own johnnies in the top jobs instead of a few Englishmen. More than half my family work in England. What was it all for? The whole thing was a cod.' (p.5)

For Moran and his generation, nothing was so clear again, and yet in another sense it was. As the novel's title suggests, there is a counter to masculine power, and it is based amongst women, women as mediators, consolers, pacifiers, intermediaries, and aids in battle, as in the War of Independence. Wherever else the masculine mind is, the world is here amongst women. The whole thing may be a 'cod' but, in their struggle for a sense of belonging, his daughters provide another response to history, one linked to solidarity: 'Together they were one world and could take on the world' (p.145). The troubling of McGahern's memory makes itself felt at such moments. In *That They May Face the Rising Sun*, Jimmy Joe McKiernan's republican activities, which are monitored by Irish detectives, are dismissed by the narrator in two beautifully cadenced sentences: 'Easier still to imagine him on hunger strike and proceeding to the final self-effacement with a quiet, unbreakable resolve. Others he would use as pitilessly as tools' (p.284). We can discern in such moments how McGahern's engagement with rural Ireland is also therefore an engagement with history and a concern with what happened to the harp without the crown. But there are no outcomes, and, if pressed about the direction of his work, McGahern might well remain silent, suggesting that it's impossible to found a political party or a state on his fiction, only to accept that his fiction belongs somewhere in that ballpark. As Yeats remarked of William Carleton (cited in Chapter 4): 'The history of a nation is not in parliaments and battlefields, but in what the people say to each other on fair-days and high days, and in how they farm, and quarrel, and go on pilgrimage.'[49]

In dwelling on McGahern here, at the end of this book, my intention is to signal the way major writers reconfigure the cultural landscape. Ireland is undergoing profound changes and McGahern is part of that changing landscape. He lacks the confident outlook of the new Irish architecture as evident in the Guinness Storehouse Gallery or the O'Reilly Theatre in Joyce's old school of Belvedere, which are buildings designed to be seen and, with their rooftop views, to act as 'belvederes' across the city skyline. Furthermore, he seems disinterested in the postmodernist technique of playing with images, whether for shock, as is the case with Sean Hillen's *Irelantis* (1999), or as part of a more radical agenda, as with the photographs of Willie Doherty.[50] However, he is not the stereotypical remote figure living in a remote cottage in some remote part of County Leitrim, and he has none of the decentred forlornness that is to be found in Anthony Haughey's photographs in *The Edge of Europe* (1996).[51] McGahern's characters shop across the border in Enniskillen, enjoy coffee in Bewleys in Grafton Street, and, as with Johnny, pay rent to Indian landlords in the Home Counties. Some are successful in negotiating different worlds, while others are not. Some favourite locations of Brian Moore in his fiction – *The Temptation of Eileen Hughes* (1981) is emblematic in this regard – are the airport terminal, the hotel lobby, and the taxi, for this is where people are in transit, where a space for temptation opens up, where secrets can be revealed, innocence exposed, sins committed in public, and lives changed for ever. This is not McGahern's world. Daughters return home with teddy boys but without sin. They tell stories of their life away from home, but they are not asked to confront their existential selves. 'We're no more than a puff of wind out on the lake' (p.115) is the most that can be mustered in the face of the dark.

After Beckett life goes on, and for proof there is McGahern. To write a thesis on his Irishness or on his position within a postcolonial discourse can seem strangely beside the point. In fact, the tables are turned and it is McGahern who is doing the asking. What he places before us is a double question: what is the nature of contemporary Irish reality and where is it to be found? Many Irish writers draw on ancient myths to comprehend the world. Thus, in Marina Carr's *The Mai* (1994), at the end of the first act, Millie, The Mai's daughter, tries to make sense of her parents' failed relationship by reference to Coillte, daughter of the mountain god Bloom, who fell in love with Blath, Lord of all the flowers, and the latter's desire for the dark witch of the bog. The monologue is remarkable, not just for its searching lyricism but also for the way in which ancient myths can be successfully deployed to shed light on the dark side of modern psychology. After retelling the myth Millie concludes:

> I knew that story as a child. So did The Mai and Robert. But we were unaffected by it and in our blindness moved along with it like sleepwalkers along a precipice and all around gods and mortals called out for us to change our course and, not listening, we walked on and on.[52]

Carr effectively deploys Irish myth (including myths about lakes) to produce a domestic tragedy in the Eugene O'Neill mould. McGahern, by contrast, has largely avoided the great quarry of Irish myths for Irish writers and refuses to take his work into tragedy. Ritual is his true Penelope, the *nostos* or return his favourite motif, and exile a frequent fate that befalls his characters. Homer's *Odyssey* and the Prodigal Son are the great informing stories in his work. The son returns home in 'Gold Watch' to find his father has married another woman; in *Amongst Women*, Luke never returns to Ireland to become reconciled with his father; in *That They May Face the Rising Sun*, Johnny would like to return home from England but is persuaded not to by his parents. All these stories could be turned into tragedies, but McGahern, a writer of slow airs rather than laments, seems to take the view that tragedy belongs to narrative, rather than the other way round, and that tragedy heightens a moment, whereas a narrative tends to stress a state or condition and therefore seems closer to the truth.

It is a good moment to end on. Ritual, not tragedy, stalks the Irish countryside. From his base in County Leitrim, McGahern is not given to excess, as he might have been if he were writing in the 1930s about the Western seaboard. His land-

LIFE IN THE FAST LANE!

On the reverse of this card someone has written, 'People are very friendly here and have a great sense of humour. The guy on the front is the CEO of one of Ireland's largest financial advisor-consulting firms. It's his rush hour.'

scape is a watery one of meadows and lakes, and there is time to observe animal tracks and the movement of the seasons. This is rural Ireland at its best, about two to three hours from the gridlock of Dublin traffic and the fast world of Temple Bar and the remains of the Celtic Tiger. It can be readily conceded that for some McGahern simply fits in with a touristy or weekender's view of Ireland, with the crown's view of the harp – though I hope I have done enough to suggest otherwise. Equally, we can never forget that the flipside is the claustrophobic world from which O'Brien's country girls sought – and still seek – to escape. But as Ireland tilts ever more surely into Dublin Bay, there is much to recommend in the recuperative vision of a writer such as McGahern, for he has already begun the task at the level of culture of countering the magnetic pull of the dark pool that inheres in the name of Ireland's capital city.

NOTES

Chapter 1 THE HARP WITHOUT THE CROWN

1 Thomas Moore, *A Selection of Irish Melodies with Symphonies and Accompaniments by Sir John Stevenson*, 6th Number (London and Dublin: J. Power's, 1815), 111.

2 John Gregory Dunne, *Harp* (1989; Cambridge: Granta, 1990), 26.

3 Speech delivered 11 October 1614. *Calendar of State Papers, Ireland, James I 1611–1614* (eds C. W. Russell and John P. Prendergast) (London: Longman, 1877), 517–18.

4 Sean O'Casey, 'There Go The Irish', in Leslie Daiken (ed.), *They Go, The Irish* (London: Nicholson & Watson, 1944), 20.

5 For words to 'Down Erin's Lovely Lee', see *http://celtic-lyrics.com/lyrics/172*. I first heard it sung by Michael Malone at a house dance in Liscannor, County Clare in the 1950s.

6 Seamus Deane, *Reading in the Dark* (London: Jonathan Cape, 1996), 141.

7 Fredric Jameson, *The Political Unconscious: Narrative as a Socially Symbolic Act* (Ithaca: Cornell University Press, 1981), 9.

8 For the phrase 'outside history', see Eavan Boland, *Outside History* (Manchester: Carcanet, 1990).

9 See D. P. Moran *The Philosophy of Irish Ireland* (Dublin: James Duffy, 1905).

10 W. B. Yeats, *A Vision* (New York: Collier, 1966), 270–1.

11 Michael Longley, 'According to Pythagoras', in *The Ghost Orchid* (London: Jonathan Cape, 1995), 8.

12 Flannery O'Connor, *Everything That Rises Must Converge* (London: Faber and Faber, 1980).

13 Eavan Boland, *In a Time of Violence* (Manchester: Carcanet, 1994), 5.

14 John A. O'Brien (ed.), *The Vanishing Irish: The Enigma of the Modern World* (London: W. H. Allen, 1954), 7.

15 Christine Kinealy, *A Death-Dealing Famine: The Great Hunger in Ireland* (London: Pluto, 1997), 2.

16 Cited in Colm Lincoln, 'City of Culture: Dublin and the Discovery of Urban Heritage', in Barbara O'Connor and Michael Cronin (eds), *Tourism in Ireland: A Critical Analysis* (Cork: Cork University Press, 1993), 219.

17 Thomas Kinsella, *Nightwalker and Other Poems* (Dublin: Dolmen, 1968), 66.

18 *The Irish Commonwealth* 1:1, St Patrick's Day, 1919.

19 For further discussion, see Fintan O'Toole, 'The Means of Production', in *Labour in Art: Representations of Labour in Ireland*

1870–1970 (Exhibition Catalogue) (Dublin: Irish Museum of Modern Art, 1994).

20 George Moore, *Hail and Farewell: Ave* (London: William Heinemann, 1911), 5.

21 Tom Stoppard, *Shipwreck* (London: Faber and Faber, 2002), 57.

22 See Maud Gonne, 'Yeats and Ireland', in Stephen Gwynn (ed.), *Scattering Branches: Tributes to the Memory of W. B. Yeats* (London: Macmillan, 1940), 27.

23 See W. B. Yeats, *Autobiographies* (London: Macmillan, 1977), 559.

24 Ibid., 199.

25 See *Gaelic American* 5 March 1904. Cited in my *Yeats's Worlds: Ireland, England and the Poetic Imagination* (New Haven and London: Yale University Press, 1995), 69.

26 Lionel Pilkington, *Theatre and the State in Twentieth-Century Ireland: Cultivating the People* (London: Routledge, 2001), 71. He has in mind the years 1909–12.

27 Lady Gregory, *The Collected Plays of Lady Gregory*, Vol 1 (ed. Anne Saddlemyer) (Gerrards Cross: Colin Smythe, 1970), 262. The play was also too long for the Abbey.

28 W. B. Yeats, *The Secret Rose* (London: Lawrence & Bullen, 1897), vii.

29 Stephen Gwynn, *Irish Literature and Drama in the English Language* (London: Nelson, 1936), 158.

30 For popularity of the game in Philadelphia, see J. A. Lester (ed), *A Century of Philadelphia Cricket* (Philadelphia: University of Pennsylvania Press, 1951). When he toured North America in 1859, Fred Lillywhite believed cricket in Philadelphia 'had every prospect of becoming a national game'. See *The English Cricketers' Trip To Canada and the United States* (London: F. Lillywhite, 1860), 44. The problem, as Jones Wister recognised in the 1890s in an early comparison between the two games, was that cricket was played almost exclusively in the United States by amateurs, while 'base ball' was already a professional game. See *A 'Bawl' for American Cricket* (Philadelphia,

1893). Cricket's fortunes in the United States have begun to change with the influx of new immigrants from the Caribbean and the Indian sub-continent (and the United Kingdom). For a useful site on the game today, see http://www.uscricket.com

31 See W. P. Hone, *Cricket in Ireland* (Kerryman Tralee, 1955), 88, 106. In recent years, cricket's fortunes have revived in Ireland.

32 Ramachandra Guha, *A Corner of a Foreign Field: The Indian History of a British Sport* (London: Pan Macmillan, 2002), xiii.

33 Kathleen Coyle, *Youth in the Saddle* (London: Jonathan Cape, 1927), 235. The remark by Shule and Roddy's Protestant grandmother Mrs Macedoine is an apt response to the Boundary Commission. Elsewhere, Mrs Macedoine's Northern snobbishness gets the better of her and she wants to know if they've managed to sweep the streets in Dublin and put a tax on beggars (p.59).

34 John Banville, *Eclipse* (London: Picador, 2000), 130.

35 John McGahern, *Amongst Women* (London: Faber and Faber, 1900), 5.

Chapter 2: The Hybrid Character of Modern Irish Writing

1 For a brief survey and discussion of the term 'hybridity', see Ania Loomba, *Colonialism/Postcolonialism* (London: Routledge, 1998), 173–83.

2 Tom Murphy, *The Wake* (London: Methuen, 1998), 71.

3 James Joyce, *A Portrait of the Artist as a Young Man* (ed. Chester Anderson) (New York: Viking, 1968), 189.

4 For a related discussion in which I discuss the look of translation in Joyce's writing – another way in which he forces the language on the reader – see 'The Issue of Translation', *James Joyce Quarterly* 40:3, 2005.

5 Bernard O'Donoghue, *Here Nor There* (London: Chatto and Windus, 1999), 17–8.

6 The word has a wider distribution, but its emotional field is similar. In Muriel Spark's childhood in Edinburgh in the 1920s, 'shopping' is the word the 'superficial' and 'hypocritical' English used; 'messages' is the word of the tribe. See *Curriculum Vitae* (Harmondsworth: Penguin, 1993), 21.

7 John Banville, *Mefisto* (1986; London: Minerva, 1993), 60.

8 See John Waters, *An Intelligent Person's Guide to Modern Ireland* (1997).

9 Terence Patrick Dolan, *A Dictionary of Hiberno-English* (Dublin: Gill and Macmillan, 1999).

10 Roddy Doyle, *The Barrytown Trilogy* (London: Secker and Warburg, 1991), 13.

11 Ursula Rani Sarma, *Touched/Blue* (London: Oberon, 2002), 40.

12 See Paul Durcan, *Cries of an Irish Caveman* (London: Harvill, 2001), 147. The sequence is used for a title to the volume.

13 For further discussion, see my article, 'The Irish Theme in the Writings of Bill Naughton', in the first issue of *Estudios Irlandeses*, an internet journal edited by Rosa González at www.estudiosirlandeses.org (2005).

14 Justin McCarthy *et al.*, *Irish Literature* 10 vols. (New York: P. F. Collier, 1904). Taylor's essay, in which he lamented the decline in Irish oratory since the eighteenth century, was printed in Volume 7.

15 J. M. Synge, *The Playboy of the Western World* (1907; London: Methuen, 1971), 64.

16 Martin McDonagh, *The Lonesome West* (London: Methuen, 1997), 10.

17 Christy Brown, *Down All the Days* (1970; London: Minerva, 1990), 95.

18 For a recent discussion, see the chapter 'The Difficult Birth of Irish Language Television', in Farrell Corcoran, *RTÉ and the Globalisation of Irish Television* (Bristol and Portland: Intellect Books, 2004), 177–96.

19 James Stephens, *Reincarnations* (London and New York: Macmillan, 1918).

20 See Ciaran Carson, *The Inferno of Dante Alighieri* (London: Granta, 2002) and *The Star Factory* (London: Granta, 1997). Ian Duhig, *The Bradford Count* (Newcastle-upon-Tyne: Bloodaxe, 1991).

21 Nuala Ní Dhomnaill, *Pharaoh's Daughter* (Oldcastle, Co Meath: Gallery Press, 1990), 155. The translation is by Paul Muldoon.

22 See 'Déagóir Ag Driftáil' (Drifting) in Cathal Ó Searcaigh, *Out in the Open* (tr. Frank Sewell) (Indreabhán, Conamara: Cló Iar-Chonnachta, 1997), 153–9.

23 My focus in this book is on Irish writing in English, but my remarks here and elsewhere are pointers to a wider cultural history and to a shared terrain.

24 Ibid., 52–3. 'An tAngelus' is translated by Heather Allen.

25 See Ciaran Carson, *The Irish For No* (Newcastle-upon-Tyne: Bloodaxe, 1988), 49–50.

26 For examples of macaronic verse, see Andrew Carpenter (ed.), *Verse in English from Eighteenth-Century Ireland* (Cork: Cork University Press, 1998).

27 In an essay on his Catholic upbringing in Protestant Portadown, George Watson suggests the lively use of English 'did much to compensate for the austerities of Presbyterian Sundays'. See 'Countries of the Mind', *Irish Pages: Inaugural Issue* (Belfast: Linen Hall Library, 2002), 56.

28 Michael Longley, *The Weather in Japan* (London: Jonathan Cape, 2000), 11. *Hurlygush* is also a Scottish dance, and the sound of a running burn.

29 See title poem in Paul Muldoon, *Quoof* (London: Faber, 1983).

30 Marina Carr, *On Raftery's Hill* (London: Faber, 2000), 32.

31 *I'm Alan Partridge. Episode 5 – To Kill A Mocking Alan.* For more, see http://www.alan-partridge.co.uk/scripts/scripts.htm

32 See Lewis P. Curtis Jr, *Apes and Angels: The Irishman in Victorian Caricature*

(Newton Abbot: David & Charles, 1971), *passim.*

33 By Christina Reid.

34 David Park, *Swallowing the Sun* (London: Bloomsbury, 2004), 34.

35 G. B. Shaw, *John Bull's Other Island with How She Lied to Her Husband and Major Barbara* (London: Constable, 1947), 111.

36 Sean O'Casey, *Two Plays: Juno and the Paycock and The Plough and the Stars* (London: Macmillan, 1966), 73

37 Martin McDonagh, *The Lieutenant of Inishmore* (London: Methuen, 2001), 11.

38 James Joyce, *Ulysse* (tr. August Morel with the assistance of Stuart Gilbert) (Paris: Gallimard, 1957), 413.

39 Paul Muldoon, *Why Brownlee Left* (London: Faber and Faber, 1980), 19.

40 For image and commentary on Willie Doherty's *Border Incident* (1994) see *http://www.3corneredgallery.com/ details_on_article_number/w1171.html*

41 Michael Pickering, *Stereotyping: The Politics of Representation* (Basingstoke: Palgrave, 2001), 2–3. Pickering devotes a short section to nineteenth-century stereotypes of the Irish, which he places within a context of Victorian fears about cheap labour. What is missing from his analysis is, as is evident from my remarks on Spenser in Chapter 2, a much longer history – and, equally, an awareness of the continuation of prejudice long after the economic cause has disappeared.

42 Edna O'Brien, *The Country Girls* (1960; Harmondsworth: Penguin, 1966), 174.

43 Brian Harvey, *Rights and Justice Work in Ireland: A New Base Line* 2nd edition (York: Joseph Rowntree Charitable Trust, 2002). Among the many indictments in this hard-hitting report there is a suggestion that some ten per cent of potential foreign investment into Ireland has been lost because of the country's 'bad international reputation', corruption being 'a central theme of Irish life and politics' (p.45). For a down-to-earth view of contemporary Ireland in the context of transnational corporations, see Colin Coulter and Steve Coleman (eds), *The End of Irish History: Critical Reflections on the Celtic Tiger* (Manchester: Manchester University Press, 2003).

44 Raymond Williams, *Keywords: A Vocabulary of Culture and Society* (Glasgow: Fontana, 1976), 80.

45 See, for example, Brendan Behan, *Brendan Behan's Island: An Irish Sketchbook* (Drawings by Paul Hogarth) (London: Hutchinson, 1962), 18.

46 Tom Murphy, *The Wake* (London: Methuen, 1998), 9.

47 See Matthew Arnold, *Culture and Anarchy: An Essay in Political and Social Criticism* (London: Smith, Elder, 1869). For Arnold's views on the Irish, see *On the Study of Celtic Literature* (London: Smith, Elder, 1867).

48 Cited in Frank Sewell, *Modern Irish Poetry: A New Alhambra* (Oxford: Oxford University Press, 2000), 14.

49 F. S. L. Lyons, *Culture and Anarchy in Ireland, 1890–1939* (Oxford: Clarendon, 1979), 83. Lyons's stress on disenchantment resembles Arnold's remarks on the melancholy of the Celts.

50 Kathleen Coyle, *The Magical Realm* (New York: E. P. Dutton, 1942), 98.

51 Oscar Wilde, *The Portrait of Mr W. H.* (1921; London: Hesperus, 2003), 75. Originally published in *Blackwoods Magazine* in 1889.

52 Samuel Beckett, *The Complete Dramatic Works* (London: Faber and Faber, 1986), 220.

53 John Banville, *Shroud* (London: Picador, 2002), 338.

54 Marina Carr, *On Raftery's Hill* (London: Faber, 2000), 57.

55 Colm Tóibín, *The Master* (London: Picador, 2004), 26.

56 Frank McGuinness, *Plays One: The Factory Girls, Observe the Sons of Ulster Marching Towards the Somme, Innocence, Carthaginians, Baglady* (London: Faber and Faber, 1996), 164. 'There are hounds

about me, and I'm following them to death,' says Craig. 'I'm a dying breed, boy.'

57 Michael Longley, *The Ghost Orchid* (London: Cape, 1995), 52.

58 Medbh McGuckian, *The Face of the Earth* (Oldcastle, Co. Meath: Gallery, 2002), 81.

59 Stewart Parker, *Pentecost* in *Three Plays for Ireland* (Birmingham: Oberon Books, 1989), 193.

60 Marina Carr, *The Mai* (Oldcastle, Co Meath: Gallery Press, 1995), 51.

61 Paula Meehan, 'Pillow Talk' in *Mysteries of the Home* (Newcastle-upon-Tyne: Bloodaxe, 1996), 50.

62 Kathleen Coyle, *There Is a Door* (Paris: Edward W. Titus, 1931), 26.

Chapter 3 THE GREAT FAMINE AND MODERN IRISH CULTURE

1 Jesuits (Ireland), *A Page of Irish History: Story of University College Dublin 1883–1909. Compiled by Fathers of the Society of Jesus* (Dublin and Cork: Talbot Press, 1930). Among topics for inaugural addresses were 'Realism in Fiction', 'The Keltic Note in Literature', 'The University Question', 'Problems of Progress' and 'Home Rule'.

2 The Christian Brothers, *Irish History Reader* (Dublin: M. H. Gill; London: Burns & Oates, 1916), 286.

3 See the section entitled 'A Dangerous Memory?' in Christine Kinealy, *The Great Famine: Impact, Ideology and Rebellion* (Basingstoke: Palgrave, 2002), 10–7.

4 Cormac Ó Gráda, *Black '47 and Beyond: The Great Irish Famine in History, Economy, and Memory* (Princeton, New Jersey: Princeton University Press, 1999), 232.

5 See the title story, which is about the Famine, in William Trevor's *The News From Ireland and Other Stories* (London: The Bodley Head, 1986).

6 Harriet Ide Keen Roberts, *Nana: A Memory of an Old Nurse* (London: Macmillan, 1936), 52.

7 Christopher Morash, 'The Literature of the Irish Famine' in Patrick O'Sullivan (ed.), *The Meaning of the Famine* (London and Washington: Leicester University Press, 1997), 53. The texts referred to here are John Mitchel's *Jail Journal* (1854), Louis J. Walsh's historical novel *The Next Time: A Story of 'Forty Eight* (1919), and David Power Conyngham's Irish-American novel *The O'Donnells of Glen Cottage* (1903). Ryan's novel was published in 1984.

8 In recent years, doubt has been expressed over Spenser's authorship of both 'A Briefe Note of Ireland' and *A View of the Present State of Ireland*. See, in particular, Jean R. Brink, 'Constructing the *View of the Present State of Ireland*', in *Spenser Studies* II (1994), 203–30, and subsequent issues for an exchange of correspondence with Andrew Hadfield.

9 Edmund Spenser, 'A Brief Note of Ireland' (1598) in *The Works of Edmund Spenser: A Variorum Edition* (Baltimore: The Johns Hopkins Press, 1949), 244.

10 Theodor Adorno, 'Essay on Cultural Criticism and Society', in Theodor Adorno, *Prism* (tr. Samuel and Shierry Weber) (Cambridge, Mass.: MIT Press, 1967), 19.

11 See Thomas Kinsella, 'The Irish Writer', in W. B. Yeats and Thomas Kinsella, *Davis, Mangan, Ferguson?: Tradition and the Irish Writer* (Dublin: Dolmen, 1970), 58.

12 George Steiner, *Language and Silence: Essays on Language, Literature and the Inhuman* (New York: Atheneum, 1970), 165.

13 The reasons for the delay in publication are not wholly clear – it was possibly due to censorship in the 1590s, or possibly because Spenser's opinions were too out-spoken. Perhaps it was published when it was because it served the interests of Calvinist-inspired Protestants in the 1630s. For a recent discussion, see Andrew Hadfield, *Edmund Spenser's Irish Experience: Wilde Fruit and Salvage Soyl* (Oxford: Clarendon, 1997), 78–84, and Richard A. McCabe, *Spenser's Monstrous*

Regiment: Elizabethan Ireland and the Poetics of Difference (Oxford: Oxford University Press, 2002), 270–87.

14 Edmund Spenser, *A View of the Present State of Ireland* (1596), in *The Works of Edmund Spenser: A Variorum Edition*, 158.

15 *The Poems of Spenser* (Selected and Introduced by W. B. Yeats) (London: Caxton: 1906), xx, xxxiv.

16 Constantia Maxwell, *The Stranger in Ireland: From the Reign of Elizabeth to the Great Famine* (London: Jonathan Cape, 1954), 30.

17 Nicholas Canny, *Making Ireland British 1580–1650* (Oxford: Oxford University Press, 2001), 31.

18 See Edmund Spenser, *A View of the State of Ireland* (eds Andrew Hadfield and Willy Maley), (Oxford: Blackwell, 1997), xxi–xxii.

19 I am using 'awful' in the way it is used by the pro-nationalist writer Emily Lawless when she quotes this passage in *Ireland* (London: T. Fisher Unwin, 1887): '[N]o other words will bring the picture before us in the same simple, awful vividness' (p.193).

20 *Illustrated London News*, 22 December 1849, 404. The journalist is describing Moveen, Kilrush in County Clare.

21 Alexander Somerville, *Letters From Ireland During the Famine of 1847* (ed. K. D. M. Snell) (Blackrock, Co Dublin: Irish Academic Press, 1994), 56. Letter dated 9 February 1847 from Limerick.

22 Cecil Woodham-Smith, *The Great Hunger: Ireland 1845–9* (1962; London: New English Library, 1968), 190.

23 Canon P. A. Sheehan, *Glenanaar: A Story of Irish Life* (1902; London: Longmans, Green, 1929), 198.

24 Anthony Trollope, *Castle Richmond* (1860; London: The Folio Society, 1994), 359.

25 Margaret Kelleher, *The Feminization of the Famine: Expressions of the Inexpressible* (Cork: Cork University Press, 1997), 56.

26 William Carleton, *The Black Prophet: A Tale of Irish Famine* (1847; London: Thomas Hodgson, 1854), 109.

27 Charlotte Brontë, *Shirley* (1849; Harmondsworth: Penguin, 1974), 128.

28 For a discussion of another kind of narrative bursting through its setting – Carleton's castigation of those responsible for the Famine – see Margaret Kelleher, *The Feminization of the Famine*, 31–3.

29 For a useful critical survey, see Margaret Kelleher, 'Irish Famine in Literature' in Cathal Póirtéir (ed.), *The Great Irish Famine* (Dublin: Mercier, 1995), 232–47. In 'Stopping the Hunt: Trollope and the Memory of Ireland', Roy Foster writes about Trollope's 'suppressed sense of contradiction', but his enquiry cannot be satisfactorily answered in biographical terms. See *The Irish Story: Telling and Making It Up in Ireland* (Harmondsworth: Penguin, 2001). For some excellent comments on the uneven texture in *Castle Richmond*, see Melissa Fegan, *Literature and the Irish Famine 1845–1919* (Oxford: Clarendon Press, 2002), 123. See also Bridget Matthews-Kane, 'Love's Labour's Lost: Romantic Allegory in Trollope's *Castle Richmond*', *Victorian Literature and Culture* 32:1 , March 2004, 117–31.

30 James Joyce, 'James Clarence Mangan' (1907) in *The Critical Writings of James Joyce* (eds Ellsworth Mason and Richard Ellmann) (New York: Viking, 1966), 186.

31 Louis D'Alton, *Two Irish Plays: The Man in the Cloak and The Mousetrap* (London: Macmillan, 1938), 96 and 129.

32 Ellen Shannon-Mangan, *James Clarence Mangan: A Biography* (Blackrock, County Dublin: Irish Academic Press, 1996), 206–7.

33 Stanzas 2 and 3 of 'The Funerals', *Irishman* 31 March 1849, 203. Cited in Ellen Shannon-Mangan, *James Clarence Mangan: A Biography*, 206.

34 Sir Samuel Ferguson, 'Hardiman's Irish Minstrelsy II', *The Dublin University Magazine* Vol IV, August 1834, 158.

35 Rev. John O'Rourke, *The History of the Great Irish Famine of 1847, With Notices of*

Earlier Irish Famines (Dublin: McGlashan and Gill, 1875), 276.

36 *Illustrated London News*, 15 December 1849, 394.

37 Rev. John O'Rourke, *The History of the Great Irish Famine of 1847*, 276–7.

38 Mary Carbery, *The Farm By Lough Gurr: The Story of Mary Fogarty* (Sissy O'Brien) (London: Longmans, Green, 1937), 156. Sissy was born in 1858 into a well-to-do farming family in County Limerick.

39 Emily Lawless, *Traits and Confidences* (London: Methuen, 1898), 151.

40 Sean O'Faolain, *Bird Alone* (1936; Oxford: Oxford University Press, 1985), 15.

41 Thomas Keneally, *The Great Shame: The Story of the Irish in the Old World and the New* (London: Chatto and Windus, 1998), 299.

42 Kathleen Coyle, *Piccadilly* (London: Jonathan Cape, 1923), 6.

43 See Christine Kinealy, *The Great Famine: Impact, Ideology and Rebellion* (Basingstoke: Palgrave, 2002), 5–6.

44 James J. Mangan (ed.), *Gerald Keegan's Famine Diary* (Dublin: Wolfhound, 1992), 122.

45 Robert Sellar, *The Summer of Sorrow: Abner's Device and Other Stories* (Huntington, Quebec: 1895), frontispiece.

46 Terry Eagleton, *Heathcliff and the Great Hunger* (London: Verso, 1995), 13.

47 Margaret Kelleher, *The Feminization of the Famine*, 4–5.

48 W. B. Yeats (ed.), *Stories from Carleton* (London: Walter Scott, n.d. [1889]), xvi.

49 *The Variorum Edition of the Plays of W. B. Yeats* (ed. Russell K. Alspach) (1966; London: Macmillan, 1979), 1081.

50 John P. Frayne (ed.), *Uncollected Prose by W. B. Yeats* 1 (New York: Columbia University Press, 1970), 173.

51 Margaret Kelleher, *The Feminization of the Famine*, 113.

52 For more on 'Lilly Dale', see Richard Pearce, 'Simon's Irish Rose: Famine Songs, Blackfaced Minstrels, and Woman's Repression in *A Portrait*' in Susan Stanford Friedman (ed.), *Joyce: The Return of the Repressed* (Ithaca and London: Cornell University Press, 1993), 128–48.

53 See, for example, the pauper's rhyme in the Scariff workhouse in County Clare which included the lines: 'Pauper, pauper, don't you fret,/The stirabout you will surely get./The meal so thick and milk so sour/That's what you'll get at the regular hour.' Cited in Cormac Ó Gráda, *Black '47 and Beyond: The Great Irish Famine in History, Economy, and Memory* (Princeton, New Jersey: Princeton University Press, 1999), 69.

54 Asenath Nicholson, *Lights and Shades of Ireland* (London: Charles Gilpin, 1850), 364.

55 James Joyce, '*Dubliners*': *Text, Criticism, and Notes* (eds Robert Scholes and A. Walton Litz) (New York: Viking, 1979), 196.

56 For a related discussion, see 'Reading Dublin 1904,' a chapter on the city in *Joyce and Company* (London and New York: Continuum, 2006).

57 Liam O'Flaherty, *Famine* (London: Victor Gollancz, 1937), 366.

58 Sean O'Faolain, Review of *Famine*, in *Ireland To-Day* 2: 2, February 1937, 81.

59 Ciaran Ó Murchadha, *Sable Wings Over the Land: Ennis County Clare and its Wider Community During the Great Famine* (Ennis, Co Clare: Clasp, 1998). Ó Murchadha stays close to the texture of life as recorded in local newspaper accounts, including criminal activities such as pickpocketing and youngsters smashing shopwindows. He also notices the consorting of street prostitutes with the Scottish regiments stationed in the town.

60 See Peter Costello, 'Land and Liam O'Flaherty', in Carla King (ed.), *Famine, Land and Culture in Ireland* (Dublin: University College Dublin Press, 2000), 169.

61 Louis J. Walsh, *The Next Time: A Story of 'Forty-Eight* (Dublin: M. H. Gill, 1919), 227.

62 Gerard Healy, *The Black Stranger* (Dublin: James Duffy, 1950), 42.

63 Andrew Merry [Mrs Mildred H. G.

Darby], *The Hunger: Being Realities of the Famine Years in Ireland 1845 to 1848* (London: Andrew Melrose, 1910), 236.

64 The historian Austin Bourke makes the same point in '*The Visitation of God*'?: *The Potato and the Great Irish Famine* (eds Jacqueline Hill and Cormac Ó Gráda) (Dublin: Lilliput, 1993), 24.

65 Patrick Kavanagh, *Collected Poems* (1964; New York: Norton, 1973), 34–55.

66 *The Complete Poems of Patrick Kavanagh* (ed. Peter Kavanagh) (New York: The Peter Kavanagh Hand Press, 1996), 420. By 'these', Peter Kavanagh means *The Great Hunger*, 'Lough Derg', and 'Why Sorrow?'.

67 See Frank O'Connor, *The Midnight Court* (London and Dublin: Maurice Fridberg, 1945). The translation, but not the original Irish language version, was banned.

68 'Introducing *The Great Hunger*' in *November Haggard: Uncollected Prose and Verse of Patrick Kavanagh* (ed. Peter Kavanagh) (New York: The Peter Kavanagh Hand Press, 1971), 15–6. Date of broadcast: 13 May 1960.

69 See Thomas Kinsella, 'The Irish Writer', in W. B. Yeats and Thomas Kinsella, *Davis, Mangan, Ferguson?*, 57–66.

70 Thomas Kinsella, *Nightwalker and Other Poems* (Dublin: Dolmen, 1968), 67. The initial letters of the three words of the last line – HCE – recall the Humphrey Chimpden Earwicker figure in *Finnegans Wake*. Kinsella's debt to William Carlos Williams and T. S. Eliot is also apparent in these lines.

71 Ibid., 66. These lines have been altered in his *Collected Poems 1956–1994* (Oxford: Oxford University Press, 1996).

72 Cathy Carruth, *Trauma: Explorations in Memory* (Baltimore: Johns Hopkins University Press, 1995), 5.

73 Brendan Kennelly, *The Book of Judas* (Newcastle-upon-Tyne: Bloodaxe, 1991), 14.

74 Susan Howe, *The Nonconformist's Memorial* (New York: New Directions, 1993), 125.

75 Cited in D. J. O'Donoghue, *Poems of James Clarence Mangan* (Dublin: O'Donoghue; London: A. H. Bullen, 1903), xxv.

76 John Mitchel, 'Introduction', in D. J. O'Donoghue, *Poems of James Clarence Mangan*, xlii.

77 Denis Florence MacCarthy, 'A Mystery', in *Poems* (Dublin: M. H. Gill, 1882), 172.

78 Tom Murphy, *Plays: One: Famine, The Patriot Game, The Blue Macushla* (London: Methuen, 1992), 5.

79 Seamus Deane, *Strange Country: Modernity and Nationhood in Irish Writing Since 1790* (Oxford: Clarendon, 1997), 50.

80 Asenath Nicholson, *Lights and Shades of Ireland*, 6. For a recent discussion on this 'gulf', see Kevin Whelan, 'Pre- and Post-Famine Landscape Change' in Cathal Póirtéir (ed.), *The Great Irish Famine* (Dublin: Mercier, 1995), 19–33. 'A certain amount of iron entered the Irish soul in the Famine holocaust.' (32)

81 Brian Friel, *Translations* (London: Faber and Faber, 1981), 63.

82 Asenath Nicholson, *Lights and Shades of Ireland*, 3.

83 Peadar O'Donnell, *Adrigoole* (London: Jonathan Cape, 1929), 276–7.

84 Liam O'Flaherty, *Famine* (London: Victor Gollancz, 1937), 176.

85 Cited in Roger McHugh, 'The Famine in Irish Oral Tradition', in R. Dudley Edwards and T. Desmond Williams (eds), *The Great Famine: Studies in Irish History 1845–52* (Dublin: Irish Committee of Historical Sciences, 1962), 421. I give the English translation.

86 Cormac Ó Gráda, *Black '47 and Beyond*, 222.

87 Alexander Irvine, *My Lady of the Chimney Corner* (London: Eveleigh Nash, 1913), 32.

88 Andrew Merry, *The Hunger*, 111.

89 *Strictures on the Proposed Poor Law for Ireland As Recommended in the Report of George Nicholls Esq* (London: James Ridgway and Sons, 1837), 21.

90 Words of Malachi Horan, a small farmer

in the Wicklow Mountains. Cited in Kevin Whelan, 'Pre- and Post-Famine Landscape Change' in Cathal Póirtéir (ed.), *The Great Irish Famine*, 32.

91 The other word for hunger, *ocras*, also includes a moral attitude: hungry, starved, greedy, miserly. See Patrick S. Dinneen, *Foclóir Gaedilge Agus Bearla: An Irish-English Dictionary* (Dublin: Irish Texts Society, 1927).

92 Gerard Healy, *The Black Stranger*, 27.

93 William Carleton, *The Black Prophet*, 30–1.

94 See Terence Patrick Dolan, *A Dictionary of Hiberno-English: The Irish Use of English* (Dublin: Gill and Macmillan, 1999).

95 'Fair Gurtha; Or the Hungry Grass: The Legend of the Dumb Grass' was first published in the *Dublin University Magazine* in April 1856, 414–35.

96 According to Cormac Ó Gráda, the Irish were disastrously unlucky in the timing of the blight. After 1850, the demand for labour in Britain and North America could have absorbed many of those who in fact perished. See Cormac Ó Gráda, *Ireland Before and After the Famine: Explorations in Economic History 1800–1925* (Manchester: Manchester University Press, 1993), 41ff.

97 In his thoroughgoing analysis of the causes of the Famine, Joel Mokyr lists among the factors geographical, political and institutional, social and ethnic, population, capital formation, entrepreneurial, and emigration. Joel Mokyr, *Why Ireland Starved: A Quantitative and Analytical History of the Irish Economy, 1800–1850* (London: George Allen and Unwin, 1985), 2–3.

98 Alexander Somerville, *Letters From Ireland During the Famine of 1847* (ed. K. D. M. Snell), 28. Letter dated 23 January 1847 from Dublin.

99 See, for example, Cathal Póirtéir, *Famine Echoes* (Dublin: Gill and Macmillan, 1995), 91.

100 From George Cooper, 'The Irish Mother's Lament Over Her Child', in *Howitt's Journal of Literature and Popular Progress* Vol II (1847), 262.

101 The sketch is frequently reproduced. See, for example, John Killen (ed.), *The Famine Decade: Contemporary Accounts 1841–1851* (Belfast: Blackstaff, 1995), 232.

102 Peter O'Leary, *My Story* (tr. Cyril Ó Céirin) (1915; Oxford: Oxford University Press, 1987), 51.

103 Cathy Carruth, *Trauma*, 5.

104 Mike Cronin, *A History of Ireland* (Basingstoke: Palgrave, 2001), 135–6.

105 See graph in Cormac Ó Gráda, *Black '47 and Beyond*, 89. See also 'The Burden of Disease' section, in Liam Kennedy, Paul S. Ell, E. M. Crawford, and L. A. Clarkson, *Mapping the Great Irish Famine* (Dublin: Four Courts, 1999).

106 Maggie O'Sullivan, 'that bread should be' in Maggie O'Sullivan, David Gascoyne, Barry MacSweeney, *Etruscan Reader III* (Newcastle-under-Lyme: Etruscan Books, 1997), 39–40. Her title comes from a phrase often heard at the time of the Famine: 'that bread should be so dear and human flesh so cheap'.

107 Theodor Adorno, *Negative Dialectics* (tr. E. B. Ashton) (New York: Continuum Books, 1973), 362.

108 Michael Davitt, *The Fall of Feudalism in Ireland: Or the Story of the Land League Revolution* (London and New York: Harper, 1904), 50.

109 Zygmunt Bauman, *Modernity and the Holocaust* (1989; Cambridge: Polity Press, 2000), 233. The remark appears in his 2000 Afterword (my italics). There is virtually no mention of the Irish Famine in Mike Davis, *Late Victorian Holocausts: El Niño Famines and the Making of the Third World* (London: Verso, 2001).

110 Ciarán Ó Murchadha, 'The Bad Times in Clare: Emigration and Aftermath', in *The Other Clare* 27 (2003), 55–8.

111 Melissa Fegan, *Literature and the Irish Famine 1845–1919*, 32.

112 See Philip Knightley, *The First Casualty: From Crimea to Vietnam: The War*

Correspondent as Hero, Propagandist, and Myth Maker (London: Quartet, 1978), 329.

113 *New Statesman and Nation*, 7 April 1945. Cited in Knightley, 328.

114 Eva Hoffman, *After Such Knowledge: Memory, History, and the Legacy of the Holocaust* (London: Secker and Warburg, 2004), 66.

115 For a discussion of Rich in the context of identity and the Nazi Holocaust, see Mary Eagleton, 'Adrienne Rich, Location and the Body', *Journal of Gender Studies* 9: 3, 2000, 299–312.

116 Cathy Carruth, *Trauma*, 145. 'Interview with Robert Jay Lifton'.

Chapter 4   THE IMPACT OF CULTURAL NATIONALISM

1 Godwin Smith, 'The Administration of Ireland' in the *Contemporary Review*, July 1885, 7.

2 George Bernard Shaw, *O'Flaherty V. C.*, in *The Complete Plays of Bernard Shaw* (London: Odhams, 1934), 821. As if by way of riposte to Yeats's play *Cathleen Ni Houlihan* (1902), Shaw includes a reference to O'Flaherty's mother thinking her son is fighting the English and going about the house imagining the French are on the sea and the 1798 Rising is about to be repeated.

3 See 'Thomas McDonagh' (sic) in *The Complete Poems of Francis Ledwidge* (Introduction Lord Dunsany) (London: Herbert Jenkins, 1919), 210.

4 Roddy Doyle, *A Star Called Henry* (London: Jonathan Cape, 1999), 52.

5 I have taken this phrase from Robert Lynd, *Ireland A Nation* (London: Grant Richards, 1919), 70.

6 Bobby Sands, *One Day in My Life* (Dublin and Cork: The Mercier Press, 1982), 60. Elsewhere, on the other side of the fence, when the RUC officer Caroline, in Gary Mitchell's play *The Force of Change* (2000), is interrogating Stanley about his membership of the UDA and his role in directing terrorism, she makes a telling observation that sounds especially odd to audiences abroad: 'You don't think of yourself as Irish, do you?' (19)

7 See Anthony D. Smith, *The Nation in History: Historiographical Debates about Ethnicity and Nationalism* (Cambridge: Polity, 2000). Smith provides a useful introduction to the modernist v perennialist debate about the antiquity or otherwise of nations. See also the same author's *The Antiquity of Nations* (Cambridge: Polity, 2004).

8 W. B. Yeats, *Essays and Introductions* (New York: Collier, 1968), 210.

9 W. B. Yeats, *On the Boiler* (Dublin: Cuala Press, 1938), 21.

10 W. B. Yeats, *Reveries Over Childhood and Youth* (London: Macmillan, 1916), 60.

11 Donald R. Pearce (ed.), *The Senate Speeches of W. B. Yeats* (London: Faber and Faber, 1961), 172.

12 W. B. Yeats, *On the Boiler* (Dublin: Cuala Press, 1938), 31.

13 See Declan Kiberd, *Inventing Ireland* (London: Jonathan Cape, 1995), 51–66. It's worth recalling that British imperial attitudes towards Shaw's play died slowly. In an editorial in the *Listener* on 12 July 1951 entitled 'The Irish in Us', much is made of 'the Irish character': 'If (as at any rate the leaders in Eire aver) there is still an Irish problem, is it not largely a problem of the Irish character, the problem posed by Shaw in "John Bull's Other Island"?'

14 George Bernard Shaw, *John Bull's Other Island*, 83.

15 See Mario Borsa, *The English Stage of Today* (tr. Selwyn Brinton) (London: John Lane, 1908), 158.

16 George Bernard Shaw, *John Bull's Other Island*, 174.

17 For an informative discussion of Boazio's map, see J. H. Andrews, *Shapes of Ireland: Maps and Their Makers 1564–1839* (Dublin: Geography Publications, 1997), 75–85.

18 Reproduced in Angela Bourke, *et al.* (eds), *The Field Day Anthology of Irish Writing Volume V: Irish Women's Writing and Traditions* (Cork: Cork University Press; New York: New York University Press, 2002), 1313.

19 Hugo Hamilton, *The Speckled People* (London and New York: Fourth Estate, 2003), 108.

20 The original story is reproduced in my *James Joyce's Ireland* (New Haven and London: Yale University Press, 1992).

21 Virginia Woolf, 'The Leaning Tower', *A Woman's Essays: Selected Essays* Vol 1, (ed. Rachel Bowlby) (Harmondsworth: Penguin, 1992), 168.

22 W. B. Yeats, 'Letters to the New Island', 22 February 1890, in George Bornstein and Hugh Witemeyer (eds), *The Collected Works of W. B. Yeats* Vol VII (New York: Macmillan, 1989), 30.

23 W. B. Yeats, 'Ireland and the Arts', in *Ideas of Good and Evil* (London: A. H. Bullen; Dublin: Munsel, 1907), 324.

24 Ernest Renan, *Poetry of the Celtic Races and Other Studies* (tr. William G. Hutchison) (London: Walter Scott, 1896), 80.

25 *The Popular Works of Johann Gottlieb Fichte*, Volume 1 (tr. William Smith) (London: Trübner, 1889), 132.

26 W. B. Yeats, 'A General Introduction for My Work', in *Essays and Introductions* (New York: Collier, 1968), 513.

27 See E. J. Hobsbawm, *Nations and Nationalism Since 1870*, 2nd edition (Cambridge: Cambridge University Press, 2000), 102.

28 W. B. Yeats, 'A General Introduction for My Work', in *Essays and Introductions*, 519.

29 Ernest Renan, *Recollections of My Youth* (tr. C. B. Pitman) (London: Chapman and Hall, 1892), 65.

30 W. B. Yeats, 'The Literary Movement in Ireland', in Lady Gregory (ed.), *Ideals in Ireland* (London: Unicorn, 1901), 98.

31 Perry Anderson, 'Internationalism: A Breviary', *New Left Review*, 14 March/April 2002, 5.

32 Anthony D. Smith, *Nationalism and Modernism: A Critical Survey of Recent Theories of Nations and Nationalism* (London and New York: Routledge, 1998), 1.

33 Canon P. A. Sheehan, *Glenanaar: A Story of Irish Life* (1902; London: Longmans, Green, 1929), 42.

34 Robert Lynd, *Ireland A Nation* (London: Grant Richards, 1919).

35 J. O. Bartley speculates that Macmorris belonged to one of the older settler families in Ireland who substituted the Gaelic 'Mac' for the Norman 'Fitz' in their surnames. Macmorris may also have been educated in England. See *Teague, Shenkin and Sawney* (Cork: Cork University Press, 1954), 16.

36 M. J. MacManus, *Eamon de Valera: A Biography* (Dublin: Talbot, 1947), 347.

37 Liam de Paor, *Landscapes with Figures: People, Culture and Art in Ireland and the Modern World* (Dublin: Four Courts, 1998), 143. The comment was originally made in an article entitled 'A Terrible Beauty is Born' and published in the *Irish Times* on 29 April 1975.

38 Ernie O'Malley, *Army Without Banners* (London: New English Library, 1967), 50. First published in 1936 under the title *On Another Man's Wounds*.

39 Brinsley MacNamara, 'MacNamara on Yeats', *Irish Commonwealth*, 1: 3 May 1919, 172–3. This was a review of *The Wild Swans at Coole* (1919).

40 George O'Brien, *The Four Green Fields* (Dublin and Cork: Talbot, 1936), 74.

41 Tom Garvin, *1922: The Birth of Irish Democracy* (Dublin: Gill and Macmillan, 1996).

42 See Rick Wilford (ed.), *Aspects of the Belfast Agreement* (Oxford: Oxford University Press, 2001), 6.

43 Ray Ryan, *Ireland and Scotland: Literature and Culture, State and Nation 1966–2000* (Oxford: Clarendon, 2002), 290–1.

44 David Fitzpatrick, *The Two Irelands 1912–1939* (Oxford: Opus, 1998).

45 Sean O'Casey, *Autobiographies* 2 (London: Pan, 1980), 3.

46 Frank McGuinness, *Plays One: The Factory Girls, Observe the Sons of Ulster Marching Towards the Somme, Innocence, Carthaginians, Baglady* (London: Faber and Faber, 1996), 175.

47 Ernest Gellner, *Nationalism* (London: Phoenix, 1997), 90–101.

48 The front page of the *Connacht Tribune* is reproduced on the back cover of Tim Pat Coogan, *1916: The Easter Rising* (London: Weidenfeld and Nicolson, 2001).

49 Douglas Hyde, 'The Necessity for De-Anglicising Ireland' (1892), reprinted in Charles Gavan Duffy, George Sigerson, and Douglas Hyde, *The Revival of Irish Literature* (London: T. Fisher Unwin, 1894), 136–7.

50 Horace Plunkett, *Ireland in the New Century* (1904; London: John Murray, 1905), x.

51 George Moore, *Hail and Farewell: Ave* (London: William Heinemann, 1911), 42.

52 Jeanne Sheehy, *The Rediscovery of Ireland's Past: The Celtic Revival 1830–1930* (London: Thames and Hudson, 1980), *passim.*

53 George Russell, *Imaginations and Reveries* (Dublin and London: Maunsel and Roberts, 1921), 5; Maurice Goldring, *Pleasant the Scholar's Life: Irish Intellectuals and the Construction of the Irish State* (London: Serif, 1993), 28.

54 George Russell, 'Nationality and Imperialism' in Lady Gregory (ed.), *Ideals in Ireland*, 22.

55 See Margaret Digby, *Horace Plunkett: An Anglo-American Irishman* (Oxford: Basil Blackwell, 1949), *passim.*

56 'Ethna Carbery' [Anna MacManus], *The Four Winds of Erinn* (ed. Seamas MacManus) (Dublin: M. H. Gill, 1902), 82.

57 W. B. Yeats, *The Wind Among the Reeds* (1899; London: Elkin Mathews, 1903), 1 and 35.

58 The '1860s generation' is my own term. The following were all born in this decade: Hyde (1860), Katharine Tynan (1861), Yeats (1865), Carbery (1866), Alice Milligan (1866), George Russell (1867), John Eglinton (1868), Constance Markievicz (1868).

59 George Bernard Shaw, *John Bull's Other Island*, 81.

60 Oscar Wilde, *The Importance of Being Earnest*, in *Complete Works of Oscar Wilde* (Introduction Vyvyan Holland) (London: Book Club Associates, 1976), 321, 326.

61 Hugo Hamilton, *The Speckled People.*

62 Lines from Pound's *Pisan Cantos*. See my *Yeats's Worlds* for copy of original type-script (p.175).

63 W. B. Yeats, *Explorations* (Selected by Mrs W. B. Yeats) (New York: Collier, 1973), 263.

64 W. B. Yeats, *Dramatis Personae 1896–1902* (London: Macmillan, 1936), 52.

65 W. B. Yeats, 'Four Years: 1887–1891', *Autobiographies* (London: Macmillan, 1977), 135. 'Four Years: 1887–1891' was first published in the *London Mercury* in June 1921. It would be interesting to know if, when composing his memory of this encounter with Wilde, he consulted Sherard.

66 Robert Harborough Sherard, *The Life of Oscar Wilde* (London: T. Werner Laurie, 1906), 295.

67 W. B. Yeats, *A Vision* (1937; New York: Collier, 1977), 147–8.

68 See Frank Harris, *Oscar Wilde: His Life and Confessions* (New York: The Author, 1918), 125–6. The interview was conducted by Robert Ross in the *Pall Mall Budget* in June 1892. See also Richard Ellmann, *Oscar Wilde* (London: Hamish Hamilton, 1987), 351–2.

69 Samuel Beckett, *Three Novels: Molloy, Malone Dies, The Unnamable* (1955; New York: Grove Press, 1977), 69–74.

70 *All That Fall* (1957) is Beckett's most Irish play, in that Irish voices can be heard throughout.

71 The town adjacent to Lady Gregory's estate in the west of Ireland was Kiltartan; 'Kiltartanese' is the name given to the form of Hiberno-English in her writings. The 'apple' phrase is an image Synge himself

used in his preface to *The Playboy of the Western World*, where he is really talking about his own work.

72 George Fitzmaurice, *The Dandy Dolls* in *The Plays of George Fitzmaurice: Dramatic Fantasies* (Introduction Austin Clarke) (Dublin: Dolmen, 1967), 21.

73 P. W. Joyce, *English as We Speak it in Ireland* (Introduction Terence Dolan) (1910; Portmarnock, Co Dublin, 1979). In his Preface, Joyce refers to the life of the people pictured in language and how 'our picture ought to be a good one, for two languages were concerned in it' (v).

74 For a recent discussion of accumulation by dispossession in the context of American imperialism, see David Harvey, *The New Imperialism* (Oxford: Oxford University Press, 2003).

75 See Ernest Boyd, *Ireland's Literary Renaissance* (New York: Alfred Knopf, 1922).

76 Report in *Punch* 17 May 1916, 331.

77 D. George Boyce, *Nationalism in Ireland* (London: Croom Helm, 1982), 312.

78 Jamie O'Neill, *At Swim, Two Boys* (London: Scribner, 2001), 567. As this novel suggests, 1916 initiated – or should have done – a new kind of Ireland, freedom from Britain and freedom from sexual oppression, especially, with its epigraph from Whitman, for gays.

79 Iris Murdoch, *The Red and the Green* (Harmondsworth: Penguin, 1967), 77.

80 Roddy Doyle, *A Star Called Henry*, 112.

81 Kathleen Clarke, *Revolutionary Woman: Kathleen Clarke* (ed. Helen Litton) (Dublin: O'Brien, 1991), 93.

82 Francis Shaw S. J., 'The Canon of Irish History – A Challenge', in *Studies: An Irish Quarterly Review* 61: 242, Summer 1972, 123. Martin Mansergh puts a different gloss on this, arguing that Pearse 'was more respectful of religion than almost any previous Irish revolutionary'. See 'Republicanism in a Christian Country – Past, Present and Future', in *Studies: An Irish Quarterly Review* 89: 355, Autumn 2000, 255.

83 See, for example, Desmond Fennell, *Heresy: The Battle of Ideas in Modern Ireland* (Belfast: Blackstaff, 1993) and Maurice Goldring, *Pleasant the Scholar's Life*.

84 See Michael Laffan, 'The Sacred Memory: Religion, Revisionists and the Easter Rising', in Judith Devlin and Ronan Fanning (eds), *Religion and Rebellion* (Dublin: University College Dublin Press, 1997), 177.

85 David Fitzpatrick, *The Two Irelands 1912–1939*, 4.

86 *Catholic Bulletin* 25: 4, April 1935, 273.

87 Cited in Jonathan Bardon, *A History of Ulster* (Belfast: Blackstaff, 1992), 539.

88 According to George O'Brien, 'The identification [of nationalism and Catholicism in the nineteenth century] was of the greatest service to the opponents of home rule in Ireland.' See *The Four Green Fields* (Dublin and Cork: Talbot, 1936), 70.

89 John O'Leary, *Recollections of Fenians and Fenianism,* Vol 2 (London: Downey, 1896), 33 and 66.

90 D. George Boyce and Alan O'Day (eds), *Defenders of the Union: A Survey of British and Irish Unionism Since 1801* (London: Routledge, 2001), 9.

91 Terence Brown, 'Cultural Nationalism 1880–1930', in the *Field Day Anthology of Irish Writing, Volume II*, eds Seamus Deane, Andrew Carpenter and Jonathan Williams (Derry: Field Day, 1991), 517.

92 Joep Leerssen, *Remembrance and Imagination: Patterns in the Historical and Literary Representation of Ireland in the Nineteenth Century* (Cork: Cork University Press, 1996), 5.

93 From George Russell, 'Lessons of Revolution', *Studies: An Irish Quarterly Review*, March 1923.

94 See my *Yeats's Worlds*, pp.218–20, for details and my interpretation. For transcript of correspondence, see Anne Saddlemyer, *Becoming George: The Life of Mrs W. B. Yeats* (Oxford University Press, 2002), 315 and Roy F. Foster, *W. B. Yeats: A Life II: The Arch-Poet, 1915–1939*

(Oxford: Oxford University Press, 2003), 232.

95 V. S. Pritchett, *Dublin: A Portrait* (Photographs by Evelyn Hofer) (London: The Bodley Head, 1967), 11–12.

96 Sir John Lavery, *The Life of a Painter* (London: Cassell, 1940), 217.

97 George O'Brien, *The Four Green Fields*, 16.

98 Denis Devlin, 'The Tomb of Michael Collins', *Sewanee Review*, October 1956.

99 This was written by R. A. Stewart Macalister, Professor of Celtic Archaeology at University College Dublin. See George Fletcher (ed.), *Ireland* (Cambridge: Cambridge University Press, 1922), 116.

100 Daniel Corkery, *Synge and Anglo-Irish Literature* (1931; Cork: Mercier, 1966), 19.

101 Thomas McGreevy, *Richard Aldington: An Englishman* (London: Chatto and Windus, 1931), 53.

102 Máire Cruise O'Brien, *The Same Age as the State* (Dublin: The O'Brien Press, 2003), 100–1.

103 Cited in Frank Sewell, *Modern Irish Poetry: A New Alhambra* (Oxford: Oxford University Press, 2000), 13.

104 *Dublin Opinion*, 3: 36, February 1925, 234–5. De Valera had refused to ratify the Anglo-Irish Treaty, and instead proposed Document No 2. The Republicans insisted on deleting any reference to an oath of allegiance or to the position of Governor-General. The refusal to sign Document No 1 in turn led to the Civil War.

105 See Sean Rothery, *Ireland and the New Architecture 1900–1940* (Dublin: Lilliput, 1991), 76–8. In Roddy Doyle's *A Star Called Henry* (1999), Henry – on Collins's instruction – buys a suit in Clery's after the funeral of Thomas Ashe in 1917 (see p.191). I wonder if this is an error on the author's part.

106 See Robert Lynd, *Ireland A Nation*, 197.

107 Stephen Howe, *Ireland and Empire: Colonial Legacies in Irish History and Culture* (Oxford: Oxford University Press, 2000), 44.

108 F. Sheehy-Skeffington, 'Frederick Ryan', the *Irish Review*, May 1913, 113.

109 Terry Eagleton, 'The Ryan Line' in *Crazy John and the Bishop And Other Essays on Irish Culture* (Cork: Cork University Press, 1998), 263.

110 See Joseph Holloway's Diary, 15 May 1906. Cited in Robert Hogan and James Kilroy (eds), *The Abbey Theatre: The Years of Synge 1905–1909* (Dublin: Dolmen, 1978), 102.

111 There is a thumb-nail sketch of Ryan in Desmond Ryan, *Remembering Sion: A Chronicle of Storm and Quiet* (London: Arthur Barker, 1934) where the author recalls his childhood amid the voices of dissent: 'One, Fred Ryan, returned from Egypt, wars upon all physical forces and Nationalists and Gaelic Leaguers and clergymen and Marxian Socialists with the utmost courtesy and persuasiveness . . . . "Irial" is his pen name all the world knows. He hurls his weekly javelin at Arthur Griffith his former ally . . . . The Gaels like him not . . . . The Socialists bristle weekly and hurl shibboleths at him . . . . He is a militant agnostic and it is said his father took the utmost pains with his upbringing to produce this result' (p.53). The irony is that Ryan, the author of one of the lost plays of the Abbey (one Act is extant), has been subjected to an equal carelessness concerning the facts of his life. The omens were not good. Within ten years of his death 'M. C. S.' [?the bibliographer Michael Sadleir] in *The Irish Book Lover* wanted to know if Ryan was Frederick W. Ryan, author of a pamphlet 'A Plea for Irish Studies' (1908), which he wasn't (see 13: 6, January 1922, 115). A generation ago, Ann Saddlemyer implied that Ryan wrote for the Abbey Theatre after its establishment in 1904, when his only known play was produced under the auspices of the Irish National Dramatic Company in October 1902. (See Ann

Saddlemyer, '"Worn-Out With Dreams": Dublin's Abbey Theatre' in Robin Skelton and Ann Saddlemyer (eds), *The World of W. B. Yeats*, (Seattle: University of Washington Press, 1967), 87. For the date of Ryan's play, see Lady Gregory, *Our Irish Theatre* (1913; New York: Capricorn, 1965), 262. Herbert Kenny refers to Ryan as Secretary of the Irish National Theatre Society, but then adds he was 'a playwright who would die too soon'. (See Herbert Kenny, *Literary Dublin: A History* (New York: Taplinger; Dublin: Gill & Macmillan, 1974), 189.) The editors of Yeats's *Uncollected Prose* Volume 2 (London: Macmillan, 1975), claim that he died some time after the demise of *Dana* in 1905. They also seem unaware that Ryan wrote under at least two pseudonyms, 'Irial', whom they describe as a 'shrewd and pseudonymous commentator' (p.262) and 'Finian'. The identity of 'Irial' was known at least as early as May 1913, when it was revealed by Sheehy-Skeffington in his tribute to Ryan in the *Irish Review*. Dominic Manganiello repeatedly refers to the 'pseudonymous columnist of the *United Irishman*' as 'Trial', not 'Irial', but it is clear from Yeats's *Uncollected Prose* Volume 2 (eds John P. Frayne and Colton Johnson) (London: Macmillan, 1975) that 'Irial' is his name. (See Dominic Manganiello, *Joyce's Politics* (London: Routledge & Kegan Paul, 1980), 215–17.) Bonnie Kime Scott refers to Frank Ryan as co-editor of *Dana*. (See Bonnie Kime Scott, *Joyce and Feminism* (Bloomington, IN: Indiana University Press; Brighton: Harvester, 1984), 86.)

112 Fred Ryan to Frank Sheehy-Skeffington, 13 July 1908. From Cairo. Sheehy-Skeffington Papers. National Library of Ireland. Ms 21, 619(i). Thomas Kettle (1880–1916), was an Irish nationalist politician and poet, who died in the Great War. For the Ryan and Joyce generation, Kettle was held in high esteem, particularly for his integrity.

113 Fred Ryan, 'On Language and Political Ideals', *Dana: An Irish Magazine of Independent Thought*, 9 January 1905, 278.

Chapter 5 YEATS'S REVERIES ON THE EASTER RISING

1 W. B. Yeats, *Reveries Over Childhood and Youth* (London: Macmillan, 1916), vii–viii.

2 Ernest Renan, *Recollections of My Youth* (tr. C. B. Pitman) (London: Chapman and Hall, 1892), viii.

3 The Complete Autograph Manuscript of *Reveries* can be consulted in the James Augustine Healy Collection at Colby College Library, Waterville, Maine.

4 St Augustine, *Confessions*, Book 10: 8 (tr. R. S. Pine-Coffin) (Harmondsworth: Penguin, 1961), 215

5 Manuscript, 33a. The deletion originally appeared before the sentence beginning: 'She would spend hours listening to stories. . . .' Macmillan 1916 edition, 54.

6 Manuscript, 45.

7 George Russell. Letter to George Moore, 6 April 1916. In Alan Denson (ed.), *The Letters of A E* (London, New York, Toronto: Abelard-Schuman), 1961.

8 'Lord Clonbrony, who was somebody in Ireland, who was a great person in Dublin, found himself nobody in England, a mere cipher in London.' Maria Edgeworth, *The Absentee* (Oxford: Oxford University Press, 1988), 22.

9 Edwin Thumboo, 'W. B. Yeats as Third World Paradigm', in Robbie B. H. Goh (ed.), *Conflicting Identities: Essays on Modern Irish Literature* (Singapore: UniPress, 1997), 230.

10 Manuscript, 80.

11 James Connolly, 'The Glories of War', in *The Irish Worker* 21 November 1914. MacDonagh's Last Address is cited in Patrick Galvin (ed.) *The Songs and Ballads of Irish Freedom* (Cork: The Fountain Bookshop, 1919), 61.

12 Pádraic H. Pearse, *Political Writings and*

Speeches (Dublin: Talbot, 1952), 38–9. At the end of the Boer War – significantly recalled in the entry on his biography in *Sinn Féin Handbook* (Dublin, 1917) – MacBride was presented with the flag of the Irish Brigade with the inscription ''Tis better to have fought and lost/Than never to have fought at all.' (p.269)

13 For words and tune, see http://www.bbc.co.uk/history/war/easterrising/songs/rs_song06.shtml.

14 The two great figures in the making of modern Ireland tended to ignore each other. In his public speeches de Valera made, it appears, only one reference to Yeats, when he quoted from the final lines of *Cathleen ni Houlihan* ('They shall be remembered for ever') at the time of the deaths of Terence MacSwiney and Kevin Barry. See Maurice Moynihan (ed.), *Speeches and Statements by Eamon de Valera 1917–73* (Dublin: Gill and Macmillan; New York: St Martin's Press, 1980), 47. But he led the nation when Yeats's body was returned to Ireland in 1948.

15 Edna C. Fitzhenry (ed.), *Nineteen-Sixteen: An Anthology* (Dublin: Brown and Nolan; London: Geo. G. Harrap, 1935), 60.

16 William Rothenstein, *Men and Memories: Recollections of William Rothenstein, 1900–1922* (London: Faber and Faber, 1932), 321.

17 W. B. Yeats, 'What is Popular Poetry', in W. B. Yeats, *Essays and Introductions* (New York: Macmillan, 1977), 10.

18 See Joseph Hone (ed.), *J. B. Yeats: Letters to his Son W. B. Yeats and Others, 1869–1922, 1865–1939* (London: Faber and Faber, 1944), 300.

19 See, for example, *Sinn Féin Handbook* (Dublin, 1917), 11; *Revolutionary Woman: Kathleen Clarke 1878–1972* (ed. Helen Litton) (Dublin: O'Brien, 1991), 116.

20 Michael Laffan, *The Resurrection of Ireland: The Sinn Féin Party 1916–1923* (Cambridge: Cambridge University Press, 1999), 36.

21 Standish James O'Grady, 'The Great Enchantment', in *All Ireland Review*, 17 February 1900.

22 *Sphere*, 6 May 1916, 124.

23 Gillian McIntosh, *The Force of Culture: Unionist Identities in Twentieth-Century Ireland* (Cork: Cork University Press, 1999), 15.

24 C. Desmond Greaves, *The Easter Rising in Song and Ballad* (London: Kahn & Averill, 1982), 54–5.

25 Michael Foy and Brian Barton, *The Easter Rising* (Stroud, Gloucestershire: Sutton, 2004), 42.

26 *Revolutionary Woman: Kathleen Clarke 1878–1972*, 64.

27 W. B. Yeats, *Responsibilities* (London: Macmillan, 1916), 187. I am grateful to Eamonn Cantwell for pointing this out to me.

28 Cited in the *Irish Independent*, 11 May 1916, p.3.

29 See, for example, Eva Gore-Booth's 'Dedication to "The Death of Fionavar"', in Edna C. Fitzhenry (ed.), *Nineteen-Sixteen; An Anthology* (Dublin: Brown and Nolan; London: Geo. G. Harrap, 1935), 73.

30 Kathleen Coyle, *Piccadilly* (London: Jonathan Cape, 1923), 89, 129.

31 See 'The New Irish Revolutionary', in the *Daily Chronicle* 9 May 1916.

32 Liam de Paor, 'A Terrible Beauty Is Born', in *Landscapes with Figures: People, Culture and Art in Ireland and the Modern World* (Dublin: Four Courts, 1998), 143. The article first appeared in the *Irish Times* on 29 April 1975.

33 Niall Ferguson, *Empire: The Rise and Demise of the British World Order* (London: Allen Lane, 2003), 323. I think the phrase should read 'advanced nationalist', which carries none of the reactionary associations of 'extreme'.

34 Ernest Renan, *Poetry of the Celtic Races and Other Studies*, 9.

35 According to Cornelius F. Smith, Yeats resigned in protest against the burning of the great houses (including Plunkett's,

who also changed clubs at this time) by the Irregulars. The year was presumably 1923. See Cornelius F. Smith and Bernard Share (eds), *Whigs on the Green: The Stephen's Green Club 1840–1990* (Dublin: Gill and Macmillan, 1990), 48. Yeats was also keen to socialise with the Southern Unionists, with whom he voted in the Senate. See Joseph Hone, *W. B. Yeats 1865–1939* (London: Macmillan, 1942), 352.

36 See ALS Letter to Lady Gregory, 10 February 1917. In Henry W. and Albert A. Berg Collection, the New York Public Library, Astor, Lenox, and Tilden Foundations.

37 See Brian Inglis, *West Briton* (London: Faber and Faber, 1962), 9–35.

38 See *British and Irish Biographies 1840–1945* (ed. David Lewis Jones) (Cambridge: Chadwyck-Healey microfiche).

39 Mark Bence-Jones, *Twilight of the Ascendancy* (London: Constable, 1987), 109. Of the 700 or 800 members, only some 80 were not from the Ascendancy. For details on senior resident magistrates and serving English officers, see Penny Bonsall, *The Irish RMs: The Resident Magistrates in the British Administration of Ireland* (Dublin: Four Courts, 1997), 89.

40 Nora Robertson, *Crowned Harp: Memories of the Last Years of the Crown in Ireland* (Dublin: Allen, Figgis, 1960), 76. L. P. Curtis Jr., 'The Anglo-Irish Predicament', in *20ᵗʰ Century Studies*, volume 4, November 1970, 43.

41 A. Norman Jeffares, *A Commentary on the Collected Poems of W. B. Yeats* (London: Macmillan, 1968), 226 and *W. B. Yeats: A New Biography* (London: Hutchinson, 1988), 215.

42 Cornelius F. Smith and Bernard Share (eds), *Whigs on the Green*, 41–2.

43 Ibid., 76. Interestingly, the term Yeats used to refer to 'Easter 1916' was the 'rebellion' poem. See my *Yeats's Worlds*, 190.

44 See Roy F. Foster, *W. B. Yeats: A Life II*, 54.

For details on the police pass, see MS 30, 693 in the National Library of Ireland.

45 See the website of the United Arts Club at http://www.dublinarts.com/history.htm.

46 P. L. Dickinson, *The Dublin of Yesterday* (London: Methuen, 1929), 54.

47 See Maud Gonne's letter to Yeats March 1911, in Anna MacBride White and A. Norman Jeffares (eds), *Always Your Friend: The Gonne–Yeats Letters 1893–1938* (London: Pimlico, 1993), 298.

48 This was not the view of the rebels, who, like Connolly, were inclined to politicise art rather than aestheticise politics (as was Yeats's tendency).

49 Nora Robertson, *Crowned Harp*, 108–23.

50 *The Gonne–Yeats Letters, 1893–1938* (ed. Anna MacBride White and A. N. Jeffares) (London: Pimlico, 1993), 372, 373, 377.

51 Casement's speech is reproduced in Brian Inglis, *Roger Casement* (London: Hodder and Stoughton, 1973), 410. For Quinn's remark, see Maud Gonne's letter to John Quinn, 30 April 1916, in Janis Londraville and Richard Londraville (eds), *Too Long A Sacrifice: The Letters of Maud Gonne and John Quinn* (Sleinsgrove: Susquehanna University Press; London: Associated University Press, 1999), 167.

52 See Joan Towey Mitchell, 'Yeats, Pearse and Cuchulain', in *Eire-Ireland* XI: 4, 1976, 51–65. See also John Wilson Foster, *Colonial Consequences: Essays in Irish Literature and Culture* (Dublin: Lilliput, 1991), 139–40.

53 Austin Clarke, *A Penny in the Clouds: More Memories of Ireland and England* (London: Routledge & Kegan Paul, 1968), 25.

54 See my *Yeats's Worlds*, 91 and 284–5.

55 'Standing by the seashore in Normandy in September 1916 he read me that poem; he had worked on it all the night before. . . .' See Maud Gonne, 'Yeats and Ireland', in Stephen Gwynn (ed.), *Scattering Branches: Tributes to the Memory of W. B. Yeats* (London: Macmillan, 1940), 31–2.

56 Roy F. Foster, *W. B. Yeats: A Life 1: The Apprentice Mage 1965–1914* (Oxford: Oxford University Press, 1997), 180–1.

57 W. B. Yeats, *Memoirs* (ed. Denis Donoghue) (New York: Macmillan, 1973), 77–8.

58 Anne Marreco, *The Rebel Countess: The Life and Times of Constance Markievicz* (London: Corgi, 1969), 257.

59 C. S. Andrews, *Man of No Property: An Autobiography* (Volume Two) (Dublin and Cork: Mercier, 1982), 50.

60 See Diana Norman, *Terrible Beauty: A Life of Constance Markievicz 1868–1927* (London: Hodder and Stoughton, 1987), 139. Norman believes Constance did not pull the trigger.

61 Ibid., 129. Kathleen Clarke was less impressed and she was irritated by Constance's condescension towards her. See *Revolutionary Woman: Kathleen Clarke 1878–1972*, 164. She also comments on the social snobbery of both Constance and Maud Gonne, mentioning how once, in the exercise yard of Holloway Prison, she caught the two arguing about which had the higher social status (159).

62 See 'The New Irish Revolutionary', the *Daily Chronicle*, 9 May 1916.

63 Roy F. Foster, *W. B. Yeats: A Life II*, 62.

64 See TS 30,216 in the National Library of Ireland. Cited in Foster, 60.

65 Gifford Lewis, *Eva Gore-Booth and Esther Roper: A Biography* (London: Pandora, 1988), 12.

66 Edna Longley, *From Cathleen to Anorexia: The Breakdowns of Ireland* (Dublin: Attic, 1990), 17.

67 Ibid., 1082.

68 For text and commentary on this play, see Cheryl Herr (ed.), *For the Land They Loved: Irish Political Melodramas 1890–1925* (Syracuse: Syracuse University Press, 1991).

69 See Maud Gonne, 'Yeats and Ireland', in Stephen Gwynn (ed.), *Scattering Branches*, 32.

70 Seán Ó Tuama, 'Abair Do Phaidir' (Say a Prayer) in *An Bás I dTír na nÓg* (Baile Átha Cliath: Coiscéim, 1988). Reproduced in my Cork *Reader*, 1065.

71 David Lloyd, *Anomalous States: Irish Writing and the Post-Colonial Moment* (Dublin: Lilliput, 1993), 69. Lloyd seems to use 'nation' and 'State' as interchangeable on this page.

72 Reported in the *Irishman*, 21 April 1917. The play was staged at the Abbey the week before Easter, 2–7 April.

73 For a discussion concerning the reasons for his delay, see my *Yeats's Worlds*, 189–90.

74 Leon Uris, *Trinity* (Garden City, New York: Doubleday, 1976), 751.

75 The opening stanza first appeared in Ernest A. Boyd's 'The Drift of Anglo-Irish Literature', published in a short-lived Dublin-based journal, *The Irish Commonwealth*, on St Patrick's Day 1919, 20–8, at 24.

Chapter 6 Beyond a Boundary

1 Frank Budgen, *James Joyce and the Making of 'Ulysses'* (Introduction Clive Hart) (1934; London: Oxford University Press, 1972), 15.

2 See Katharine O'Shea, *Charles Stewart Parnell: His Love Story and Political Life* Vol. I (London: Cassell, 1914), 49.

3 Stanislaus Joyce, *My Brother's Keeper* (ed. Richard Ellmann) (London: Faber and Faber, 1982), 61.

4 At least this is what happened in the period after 1916 when the IRA began to recruit in the Cork area. 'An analysis of IRA unit rolls bears out this impression of clannishness' (209). 'Football and hurling teams were another important source of recruits' (210). See Peter Hart, *The IRA and Its Enemies: Violence and Community in Cork, 1916–1923* (Oxford: Oxford University Press, 1999). The point had been made by Padraic de Burca in 'Gaelic Sports and the National Revival' that 'the first school of nationality was the G.A.A' (p.580). See William G. Fitzgerald (ed.), *The Voice of Ireland* (Dublin and London: Virtue, 1924).

5 Timothy Corcoran, *The Story of Clongowes*

Wood: A.D. 1450–1900 (Dublin: Catholic Truth Society, 1911), 32. Apparently, the only time Joyce ventured inside the gates of Trinity was to watch a cricket match.

6 James Joyce, *A Portrait of the Artist as a Young Man* (ed. Chester Anderson) (New York: Viking, 1968), 59.

7 For a description of lob-bowling and its status in the 1890s, see K. S. Ranjitsinghi, *The Jubilee Book of Cricket* (Edinburgh and London: William Blackwood, 1898), 94.

8 See Stanislaus Joyce, *My Brother's Keeper*, 238.

9 See Fleming's comments in Stephen's geography book in James Joyce, *A Portrait of the Artist as a Young Man*, 41.

10 W. P. Hone, *Cricket in Ireland* (Tralee: Kerryman, 1955), 88.

11 Jamie O'Neill, *At Swim, Two Boys* (London: Scribner, 2001), 306. 'Castle' Catholics were those who supported British rule in Ireland (which was administered from Dublin Castle).

12 For elucidation, see Roland McHugh, *Annotations to Finnegans Wake* (rev. ed.) (Baltimore and London: Johns Hopkins University Press, 1991).

13 Edward Thomas, *Poems and Last Poems* (ed. Edna Longley) (London: Collins, 1973), 68.

14 For other 'Grace notes', see Derek Birley, *A Social History of English Cricket* (London: Aurum, 1999), 112.

15 This is probably an apocryphal story. See Roy Clement's booklet entitled *Re Joyce and Cricket* (Hampton: Dari Press, 1999), 30.

16 For details, see Cornelius F. Smith and Bernard Share (eds), *Whigs on the Green*, 118.

17 W. G. Grace, *Cricket* (Bristol: J. W. Arrowsmith; London: Simpkin, Marshall, Hamilton, Kent, 1891), 2.

18 I am indebted to Pieter Bekker for this suggestion. For general discussion of sigla, see Roland McHugh, *The Sigla of 'Finnegans Wake'* (London: Edward Arnold, 1976).

19 James S. Atherton, 'Sport and Games in *Finnegans Wake*', in Jack P. Dalton and Clive Hart (eds), *Twelve and a Tilly* (London: Faber and Faber, 1966), 56. For more on the significance of this passage in terms of themes in the Wake, see Ron Malings, 'Cricketers at the Wake', in *James Joyce Quarterly* 7:4 Summer 1970, 333–49.

20 K. S. Ranjitsinghi, *The Jubilee Book of Cricket*, 160.

21 James Joyce, *Stephen Hero* (eds John J. Slocum and Herbert Cahoon) (New York: New Directions, 1963), 30.

22 For the term, see Bernard Share, *Slanguage: A Dictionary of Irish Slang* (Dublin: Gill and Macmillan, 1998). Share cites Joyce and only Joyce as his exemplum, which is not always a wise move.

23 See Ezra Pound, Review of *Dubliners*, in the *Egoist* 1: 14, 15 June 1914.

24 For a related discussion, see Trevor L. Williams, *Reading Joyce Politically* (Gainesville: University Press of Florida, 1997), 104–5.

25 James Pycroft, *The Cricket Field: Or the History and the Science of Cricket* (London: Longman, Brown, Green and Longmans, 1851), 14–15.

26 Ibid., 16–17.

27 Matthew Arnold, *On the Study of Celtic Literature* (London: Smith, Elder, 1867), 102.

28 Ramachandra Guha, *A Corner of a Foreign Field: The Indian History of a British Sport* (London: Pan Macmillan, 2002).

29 See *The Irishman* (ed. Herbert Moore Pim), 2: 26, 30 June, 1917, 1.

30 For a more upbeat assessment, albeit now a quarter of a century out of date, see Karl Johnston, 'Cricket for All', in *Hibernia*, 24 May 1979, who claimed that the game was played 'in far more counties than hurling'.

31 C. L. R. James, *Beyond a Boundary* (London: Sportsmans Book Club, 1964), 17.

32 Hobbs is spelt without the e, not Thomas

Hobbes, the author of *Leviathan*, but Sir Jack Hobbs. As for Rhodes, I think James has in mind the Yorkshire all-rounder Wilfred, rather than Cecil Rhodes.

33 Hilary McD. Beckles, *The Development of West Indies Cricket: Vol 1 The Age of Nationalism* (Kingston, Jamaica: The Press University of the West Indies; London: Pluto, 1998), 178.

34 Hilary McD. Beckles, *The Development of West Indies Cricket: Vol 2 The Age of Globalization* (Kingston, Jamaica: The Press University of the West Indies; London: Pluto, 1998), xviii.

35 Patrick McGee, *Cinema, Theory and Political Responsibility in Contemporary Culture* (Cambridge: Cambridge University Press, 1997), 134. For an extended discussion of the film, including remarks on C. L. R. James and cricket, see his chapter 'Sexual Nations: History and the Division of Hope in *The Crying Game*', 79–160.

36 Alan A. Stone in the *Boston Review*. See http://bostonreview.mit.edu/film/cryinggame.html.

37 Elizabeth Butler Cullingford, *Ireland's Others: Gender and Ethnicity in Irish Literature and Popular Culture* (Cork: Cork University Press, 2001), 61. Surprisingly, little is made of cricket in the comments which follow this remark.

Chapter 7 IRELAND IN THE 1930s

1 *The Letters of W. B. Yeats* (ed. Allan Wade) (London: Rupert Hart-Davis, 1954), 690. Letter dated 9 October 1922.

2 Hanna Sheehy-Skeffington, 'Woman in the Free State', in the *Irish People*, 29 February 1936, 4.

3 Patrick McGinley, *The Lost Soldier's Song* (London: Sinclair-Stevenson, 1994), 187.

4 H. V. Morton, *In Search of Ireland* (London: Methuen, 1930), 62. There is also a reference to half-ruined barracks in Sean O'Faolain, *Come Back to Erin* (New York: Viking, 1940), 329.

5 Terence de Vere White, *The Fretful Midge* (London: Routledge & Kegan Paul, 1957), 85.

6 Maurice Moynihan (ed.), *Speeches and Statements by Eamon de Valera 1917–73* (Dublin: Gill and Macmillan; New York: St Martin's Press, 1980), 466. Reported in de Valera's newspaper *Irish Press*, 18 March 1943.

7 From a speech made by de Valera at Blackrock Town Hall, Dublin, 22 August 1927. Ibid., 155.

8 Sean O'Faolain, *De Valera* (Harmondsworth: Penguin, 1939), 181.

9 Terence de Vere White, *The Fretful Midge*, 87.

10 Sean O'Faolain, *De Valera*, 180.

11 For more on Vocationalism in the 1930s, see Kieren Mullarkey, 'Ireland, the Pope and Vocationalism: The Impact of the Encyclical *Quadragesimo Anno*' in Joost Augusteijn (ed.), *Ireland in the 1930s: New Perspectives* (Dublin: Four Courts, 1999), 96–116.

12 The phrase is a translation of Geoffrey Keating's *domhan beag innti féin*. See Pádraic H. Pearse, *Political Writings and Speeches* (Dublin: Talbot, 1952), 228.

13 S. J. Brown, 'But Why Catholic Reading?', *Irish Rosary* 45: 7, July 1941, 523. Cited in Susannah Riordan, 'The Unpopular Front: Catholic Revival and Irish Cultural Identity, 1932–48', in Mike Cronin and John M. Regan (eds), *Ireland: The Politics of Independence, 1922–49* (Basingstoke: Macmillan, 2000), 111.

14 Thomas McCarthy, *The First Convention* (Dublin: Dolmen, 1978), 10.

15 See Alfred Dennis, 'A Memory of Patrick Pearse', in the *Capuchin Annual* 1934, 181–5.

16 Sean O'Faolain, 'The Dangers of Censorship', in *Ireland To-Day* 1: 6, November 1936, 60.

17 See Kevin Rockett, 'From Radicalism to Conservatism: Contradictions within Fianna Fáil Film Policies in the 1930s', in *Irish Studies Review* 9: 2, August 2001, 161.

18 See Julia Carlson, *Banned in Ireland: Censorship and the Irish Writer* (London: Routledge, 1990).

19 Donald S. Connery, *The Irish* (London: Eyre and Spottiswoode, 1968). The Censorship of Publications Act 1967 modified the previous two Censorship Acts of 1929 and 1946, reducing among other things the time span of a ban from twenty to twelve years, which meant that some 5,000–6,000 books were immediately 'unbanned'. Since the late 1960s the work of the censor in the field of literature has been increasingly less active, which has meant, in passing, that a cultural history such as mine can spend more time discussing the literature itself rather than issues of censorship.

20 See, for example, John Heuston, 'Kilkee: The Origins and Development of a West Coast Resort', in Barbara O'Connor and Michael Cronin (eds), *Tourism in Ireland: A Critical Analysis* (Cork: Cork University Press, 1993), 23. The sermon, which was reproduced in the *Clare Champion* on 1 August 1935, was entitled 'Seaside Immodesty – Modern Laxity of Morals'.

21 For a more recent discussion, see Kevin Rockett, 'Disguising Dependence: Separatism and Foreign Mass Culture', in *Circa* 49, January/February 1990, 20–5.

22 See the *Capuchin Annual* (1938), 248–71.

23 Gabriel Fallon, 'Celluloid Menace', in the *Capuchin Annual* (1938), 253.

24 Much of the programming was of a high if middle-brow order: regular talks and discussion programmes in both English and Irish, music from a permanent Radio Orchestra, and drama relayed from the Gate, the Peacock, and the Abbey. The successful variety show 'We Have With Us Tonight' began in 1936, while 1938 saw the launch of one of Irish radio's longest running series 'Question Time'. News also featured prominently, with 169 hours of news in 1935 broadcast in two slots at 6.45 and 10.30; and children were catered for with 185 hours. Religious programmes, on the other hand, accounted for less than one per cent of air time. For statistical details, see Alacoque Kealy, 'Radio Telefís Éireann Occasional Papers No 1: Irish Radio Data: 1926–1980' (Dublin, May 1981).

25 Brian Friel, *Dancing at Lughnasa* (London: Faber and Faber, 1990), 1.

26 The phrase is from the poem 'My Fields This Springtime'. The poet has in mind the way Beckett, MacNeice and Kavanagh provided a new direction for Irish poetry after Yeats had 'left his generation knackered'. See Desmond O'Grady, *The Road Taken: Poems 1956–1996* (Salzburg, Oxford, Portland: University of Salzburg Press, 1996), 291.

27 Francis Stuart, *Things to Live For: Notes for an Autobiography* (London: Jonathan Cape, 1934), 253–4.

28 Sean Keating, 'Art Does Not Get A Chance in Ireland!', the *Irish People*, 29 February 1936, 4. Thomas Bodkin, *The Importance of Art to Ireland* (Dublin: At the Sign of the Three Candles, 1935), 2. The corollary was that without such an art 'we can scarcely claim the right to assert our separate nationality'.

29 Norah Hoult, *Coming From The Fair* (London: William Heinemann, 1937), 278–9.

30 Kate O'Brien, *Pray for the Wanderer* (1938; Harmondsworth: Penguin, 1951), 98.

31 These writers, too, had their own contribution to make to 'the lost generation'.

32 Frank O'Connor, *Dutch Interior* (New York: Alfred A. Knopf, 1940), 269.

33 Sean O'Faolain, *Bird Alone* (1936; Oxford: Oxford University Press, 1985), 292.

34 Sean O'Faolain, *Come Back to Erin* (New York: Viking, 1940), 11.

35 Elizabeth Bowen, Review of *Come Back to Erin*, in the *Bell* 1: 3, December 1940, 89.

36 Kate O'Brien, *Without My Cloak* (1931; Harmondsworth: Penguin, 1949), 415.

37 From 'Carrickfergus' (1937) in *The Collected Poems of Louis MacNeice* (ed. E. R. Dodds) (London: Faber and Faber, 1979), 69.

38 See Declan Kiberd, *Irish Classics* (London: Granta, 2000), 543–55.

39 Thomas McCarthy, *Mr Dineen's Careful Parade: New and Selected Poems* (London: Anvil, 1999), 20.

40 See report in *People's: Ireland's Magazine Weekly*, 8 July 1950, 6.

41 Honor Tracy, *Mind You, I've Said Nothing!: Forays in the Irish Republic* (London: Methuen, 1953), 29.

42 For a survey of the close association of the Irish exiles Beckett and Joyce with the appropriately named *transition*, the avant-garde literary magazine published in Paris from 1927 to 1938, see Dougald McMillan, *transition: The History of a Literary Era 1927–1938* (London: Calder and Boyars, 1975).

43 Austin Clarke, *Collected Poems* (ed. Liam Miller) (Dublin: Dolmen; Oxford: Oxford University Press, 1974), 206.

44 Samuel Beckett, *Watt* (Paris: Merlin Press, 1953), 248.

45 Fintan O'Toole in Martin Parr, *A Fair Day: Photographs from the West of Ireland* (Wallesey, Merseyside: Promenade Press, 1984), 11–12.

46 Robert Ballagh, 'The Irishness of Irish Art' (1980) [unpublished lecture]. Cited in Luke Gibbons, *Transformations in Irish Culture* (Notre Dame, IN: University of Notre Dame Press, 1996), 23.

47 Máire Cruise O'Brien, *The Same Age as the State*, 114.

48 See Kevin Whelan, 'Settlement Patterns in the West of Ireland in the Pre-Famine Period', in Timothy Collins (ed.), *Decoding the Landscape: Contributions Towards the Synthesis of Thinking in Irish Studies on the Landscape* (NUI, Galway: Centre for Landscape Studies, 2003), 60–78.

49 Aodh de Blacám, *From a Gaelic Outpost* (Dublin: Catholic Truth Society of Ireland, 1921), xi.

50 Michael Collins, *The Path to Freedom* (Dublin: Talbot, 1922), 119.

51 I am indebted at this point to Lawrence Buell, *The Environmental Imagination: Thoreau, Nature Writing, and the Form-ation of American Culture* (Cambridge, Mass.: The Belknap Press of Harvard University Press, 1995), 32ff. Buell doesn't refer to Ireland but many of his comments are highly suggestive in the context of modern Irish culture.

52 See *Hinde*sight (Exhibition Catalogue) (Dublin: Irish Museum of Modern Art, 1993), 34, 40. The first six postcards appeared in 1957. The Liffey, which resembled the colour of Guinness, was given a blue makeover by Hinde.

53 See R. A. Stewart Macalister, *The Secret Languages of Ireland* (Cambridge: Cambridge University Press, 1937). The Shelta language in particular, the language of the travelling community in Ireland, is the focus. One of the few stories about itinerants at this time was O'Flaherty's 'The Tent'. See *The Tent* (London: Jonathan Cape, 1926).

54 'The Artist Speaks', in the *Bell* 4: 15, February 1951, 39.

55 Paul Henry, *An Irish Portrait* (London: Batsford, 1951), 51.

56 See Heaney's Introduction to the exhibition *Seamus Heaney: A Personal Selection*, Ulster Museum Belfast, 1982. Cited in Reviews, *Circa* 7, November/December 1982, 20.

57 Jennifer Johnston, *The Railway Station Man* (1984; Harmondsworth: Penguin, 1989), 87. 'How can anyone bear to live facing to the East?' asks the painter Helen.

58 I am reminded of a comment made by Chris Curtin, Hastings Donnan, and Thomas M. Wilson, the editors of *Irish Urban Cultures* (Queen's University Belfast: Institute for Irish Studies, 1993) lamenting the dominance of two myths about Ireland in twentieth-century anthropological studies, one of the dying peasant community of the West, North West and South (where anomic rural change has been the order of the day), and the other of the two tribes in the North (pp.11–12).

59 See, for example, Brian Winston, *Claiming the Real: The Documentary Film*

Revisited (London: British Film Institute, 1999), Marcus Banks and Howard Morphy (eds), *Rethinking Visual Anthropology* (New Haven and London: Yale University Press, 1997), Arthur Calder-Marshall, *The Innocent Eye: A Life of Robert Flaherty* (London: W. H. Allen, 1963), and Paul Rotha, *Robert J. Flaherty: A Biography* (ed. J. Ruby) (Philadelphia: University of Pennsylvania Press, 1983).

60 *Ireland* (Dublin: Irish Tourist Association, 1939), 195. This entry can be contrasted with Baddeley's *Thorough Guide to Ireland: Part II* (London: Thomas Nelson, 1911): 'As scenery the Arans have few attractions. . .. It is for their ancient forts, cromlechs, and cloghauns (stone-roofed houses), and very early Christian ruins that the Arans are interesting.' (187–8)

61 Cited in Brian Winston, *Claiming the Real*, 219. To the islanders, *Man of Aran* was/is known simply as 'the Film'. See Tim Robinson, *Stones of Aran: Labyrinth* (1986; Harmondsworth: Penguin, 1990), 162.

62 J. Norris Davidson in note to Rotha, July 1959. See Paul Rotha, *Robert J. Flaherty: A Biography*, 139.

63 John Goldman, who helped edit the film, does not mention this; instead, he concentrates on the 'extraordinary sequence' and how it gave expression to 'the whole pent-up fury of Flaherty's genius'. See Paul Rotha, *Robert J. Flaherty: A Biography*, 133. Rotha's account corroborates the accuracy of Johnston's play, although the play itself is not discussed (see pp.119–39).

64 Tim Robinson, *Stones of Aran: Labyrinth*, 138. For further discussion, see Martin McLoone, *Irish Film: The Emergence of a Contemporary Cinema* (London: British Film Institute, 2000), 42–4.

65 D. H. Greene and E. M. Stephens, *J. M. Synge 1871–1909* (New York: Macmillan, 1959), 96.

66 See Frank Delaney, 'Endpiece', the *Listener*, 31 May 1984, 39. Delaney first saw *Man of Aran* at school in 1956. On seeing it again on Channel 4 in 1984, he connected the film with the Irish tradition of story-telling, which was 'safety itself' for 'young Catholics mustn't be allowed to think'.

67 Darrell Figgis, *Children of Earth* (Dublin and London: Maunsel, 1918), 1–5.

68 Ernie O'Malley, *Army Without Banners* (London: New English Library, 1967), 66. First published in 1936 under the title *On Another Man's Wounds*.

69 Johnston had been present while *Man of Aran* was being made. See Paul Rotha, *Robert J. Flaherty*, 123.

70 Denis Johnston, *Storm Song and A Bride for the Unicorn* (London: Jonathan Cape, 1935), 42, 100 and 78–9.

71 I have in mind Johnston's *The Old Lady Says 'No!'* (1929), an anti-romantic play reminiscent of the 'Nighttown' episode of *Ulysses*. Rejected by Lady Gregory for the Abbey, the play went on to become one of the Gate Theatre's most popular plays in the 1930s.

72 *The Best of Myles: A Selection from 'Cruiskeen Lawn'* (ed. Kevin O'Nolan) (London: Picador, 1977), 234–5.

73 For information on Tyrell and Reid, see my Cork *Reader* 213–6, 361–4. For a recent discussion of Reid, see Colin Cruise, 'Error and Eros: The Fiction of Forrest Reid as a Defence of Homosexuality', in Éibhear Walshe (ed.), *Sex, Nation and Dissent in Irish Writing* (Cork: Cork University Press, 1997), 60–86.

74 Kathleen Coyle, *A Flock of Birds* (1930; Dublin: Wolfhound, 1995), 5. The contrast between Woolf and Coyle also deserves to be noticed. It is especially evident in the juxtaposition of *Piccadilly* (1923), Coyle's London novel of deprivation and social exclusion, with *Mrs Dalloway* (1925).

75 Kate O'Brien, *Pray for the Wanderer*, 21.

76 Coyle, deliberately, I suspect, is imprecise about dates and setting. The blurb on the Jonathan Cape first edition claims the novel is set in Dublin during the regime of the Black and Tans in 1919, while the 1995 Wolfhound edition states that the place is Northern Ireland, and that the

year is 1918. References in the novel to the Great War suggest it is 1918, while mention of the Mayor of Cork in the context of heroes (from William Tell to the Mayor of Cork) must mean 1920, when Terence McSwiney died on hunger strike during the War of Independence. The one date mentioned is 1919, in connection with bottling strawberries (which could mean to be opened in 1919). Christy's guilt is also not dealt with, nor indeed is the question of whether he has been acting as a spy for the British Government (who are perhaps prepared to see him hanged to prevent anyone thinking he was their man). Such imprecision is part of Coyle's intention to concentrate on the effects of war, whether civil war or the Great War or the War of Independence.

77 Cicely is Christy's girlfriend.

78 Kathleen Coyle, *The Widow's House* (London: Jonathan Cape, 1924), 160.

79 Kate O'Brien, *Pray for the Wanderer*, 21.

80 *Nationality: Economic, Cultural, Political. An Organ of Opinion Not of Party* 23 July 1932, 13.

81 *Signpost: A Monthly Magazine for the Irish-Home-Circle* 1: 1 April 1936, 6.

82 Ibid., 1:2 May 1936, 32.

83 Kathleen Coyle, *Liv* (1929; London: Jonathan Cape, 1930), 252.

84 Kathleen Coyle, *The Skeleton* (New York: E. P. Dutton, 1933), 251.

85 Kathleen Coyle, *The French Husband* (London: Pharos, 1932), 9.

86 Kathleen Coyle, *To Hold Against Famine* (New York: E. P. Dutton, 1942).

87 For a wartime anthology produced at home in support of the Irish who 'rushed to the aid, under arms, of fascism's victims', see Leslie Daiken (ed.), *They Go, The Irish* (London: Nicholson & Watson, 1944).

88 See James Knowlson, *Damned to Fame: The Life of Samuel Beckett* (London: Bloomsbury, 1996), 304.

89 Denis Johnston, 'Buchenwald', in the *Bell* 16: 6, March 1951, 40.

90 See Hubert Butler, *The Sub-Prefect Should Have Held His Tongue And Other Essays* (ed. R. F. Foster) (Harmondsworth: Penguin, 1990).

91 See Máire Cruise O'Brien, *The Same Age as the State* (Dublin: The O'Brien Press, 2003), 150. By 'West British', O'Brien means well-to-do Catholics, professional people, lawyers, doctors, and big landowners.

92 For texts of his broadcasts from 1942 to 1944, see Brendan Barrington (ed.), *The Wartime Broadcasts of Francis Stuart* (Dublin: Lilliput, 2000). For context, see David O'Donoghue, *Hitler's Irish Voices: The Story of German Radio's Wartime Irish Service* (Belfast: Beyond the Pale, 1998). Stuart defended Irish neutrality, but when he refused to make propaganda against the Soviet Union he fell out of favour with his Nazi handlers and his passport was confiscated.

93 Francis Stuart, *Redemption* (1949; Dublin: New Island Books, 1994), 7.

94 Francis Stuart, *The Pillar of Cloud* (1948; Dublin: New Island Books, 1994), 130.

95 For details, see Appendix 1 'Aosdána and Francis Stuart' in Máire Cruise O'Brien, *The Same Age as the State*, 330–8.

96 In a contemporary review of *Redemption* in the *Listener* 2 June 1949, P. H. Newby claimed Stuart 'romanticised violence': 'He abhors it, of course, yet he seems to have the same superstitious regard for it as certain other writers have for sex.'

97 Frank O'Connor, 'An Irishman Looks at England', the *Listener*, 2 January 1941.

98 Ewart Milne, *Letter from Ireland* (Dublin: Gayfield Press, 1940), 75–7. 'Thinking of Artolas' (pp.27–9) contains his elegy to Donnelly.

99 John Hewitt, *No Rebel Word* (London: Frederick Muller, 1948), 9.

100 See Elizabeth Bowen, *The Demon Lover and Other Stories* (1945; Harmondsworth: Penguin, 1966), 178.

101 Elizabeth Bowen, *A World of Love* (1955; Harmondsworth, 1983), 48.

102 Ibid., 45. The passage I have in mind is the beginning of Chapter 4.

103 For a first-hand account of this period,

see John Montague, *Company: A Chosen Life* (London: Duckworth, 2001).

104 Brian Nolan, 'A Bash in the Tunnel', in *Envoy* 5: 17, April 1951, 9.

105 Arguably the best Irish anthology in this decade was compiled by a Scot. See Ronald MacDonald Douglas, *The Irish Book* (Dublin and Cork: Talbot, 1936).

106 This is the title of Joseph M. Curran's study published by Greenwood Press in 1989.

107 The play was completed in 1940, but O'Neill stipulated that it was not to be performed until after his death. See Arthur and Barbara Geld, *O'Neill* (London: Jonathan Cape, 1962), 836–8.

108 See Andrew Turnbull, ed. *The Letters of F. Scott Fitzgerald* (Harmondsworth: Penguin, 1967), 522. Letter to John O'Hara dated 18 July 1933.

109 It's not often noticed that MacSpaunday (MacNeice, Spender, Auden, Cecil Day-Lewis) included two Irishmen. Between 1896 and 1907, most of the key players who came to prominence in the 1930s were born: Austin Clarke (1896), Liam O'Flaherty (1896), L. A. G. Strong (1896), F. R. Higgins (1896), Kate O'Brien (1897), Nora Hoult (1898), Sean O'Faolain (1900), Denis Johnston (1901), Francis Stuart (1902), Frank O'Connor (1903), Ewart Milne (1903), Patrick Kavanagh (1904), Maurice O'Sullivan (1904), C. Day-Lewis (1904), Padraic Fallon (1905), Samuel Beckett (1906), Michael McLaverty (1907), John Hewitt (1907), Louis MacNeice (1907). In the United States, we might extend the dates and add Sean Aloysius O'Fearna (aka John Ford) (1894), James T. Farrell (1904) and John O'Hara (1905). The names of painters born during this period included Mainie Jellet (1897), Harry Kernoff (1900), Norah McGuiness (1903), Elizabeth Rivers (1904), Cecil Salkeld (1904), Nano Reid (1905), not forgetting the architect Michael Scott (1905).

110 Samuel Beckett, 'Dante . . . Bruno. Vico . . . Joyce' in Samuel Beckett, *et al.*, *Our Exagmination Round His Factification for Incamination of Work in Progress* (1929; New York: New Directions, 1972), 14.

111 For a brief account, see Nicholas Sheaff, 'The Shamrock Building', in *Irish Arts Review*, 1: 1, Spring 1984, 26–9. Eric Gill's hand is behind the lettering on the building.

Chapter 8 Ireland in the 1980s

1 Julia O'Faolain, *No Country for Young Men* (Harmondsworth: Penguin, 1980), 192–3.

2 For the comparison between Owen and de Valera, see Elizabeth Butler Cullingford, *Ireland's Others: Gender and Ethnicity in Irish Literature and Popular Culture* (Cork: Cork University Press, 2001), 226–8.

3 Rosita Sweetman, *On Our Backs: Sexual Attitudes in a Changing Ireland* (London: Pan, 1979), 192 and 237.

4 See the issue devoted to 'The Story of Ireland', in *Picture Post*, 27 July 1940. The front cover is reproduced in my *Yeats's Worlds*, 255.

5 Red Saunders and Syd Shelton, *Ireland: A Week in the Life of the Nation* (Text Anthony Cronin) (London: Century, 1986), 270–1. The woman spoke no English and watched television which broadcast for the most part only in English.

6 *Ireland in the Year 2000: Towards a National Strategy* (Dublin: An Foras Forbartha, 1983).

7 I am thinking here in particular of articles by David Brett and Joan Fowler on the local, regional, and global, Luke Gibbon on ideology and contemporary art criticism, Belinda Loftus on murals and other public displays of visual art, Kevin Rockett on Irish film, and reviews of new work by Willie Doherty, Martin Parr, and other graphic artists. The other

arts magazine launched in these years was the more weighty Dublin-based *Irish Arts Review*, which began publication in 1984.

8 See John Stephenson's Introduction to *A Sense of Ireland* (Exhibition Catalogue) (Dublin: A Sense of Ireland, 1980), 12–3.

9 Richard Broad, *et al.*, *The Troubles* (London: Thames/MacDonald Futura, 1980), 181–2. Robert Kee, *Ireland: A History* (London: Weidenfeld and Nicolson, 1980).

10 Dermot Bolger, *Invisible Cities: The New Dubliners: A Journey Through Unofficial Dublin* (Dublin: Ravens Art, 1988), 8.

11 Robert Johnstone (Photos Bill Kirk), *Images of Belfast* (Belfast: Blackstaff, 1983), 105.

12 Frank McGuinness, *Plays One*, 344.

13 Henry Glassie, *Passing the Time in Ballymenone: Culture and History of an Irish Ulster Community* (1982; Bloomington and Indianapolis: Indiana University Press, 1995), 15.

14 John Montague, *The Dead Kingdom* (Oxford: Oxford University Press, 1984), 75. Phrases taken from 'Last Journey', a poem in memory of the poet's father. The last section is entitled 'A Flowering Absence'.

15 Michael Longley, *Gorse Fires* (London: Secker and Warburg, 1991), 10.

16 Thomas Kilroy, *Talbot's Box* (1979; Old Castle, County Meath: Gallery Press, 1997), 48. The subject of the play is Matt Talbot (1856–1925), the reformed alcoholic who, when he died, was found wearing a chain under his clothes to atone for his sins.

17 Brendan Murphy, *Eyewitness: Four Decades of Northern Life* (text Seamus Kelters) (Dublin: O'Brien Press, 2003).

18 For details, see Mary Kelly, 'Twenty Years of Current Affairs on RTE', in Martin McLoone and John MacMahon (eds), *Television and Irish Society: 21 Years of Irish Television* (Dublin: RTÉ/IFI, 1984), 107–122.

19 Christina Reid, *Plays: 1* (London: Methuen, 1997), 13.

20 Eithne Strong, *Flesh . . . the Greatest Sin* (Monkstown: Runa, 1982).

21 Nancy Scheper-Hughes, *Saints, Scholars and Schizophrenics: Mental Illness in Rural Ireland* (Berkeley and Los Angeles: University of California Press, 1979), 8. Her study met with considerable criticism in Ireland, partly because she was an outsider and partly because she had raised an issue which was considered 'family' or, as she put it in an article in the *Irish Times* on 21 February 1981, 'delicate'.

22 Maeve Kelly, *Necessary Treasons* (London: Methuen, 1985).

23 *A Sense of Ireland*, 51. For Farrell's comments, see Maev Kennedy, 'Maev Kennedy Talks to the Painter Micheal Farrell', *Irish Times*, 27 August 1977, 12. Cited in *When Time Began to Rant and Rave*, 234.

24 See interview with Farrell in Gerry Walker, 'The Journal of a Meathman as an Intellectual', in John O'Regan (ed.), *Micheal Farrell* (Kinsale: Gandon, 1998), 43.

25 Dave Eggers, *A Heartbreaking Work of Staggering Genius* (London: Picador, 2001), 201–2.

26 Cited in Ciaran Carty, *Robert Ballagh* (Dublin: Magill, 1986), 11.

27 Sissela Bok, *Secrets: On the Ethics of Concealment and Revelation* (Oxford: Oxford University Press, 1982), 10.

28 On seriality, see Jean-Paul Sartre, *Critique of Dialectical Reason* (tr. Alan Sheridan-Smith) (ed Jonathan Ree) (London: NLB, 1976), 253–76.

29 Aidan Mathews, *Lipstick on the Host* (London: Secker and Warburg, 1992), 233.

30 William Trevor, *The News from Ireland and Other Stories* (London: The Bodley Head, 1986), 160–1.

31 Ruth Barton, *Irish National Cinema* (London and New York: Routledge, 2004), 119.

32 See the Channel 4 documentary 'Sex in a Cold Climate' shown in 1993.

33 Tommy Williams was a member of the

Belfast Brigade of the Irish Republican Army. He was arrested after a gun battle, where he was wounded and later hanged on 2 September 1942. The song can be found in Dominic Behan, *The Singing Irish* (London: Scott Solomon, 1967), 105–6.

34 See 'Image Making, Image Breaking' (a roundtable discussion between Ailbhe Smyth, Pauline Cummins, Beverley Jones, and Pat Murphy), in *Circa* 32, Jan.–Feb. 1987, 13–19. For a related discussion, see Martin McLoone, *Irish Film: The Emergence of a Contemporary Cinema* (London: British Film Institute, 2000), 142–7.

35 In *Modernisation, Crisis and Culture in Ireland, 1969–1992* (Dublin: Lilliput, 2000), Conor McCarthy suggests that this debate between Maeve and Liam is 'self-conscious, jargon-laden' (192). I don't think that was the case at the time, when intense conversations such as this were, I suspect, not uncommon.

36 Pierre Bourdieu, *Masculine Domination* (tr. Richard Nice) (Cambridge: Polity, 2001). By symbolic violence Bourdieu means the 'gentle', invisible violence that makes it look as if masculine domination is natural and, as it were, eternal.

37 See Belinda Loftus, *Mirrors: William III & Mother Ireland* (Dundrum, Co Dublin: Picture Press, 1990), 77–8.

38 See Antoinette Quinn, 'New Noises from the Woodshed: The Novels of Emma Donoghue', in Liam Harte and Michael Parker (eds), *Contemporary Irish Fiction: Themes, Tropes, Theories* (Basingstoke: Macmillan, 2000), 146–7.

39 Between 1967 and 1998 almost 95,000 women who had terminations in Britain gave Irish addresses. See Sinéad Kennedy, 'Irish Women and the Celtic Tiger Economy', in Colin Coulter and Steve Coleman (eds), *The End of Irish History: Critical Reflections on the Celtic Tiger* (Manchester: Manchester University Press, 2003), 99.

40 See, for example, the extracts in the sections entitled 'The Women's Movement

and Women Politicians in the Republic of Ireland, 1980–2000' and 'Women and Politics in Northern Ireland 1993–2000' in Angela Bourke, *et al* (eds), *The Field Day Anthology of Irish Writing*, Volume V.

41 Ursula Barry, 'Movement, Change and Reaction: The Struggle Over Reproductive Rights in Ireland' in Ailbhe Smyth (ed.), *The Abortion Papers Ireland* (Dublin: Attic Press, 1992), 117.

42 Rosita Sweetman, '*On Our Knees': Ireland 1972* (London: Pan, 1972), 43.

43 Paula Meehan, 'The Statue of the Virgin at Granard Speaks', in *Mysteries of the Home* (Newcastle-upon-Tyne: Bloodaxe, 1996), 24.

44 Jane Gallop, *Around 1981: Academic Feminist Literary Theory* (New York and London: Routledge, 1992). By 1987 'the theoretical action had moved to "institutions" and "history"' (3).

45 Kathleen Coyle, *Youth in the Saddle* (London: Jonathan Cape, 1927), 215.

46 Kathleen Coyle, *Who Dwell With Wonder* (New York: E. P. Dutton, 1940), 47.

47 Frank McGuinness, *Plays One*, 314.

48 See Richard English, 'Left on the Shelf', *Fortnight* 388, September 2000, 32–3. For a qualification to this view, see Patrick Magee, 'Do They Mean Us?', in the *Guardian* 3 September 1997, 12–3.

49 See David McKittrick and David McVea, *Making Sense of the Troubles* (Harmondsworth: Penguin, 2001), 139.

50 Allen Feldman, *Formations of Violence: The Narrative of the Body and Political Terror in Northern Ireland* (Chicago and London: University of Chicago Press, 1991), 259.

51 Anne Devlin, *Ourselves Alone* (with *The Long March* and *A Woman Calling*) (London: Faber and Faber, 1986), 148.

52 For a recent up-to-date survey of these various attempts at negotiating a settlement, see Martin Mansergh, 'The Background to the Irish Peace Process', in Michael Cox, Adrian Guelke and Fiona Stephen (eds), *A Farewell to Arms?: From 'Long War' to Long Peace in Northern*

Ireland (Manchester: Manchester University Press, 2000), 8–23. It was Seamus Mallon who made the famous remark about the Belfast Agreement being 'Sunningdale for slow learners'. Cited in the Introduction to Rick Wilford (ed.), *Aspects of the Belfast Agreement* (Oxford: Oxford University Press, 2001), 6.

53 Richard Broad, *et al*, *The Troubles*, 181–2.

54 For list, see Bill Rolston, 'Literature of the "Troubles": Novels' at http://cain.ulst.ac.uk/bibdbs/chrnovel.htm

55 Robert Kee, *Ireland: A History* (London: Weidenfeld and Nicolson, 1980), 238.

56 See Philip Schlesinger, 'Television and Terrorism', the *Listener*, 2 February 1984, 9–11.

57 John McDonnell, Labour MP and chair of the Labour Party's Irish Society recently claimed what he described as 'the harsh truth', namely that 'the negotiations on the future of Northern Ireland would not be taking place if it had not been for the military action of the IRA' (see the *Guardian*, 3 June 2003). The harsh truth is even harsher to my mind: were any of the deaths between Sunningdale and the Good Friday Agreement necessary?

58 Gerry Foley, 'Bernadette and the Politics of the H-Block', in *Magill*, April 1981, 20. Twelve years later, writing in 1993, Bernadette Devlin McAliskey was more sanguine: 'No deaths have been harder for me to come to terms with than the deaths of the hunger strikers.' See her Foreword to Bruce Campbell, Laurence McKeown, Felim O'Hagan (eds), *Nor Meekly Serve My Turn: The H-Block Struggle 1976–1981* (Belfast: Beyond the Pale, 1998), xiii.

59 Bobby Sands, *One Day in My Life* (Introduction Sean MacBride) (Dublin and Cork, Mercier, 1982), 23.

60 Margaretta D'Arcy, *Tell Them Everything: A Sojourn in the Prison of Her Majesty Queen Elizabeth II at Ard Macha (Armagh)* (London: Pluto, 1981), 80.

61 See Padraig O'Malley, *Biting at the Grave: The Irish Hunger Strikes and the Politics of Despair* (Belfast: Blackstaff, 1990).

62 Quoted in Gerry Northam, 'Support for Sinn Fein', the *Listener*, 19 July 1984, 2–4.

63 See *Endgame in Ireland* (four documentary programmes shown on the BBC, June 2001). Twenty minutes into the first programme – entitled *Bomb and Ballot Box* – Mrs Thatcher's provocative views were being discussed (and discounted) by her Private Secretary, Charles Powell, the Cabinet Secretary, Robert Armstrong, and David Goodall, the Deputy Secretary to the Cabinet Office. For changes in Mrs Thatcher's position on the North while she was in office, see Paul Bew, Peter Gibbon, Henry Patterson, *Northern Ireland 1921–1996* (London: Serif, 1996), 204ff. The idea of redrawing the map of Northern Ireland and forcibly removing people according to their religion was also proposed in 1972, when Edward Heath was Prime Minister.

64 For statistics, see Marie Smyth, 'The Human Consequences of Armed Conflict: Constructing "Victimhood" in the Context of Northern Ireland's Troubles' in Michael Cox, Adrian Guelke, and Fiona Stephen (eds), *A Farewell to Arms*, 119.

65 For graph showing distribution of deaths 1969–1998, see Marie-Therese Fay, Mike Morrissey and Marie Smyth, *Northern Ireland's Troubles: The Human Costs* (London: Pluto, 1999), 137.

66 'Republicanisation', the attempt to persuade the Irish people as a whole to support Republicanism, was a term first used by Gerry Adams in 1976. For a history of the shift among the IRA towards politics, see Richard Bourke, *Peace in Ireland: The War of Ideas* (London: Pimlico, 2003), 171–80.

67 See Gerry Northam, 'Support for Sinn Fein', in the *Listener*, 19 July 1984, 2–4.

68 John Montague, *The Dead Kingdom*, 50.

69 In the 1880s, Richard Pigott was revealed as the forger behind a letter purportedly written by Parnell in which he didn't wholly condemn the Phoenix Park murders in 1882. In court, Pigott was asked to

write the word 'hesitancy' and spelt it wrongly, as he had in the letter, with an 'e' before the 'c'. (For more details, see my *James Joyce's Ireland*, 19–20.)

70 Cited in Susan McKay, *Northern Protestants: An Unsettled People* (Belfast: Blackstaff, 2000), 41. Fr Edward Daly makes a similar point in a recent interview: 'When you have seen people lying dead on the street, and you've seen what a high-velocity bullet does to a person, or you've been at the scene of a bombing immediately after, it does have a considerable impact on you'. See the *Independent*, 9 January 2002, Review Section, 7.

71 Jennifer Johnston, *The Railway Station Man* (1984; Harmondsworth: Penguin, 1989), 88.

72 Maeve McGuckian, *Drawing Ballerinas* (Oldcastle, Co Meath: Gallery, 2001), 15.

73 Seamus Heaney, *North* (London: Faber and Faber, 1975), 16.

74 The most famous attack on Heaney is based in part on the view that Heaney has said little about his native province. See Desmond Fennell, *Heresy* (Dublin: Lilliput, 1993), 130–77. Heaney's phrase appears in *North*, 59.

75 Seamus Heaney, *The Cure at Troy* (London: Faber and Faber, 1990), 77.

76 *Listener*, October 1971, 496–7.

77 Conor Cruise O'Brien, 'A Slow North-East Wind', in the *Listener*, 25 September 1975. This article was a review of *North*.

78 See *Hibernia*, 21 November 1969.

79 Frank O'Connor, *The Lonely Voice: A Study of the Short Story* (London: Macmillan, 1963), 18–21.

80 With one or two exceptions, such as two *This Week* reports, there had been virtually no current affairs programmes devoted to Northern Ireland on British television. In 1959 Alan Wicker made eight ten-minute programmes for *Tonight*, but only managed to get one broadcast because of the ensuing storm. See Liz Curtis, *Ireland: The Propaganda War* (London: Pluto, 1984), 203.

81 Daniel Corkery, *The Hidden Ireland: A Study of Gaelic Munster in the Eighteenth Century* (Dublin: Gill, 1924). The suggestive word 'underlife' – not undergrowth or undercurrents – was used by Heaney at a reading at the University of Leeds on 30 January 2002.

82 See, for example, 'The Placeless Heaven: Another Look at Kavanagh' in his *Finders Keepers: Selected Prose 1971–2001* (London: Faber and Faber, 2002), 134–44. See also 'After Synge-song – Seamus Heaney on the Writings of Patrick Kavanagh', the *Listener*, 13 January 1972 and 'A Poet's Blessing,' 19 April 1984.

83 Seamus Heaney, *Electric Light* (London: Faber and Faber, 2001), 14.

84 Not everyone was conscious of this. Heaney took exception to being included as 'British' in Blake Morrison and Andrew Motion's *Penguin Book of Contemporary British Poetry* (1982). For further details, see Neil Corcoran, *The Poetry of Seamus Heaney: A Critical Study* (London: Faber and Faber, 1998), 261–2.

85 Seamus Heaney, *The Cure at Troy*, 77.

86 Derek Mahon, *Collected Poems* (Oldcastle, Co Meath: Gallery Press, 1999), 45.

87 The word 'torc' appears in Heaney's 'The Tollund Man'.

88 'Doorstep killings', another example of the neighbourly murder, where the victim was shot as h/she opened the door of their home (as in McLaverty's *Cal*), were also a common feature in Belfast and Derry in the 1970s. See 'Understanding Political Violence in Northern Ireland', in Marie-Therese Fay, Mike Morrissey and Marie Smyth, *Northern Ireland's Troubles*, 73–94.

89 'Neighbourly' appears but once in Yeats's verse, in a rather awkward line in 'The Curse of Cromwell': 'All neighbourly content and easy talk are gone'. The nomadic Yeats understood friends and friendship but not neighbours or neighbourliness. Only someone who had lived among a community that practised funeral rites could stumble upon the naturalness of the phrase 'neighbourly murder'.

90 Padraic Fiacc, *Missa Terribilis* (Belfast: Blackstaff, 1986), 21. When published in *The Selected Padraic Fiacc* (Introduction Terence Brown) (Belfast: Blackstaff, 1979), the title of this poem was 'Christ Goodbye' and its subtitle '*or how we turn Christ into an "inhuman martyr" in Belfast*'. By delaying the revelation of the subject's identity, Fiacc achieves a more disturbing poem.

91 For an account of the Shankill Butchers, see 'The Butchers' in Allen Feldman, *Formations of Violence*, 59–65. During one torture session, Lenny Murphy and his gang stopped for tea, gave a cup to the victim, and started again.

92 Ibid., 64.

93 Padraic Fiacc, *Missa Terribilis*, 1.

94 For other terms, see Glossary in Appendix 1 in Allen Feldman, *Formations of Violence*.

95 See James Simmons, *West Strand Visions* (Belfast: Blackstaff, 1974), and David McKittrick, *et al.*, *Lost Lives: The Stories of the Men, Women and Children Who Died as a Result of the Northern Ireland Troubles* (Edinburgh and London: Mainstream, 1999).

96 See Laura Pelaschiar, *Writing the North: The Contemporary Novel in Northern Ireland* (Trieste: Edizione Parnaso, 1998), 113.

97 Robert McLiam Wilson, *Eureka Street* (1996; London: Minerva, 1997), 222.

98 See Roderic Knowles, *Contemporary Irish Art* (Dublin: Wolfhound, 1982), 130–1.

99 Robert McLiam Wilson, *Eureka Street*, 231.

100 I am thinking here in particular of John Sommerfield's *May Day* (1936), a novel which over the course of three days traces the coming together of a disparate group of people in London to celebrate May Day.

101 Glenn Patterson, *Burning Your Own* (1988; London: Abacus, 1989), 136.

102 Glenn Patterson, *Fat Lad* (London: Chatto and Windus, 1992), 119–20.

103 Glenn Patterson, *That Which Was* (London: Hamish Hamilton, 2004), 134.

104 See Niall McGrath, 'Interview with Glenn Patterson', *Edinburgh Review* 93, Spring 1995, 50. Cited in Gerry Smyth, *The Novel and the Nation: Studies in the New Irish Fiction* (London: Pluto, 1997), 114.

105 See Richard Kirkland, 'Bourgeois Redemptions: The Fictions of Glenn Patterson and Robert McLiam Wilson' in Liam Harte and Michael Parker (eds), *Contemporary Irish Fiction*, 224.

106 Glenn Patterson, *That Which Was* (London: Hamish Hamilton, 2004), 69.

107 See Allen Feldman, *Formations of Violence*, 41–5.

108 Benedict Kiely, *Nothing Happens in Carmincross* (London: Methuen, 1985), 182.

109 Eugene McCabe, *Heritage* (1978; rpt in *Christ in the Fields* London: Minerva, 1993), 79.

110 See R. H. Tawney, *Religion and the Rise of Capitalism* (London: John Murray, 1936), 231–2. Sir Walter Scott's remark, made in 1825, is used as an epigraph to A. T. Q. Stewart's *The Narrow Ground: The Roots of Conflict in Ulster* (1977; rev. ed. London: Faber and Faber, 1989).

111 Eve Patten, 'Fiction in Conflict: Northern Ireland's Prodigal Novelists', in I. A. Bell (ed.), *Peripheral Visions: Images of Nationhood in Contemporary British Fiction* (Cardiff: University of Wales Press, 1995), 132.

112 Gerry Smyth, *The Novel and the Nation*, 116.

113 Colin Bateman, *Divorcing Jack* (1995; London: HarperCollins, 2001), 13.

114 Colin Bateman, *Cycle of Violence* (London: HarperCollins, 1995), 211, 219.

115 For examples of Turner's work, see *Pack Up Your Troubles: 25 Years of Northern Ireland Cartoons* (Belfast: Blackstaff, 1995) and *The NOble Art of Politics* (Belfast: Blackstaff, 1998). For discussion of his work, see John Darby, *Scorpions in a Bottle: Conflicting Cultures in Northern*

Ireland (London: Minority Rights, 1997) and Roy Douglas, Liam Harte, Jim O'Hara, *Drawing Conclusions: A Cartoon History of Anglo-Irish Relations 1798–1998* (Belfast: Blackstaff, 1998).

116 Glenn Patterson, *The International* (London: Anchor, 1999), 318.

117 John Morrow, *Northern Myths* (Belfast: Blackstaff, 1979), 93.

118 See Georg Lukács, *Writer and Critic and Other Essays* (tr. Arthur Kahn) (London: Merlin, 1970).

119 Eoin McNamee, *Resurrection Man* (London: Picador, 1994), 3–4.

120 Richard Haslam makes a similar point when he writes that 'the cinematic mode pervades *Resurrection Man* to such a degree that the third-person narrator seems complicit with Kelly's narcissistic sadism.' See '"The Pose Arranged and Lingered Over": Visualizing the "Troubles"' in Liam Harte and Michael Parker (eds), *Contemporary Irish Fiction*, 205.

121 Eoin McNamee, *The Ultras* (London: Faber and Faber, 2004), 21.

122 David Park, *Stone Kingdoms* (London: Phoenix House, 1996), 64.

Chapter 9   Conclusion

1 See title poem in Michael S. Harper, *History Is Your Own Heartbeat: Poems* (Urbana: University of Illinois Press, 1971). Francis Mulhern, *The Present Lasts a Long Time: Essays in Cultural Politics* (Cork: Cork University Press, 1998). For Althusser it was the future that lasted a long time.

2 Thomas Kinsella, *The Pen Shop* (Dublin: Dedalus; Manchester: Carcanet, 1997).

3 There is a suggestive analogy at one point in *The Book of Evidence*, when Freddie Montgomery remarks: 'A long time ago, it seems, I have committed a crime. . . . Now, years later, the evidence has been found, and they have come to question me' (123). Here is another way of thinking about the past, the colonial encounter, a postmodern, second-hand discourse and original sin.

4 Kathleen Coyle, *Youth in the Saddle* (London: Jonathan Cape, 1927), 50.

5 See Laura P. Z. Izarra, 'Interviewing John Banville', in Munira H. Mutran and Laura P. Z. Zarra (eds), *Kaleidoscopic Views of Ireland* (Sao Paulo: Universidade de Sao Paulo, 2003), 229. In the same interview, Banville refers to *Birchwood* as his 'Irish novel', adding, 'I didn't know where to go after that' (228).

6 John Banville, *Eclipse* (London: Picador, 2000), 3.

7 John Banville, *Shroud* (London: Picador, 2002), 365.

8 It's also worth noting the suggestive passage in Coyle's *The Magical Realm* (1942), in which she discusses her family's Irish pride and what made them 'untouchable' (see p.279).

9 Louis MacNeice, *Collected Poems*, 110.

10 John Banville, *The Untouchable* (London: Picador, 1997), 57.

11 It would be interesting to know if MacNeice intended the pun when he refers to 'blunt [i]deals' in his section on Spain.

12 Derek Mahon, *Collected Poems* (Oldcastle, Co Meath: Gallery Press, 1999).

13 Austin Clarke, 'Mnemosyne Lay in Dust' (1966) in *Collected Poems*, 328.

14 See Tom Paulin's letter 'Modern Classic', in *London Review of Books*, 8 March 2001. Paulin first read the poem in the *Listener* in September 1973, when the Troubles were in full swing, but this is a retrospective reading.

15 Paul Muldoon, *Moy Sand and Gravel* (London: Faber and Faber, 2002).

16 Michael Longley, *The Weather in Japan* (London: Jonathan Cape, 2000), 9.

17 Jody Allen Randolph, 'Michael Longley in Conversation', *PN Review* 31:2 November–December, 2004, 26.

18 Michael Longley, *The Ghost Orchid* (London: Jonathan Cape, 1995), 39.

19 Medbh McGuckian, *Drawing Ballerinas* (Oldcastle, Co Meath: Gallery, 2001), 14.

20 Brendan Kennelly, *The Book of Judas* (Newcastle-upon-Tyne: Bloodaxe, 1991), 11.

21 Brendan Kennelly, *Begin* (Newcastle-upon-Tyne: Bloodaxe, 1999), 68.

22 Tom Murphy, *The Wake* (London: Methuen, 1998), 88.

23 Angela Bourke, *et al.* (eds), *The Field Day Anthology of Irish Writing Volumes IV and V: Irish Women's Writing and Traditions* (Cork: Cork University Press; New York: New York University Press, 2002).

24 Jimmy Murphy, *Two Plays: The Kings of the Kilburn High Road* and *Brothers of the Brush* (London: Oberon Books, 2001), 46. 'This tiger bastard', says Jap, an Irishman working on building sites in London and thinking of returning home, 'want to get a piece of it before it's made extinct.'

25 Paula Meehan, *Mrs Sweeney* in *Rough Magic: First Plays* (ed. Siobhán Bourke) (Dublin: New Island Books, 1997), 433.

26 Paula Meehan, *Cell* (Dublin: New Island Books, 2000), 36.

27 Conor McPherson, *Shining City* (London: Nick Hern Books, 2004), 64.

28 Anne Devlin, *After Easter* (London: Faber and Faber, 1996), 11.

29 Paula Meehan, *Dharmakaya* (Manchester: Carcanet, 2000), 39.

30 Anne Enright, *The Pleasure of Eliza Lynch* (London: Jonathan Cape, 2002), 1.

31 Roland Barthes, *The Pleasure of the Text* (tr. Richard Miller) (London: Jonathan Cape, 1976).

32 Paul Durcan, *Cries of an Irish Caveman* (London: Harvill, 2001), 121.

33 Cathal Ó Searcaigh, *Homecoming An Bealach 'na bhaile* (ed. Gabriel Fitzmaurice) (Indreabhán: Cló Iar-Chonnachta, 1993), 141.

34 Cathal Ó Searcaigh, 'Déagóir Ag Driftáil' ('Drifting'), *Out in the Open* (tr. Frank Sewell) (Indreabhán: Cló Iar-Chonnachta, 1997), 157.

35 O'Neill might have developed the gay theme by making more of Roger Casement, whose afterlife continues to intrigue scholars.

36 See, for example, Rosa González, 'The Cultural Greening of Britain' in *Irlanda Ante Un Nuevo Milenio* (ed. Ines Praga Terente) (Burgos: AEDEI, 2002). The success of plays such as Marion Jones's *Stones in Their Pockets* or the television soap *Father Ted*, or the presence of Irish voices in cold calling centres, or the fine conscience-driven reports of Irish correspondents (such as Fergal Keane, Maggie O'Kane, Orla Guerin) from the troublespots of the world, are reminders of a reverse form of colonisation now at work in Britain.

37 John McGahern, *Amongst Women* (London: Faber and Faber, 1990), 106.

38 St Augustine, *Confessions* (tr. R. S. Pine-Coffin) (Harmondsworth: Penguin, 1961), 220.

39 In the United States the novel carries the simpler title *By the Lake* (New York: Knopf, 2002).

40 John McGahern, *That They May Face the Rising Sun* (London: Faber and Faber, 2002), 73.

41 I am reminded of a remark by David Fitzpatrick in *Politics and Irish Life 1913–1921* (Dublin: Gill and Macmillan, 1977): 'The eyes of Clare people were turned either inwards or outwards, but seldom sideways towards Dublin' (xi).

42 Michael Viney, *A Year's Turning* (Belfast: Blackstaff, 1996), 224.

43 See interview with McGahern in Julia Carlson (ed.), *Banned in Ireland: Censorship and the Irish Writer* (London: Routledge, 1990), 53–68.

44 Paul Durcan, *Cries of an Irish Caveman*, 35.

45 Timothy O'Grady and Steve Pyke (photographer), *I Could Read the Sky* (London: Harvill, 1997), 63.

46 John McGahern, *Amongst Women*, 93.

47 Hugh Maxton, *Waking: An Irish Protestant Upbringing* (Belfast: Lagan Press, 1997), 21.

48 Eamon Maher, 'Catholicism and National Identity in the Works of John McGahern', in *Studies: An Irish Quarterly Review* 90: 357, Spring 2001, 78.

49 W. B. Yeats (ed.), *Stories from Carleton* (London: Walter Scott, n.d. [1889]), xvi.

50 Sean Hillen, *Irelantis* (Dublin: Irelantis, 1999); for Willie Doherty, see Ian Hunt and Camilla Jackson, *Willie Doherty: Somewhere Else* (London: Tate, 1999).

51 Anthony Haughey, *The Edge of Europe* (Text by Fintan O'Toole) (Dublin: An Roinn Ealaíon, Cultúir Agus Gaeltachta, 1996). The abiding image I have of McGahern is of him standing pouring tea in his kitchen in County Leitrim responding to a question I had put to him about the influence of D. H. Lawrence on his work. The year was 1985, the month October, the morning still, his answer patient.

52 Marina Carr, *The Mai* (Oldcastle, Co Meath: Gallery Press, 1995), 42.

SELECT BIBLIOGRAPHY

A New Tradition: Irish Art of the Eighties (Dublin: Douglas Hyde Galleries, 1990).

A Sense of Ireland (Exhibition Catalogue) (Dublin: A Sense of Ireland, 1980).

Adorno, Theodor, *Prism* (tr. Samuel and Shierry Weber) (Cambridge, Mass.: MIT Press, 1967).

—— *Negative Dialectics* (tr. E. B. Ashton) (New York: Continuum Books, 1973).

Anderson, Perry, 'Internationalism: A Breviary', *New Left Review*, 14 March/April 2002.

Andrews, C. S., *Man of No Property: An Autobiography* (Volume Two) (Dublin and Cork: Mercier, 1982).

Arensberg, Conrad, *The Irish Countryman: An Anthropological Study* (London: Macmillan, 1937).

Arnold, Matthew, *On the Study of Celtic Literature* (London: Smith, Elder, 1867).

—— *Culture and Anarchy: An Essay in Political and Social Criticism* (London: Smith, Elder, 1869).

Atherton, James S., 'Sport and Games in *Finnegans Wake*', in Jack P. Dalton and Clive Hart (eds), *Twelve and a Tilly* (London: Faber and Faber, 1966).

Augusteijn, Joost, ed., *Ireland in the 1930s: New Perspectives* (Dublin: Four Courts, 1999).

Augustine, St., *Confessions* (tr. R. S. Pine-Coffin) (Harmondsworth: Penguin, 1961).

Banville, John, *Birchwood* (London: Secker and Warburg, 1973).

—— *Mefisto* (1986; London: Minerva, 1993).

—— *The Book of Evidence* (London: Secker and Warburg, 1989).

—— *The Untouchable* (London: Picador, 1997).

—— *Eclipse* (London: Picador, 2000).

—— *Shroud* (London: Picador, 2002).

—— *The Sea* (London: Picador, 2005).

Barrett, Cyril, 'Irish Nationalism and Art 1800–1921', *Studies: An Irish Quarterly Review* 64: 256, winter 1975.

Barry, Sebastian, *The Steward of Christendom* (London: Methuen, 1995).

—— *Our Lady of Sligo* (London: Methuen, 1998).

Barton, Ruth, *Irish National Cinema* (London and New York: Routledge, 2004).

Bauman, Zygmunt, *Modernity and the Holocaust* (1989; Cambridge: Polity Press, 2000).

Bateman, Colin, *Cycle of Violence* (London: HarperCollins, 1995).

—— *Divorcing Jack* (1995; London: HarperCollins, 2001).

Beckett, Samuel, *Murphy* (1938; London: John Calder, 1963).

—— *Watt* (Paris: Merlin Press, 1953).

—— *Three Novels: Molloy, Malone Dies, The Unnamable* (1955; New York: Grove Press, 1977).

—— *The Complete Dramatic Works* (London: Faber and Faber, 1986).

Beckett, Samuel *et al., Our Exagmination Round His Factification for Incamination of Work in Progress* (1929; New York: New Directions, 1972).

Beckles, Hilary McD., *The Development of West Indies Cricket: Vol 1 The Age of Nationalism* (Kingston, Jamaica: The Press University of the West Indies; London: Pluto, 1998).

—— *The Development of West Indies Cricket: Vol 2 The Age of Globalization* (Kingston, Jamaica: The Press University of the West Indies; London: Pluto, 1998).

Behan, Brendan, *Borstal Boy* (London: Hutchinson, 1958).

—— *Brendan Behan's Island: An Irish Sketch-book* (Drawings by Paul Hogarth) (London: Hutchinson, 1962).

—— *The Complete Plays* (London: Methuen, 1978).

Behan, Dominic, *The Singing Irish* (London: Scott Solomon, 1967).

Bew, Paul, *Ideology and the Irish Question: Ulster Unionism and Irish Nationalism 1912–1916* (Oxford: Clarendon, 1994).

Bew, Paul, Peter Gibbon, Henry Patterson, *Northern Ireland 1921–1996* (London: Serif, 1996).

Binchy, Maeve, *Echoes* (London: Century, 1985).

Birley, Derek, *A Social History of English Cricket* (London: Aurum, 1999).

Birmingham, George E., *The Inviolable Sanctuary* (London: Nelson, 1912).

Blake, Liam, *Real Ireland* (text by Brendan Kennelly) (Belfast: Appletree, 1984).

Bodkin, Thomas, *The Importance of Art to Ireland* (Dublin: At the Sign of the Three Candles, 1935).

Bok, Sissela, *Secrets: On the Ethics of Concealment and Revelation* (Oxford: Oxford University Press, 1982).

Boland, Eavan, *Outside History* (Manchester: Carcanet, 1990).

—— *In a Time of Violence* (Manchester: Carcanet, 1994).

Bolger, Dermot, *Invisible Cities: The New Dubliners: A Journey Through Unofficial Dublin* (Dublin: Ravens Art, 1988).

—— *Father's Music* (London: Flamingo, 1997).

Boucicault, Dion, *Selected Plays of Dion Boucicault* (ed. Andrew Parkin) (Gerrards Cross: Colin Smythe, 1989).

Bourdieu, Pierre, *Masculine Domination* (tr. Richard Nice) (Cambridge: Polity, 2001).

Bourke Angela, *et al.,* eds, *The Field Day Anthology of Irish Writing Volumes IV and V: Irish Women's Writing and Traditions* (Cork: Cork University Press; New York: New York University Press, 2002).

Bowen, Elizabeth, *The Last September* (London: Constable, 1929).

—— *The Demon Lover and Other Stories* (1945; Harmondsworth: Penguin, 1966).

—— *The Heat of the Day* (London: Jonathan Cape, 1949).

—— *A World of Love* (1955; Harmondsworth, 1983).

Boyce, D. George, *Nationalism in Ireland* (London: Croom Helm, 1982).

Boyce, D. George and Alan O'Day, eds, *Defenders of the Union: A Survey of British and Irish Unionism Since 1801* (London: Routledge, 2001).

Boyd, Ernest, *Ireland's Literary Renaissance* (1916; New York: Alfred A. Knopf, 1922).

Broad, Richard, *et al., The Troubles* (London: Thames/MacDonald Futura, 1980).

Brown, Christy, *Down All the Days* (1970; London: Minerva, 1990).

Brown, Stephen S. J., 'Guide to Books on Ireland', the *Irish Book Lover* 1:8, March 1910.

Brown, Terence, *Ireland: A Social and Cultural History 1922–85* (London: Fontana, 1985).

Budgen, Frank, *James Joyce and the Making of 'Ulysses'* (Introduction Clive Hart) (1934; London: Oxford University Press, 1972).

Butler, Hubert, *The Sub-Prefect Should Have Held His Tongue And Other Essays* (ed. R. F. Foster) (Harmondsworth: Penguin, 1990).

Campbell, Bruce, Laurence McKeown, Felim O'Hagan, eds, *Nor Meekly Serve My Turn: The H-Block Struggle 1976–1981* (Belfast: Beyond the Pale, 1998).

Campbell, Joseph, *The Mountainy Singer* (Dublin: Maunsel, 1909).

Canny, Nicholas, *Making Ireland British 1580–1650* (Oxford: Oxford University Press, 2001).

Carbery, Ethna [Anna MacManus], *The Four Winds of Eirinn* (ed. Seamas MacManus) (Dublin: M. H. Gill, 1902).

Carbery, Mary, *The Farm By Lough Gurr: The Story of Mary Fogarty* (Sissy O'Brien) (London: Longmans, Green, 1937).

Carleton, William, *Traits and Stories of the Irish Peasantry* (Dublin: William Curry, 1830).

—— *The Black Prophet: A Tale of Irish Famine* (1847; London: Thomas Hodgson, 1854).

Carlson, Julia, *Banned in Ireland: Censorship and the Irish Writer* (London: Routledge, 1990).

Carr, Marina, *The Mai* (Oldcastle, Co Meath: Gallery Press, 1995).

—— *On Raftery's Hill* (London: Faber, 2000).

Carruth, Cathy, *Trauma: Explorations in Memory* (Baltimore: Johns Hopkins University Press, 1995).

Carson, Ciaran, *The Irish For No* (Newcastle-upon-Tyne: Bloodaxe, 1988).

—— *The Star Factory* (London: Granta, 1997).

—— *The Inferno of Dante Alighieri* (London: Granta, 2002).

—— *Breaking News* (Winston-Salem, NC: Wake Forest, 2003).

Carty, Ciaran, *Robert Ballagh* (Dublin: Magill, 1986).

Clarke, Austin, *The Bright Temptation* (1932; Dublin: Dolmen, 1965).

—— *A Penny in the Clouds: More Memories of Ireland and England* (London: Routledge & Kegan Paul, 1968).

—— *Collected Poems* (ed. Liam Miller) (Dublin: Dolmen; Oxford: Oxford University Press, 1974).

Clarke, Kathleen, *Revolutionary Woman: Kathleen Clarke 1878–1939* (ed. Helen Litton) (Dublin: O'Brien, 1991).

Clement, Roy, *Re Joyce and Cricket* (Hampton: Dari Press, 1999).

Collins, Michael, *The Path to Freedom* (Dublin: Talbot, 1922).

Collins, Thomas J. and Charles E. Kelly, eds, *Fifteen Years of Dublin Opinion* (Dublin: Dublin Opinion, 1937).

Colum, Padraic, *Three Plays: The Land, Thomas Muskerry, The Fiddler's House* (Dublin: Allen Figgis, 1963).

Connery, Donald S., *The Irish* (London: Eyre and Spottiswoode, 1968).

Connolly, James, *Selected Writings* (ed. Peter Berresford-Ellis) (London: Pluto, 1997).

Coogan, Tim Pat, *1916: The Easter Rising* (London: Weidenfeld and Nicolson, 2001).

Corcoran, Neil, *The Poetry of Seamus Heaney: A Critical Study* (London: Faber and Faber, 1998).

Corcoran, Timothy, *The Story of Clongowes Wood: A.D. 1450–1900* (Dublin: Catholic Truth Society, 1911).

Corkery, Daniel, *A Munster Twilight* (Dublin: Talbot, 1916).

—— *The Hidden Ireland: A Study of Gaelic Munster in the Eighteenth Century* (Dublin: Gill, 1924).

—— *Synge and Anglo-Irish Literature* (1931; Cork: Mercier, 1966).

Coulter, Colin and Steve Coleman, eds, *The End of Irish History: Critical Reflections on the Celtic Tiger* (Manchester: Manchester University Press, 2003).

Coyle, Kathleen, *Piccadilly* (London: Jonathan Cape, 1923).
—— *The Widow's House* (London: Jonathan Cape, 1924).
—— *Youth in the Saddle* (London: Jonathan Cape, 1927).
—— *Liv* (1929; London: Jonathan Cape, 1930).
—— *A Flock of Birds* (1930; Dublin: Wolfhound, 1995).
—— *There Is a Door* (Paris: Edward W. Titus, 1931).
—— *The French Husband* (London: Pharos, 1932).
—— *The Skeleton* (New York: E. P. Dutton, 1933).
—— *Who Dwell With Wonder* (New York: E. P. Dutton, 1940).
—— *To Hold Against Famine* (New York: E. P. Dutton, 1942).
—— *The Magical Realm* (New York: E. P. Dutton, 1943),
Cronin, Mike, *Sport and Nationalism in Ireland* (Dublin: Four Courts, 1999).
—— *A History of Ireland* (Basingstoke: Palgrave, 2001).
Cullingford, Elizabeth Butler, *Ireland's Others: Gender and Ethnicity in Irish Literature and Popular Culture* (Cork: Cork University Press, 2001).
Curtin, Chris, Hastings Donnan, and Thomas M. Wilson, eds, *Irish Urban Cultures* (Belfast: Institute for Irish Studies at Queen's University, 1993).
Curtis, L. P. Jr., 'The Anglo-Irish Predicament,' *20th Century Studies*, Volume 4, November 1970.
—— *Apes and Angels: The Irishman in Victorian Caricature* (Newton Abbot: David & Charles, 1971).
Curtis, Liz, *Ireland: The Propaganda War* (London: Pluto, 1984).
Daiken, Leslie, ed., *They Go, The Irish* (London: Nicholson & Watson, 1944).
D'Alton, Louis, *Two Irish Plays: The Man in the Cloak and The Mousetrap* (London: Macmillan, 1938).
Dana: An Irish Magazine of Independent Thought (eds John Eglinton and Fred Ryan) (Dublin: Hodges Figgis; London: David Nutt, 1904–5).
Darby, John, *Scorpions in a Bottle: Conflicting Cultures in Northern Ireland* (London: Minority Rights, 1997).
D'Arcy, Margaretta, *Tell Them Everything: A Sojourn in the Prison of Her Majesty Queen Elizabeth II at Ard Macha (Armagh)* (London: Pluto, 1981).
Davitt, Michael, *The Fall of Feudalism in Ireland: Or the Story of the Land League Revolution* (London and New York: Harper, 1904).
De Blácam, Aodh, *From a Gaelic Outpost* (Dublin: Catholic Truth Society of Ireland, 1921).
de Paor, Liam, *Landscapes with Figures: People, Culture and Art in Ireland and the Modern World* (Dublin: Four Courts, 1998).
Deane, Seamus, *Reading in the Dark* (London: Jonathan Cape, 1996).
—— *Strange Country: Modernity and Nationhood in Irish Writing Since 1790* (Oxford: Clarendon, 1997).
Deane, Seamus (general editor), *The Field Day Anthology of Irish Writing*, 3 volumes (Derry: Field Day, 1991).
Dennis, Alfred, 'A Memory of Patrick Pearse', in the *Capuchin Annual*, 1934.
Devlin, Anne, *Ourselves Alone* (with *The Long March* and *A Woman Calling*) (London: Faber and Faber, 1986).
—— *After Easter* (London: Faber and Faber, 1994).
Devlin, Denis, *Intercessions* (London: Europa, 1937).
—— *Lough Derg and Other Poems* (New York: Reynal and Hitchcock, 1946).
Dickinson, P. L., *The Dublin of Yesterday* (London: Methuen, 1929).
Dinneen, Joseph F., *Ward Eight* (New York: Harper, 1936).
Dinneen, Patrick S., *Foclóir Gaedilge Agus Bearla: An Irish-English Dictionary* (Dublin: Irish Texts Society, 1927).

Dolan, Terence Patrick, *A Dictionary of Hiberno-English: The Irish Use of English* (Dublin: Gill and Macmillan, 1999).

Donaghy, Michael, *Dances Learned Last Night: Poems, 1975–1995* (London: Picador, 2000).

Donleavy, J. P., *The Ginger Man* (1955; London: Abacus, 1997).

Donoghue, Emma, *Hood* (Harmondsworth: Penguin, 1996).

Douglas, Ronald MacDonald, *The Irish Book* (Dublin and Cork: Talbot, 1936).

Douglas, Roy, Liam Harte, and Jim O'Hara, *Drawing Conclusions: A Cartoon History of Anglo-Irish Relations 1798–1998* (Belfast: Blackstaff, 1998).

Doyle, Roddy, *The Barrytown Trilogy* (London: Secker and Warburg, 1991).

—— *The Woman Who Walked Into Doors* (London: Jonathan Cape, 1996).

—— *A Star Called Henry* (London: Jonathan Cape, 1999).

Duhig, Ian, *The Bradford Count* (Newcastle-upon-Tyne: Bloodaxe, 1991).

Durcan, Paul, *Cries of an Irish Caveman* (London: Harvill, 2001).

Eagleton, Terry, *Heathcliff and the Great Hunger* (London: Verso, 1995).

—— *Crazy John and the Bishop And Other Essays on Irish Culture* (Cork: Cork University Press, 1998).

Edgeworth, Maria, *Castle Rackrent* (1800; Oxford: Oxford University Press, 1995).

—— *The Absentee* (1812; Oxford: Oxford University Press, 1988).

Edwards, R. Dudley and T. Desmond Williams, eds, *The Great Famine: Studies in Irish History 1845–52* (Dublin: Irish Committee of Historical Sciences, 1962).

Eggers, Dave, *A Heartbreaking Work of Staggering Genius* (London: Picador, 2001).

Endgame in Ireland (four documentary programmes shown on the BBC, June 2001).

English, Richard, 'Left on the Shelf', *Fortnight*, September 2000.

Enright, Anne, *The Pleasure of Eliza Lynch* (London: Jonathan Cape, 2002).

Ervine, St John, Greer, *Mixed Marriage* (Dublin: Maunsel, 1911).

Fallon, Brian, *An Age of Innocence: Irish Culture 1930–1960* (Dublin: Gill and Macmillan, 1999).

Fallon, Gabriel, 'Celluloid Menace', the *Capuchin Annual*, 1938.

Farrell, James T., *Studs Lonigan* (1935; New York: Signet, 1965).

Fay, Marie-Therese, Mike Morrissey and Marie Smyth, *Northern Ireland's Troubles: The Human Costs* (London: Pluto, 1999).

Fegan, Melissa, *Literature and the Irish Famine 1845–1919* (Oxford: Clarendon Press, 2002).

Feldman, Allen, *Formations of Violence: The Narrative of the Body and Political Terror in Northern Ireland* (Chicago and London: University of Chicago Press, 1991).

Fennell, Desmond, *Heresy: The Battle of Ideas in Modern Ireland* (Belfast: Blackstaff, 1993).

Fiacc, Padraic, *Missa Terribilis* (Belfast: Blackstaff, 1986).

Figgis, Darrell, *Children of Earth* (Dublin and London: Maunsel, 1918).

Finan, Thomas, *A Nation in Medieval Ireland? Perspectives on Gaelic National Identity in the Middle Ages* (Oxford: Archaeopress, 2004).

Fitzgerald, William G., ed., *The Voice of Ireland: A Survey of the Race and Nation from All Angles*, revised edition, (Dublin and London: Virtue, 1924).

Fitzhenry Edna C., ed., *Nineteen-Sixteen: An Anthology* (Dublin: Brown and Nolan; London: Geo. G. Harrap, 1935).

Fitzmaurice, George, *The Plays of George Fitzmaurice: Dramatic Fantasies* (Introduction Austin Clarke) (Dublin: Dolmen, 1967).

Fitzpatrick, David, *Politics and Irish Life 1913–1921* (Dublin: Gill and Macmillan, 1977).

—— *The Two Irelands 1912–1939* (Oxford: Opus, 1998).

Floyd, Michael, *The Face of Ireland*, (London: Batsford, 1937).

Foley, Gerry, 'Bernadette and the Politics of the H-Block', *Magill*, April 1981.

Foster, John Wilson, *Colonial Consequences: Essays in Irish Literature and Culture* (Dublin: Lilliput, 1991).

Foster, Roy, *W. B. Yeats: A Life I: The Apprentice Mage 1965–1914* (Oxford: Oxford University Press, 1997).

—— *W. B. Yeats: A Life II: The Arch-Poet, 1915–1939* (Oxford: Oxford University Press, 2003).

—— *The Irish Story: Telling and Making It Up In Ireland* (Harmondsworth: Penguin, 2001).

Foy, Michael and Brian Barton, *The Easter Rising* (Stroud, Gloucestershire: Sutton, 2004).

Franklin, Miles, *All That Swagger* (Sydney: The Bulletin, 1936).

Friel, Brian, *Faith Healer* (London: Faber and Faber, 1980).

—— *Translations* (London: Faber and Faber, 1981).

—— *Dancing at Lughnasa* (London: Faber and Faber, 1990).

Fry, C. B., *The Book of Cricket* (London: George Newnes, 1899).

Gallop, Jane, *Around 1981: Academic Feminist Literary Theory* (London: Routledge, 1992).

Galvin, Patrick, *Irish Songs of Resistance* (London: Workers' Music Association, 1955).

—— *Song for a Poor Boy: A Cork Childhood* (Dublin: Raven Arts, 1990).

Garvin, Tom, *1922: The Birth of Irish Democracy* (Dublin: Gill and Macmillan, 1996).

—— 'Democratic Politics in Independent Ireland', in John Coakley and Michael Gallagher (eds), *Politics in the Republic of Ireland* (London and New York: Routledge, 1999).

Gellner, Ernest, *Nationalism* (London: Phoenix, 1997).

Gibbon, Lewis Grassic, *Sunset Song* (London: Jarrolds, 1932).

Gibbon, Monk, *The Seals* (London: Jonathan Cape, 1935).

Gibbons, Luke, *Transformations in Irish Culture* (Notre Dame, IN: University of Notre Dame Press, 1996).

Glassie, Henry, *Passing the Time in Ballymenone: Culture and History of an Irish Ulster Community* (1982; Bloomington and Indianapolis: Indiana University Press, 1995).

Goldring, Maurice, *Pleasant the Scholar's Life: Irish Intellectuals and the Construction of the Irish State* (London: Serif, 1993).

Gonne, Maud, [MacBride] 'Yeats and Ireland', in Stephen Gwynn (ed.), *Scattering Branches: Tributes to the Memory of W. B. Yeats* (London: Macmillan, 1940).

González, Rosa, 'The Cultural Greening of Britain', in Ines Praga Terente (ed.) *Irlanda Ante Un Nuevo Milenio* (Burgos: AEDEI, 2002).

—— ed., *The Representations of Ireland/s* (Barcelona: PPU, 2003).

Grace, W. G., *Cricket* (Bristol: J. W. Arrowsmith; London: Simpkin, Marshall, Hamilton, Kent, 1891).

Graham, Brendan, *The Whitest Flower* (London: HarperCollins, 1998).

Greaves, C. Desmond, *The Easter Rising in Song and Ballad* (London: Kahn & Averill, 1982).

Greene, D. H., and E. M. Stephens, *J. M. Synge 1871–1909* (New York: Macmillan, 1959).

Gregory, Lady, ed., *Ideals in Ireland* (London: Unicorn, 1901).

—— *Cuchulain of Muirthemne* (1902; Gerrards Cross: Colin Smythe, 1970).

—— *Seven Short Plays* (Dublin: Maunsel, 1909).

Guha, Ramachandra, *A Corner of a Foreign Field: The Indian History of a British Sport* (London: Pan Macmillan, 2002).

Gwynn, Stephen, *The Charm of Ireland* (rev. ed. London: George Harrap, 1934).

—— *Irish Literature and Drama in the English Language* (London: Nelson, 1936).

Hamilton, Hugo, *The Speckled People* (London and New York: Fourth Estate, 2003).

Hamsun, Knut, *Hunger* (tr. Sverre Lyngstad) (1890; Edinburgh: Canongate Books, 2001).

Harper, Michael S., *History Is Your Own Heartbeat: Poems* (Urbana: University of Illinois Press, 1971).

Hart, Peter, *The IRA and Its Enemies: Violence and Community in Cork, 1916–1923* (Oxford: Oxford University Press, 1999).

Harte, Liam and Michael Parker, eds, *Contemporary Irish Fiction: Themes, Tropes, Theories* (Basingstoke: Macmillan, 2000).

Harvey, Brian, *Rights and Justice Work in Ireland: A New Base Line* 2nd edition (York: Joseph Rowntree Charitable Trust, 2002).

Haughey, Anthony, *The Edge of Europe* (Text by Fintan O'Toole) (Dublin: An Roinn Ealaíon, Cultúir Agus Gaeltachta, 1996).

Healy, Gerard, *The Black Stranger* (Dublin: James Duffy, 1950).

Heaney, Seamus, *North* (London: Faber and Faber, 1975).

—— *Field Work* (London: Faber and Faber, 1979).

—— *Station Island* (London: Faber and Faber, 1984).

—— *The Cure at Troy* (London: Faber and Faber, 1990).

—— *Electric Light* (London: Faber and Faber, 2001).

—— *Finders Keepers: Selected Prose 1971–2001* (London: Faber and Faber, 2002).

Hederman, M. P., and R. Kearney, eds, *The Crane Bag Book of Irish Studies* (1977–81; Dublin: Blackwater Press, 1982).

Henry, Paul, *An Irish Portrait* (London: Batsford, 1951).

Herr, Cheryl, ed., *For the Land They Loved: Irish Political Melodramas 1890–1925* (Syracuse: Syracuse University Press, 1991).

Hewitt, John, *No Rebel Word* (London: Frederick Muller, 1948).

—— *Collected Poems* (Belfast: Blackstaff, 1992).

Higgins, Aidan, *Langrishe, Go Down* (London: Calder and Boyars, 1966).

Higgins, F. R., *The Dark Breed* (London: Macmillan, 1927).

Hillen, Sean, *Irelantis* (Dublin: Irelantis, 1999).

*Hinde*sight (Exhibition Catalogue) (Dublin: Irish Museum of Modern Art, 1993).

Hobsbawm, E. J., *Nations and Nationalism Since 1870* 2nd edition (Cambridge: Cambridge University Press, 2000).

Hoffman, Eva, *After Such Knowledge: Memory, History, and the Legacy of the Holocaust* (London: Secker and Warburg, 2004).

Hone, W. P., *Cricket in Ireland* (Tralee: Kerryman, 1955).

Hoult, Norah, *Holy Ireland* (London: William Heinemann, 1935).

—— *Coming From The Fair* (London: William Heinemann, 1937).

Howe, Stephen, *Ireland and Empire: Colonial Legacies in Irish History and Culture* (Oxford: Oxford University Press, 2000).

Howe, Susan, *The Nonconformist's Memorial* (New York: New Directions, 1993).

Hunt, Ian and Camilla Jackson, *Willie Doherty: Somewhere Else* (London: Tate, 1999).

Hyde, Douglas, 'The Necessity for De-Anglicising Ireland' (1892; reprinted in Charles Gavan Duffy, George Sigerson, and Douglas Hyde, *The Revival of Irish Literature*) (London: T. Fisher Unwin, 1894).

Inglis, Brian, *West Briton* (London: Faber and Faber, 1962).

—— *Roger Casement* (London: Hodder and Stoughton, 1973).

Ireland in the Year 2000: Towards a National Strategy (Dublin: An Foras Forbartha, 1983).

Irvine, Alexander, *My Lady of the Chimney Corner* (London: Eveleigh Nash, 1913).

James, C. L. R., *Beyond a Boundary* (London: Sportsmans Book Club, 1964).

Jameson, Fredric, *The Political Unconscious: Narrative as a Socially Symbolic Act* (Ithaca: Cornell University Press, 1981).

Jameson, Storm, 'Documents', *Fact* No. 4, July 1937.

Jesuits (Ireland), *A Page of Irish History: Story of University College, Dublin 1883–1909. Compiled by Fathers of the Society of Jesus* (Dublin and Cork Talbot Press, 1930).

Johnston, Denis, *Storm Song and A Bride for the Unicorn* (London: Jonathan Cape, 1935).

—— 'Buchenwald', in the *Bell* 16: 6 March 1951.

Johnston, Jennifer, *Shadows on Our Skin* (London: Hamish Hamilton, 1977).

—— *The Railway Station Man* (1984; Harmondsworth: Penguin, 1989).

—— *This Is Not a Novel* (London: Review, 2002).

Johnstone, Robert, *Images of Belfast* (Photos by Bill Kirk) (Belfast: Blackstaff, 1983).

Joyce, James, *'Dubliners': Text, Criticism, and Notes*, (eds Robert Scholes and A. Walton Litz) (New York: Viking, 1979).

—— *'A Portrait of the Artist as a Young Man': Text, Criticism, and Notes* (ed. Chester Anderson) (New York: Viking, 1968).

—— *Ulysses: The Corrected Text* (eds Hans Walter Gabler with Wolfhard Steppe and Claus Melchior) (London: The Bodley Head, 1986).

—— *Finnegans Wake* (London: Faber and Faber, 1964).

Joyce, P. W., *English as We Speak it in Ireland* (Introduction Terence Dolan) (1910; Portmarnock: Wolfhound, 1979).

Joyce, Stanislaus, *My Brother's Keeper* (ed. Richard Ellmann) (London: Faber and Faber, 1982).

Kavanagh, Patrick, *Collected Poems* (1964; New York: Norton, 1973).

Kavanagh, Peter, ed., *November Haggard: Uncollected Prose and Verse of Patrick Kavanagh* (New York: The Peter Kavanagh Hand Press, 1971).

Kealy, Alacoque, 'Radio Telefís Éireann Occasional Papers No 1: Irish Radio Data: 1926–1980' (Dublin, May 1981).

Keane, John B., *Three Plays: Sive, The Field, Big Maggie* (Dublin: Mercier, 1990).

Keane, Molly, *Good Behaviour* (London: Virago, 1981).

Keating, Sean, 'Art Does Not Get A Chance in Ireland!', the *Irish People*, 29 February 1936.

Kee, Robert, *Ireland: A History* (London: Weidenfeld and Nicolson, 1980).

Kelleher, Margaret, *The Feminization of the Famine: Expressions of the Inexpressible* (Cork: Cork University Press, 1997).

Kelly, Liam, *Thinking Long: Contemporary Art in the North of Ireland* (Kinsale: Gandon, 1996).

Kelly, Maeve, *Necessary Treasons* (London: Methuen, 1985).

Kennelly, Brendan, *Cromwell* (Newcastle-upon-Tyne: Bloodaxe, 1987).

—— *The Book of Judas* (Newcastle-upon-Tyne: Bloodaxe, 1991).

—— *Begin* (Newcastle-upon-Tyne: Bloodaxe, 1999).

Kiberd, Declan, *Inventing Ireland* (London: Jonathan Cape, 1995).

—— *Irish Classics* (London: Granta, 2000).

Kiely, Benedict, *Proxopera* (London: Gollancz, 1977).

—— *Nothing Happens in Carmincross* (London: Methuen, 1985).

Kilroy, Thomas, *Talbot's Box* (1979; Old Castle, County Meath: Gallery Press, 1997).

Kinealy, Christine, *A Death-Dealing Famine: The Great Hunger in Ireland* (London: Pluto, 1997).

—— *The Great Famine: Impact, Ideology and Rebellion* (Basingstoke: Palgrave, 2002).

King, Carla, ed., *Famine, Land and Culture in Ireland* (Dublin: University College Dublin Press, 2000).

Kinsella, Thomas, *Nightwalker and Other Poems* (Dublin: Dolmen, 1968).

—— *New Poems 1973* (Dublin: Dolmen, 1973).

—— *Collected Poems 1956–1994* (Oxford: Oxford University Press, 1996).

—— *The Pen Shop* (Dublin: Dedalus; Manchester: Carcanet, 1997).

Knightley, Philip, *The First Casualty: From Crimea to Vietnam: The War Correspondent as Hero, Propagandist, and Myth Maker* (London: Quartet, 1978).

Knowles, Roderic, *Contemporary Irish Art* (Dublin: Wolfhound, 1982).

Laffan, Michael, 'The Sacred Memory: Religion, Revisionists and the Easter Rising', in Judith Devlin and Ronan Fanning (eds), *Religion and Rebellion* (Dublin: University College Dublin Press, 1997).

—— *The Resurrection of Ireland: The Sinn Féin Party 1916–1923* (Cambridge: Cambridge University Press, 1999).

Lavery, Sir John, *The Life of a Painter* (London: Cassell, 1940).

Ledwidge, Francis, *The Complete Poems of Francis Ledwidge* (Introduction Lord Dunsany) (London: Herbert Jenkins, 1919).

Leerssen, Joep, *Remembrance and Imagination: Patterns in the Historical and Literary Representation of Ireland in the Nineteenth Century* (Cork: Cork University Press, 1996).

——— 'Monument and Trauma: Varieties of Remembrance', in Ian McBride (ed.), *History and Memory in Modern Ireland* (Cambridge: Cambridge University Press, 2001).

Lewis, Gifford, *Eva Gore-Booth and Esther Roper: A Biography* (London: Pandora, 1988).

Listener, the [BBC], 1929–1991.

Lloyd, David, *Anomalous States: Irish Writing and the Post-Colonial Moment* (Dublin: Lilliput, 1993).

Loftus, Belinda, *Mirrors: William III & Mother Ireland* (Dundrum, County Down: Picture Press, 1990).

Londraville, Janis and Richard Londraville, eds, *Too Long A Sacrifice: The Letters of Maud Gonne and John Quinn* (Sleinsgrove: Susquehanna University Press; London: Associated University Press, 1999).

Longley, Edna, *From Cathleen to Anorexia: The Breakdowns of Ireland* (Dublin: Attic, 1990).

Longley, Michael, *Gorse Fires* (London: Secker and Warburg, 1991).

——— *The Ghost Orchid* (London: Jonathan Cape, 1995).

——— *The Weather in Japan* (London: Jonathan Cape, 2000).

——— 'Michael Longley in Conversation' (with Jody Allen Randoph), *PN Review* 31:2 November–December, 2004.

Lowry, Malcolm, *Under the Volcano* (London: Jonathan Cape, 1947).

Lukács, Georg, *Writer and Critic and Other Essays* (tr. Arthur Kahn) (London: Merlin, 1970).

Lydon, John, *Rotten: No Irish, No Blacks, No Dogs* (London: Hodder and Stoughton, 1993).

Lynd, Robert, *Ireland A Nation* (London: Grant Richards, 1919).

Lyons, F. S. L., *Culture and Anarchy in Ireland, 1890–1939* (Oxford: Clarendon, 1979).

Macalister, R. A. Stewart, *The Secret Languages of Ireland* (Cambridge: Cambridge University Press, 1937).

McCabe, Eugene, *Heritage* (1978; rpt in *Christ in the Fields*, London: Minerva, 1993).

McCabe, Patrick, *The Butcher Boy* (London: Picador, 1992).

——— *The Emerald Germs of Ireland* (London: Picador, 2001).

McCarthy, Conor, *Modernisation, Crisis and Culture in Ireland, 1969–1992* (Dublin: Lilliput, 2000).

MacCarthy, Denis Florence, *Poems* (Dublin: M. H. Gill, 1882).

McCarthy, Justin, *et al.*, *Irish Literature* 10 vols. (New York: P. F. Collier, 1904).

McCarthy, Thomas, *The First Convention* (Dublin: Dolmen, 1978).

——— *Mr Dineen's Careful Parade: New and Selected Poems* (London: Anvil, 1999).

McDonagh, Martin, *The Leenane Trilogy* (London: Methuen, 1997).

——— *The Lieutenant of Inishmore* (London: Methuen, 2001).

MacDonagh, Thomas, *Literature in Ireland: Studies Irish and Anglo-Irish* (London: T. Fisher Unwin, 1916).

McGahern, John, *The Dark* (London: Faber and Faber, 1965).

——— *The Collected Stories* (London: Faber and Faber, 1992).

——— *Amongst Women* (London: Faber and Faber, 1990).

——— *That They May Face the Rising Sun* (London: Faber and Faber, 2002).

McGee, Patrick, *Cinema, Theory and Political Responsibility in Contemporary Culture* (Cambridge: Cambridge University Press, 1997).

MacGill, Patrick, *Children of the Dead End: The Autobiography of a Navvy* (London: Herbert Jenkins, 1914).

McGinley, Patrick, *The Lost Soldier's Song* (London: Sinclair-Stevenson, 1994).

McGuckian, Medbh, *Drawing Ballerinas* (Oldcastle, Co Meath: Gallery, 2001).
—— *The Face of the Earth* (Oldcastle, Co Meath: Gallery, 2002).
McGuinness, Frank, *Plays One: The Factory Girls, Observe the Sons of Ulster Marching Towards the Somme, Innocence, Carthaginians, Baglady* (London: Faber and Faber, 1996).
McIntosh, Gillian, *The Force of Culture: Unionist Identities in Twentieth-Century Ireland* (Cork: Cork University Press, 1999).
McKay, Susan, *Northern Protestants: An Unsettled People* (Belfast: Blackstaff, 2000).
Macken, Walter, *The Silent People* (London: Pan, 1969).
McKittrick, David, *et al.*, *Lost Lives: The Stories of the Men, Women and Children Who Died as a Result of the Northern Ireland Troubles* (Edinburgh and London: Mainstream, 1999).
McKittrick, David and David McVea, *Making Sense of the Troubles* (Harmondsworth: Penguin, 2001).
MacLaverty, Bernard, *Cal* (Harmondsworth: Penguin, 1983).
McLaverty, Michael, *Call My Brother Back* (London and New York: Longmans, Green, 1939).
—— *The Game Cock and Other Stories* (New York: Devin-Adair, 1947).
McLoone, Martin, *Irish Film: The Emergence of a Contemporary Cinema* (London: British Film Institute, 2000).
McLoone, Martin and John MacMahon, eds, *Television and Irish Society: 21 Years of Irish Television* (Dublin: RTÉ/IFI, 1984).
MacManus, M. J., *Eamon de Valera: A Biography* (Dublin: Talbot, 1947).
McNamee, Eoin, *Resurrection Man* (London: Picador, 1994).
—— *The Ultras* (London: Faber and Faber, 2004).
MacNeice, Louis, *The Dark Tower and Other Radio Scripts* (London: Faber and Faber, 1947).
—— *The Collected Poems of Louis MacNeice* (ed. E. R. Dodds) (London: Faber and Faber, 1979).
McPherson, Conor, *Shining City* (London: Nick Hern Books, 2004).
Madden, Deirdre, *One by One in the Darkness* (London: Faber and Faber, 1996).
Mahon, Derek, *The Hudson Letter* (Oldcastle, Co. Meath: Gallery Press, 1995).
—— *The Yellow Book* (Oldcastle, Co. Meath: Gallery Press, 1997).
—— *Collected Poems* (Oldcastle, Co. Meath: Gallery Press, 1999).
Mangan, James J., ed., *Gerald Keegan's Famine Diary: Journey to a New World* (Dublin: Wolfhound, 1992).
Mansergh Martin, 'Republicanism in a Christian Country – Past, Present and Future', *Studies: An Irish Quarterly Review* 89: 355, Autumn 2000.
—— 'The Background to the Irish Peace Process', in Michael Cox, Adrian Guelke and Fiona Stephen (eds), *A Farewell to Arms?: From 'Long War' to Long Peace in Northern Ireland* (Manchester: Manchester University Press, 2000).
Marreco, Anne, *The Rebel Countess: The Life and Times of Constance Markievicz* (London: Corgi, 1969).
Mathews, Aidan, *Lipstick on the Host* (London: Secker and Warburg, 1992).
Maxton, Hugh, *Waking: An Irish Protestant Upbringing* (Belfast: Lagan Press, 1997).
Medbh, Máighréad, *Tenant* (Cliffs of Moher, Co Clare: Salmon, 1999).
Meehan, Paula, *Mysteries of the Home* (Newcastle-upon-Tyne: Bloodaxe, 1996).
—— *Mrs Sweeney* in *Rough Magic: First Plays* (ed. Siobhán Bourke) (Dublin: New Island Books, 1997).
—— *Dharmakaya* (Manchester: Carcanet, 2000).
—— *Cell* (Dublin: New Island Books, 2000).
Merry, Andrew [Mrs Mildred H. G. Darby], *The Hunger: Being Realities of the Famine Years in Ireland 1845 to 1848* (London: Andrew Melrose, 1910).
Milne, Ewart, *Letter from Ireland: Verses* (Dublin: Gayfield, 1940).
Mitchell, Gary, *The Force of Change* (London: Nick Hern Books, 2000).

Mitchell, Joan Towey, 'Yeats, Pearse and Cuchulain', *Eire-Ireland* XI: 4, 1976.

Mokyr, Joel, *Why Ireland Starved: A Quantitative and Analytical History of the Irish Economy, 1800–1850* (London: George Allen and Unwin, 1985).

Montague, John, *The Dead Kingdom* (Oxford: Oxford University Press, 1984).

—— *Company: A Chosen Life* (London: Duckworth, 2001).

Moore, Brian, *The Temptation of Eileen Hughes* (London: Jonathan Cape, 1981).

Moore, George, *The Untilled Field* (London: T. Fisher Unwin, 1903).

—— *The Lake* (London: William Heinemann, 1905).

—— *Hail and Farewell: Ave* (London: William Heinemann, 1911).

Moore, Thomas, *A Selection of Irish Melodies with Symphonies and Accompaniments by Sir John Stevenson*, 6th Number (London and Dublin: J. Power's, 1815).

Morash, Chris, *Writing the Irish Famine* (Oxford: Clarendon Press, 1995).

Morrison, Danny, *The Wrong Man* (Cork and Dublin: Mercier, 1997).

Morrow, John, *Northern Myths* (Belfast: Blackstaff, 1979).

Morton, H. V., *In Search of Ireland* (London: Methuen, 1930).

Moynihan, Maurice, ed., *Speeches and Statements by Eamon de Valera 1917–73* (Dublin: Gill and Macmillan; New York: St Martin's Press, 1980).

Muldoon, Paul, *Why Brownlee Left* (London: Faber and Faber, 1980).

—— *Quoof* (London: Faber and Faber, 1983).

—— *Moy Sand and Gravel* (London: Faber and Faber, 2002).

Mulhern, Francis, *The Present Lasts a Long Time: Essays in Cultural Politics* (Cork: Cork University Press, 1998).

Murdoch, Iris, *The Red and the Green* (Harmondsworth: Penguin, 1967).

Murphy, Jimmy, *Two Plays: The Kings of the Kilburn High Road and Brothers of the Brush* (London: Oberon Books, 2001).

—— *The Muesli Belt*, in Judy Friel and Sanford Sternlicht (eds), *New Plays from the Abbey Theatre* (Syracuse, New York: Syracuse University Press, 2003).

Murphy, Tom, *A Whistle in the Dark* (1961; London: Methuen, 1989).

—— *Plays: One: Famine, The Patriot Game, The Blue Macushla* (London: Methuen, 1992).

—— *The Wake* (London: Methuen, 1998).

Mutran, Munira H. and Laura P. Z. Izarra, eds, *Kaleidoscopic Views of Ireland* (Sao Paulo: Universidade de Sao Paulo, 2003).

Nationality: Economic, Cultural, Political. An Organ of Opinion Not of Party, 1932.

Naughton, Bill, *One Small Boy* (London: MacGibbon & Kee, 1957).

—— *Saintly Billy* (Oxford: Oxford University Press, 1988).

Nelson, Dorothy, *In Night's City* (Dublin: Wolfhound, 1983).

Ní Dhomnaill, Nuala, *Pharaoh's Daughter* (Oldcastle, Co. Meath: Gallery Press, 1990).

Nicholson, Asenath, *Lights and Shades of Ireland* (London: Charles Gilpin, 1850).

Nolan, Brian, 'A Bash in the Tunnel', *Envoy* 5: 17, April 1951.

Norman, Diana, *Terrible Beauty: A Life of Constance Markievicz 1868–1927* (London: Hodder and Stoughton, 1987).

Northam, Gerry, 'Support for Sinn Fein', the *Listener*, 19 July 1984.

O'Brien, Edna, *The Country Girls* (1960; Harmondsworth: Penguin, 1966).

O'Brien, Flann, *At Swim-Two-Birds* (London: Longmans, Green, 1939).

—— *The Dalkey Archive* (London: MacGibbon and Kee, 1964).

—— *The Third Policeman* (London: MacGibbon and Kee, 1967).

—— *The Best of Myles: A Selection from 'Cruiskeen Lawn'* (ed. Kevin O'Nolan) (London: Picador, 1977).

O'Brien, George, *The Four Green Fields* (Dublin and Cork: Talbot, 1936).

O'Brien, John A., ed., *The Vanishing Irish: The Enigma of the Modern World* (London: W. H. Allen, 1954).

O'Brien, Kate, *Without My Cloak* (1931; Harmondsworth: Penguin, 1949).

—— *Pray for the Wanderer* (1938; Harmondsworth: Penguin, 1951).

O'Brien, Máire Cruise, *The Same Age as the State* (Dublin: The O'Brien Press, 2003).

O'Casey, Sean, *Two Plays: Juno and the Paycock, and The Plough and the Stars* (London: Macmillan, 1966).

—— *The Star Turns Red* (London: Macmillan, 1940).

—— 'There Go The Irish', in Leslie Daiken, ed, *They Go, The Irish* (London: Nicholson & Watson, 1944).

—— *Autobiographies* 2 vols. (London: Pan, 1980).

O'Connor, Barbara, and Michael Cronin, eds, *Tourism in Ireland: A Critical Analysis* (Cork: Cork University Press, 1993).

O'Connor, Frank, *Guests of the Nation* (London: Macmillan, 1931).

—— *Dutch Interior* (New York: Alfred A. Knopf, 1940).

—— *The Midnight Court* (London and Dublin: Maurice Fridberg, 1945).

—— *The Lonely Voice: A Study of the Short Story* (London: Macmillan, 1963).

O'Connor, Joseph, *Star of the Sea* (London: Secker and Warburg, 2003).

O'Crohan, Thomas, *The Islandman* (tr. Robin Flower) (Cork and Dublin: Talbot, 1934).

O'Donnell, Peadar, *Adrigoole* (London: Jonathan Cape, 1929).

—— *The Knife* (London: Jonathan Cape, 1930).

O'Donoghue, Bernard, *Here Nor There* (London: Chatto and Windus, 1999).

O'Donoghue, D. J., *Poems of James Clarence Mangan* (Dublin: O'Donoghue; London: A. H. Bullen, 1903).

O'Donovan, Gerald, *Father Ralph* (London: Macmillan, 1913).

Ó Drisceoil, Donal, *Censorship in Ireland, 1939–1945: Neutrality, Politics and Society* (Cork: Cork University Press, 1996).

O'Faolain, Julia, *No Country for Young Men* (Harmondsworth: Penguin, 1980).

O'Faolain, Sean, *A Nest of Simple Folk* (New York: Viking, 1934).

—— *Bird Alone* (1936; Oxford: Oxford University Press, 1985).

—— 'The Dangers of Censorship', *Ireland To-Day* 1: 6, November 1936.

—— *De Valera* (Harmondsworth: Penguin, 1939).

—— *Come Back to Erin* (New York: Viking, 1940).

—— *An Irish Journey* (illustrations Paul Henry) (London: Readers Union, 1941).

—— *The Irish* (1947; rev. ed. Harmondsworth: Penguin, 1969).

O'Flaherty, Liam, *The Black Soul* (London: Jonathan Cape, 1924).

—— *The Informer* (London: Jonathan Cape, 1925).

—— *The Short Stories of Liam O'Flaherty* (London: Jonathan Cape, 1937).

—— *Famine* (London: Victor Gollancz, 1937).

—— *Land* (London: Victor Gollancz, 1946).

Ó Gráda, Cormac, *Ireland Before and After the Famine: Explorations in Economic History 1800–1925* (Manchester: Manchester University Press, 1993).

—— *Black '47 and Beyond: The Great Irish Famine in History, Economy, and Memory* (Princeton, New Jersey: Princeton University Press, 1999).

O'Grady, Desmond, *The Road Taken: Poems 1956–1996* (Salzburg, Oxford, Portland: University of Salzburg Press, 1996).

O'Grady, Standish James, 'The Great Enchantment', *All Ireland Review*, 17 February 1900.

O'Grady, Timothy, and Steve Pyke (photographer), *I Could Read the Sky* (London: Harvill, 1997).

O'Hara, John, *BUtterfield 8* (New York: Harcourt Brace, 1934).

O'Leary, John, *Recollections of Fenians and Fenianism* Vol 2 (London: Downey, 1896).

O'Leary, Peter, *My Story* (tr. Cyril Ó Céirin) (1915; Oxford: Oxford University Press, 1987).

O'Malley, Ernie, *Army Without Banners* (London: New English Library, 1967).

O'Malley, Padraig, *Biting at the Grave: The Irish Hunger Strikes and the Politics of Despair* (Belfast: Blackstaff, 1990).

Ó Murchadha, Ciaran, *Sable Wings over the Land: Ennis County Clare and its Wider Community During the Great Famine* (Ennis, Co. Clare: Clasp, 1998).

O'Neill, Eugene, *Long Day's Journey into Night,* (first published 1956) (New Haven and London: Yale University Press, 1973).

O'Neill, Jamie, *At Swim, Two Boys* (London: Scribner, 2001).

O'Regan, John, ed., *Micheal Farrell* (Kinsale: Gandon, 1998).

O'Rourke, Rev. John, *The History of the Great Irish Famine of 1847, With Notices of Earlier Irish Famines* (Dublin: McGlashan and Gill, 1875).

Ó Searcaigh, Cathal, *Homecoming An Bealach 'na bhaile* (ed. Gabriel Fitzmaurice) (Indreabhán: Cló Iar-Chonnachta, 1993).

—— *Out in the Open* (tr. Frank Sewell) (Indreabhán: Cló Iar-Chonnachta, 1997).

O'Sullivan, Maggie, David Gascoyne, Barry MacSweeney, *Etruscan Reader III* (Newcastle-under-Lyme: Etruscan Books, 1997).

O'Sullivan, Maurice, *Twenty-years A-growing* (tr. Moya Llewelyn Davies and George Thomson) (London: Chatto and Windus, 1933).

O'Sullivan, Patrick, ed., *The Meaning of the Famine* (London and Washington: Leicester University Press, 1997).

O'Toole, Fintan, 'The Means of Production', in *Labour in Art: Representations of Labour in Ireland 1870–1970* (Exhibition Catalogue) (Dublin: Irish Museum of Modern Art, 1994).

Park, David, *Stone Kingdoms* (London: Phoenix House, 1996).

—— *Swallowing the Sun* (London: Bloomsbury, 2004).

Parker, Stewart, *Northern Star, Heavenly Bodies, Pentecost. Three Plays for Ireland* (London: Oberon Books, 1989).

Parr, Martin, (text by Fintan O'Toole) *A Fair Day: Photographs from the West of Ireland* (Wallesey, Merseyside: Promenade Press, 1984).

Patten, Eve, 'Fiction in Conflict: Northern Ireland's Prodigal Novelists', in I. A. Bell (ed.), *Peripheral Visions: Images of Nationhood in Contemporary British Fiction* (Cardiff: University of Wales Press, 1995).

Patterson, Glenn, *Burning Your Own* (1988; London: Abacus, 1989).

—— *Fat Lad* (London: Chatto and Windus, 1992).

—— *The International* (London: Anchor, 1999).

—— *That Which Was* (London: Hamish Hamilton, 2004).

Paulin, Tom, 'Modern Classic', *London Review of Books,* 8 March 2001.

Pearse, Pádraic H., *Political Writings and Speeches* (Dublin: Talbot, 1952).

Pelaschiar, Laura, *Writing the North: The Contemporary Novel in Northern Ireland* (Trieste: Edizione Parnaso, 1998).

Perkins, Sonya, ed., *The Irish Today: A Celebration of Ireland and the Irish Diaspora* (Dun Laoghaire: Cadogan, 2000).

Pierce, David, *James Joyce's Ireland* (New Haven and London: Yale University Press, 1992).

—— *Yeats's Worlds: Ireland, England and the Poetic Imagination* (New Haven and London: Yale University Press, 1995).

—— *W. B. Yeats: Critical Assessments* 4 vols (Robertsbridge, Sussex: Helm Information, 2000).

—— ed., *Irish Writing in the Twentieth Century: A Reader* (Cork: Cork University Press, 2000).

—— 'The Issue of Translation', *James Joyce Quarterly* 40: 3, 2005.

—— 'The Irish Theme in the Writings of Bill Naughton', *Estudios Irlandeses*, inaugural isue, 2005. http://www.estudiosirlandeses.org.

—— *Joyce and Company* (London and New York: Continuum Books, 2006).

Pilkington, Lionel, *Theatre and the State in Twentieth-Century Ireland: Cultivating the People* (London: Routledge, 2001).

Plunkett, Horace, *Ireland in the New Century* (1904; London: John Murray, 1905).

Plunkett, James, *Strumpet City* (London: Hutchinson, 1969).

Póirtéir, Cathal, ed., *The Great Irish Famine* (Dublin: Mercier, 1995).

Power, Richard, *The Hungry Grass* (London: Bodley Head, 1969).

Praeger, Robert Lloyd, *The Way That I Went* (Dublin: Hodges, Figgis & Co.; London, Methuen, 1937).

Pritchett, V. S., *Dublin: A Portrait* (Photographs by Evelyn Hofer) (London: The Bodley Head, 1967).

Pycroft, James, *The Cricket Field: Or the History and the Science of Cricket* (London: Longman, Brown, Green and Longmans, 1851).

Quinn, Hubert, *Dear Were The Days* (Dublin and Cork, 1934).

Ranjitsinghi, K. S., *The Jubilee Book of Cricket* (Edinburgh and London: William Blackwood, 1898).

Reid, Christina, *Plays: 1: Tea in a China Shop, Did You Hear The One About the Irishman. . ., Joyriders, The Belle of Belfast City, My Name, Shall I tell You My Name?, Clowns* (Introduction Maria M. Delgado) (London: Methuen, 1997).

Reid, Forrest, *Apostate* (London: Constable, 1926).

Reid, Graham, *The Plays of Graham Reid: Too Late to Talk to Billy, Dorothy, The Hidden Curriculum* (Dublin: Co-Op Books, 1982).

—— *Ties of Blood* (London: Faber and Faber, 1986).

Renan, Ernest, *Poetry of the Celtic Races and Other Studies*, tr. William G. Hutchison (London: Walter Scott, 1896).

—— *Recollections of My Youth* (tr. C. B. Pitman) (London: Chapman and Hall, 1892).

Richards, Maura, *Interlude* (Swords, Co Dublin: Ward River, 1982).

Richardson, Henry Handel, *The Fortunes of Richard Mahony* (London: William Heinemann, 1930).

Riordan, Susannah, 'The Unpopular Front: Catholic Revival and Irish Cultural Identity, 1932–48', in Mike Cronin and John M. Regan (eds), *Ireland: The Politics of Independence, 1922–49* (Basingstoke: Macmillan, 2000).

Robertson, Nora, *Crowned Harp: Memories of the Last Years of the Crown in Ireland* (Dublin: Allen, Figgis, 1960).

Robinson Tim, *Stones of Aran: Pilgrimage* (1986; Harmondsworth: Penguin, 1990).

—— *Stones of Aran: Labyrinth* (1995; Harmondsworth: Penguin, 1997).

Rockett, Kevin, 'Disguising Dependence: Separatism and Foreign Mass Culture', in *Circa* 49, January/February 1990.

—— 'From Radicalism to Conservatism: Contradictions within Fianna Fáil Film Policies in the 1930s', *Irish Studies Review* 9: 2, August 2001.

Rolston, Bill, 'Literature of the "Troubles": Novels' at http://cain.ulst.ac.uk/bibdbs/chrnovel.htm

Rotha, Paul, *Robert J. Flaherty: A Biography* (ed. J. Ruby) (Philadelphia: University of Pennsylvania Press, 1983).

Rothery, Sean, *Ireland and the New Architecture 1900–1940* (Dublin: Lilliput, 1991).

Russell, George, *Imaginations and Reveries* (Dublin and London: Maunsel and Roberts, 1921).

—— 'Lessons of Revolution', *Studies: An Irish Quarterly Review*, March 1923.

Ryan, Fred, 'On Language and Political Ideals', *Dana: An Irish Magazine of Independent Thought*, 9, January 1905.

—— *Criticism and Courage and Other Essays* (Dublin: Tower Press Booklets, 1906).

Ryan, Ray, *Ireland and Scotland: Literature and Culture, State and Nation 1966–2000* (Oxford: Clarendon, 2002).

Salkeld, Blanaid, *Hello, Eternity!* (London: Elkin Mathews and Marot, 1933).

Sands, Bobby, *One Day in My Life* (Dublin and Cork: The Mercier Press, 1982).

Sarma, Ursula Rani, *Touched/Blue* (London: Oberon Books, 2002).

Saunders, Red, and Syd Shelton (text by Anthony Cronin), *Ireland: A Week in the Life of the Nation* (London: Century, 1986).

Sayers, Peig, *An Old Woman's Reflections* (tr. Seamus Ennis) (Oxford: Oxford University Press, 1978).

Scheper-Hughes, Nancy, *Saints, Scholars and Schizophrenics: Mental Illness in Rural Ireland* (Berkeley and Los Angeles: University of California Press, 1979).

Schlesinger, Philip, 'Television and Terrorism', the *Listener*, 2 February 1984.

Sellar, Robert, *The Summer of Sorrow: Abner's Device and Other Stories* (Huntington, Quebec: [s.n.] 1895).

Sewell, Frank, *Modern Irish Poetry: A New Alhambra* (Oxford: Oxford University Press, 2000).

Shannon-Mangan, Ellen, *James Clarence Mangan: A Biography* (Blackrock, Co Dublin: Irish Academic Press, 1996).

Share, Bernard, *Slanguage: A Dictionary of Irish Slang* (Dublin: Gill and Macmillan, 1998).

Shaw, George Bernard, *The Complete Plays of Bernard Shaw* (London: Odhams, 1934).

—— 'John Bull's Other Island' with 'How He Lied to Her' and 'Major Barbara' (London: Constable 1947).

Shaw, Francis, S. J., 'The Canon of Irish History – A Challenge', *Studies: An Irish Quarterly Review* 61: 242, summer 1972.

Sheaff, Nicholas, 'The Shamrock Building', *Irish Arts Review* 1: 1, spring 1984.

Sheehan, Canon P. A., *Glenanaar: A Story of Irish Life* (1902; London: Longmans, Green, 1929).

Sheehy, Jeanne, *The Rediscovery of Ireland's Past: The Celtic Revival 1830–1930* (London: Thames and Hudson, 1980).

Sheehy-Skeffington, Hanna, 'Woman in the Free State', the *Irish People*, 29 February 1936.

Signpost: A Monthly Magazine for the Irish-Home-Circle, 1936.

Simmons, James, *West Strand Visions* (Belfast: Blackstaff, 1974).

Sinn Fein Rebellion Handbook (Dublin, 1917).

Slater, Patrick, *The Yellow Briar* (1933; Toronto: Macmillan, 1941).

Smith, Anthony D., *Nationalism and Modernism: A Critical Survey of Recent Theories of Nations and Nationalism* (London and New York: Routledge, 1998).

—— *The Nation in History: Historiographical Debates about Ethnicity and Nationalism* (Cambridge: Polity, 2000).

Smyth, Ailbhe, ed, *The Abortion Papers Ireland* (Dublin: Attic Press, 1992).

Smyth, Ailbhe, Pauline Cummins, Beverley Jones, and Pat Murphy, 'Image Making, Image Breaking', *Circa* 32, Jan–Feb 1987.

Smyth, Gerry, *The Novel and the Nation: Studies in the New Irish Fiction* (London: Pluto, 1997).

Somerville, Alexander, *Letters From Ireland During the Famine of 1847* (ed. K. D. M. Snell) (Blackrock, Co. Dublin: Irish Academic Press, 1994).

Somerville, Edith and Martin Ross, *Some Experiences of an Irish R. M.* (London: Longmans, Green, 1899).

Spenser, Edmund, *A View of the Present State of Ireland* ([1596], in *The Works of Edmund Spenser: A Variorum Edition* (Baltimore: The Johns Hopkins Press, 1949).

—— 'A Brief Note of Ireland' (1598), in *The Works of Edmund Spenser: A Variorum Edition* (Baltimore: The Johns Hopkins Press, 1949).

Stephens, James, *The Insurrection in Dublin* (Dublin and London: Maunsel, 1916).
—— *Reincarnations* (London and New York: Macmillan, 1918).
Steward, James Christen, ed., *When Time Began to Rant and Rage* (London: Merrell Holberton, 1999).
Stewart, A. T. Q., *The Narrow Ground: The Roots of Conflict in Ulster* (1977; rev. ed. London: Faber and Faber, 1989).
Stoppard, Tom, *Shipwreck* (London: Faber and Faber, 2002).
Strong, Eithne, *Flesh . . . the Greatest Sin* (Monkstown: Runa, 1982).
Stuart, Francis, *Things to Live For: Notes for an Autobiography* (London: Jonathan Cape, 1934).
—— *The Pillar of Cloud* (1948; Dublin: New Island Books, 1994).
—— *Redemption* (1949; Dublin: New Island Books, 1994).
Sweetman, Rosita, *'On Our Knees': Ireland 1972* (London: Pan, 1972).
—— *On Our Backs: Sexual Attitudes in a Changing Ireland* (London: Pan, 1979).
Swift, Jonathan, *A Modest Proposal for preventing the children of poor people from becoming a burthen to their parents or country, and for making them beneficial to the publick* (Dublin: S. Harding, 1729).
Synge, J. M., *The Playboy of the Western World* (1907; London: Methuen, 1971).
Tawney, R. H., *Religion and the Rise of Capitalism* (London: John Murray, 1936).
Thomas, Edward, *Poems and Last Poems* (ed. Edna Longley) (London: Collins, 1973).
Thumboo, Edwin, 'W. B. Yeats as Third World Paradigm', in Robbie B. H. Goh (ed.), *Conflicting Identities: Essays on Modern Irish Literature* (Singapore: UniPress, 1997).
Tóibín, Colm, *The Master* (London: Picador, 2004).
Tracy, Honor, *Mind You, I've Said Nothing!: Forays in the Irish Republic* (London: Methuen, 1953).
Trevor, William, *The Ballroom of Romance and Other Stories* (London: Bodley Head, 1972).
—— *The News From Ireland and Other Stories* (London: The Bodley Head, 1986).
Trollope, Anthony, *Castle Richmond* (1860; London: The Folio Society, 1994).
Turner, Martyn, *Pack Up Your Troubles: 25 Years of Northern Ireland Cartoons* (Belfast: Blackstaff, 1995).
—— *The NOble Art of Politics* (Belfast: Blackstaff, 1998).
Uris, Leon, *Trinity* (New York: Doubleday, 1976).
Viney, Michael, *A Year's Turning* (Belfast: Blackstaff, 1996).
Walsh, Louis J., *The Next Time: A Story of 'Forty-Eight* (Dublin: M. H. Gill, 1919).
Waters, John, *An Intelligent Person's Guide to Modern Ireland* (London: Gerald Duckworth, 1997).
Watson, George, 'Countries of the Mind', *Irish Pages: Inaugural Issue* (Belfast: Linen Hall Library, 2002).
White, Anna MacBride and A. N. Jeffares, eds, *The Gonne-Yeats Letters, 1893–1938,* (London: Pimlico, 1993).
White, Terence de Vere, *The Fretful Midge* (London: Routledge & Kegan Paul, 1957).
Wilde, Oscar, *Complete Works of Oscar Wilde* (Introduction Vyvyan Holland) (London: Book Club Associates, 1976).
—— *The Portrait of Mr W. H.* (1921; London: Hesperus, 2003).
Wilford, Rick, ed., *Aspects of the Belfast Agreement* (Oxford: Oxford University Press, 2001).
Williams, Raymond, *Keywords: A Vocabulary of Culture and Society* (Glasgow: Fontana, 1976).
—— *Politics and Letters* (London: Verso, 1981).
Williams, Trevor L., *Reading Joyce Politically* (Gainesville: University Press of Florida, 1997).
Wilson, Robert McLiam, *Ripley Bogle* (1989; London: Minerva, 1997).
—— *Eureka Street* (1996; London: Minerva, 1997).

Winston, Brian, *Claiming the Real: The Documentary Film Revisited* (London: British Film Institute, 1999).

Woodham-Smith, Cecil, *The Great Hunger: Ireland 1845–9* (1962; London: New English Library, 1968).

Yeats, W. B., *Stories from Carleton* (London: Walter Scott, 1889).

—— *The Celtic Twilight* (London: Lawrence & Bullen, 1893).

—— *The Secret Rose* (London: Lawrence & Bullen, 1897).

—— *The Wind Among the Reeds* (1899; London: Elkin Mathews, 1903).

—— *Reveries Over Childhood and Youth* (London: Macmillan, 1916).

—— *Responsibilities* (London: Macmillan, 1916).

—— *Dramatis Personae 1896–1902* (London: Macmillan, 1936).

—— *A Vision* (1937; New York: Collier, 1977).

—— *On the Boiler* (Dublin: Cuala Press, 1938).

—— *The Letters of W. B. Yeats* (ed. Allan Wade) (London: Rupert Hart-Davis, 1954).

—— *Autobiographies* (1955; London: Macmillan, 1977).

—— *The Variorum Edition of the Poems of W. B. Yeats* (eds Peter Galt and Russell K. Alspach) (1957; New York: Macmillan, 1971).

—— *The Senate Speeches of W. B. Yeats* (ed. Donald R. Pearce) (London: Faber and Faber, 1961).

—— *Essays and Introductions* (1961; New York: Collier, 1968).

—— *Explorations* (Selected by Mrs W. B. Yeats) (1962; New York: Collier, 1973).

—— *The Variorum Edition of the Plays of W. B. Yeats* (ed. Russell K. Alspach) (1966; London: Macmillan, 1979).

—— *Uncollected Prose by W. B. Yeats* 1 (ed. John P. Frayne) (New York: Columbia University Press, 1970).

—— *Memoirs* (ed. Denis Donoghue) (New York: Macmillan, 1973).

Yeats, W. B. and Thomas Kinsella, *Davis, Mangan, Ferguson?: Tradition and the Irish Writer* (Dublin: Dolmen, 1970).

Index

italic numerals refer to illustration captions